BASKET RESOURCE GUIDE

Second Edition

Sponsored by
the National Association of Basketball Coaches

Jerry V. Krause, EdD
Eastern Washington University
Stephen J. Brennan, MEd
Peak Performance Consultants, Omaha

Leisure Press
Champaign, Illinois

Library of Congress Cataloging-in-Publication Data

Basketball resource guide / edited by Jerry V. Krause, Stephen J. Brennan. -- 2nd ed.
   p.   cm.
   Rev. ed. of: The Basketball bible / by Jerry Krause. 1982.
   "Sponsored by the National Association of Basketball Coaches."
   Includes index.
   ISBN 0-88011-369-3
   1. Basketball--Bibliography.   I. Krause, Jerry.   II. Brennan,
Stephen J., 1951-   .   III. Krause, Jerry.   Basketball bible.
IV. National Association of Basketball Coaches of the United States.
Z7514.B34K7   1990
[GV885]
016.796323--dc20
                                           89-12507
                                               CIP

ISBN: 0-88011-369-3

Developmental Editor: June I. Decker, PhD
Assistant Editors: Valerie Hall, Timothy Ryan
Copyeditor: Peter Nelson
Proofreader: Bruce Owens
Production Director: Ernie Noa
Typesetter: Cindy Pritchard
Text Design: Keith Blomberg
Text Layout: Tara Welsch
Cover Design: Tim Offenstein
Cover Photo: Dave Black
Printer: Versa Press

Printed in the United States of America

10   9   8   7   6   5   4   3   2   1

Leisure Press
A Division of Human Kinetics Publishers, Inc.
Box 5076, Champaign, IL 61825-5076
1-800-342-5457
1-800-334-3665 (in Illinois)

7-16-91

■ Contents

Foreword

The National Association of Basketball Coaches (NABC) has as one of its objectives the promotion and support of projects it feels will contribute to the advancement of the great game of basketball.

In 1982 *The Basketball Bible* was one such project. However, a new version of *The Basketball Bible* has long been needed to provide updated guidance to those who are either casual or scholarly in their basketball interest.

Jerry Krause of Eastern Washington University, the NABC research chairman, has worked with research committee members, Naismith Hall of Fame personnel, and an independent consultant to complete a 6-year project to update the contents of this book. The new title, *Basketball Resource Guide*, illustrates the direction this book will take in upcoming years. I highly recommend this resource book for coaches, teachers, players, and libraries, as well as the sports-minded public. It should be on the shelf of every basketball library!

Dean Smith, Head Basketball Coach
University of North Carolina

■

Preface

A complete reference book for basketball, *The Basketball Bible*, was first developed in 1982. It was designed to satisfy a need for a central listing of basketball resource materials.

As the popularity of basketball has grown, so has the amount of resources. Thus, it was possible to carry out the difficult task of compiling the materials for the *Basketball Resource Guide* only because of the tireless efforts of many individuals. The unpublished materials were gathered through the diligent work of NABC Research Committee members, a task they have been performing for the past 14 years. Also of great assistance were executive director Joe O'Brien and research specialist Wayne Patterson at the Naismith Memorial Basketball Hall of Fame. Finally, a publication of this magnitude is possible only because of the sponsorship of the NABC Board of Directors, who have pledged to support a continuing revision of the project, with new editions of the *Basketball Resource Guide* expected every 5 years.

Readers will notice improvements in quality and quantity of resources. All materials have been updated, the periodicals section has been broadened, and the visual resources area is more complete. All materials have been placed on computer disk in order to ensure that this publication will be a reference source that can be regularly updated. Finally, the new name, *Basketball Resource Guide*, more clearly identifies the contents of the book.

It is hoped that this resource guide will continue to be helpful to basketball coaches, for professional-preparation classes in colleges and universities, to reference librarians, to graduate researchers, and to all others who need to take an in-depth look at *any* specific area of basketball.

Basketball Resource Guide—the new "bible" for today's basketball-conscious world.

Jerry Krause
Steve Brennan

■ *Chapter 1*

Books and Monographs

Chapter 1 contains all published books and monographs on basketball and basketball-related topics.

1. **AAHPER:** *Basketball for Girls*; AAHPER Publications, Washington, D.C., 1966.
2. **AAHPER:** *Basketball, Volleyball: Tips and Techniques for Teachers and Coaches*; AAHPER Publications, Washington, D.C., 1977.
3. **AAHPER:** *Handbook for Teaching Basketball Officiating*; AAHPER Publications, Washington, D.C., 1969.
4. **AAHPER:** *Selected Basketball Articles*; AAHPER Publications, Washington, D.C., 1971.
5. **AAHPERD:** *Basketball Skills Test Manual: Boys and Girls*; AAHPERD Publications, Washington, DC, 1984.
6. **AAHPERD:** *Rules for Coeducational Activities and Sports*; AAHPERD Publications, Washington, DC, 1980.
7. **Aaseng, Nathan:** *Basketball's High Flyers*; Lerner, Minneapolis, MN, 1980.
8. **Aaseng, Nathan:** *Basketball's Playmakers*; Lerner, Minneapolis, MN, 1983.
9. **Aaseng, Nathan:** *Basketball's Power Players (Sports Heroes Books)*; Lerner, Minneapolis, MN, 1985.
10. **Aaseng, Nathan:** *Basketball's Sharpshooters*; Lerner, Minneapolis, MN, 1983.
11. **Aaseng, Nathan:** *Basketball: You Are the Coach*; Lerner, Minneapolis, MN, 1983.
12. **Aaseng, Nathan:** *You Are the Coach: College Basketball*; Dell, 1984.
13. **Aberdeen, Stu:** *The Winning Edge*; Huntington House, Shreveport, LA, 1970.
14. **Abdul-Jabbar, Kareem and Knobler, Jerry:** *Giant Steps: The Autobiography of Kareem Abdul-Jabbar*; Bantam, New York, NY, 1983.
15. **Abraham, C.C.:** *Basketball for Men and Women*; YMCA, Calcutta, 1956.
16. **Adams, Chet:** *All in Sports: A Collection of Nationally Famous Cartoons*; Drake, Chicago, IL, 1958.
17. **Albeck, Stan and Anderson, Forest:** *Coaching Better Basketball*; Ronald Press Co., New York, NY, 1964.
18. **Albert, Marv and Benaugh, Jim:** *Krazy About the Knicks*; Hawthorne, New York, NY, 1973.
19. **Alden, F.D.:** *Spaulding's Official Women's Basketball Guide*; American Sports, New York, NY, 1915.
20. **Allen, Forrest C.:** *Coach "Phog" Allen's Sports Stories for You and Youth*; Allen, Lawrence, KS, 1947.
21. **Allen, Forrest Claire:** *Basketball*; Sterling, New York, NY, 1969.
22. **Allen, Forrest Claire:** *Better Basketball*; Whittlesey House, New York, NY, 1937.

23. **Allen, Forrest Claire:** *Better Basketball Technique: Tactics and Tales*; McGraw-Hill, New York, NY, 1937.
24. **Allen, Forrest Claire:** *My Basketball Bible*; Smith-Grieves, Kansas City, MO, 1924.
25. **Allen, Maury:** *Voices of Sport*; Grosset, New York, NY, 1971.
26. **Allen, Mel and Graham, Frank, Jr.:** *It Takes Heart*; Harper, New York, NY, 1959.
27. **Ambler, Vic:** *Basketball*; Merrimack Book Service, Salem, OR, 1979.
28. **Anderson, Dave:** *Sports of Our Times*; Random House, New York, NY, 1979.
29. **Anderson, Forest and Albeck, Stan:** *Coaching Better Basketball*; Ronald Press, New York, NY, 1964.
30. **Anderson, Forest and Micolean, Tyler:** *Basketball Techniques Illustrated*; A.S. Barnes, San Diego, CA, 1952.
31. **Anderson, Lou Eastwood:** *Basketball for Women With Special Reference to the Training of Teachers*; Macmillan, New York, NY, 1929.
32. **Angell, Emmett Dunn:** *Basketball for Coach, Player, and Spectator*; Thomas Wilson, New York, NY, 1918.
33. **Antonacci, Robert and Barr, Jere:** *Basketball for the Young Champions*; McGraw-Hill, New York, NY, 1979.
34. **Archer, Jay and Olgin, Joseph:** *The Scoring Twins: A Story of Biddy Basketball*; Biddy Basketball, Scranton, PA, 1956.
35. **Armstrong, Bill:** *How I Coached Championship High School Basketball*; Parker, New York, NY, 1973.
36. **Armstrong, Robert:** *The Centers*; Creative Education, Minneapolis, MN, 1977.
37. **Armstrong, Robert:** *The Coaches*; Creative Education, Minneapolis, MN, 1977.
38. **Armstrong, Robert:** *Dave Cowens*; Creative Education, Minneapolis, MN, 1978.
39. **Armstrong, Robert:** *The Forwards*; Creative Education, Minneapolis, MN, 1977.
40. **Armstrong, Robert:** *George McGinnis*; Creative Education, Minneapolis, MN, 1977.
41. **Armstrong, Robert:** *The Guards*; Creative Education, Minneapolis, MN, 1977.
42. *Asian Basketball Federation 1960–1985*; edited by special ABC editorial committee; Asian Basketball Federation, Kuala Lumpur, 1985.
43. *Asian Games: Official Report of the Seventh Asian Games*; Organizing Committee, Tehran, Iran, 1974.
44. **Associated Press:** *Official Associated Press Sports Almanac, 1974*; Dell, New York, NY, 1974.
45. **Associated Press:** *Official Associated Press Sports Almanac, 1975*; Dell, New York, NY, 1975.
46. **Associated Press:** *Official Associated Press Sports Almanac, 1976*; Associated Press, New York, NY, 1976.
47. **Associated Press:** *Official Associated Press Sports Almanac, 1977*; Associated Press, New York, NY, 1977.
48. **Athletes in Action (Ed.):** *One Way to Play Basketball*; Beta Books, San Diego, CA, 1977.
49. **Athletic Institute:** *Basketball's Instructor's Guide*; The Athletic Institute, Chicago, IL, 1958.
50. **Athletic Institute:** *Youth League Basketball*; The Athletic Institute, Chicago, IL, 1975.

51. **Athletic Institute:** *Youth League Basketball: Coaching and Playing;* The Athletic Institute, Chicago, IL, 1984.
52. **Atkins, Ken and Rainey, Ron:** *Winning Basketball Drills;* Parker, West Nyack, NY, 1985.
53. **Auerbach, Arnold:** *Red Auerbach: An Autobiography;* G.P. Putnam's Sons, New York, NY, 1977.
54. **Auerbach, Red:** *Basketball for the Player, the Fan, and the Coach;* Simon and Schuster, New York, NY, 1976.
55. **Auerbach, Red:** *Winning the Hard Way;* Little, Brown, Boston, MA, 1966.
56. **Auerbach, Red and Fitzgerald, Joe:** *On and Off the Court;* Macmillan, New York, NY, 1985.
57. **Axthelm, Pete:** *The City Game: Basketball from the Garden to the Playgrounds;* Penguin, Rochester, NY, 1982.
58. **Axthelm, Pete:** *The City Game: Basketball in New York;* Harper and Row, New York, NY, 1970.
59. **Ayars, J.S.:** *Basketball Comes to Lonesome Point;* Viking Press, New York, NY, 1952.
60. **Bachman, Carl C.:** *Basketball for High School Coaches and Players;* William C. Brown, Dubuque, IA, 1955.
61. **Bacon, Francis L., Wood, William R., and Cameron, David:** *Just for Sport;* Lippincott, New York, NY, 1943.
62. **Baisi, Neal:** *Coaching the Zone and Man-to-Man Pressing Defenses;* Prentice-Hall, Englewood Cliffs, NJ, 1961.
63. **Baker, Eugene:** *I Want to Be a Basketball Player;* Childrens Press, Chicago, IL, 1972.
64. **Baker, Kent:** *Maryland Basketball: Red, White and Amen;* Strode, Huntsville, AL, 1980.
65. **Balch, J.W.:** *California Offense for Basketball;* J.W. Balch, Santa Barbara, CA, 1949.
66. **Balch, J.W.:** *Theory for Basketball Offenses;* J.W. Balch, Santa Barbara, CA, 1949.
67. **Ball, W.H. et al.:** *Basketball Guide;* American Sports Publishing Co., New York, NY, 1916.
68. **Ballantine Books (Ed.):** *Pro Basketball Encyclopedia;* Ballantine Books, New York, NY, 1977.
69. **Balter, Sam and Rice, Cy:** *One for the Book of Sports;* Citadel, New York, NY, 1955.
70. **Bancroft, Edith:** *Jane Allen, Center;* Saalfield, Akron, OH, 1920.
71. **Bancroft, Edith:** *Jane Allen, Right Guard;* Saalfield, Akron, OH, 1918.
72. **Bancroft, Edith:** *Jane Allen of the Sub-Team;* Saalfield, Akron, OH, 1917.
73. **Bancroft, J.H. and Pulvermacher, W.D.:** *Handbook of Athletic Games;* Macmillan, New York, NY, 1929.
74. **Banks, Pam:** *Denver Nuggets;* Creative Education, Minneapolis, MN, 1984.
75. **Banks, Pam:** *Philadelphia Seventy-Sixers;* Creative Education, Minneapolis, MN, 1984.
76. **Baratto, John and Krajewski, Bob:** *Coaching Junior High School Basketball;* Mr. Studios, East Chicago, IN, 1960.
77. **Barbour, R.H. and Sarra, LaMar:** *How to Play Better Basketball;* Appleton-Century, New York, NY, 1941.
78. **Barnes, Mildred:** *Girl's Basketball;* Allyn and Bacon, Boston, MA, 1972.
79. **Barnes, Mildred:** *Girl's Basketball, Including Summary of the Official Rules;* Sterling, New York, NY, 1974.
80. **Barnes, Robert B.:** *Basketball: Sixty-Five Programmed Principles;* Bear, 1972.

81. **Barnett, Dick:** *Inside Basketball;* Contemporary Books, Chicago, IL, 1971.
82. **Barnidge, Tom and *The Sporting News:** Best Sport Stories, 1986;* The Sporting News, St. Louis, MO, 1986.
83. **Barnidge, Tom and *The Sporting News:** Best Sport Stories, 1987;* The Sporting News, St. Louis, MO, 1987.
84. **Baron, Randall and Hill, Bob:** *The Amazing Basketball Book: The First 100 Years;* Devyn Press, Louisville, KY, 1987.
85. **Baron, Randall and Rice, Russell:** *The Official University of Kentucky Basketball Book;* Devyn Press, Louisville, KY 1986.
86. **Barr, George:** *Young Scientists and Sports, Featuring Baseball, Football, Basketball;* McGraw-Hill, New York, NY, 1962.
87. **Barr, Jere and Antonacci, Robert:** *Basketball for Young Champions;* McGraw-Hill, New York, NY, 1979.
88. **Barrier, Smith:** *On Tobacco Road: Basketball in North Carolina;* Leisure Press, West Point, NY, 1983.
89. **Barry, Justin McCarthey:** *Basketball: Individual Play and Team Play;* Clio Press, Iowa City, IA, 1926.
90. **Barry, Rick and Libby, Bill:** *Confessions of a Basketball Gypsy;* Prentice-Hall, Englewood Cliffs, NJ, 1972.
91. **Barton, George:** *The Bell Haven Five;* Winston, Philadelphia, PA, 1915.
92. **Bartow, Gene and Smith, Chuck:** *Winning Basketball;* Forum Press, St. Louis, MO, 1978.
93. **Barzman, Sol:** *505 Basketball Questions Your Friends Can't Answer;* Walker, New York, NY, 1981.
94. **Basketball Clinic:** *A Coaching Treasury;* Parker Publishing Co., New York, NY, 1974.
95. **Basketball Clinic:** *Complete Book of Defensive Fundamentals and Drills;* Parker Publishing Co., West Nyack, NY, 1981.
96. **Basketball Clinic:** *Treasury of Drills;* Parker, New York, NY, 1977.
97. **Basloe, Frank J. and Rohman, D. Gordon:** *I Grew Up With Basketball;* Greenburg, New York, NY, 1952.
98. **Bastian, Ken:** *Moscow '86 Goodwill Games;* Publishing Group, New York, NY, 1986.
99. **Batson, Larry:** *An Interview With Bobby Knight;* Creative Education, Minneapolis, MN, 1977.
100. **Batson, Larry:** *Bill Walton;* Creative Education, Minneapolis, MN, 1974.
101. **Battenburg, T.D.:** *Complete Book of Basketball Post Play;* Prentice-Hall, Englewood Cliffs, NJ, 1978.
102. **Baumgartner, Richard:** *Sure-Shot Shooting Aid;* R. Baumgartner, Richmond, IN, 1968.
103. **Baumgartner, Richard:** *Techniques for Great Outside Shooting;* R. Baumgartner, Richmond, IN, 1972.
104. **Beard, Butch et al.:** *Butch Beard's Basic Basketball: The Complete Player;* Kesend, 1985.
105. **Beckett, James and Eckes, Dennis:** *Sport American Football and Basketball Card Price Guide;* William Collins, Cleveland, OH, 1979.
106. **Beddoes, Dick and O'Bryan, M.:** *Basketball and Volleyball;* Coblam of Canada, Toronto, ON, 1976.
107. **Bedichek, Roy:** *Educational Competition: The Story of the University Interscholastic League of Texas;* University of Texas, Austin, TX, 1956.
108. **Bee, C.F. and Daher, J.G.:** *Fundamentals of Basketball;* Crowder, Cheylyan, WV, 1940.

109. **Bee, Clair:** *Backboard Fever*; Grosset, New York, NY, 1953.
110. **Bee, Clair:** *Basketball*; Townsend, New York, NY, 1939.
111. **Bee, Clair:** *Basketball Annual*; Universal, New York, NY, 1948.
112. **Bee, Clair:** *Basketball for Everyone*; Ace Books, New York, NY, 1962.
113. **Bee, Clair:** *Basketball Quiz Book*; Chilton, Radnor, PA, 1950.
114. **Bee, Clair:** *Buzzer Basket*; Grosset, New York, NY, 1962.
115. **Bee, Clair:** *Championship Ball*; Grosset, New York, NY, 1948.
116. **Bee, Clair:** *Drills and Fundamentals*; A.S. Barnes, San Diego, CA, 1942.
117. **Bee, Clair:** *Hardcourt Upset*; Grosset, New York, NY, 1957.
118. **Bee, Clair:** *Hoop Crazy*; Grosset, New York, NY, 1950.
119. **Bee, Clair:** *Make the Team in Basketball*; Grosset and Dunlap, New York, NY, 1961.
120. **Bee, Clair:** *Man To Man Defense and Attack*; A.S. Barnes, San Diego, CA, 1942.
121. **Bee, Clair:** *The Science of Coaching*; A.S. Barnes, San Diego, CA, 1942.
122. **Bee, Clair:** *Tournament Crisis*; Grosset, New York, NY, 1957.
123. **Bee, Clair (Ed.):** *Winning Basketball Plays*; Ronald Press, New York, NY, 1963.
124. **Bee, Clair:** *Zone Defense and Attack*; A.S. Barnes, San Diego, CA, 1942.
125. **Bee, Clair and Lapchick, Joe:** *Fifty Years of Basketball*; Prentice-Hall, Englewood Cliffs, NJ, 1968.
126. **Bee, Clair and Norton, Ken:** *Basketball Fundamentals and Techniques*; Ronald Press, New York, NY, 1959.
127. **Bee, Clair and Norton, Ken:** *The Bee-Norton Basketball Series*; Ronald Press, New York, 1959.
128. **Bee, Clair and Norton, Ken:** *Individual and Team Basketball Drills*; Ronald Press, New York, NY, 1959.
129. **Bee, Clair and Norton, Ken:** *Man to Man Defense and Attack*; Ronald Press, New York, NY, 1959.
130. **Bee, Clair and Norton, Ken:** *The Science of Coaching*; Ronald Press, New York, NY, 1959.
131. **Bee, Clair and Norton, Ken:** *Zone Defense and Attack*; Ronald Press, New York, NY, 1959.
132. **Bell, Marty:** *The Legend of Dr. J: The Story of Julius Erving*; New American Library, New York, NY, 1981.
133. **Bell, Mary Monroe:** *Women's Basketball*; William C. Brown, Dubuque, IA, 1964.
134. **Benagh, Jim:** *Making It To #1: How College Football and Basketball Teams Get There*; Dodd-Mead, New York, NY, 1976.
135. **Benagh, Jim:** *Walt Frazier: Superguard of Pro Basketball*; Scholastic, New York, NY, 1973.
136. **Benaugh, Jim and Pratt, John Lowell:** *The Official Encyclopedia of Sports*; Franklin Watts, New York, NY, 1964.
137. **Bender, Jack H.:** *Basketball Log*; Valley, St. Louis, MO, 1959.
138. **Benington, John and Newell, Pete:** *Basketball Methods*; Ronald Press, New York, NY, 1962.
139. **Benn, Gale D.:** *Olympic Gold, Summer and Winter Games: The Official Record of Championship Performance Since 1896*; Golden, New York, NY, 1972.
140. **Berenson, S. (Ed.):** *Basketball for Women*; American Sports, New York, NY, 1902.
141. **Berenson, S. (Ed.):** *Line Basketball*; American Sports, New York, NY, 1902.
142. **Bergan, Bill:** *Championship Drills for Basketball: Vol. 1. Offensive Drills*; Championship Books, Ames, IA, 1980.

143. **Berger, Phil:** *Heros of Basketball;* Random House, New York, NY, 1968.
144. **Berger, Phil:** *Miracle on 33rd Street: The New York Knickerbockers Championship Season;* Simon and Schuster, New York, NY, 1970.
145. **Berkow, Ira:** *The Dosable Panthers;* Atheneum, New York, NY, 1978.
146. **Berkow, Ira:** *Oscar Robertson: The Golden Year: 1964;* MacFadden, New York, NY, 1972.
147. **Berkow, Ira and Frazier, Walt:** *Rockin' Steady: A Guide to Basketball and Cool;* Prentice-Hall, Englewood Cliffs, NJ, 1974.
148. **Berstein, Ralf and Loeffler, Kenneth:** *Ken Loeffler on Basketball;* Prentice-Hall, Englewood Cliffs, NJ, 1955.
149. **Beswick, Bill:** *Beginner Basketball: International Rules;* Kaye and Kaye, Fargo, ND, 1983.
150. **Bevington, Raymond H.:** *Basketball Record Book;* Interstate, Danville, IL, 1953.
151. **Bickley, G.:** *Handbook of Athletics for Coaches and Players;* A.S. Barnes, San Diego, CA, 1929.
152. **Bilik, S.E.:** *The New Trainer Bible;* Atsco, New York, NY, 1934.
153. **Binacee, Tom and Coffey, Frank:** *The Pride of Portland: The Story of the Trailblazers;* Everest House, New York, NY, 1980.
154. **Bird, Larry J. and Bischoff, John R.:** *Bird on Basketball;* Phoenix Projects, Terre Haute, IN, 1983.
155. **Bischoff, John R. and Bird, Larry J.:** *Bird on Basketball;* Phoenix Projects, Terre Haute, IN, 1983.
156. **Bishop, Curtis:** *Dribble Up;* Steck, Austin, TX, 1956.
157. **Blackwell, Lee and Wilson, Mary:** *To Benji With Love;* Independent, Chicago, IL, 1986.
158. **Bliss, James Garfield:** *Basketball;* Lea and Febiger, Philadelphia, PA, 1929.
159. **Bluth, Robert G.:** *Basketball;* The Athletic Institute, North Palm Beach, FL, 1973.
160. **Bluth, Robert G.:** *Women's Basketball;* The Athletic Institute, North Palm Beach, FL, 1974.
161. **Bluth, Robert G.:** *Youth League Basketball;* The Athletic Institute, Chicago, IL, 1976.
162. **Bocker, Dorothy:** *Basketball for Women;* T.E. Wilson, New York, NY, 1920.
163. **Boggs, Frank K.:** *A Myriad of Sports: A Profile of Oklahoma City;* All-Sports Association of Oklahoma City, Oklahoma City, OK, 1971.
164. **Bole, Robert D. and Lawrence, Alfred C.:** *From Peachbaskets to Slamdunks;* B & L, Canaan, NH, 1988.
165. **Bolton, Clyde:** *The Basketball Tide: The Story of Alabama Basketball;* Stode, Huntsville, AL, 1977.
166. **Bonder, Jim:** *How to Be a Successful Coach;* Prentice-Hall, Englewood Cliffs, NJ, 1958.
167. **Bonham, Aubrey:** *Coaching the Flexible Man-to-Man Defense;* Parker, New York, NY, 1978.
168. **Bonham, Aubrey R. and Paye, Burrall:** *Secrets of Winning Fast-Break Basketball;* Prentice-Hall, New York, NY, 1985.
169. **Bonner, M.G.:** *The Real Book About Sports;* Doubleday, Garden City, NJ, 1958.
170. **Borcherding, Jim and Langrock, Dave:** *Winning Basketball Drills;* Jim Borcherding, Rock Island, IL, 1971.
171. **Bortstein, Larry:** *McAdoo, McGinnis, Unseld, Tomjanovich: The Big Men;* Grosset, New York, NY, 1975.
172. **Bowen, Robert Sidney:** *Basket Fever;* Whitman Books, Racine, WI, 1970.

173. **Bowen, W.P. and Mitchell, E.D.**: *The Practice of Organized Play*; A.S. Barnes, San Diego, CA, 1929.
174. **Boyden, Douglas E. and Burton, Roger G.**: *Staging Successful Tournaments*; Creative Sports Books, Hollywood, CA, 1969.
175. **Boyle, Robert H.**: *Sport, Mirror of American Life*; Little Brown, Boston, MA, 1963.
176. *Boy's Life Magazine: Boy's Life Book of Basketball Stories*; Random House, New York, NY, 1976.
177. **Brace, David**: *Basketball for Boys*; AAHPER Publications, Washington DC, 1966.
178. **Bradley, William**: *Life on the Run*; New York Times Book Co., New York, NY, 1976.
179. **Braun, Thomas**: *John Havlicek*; Creative Education, Minneapolis, MN, 1976.
180. **Braun, Thomas**: *Julius Erving*; Creative Education, Minneapolis, MN, 1976.
181. **Brennan, Stephen J.**: *The Mental Edge: Basketball's Peak Performance Workbook*; Peak Performance, Omaha, NE, 1987.
182. **Brill, Jack**: *Duke Basketball: An Illustrated History*; Four Corners Press, Chapel Hill, NC, 1986.
183. **Bronfield, Jerry**: *Kareem Abdul-Jabbar, Magic Johnson, and the Los Angeles Lakers*; Scholastic, New York, NY, 1981.
184. **Bronfield, Jerry**: *The UCLA Story*; Scholastic Book Services, New York, NY, 1973.
185. **Brown, Dale**: *Dale Brown's Freak Defense*; Dale Brown Enterprises, Baton Rouge, LA, 1988.
186. **Brown, Dale**: *LSU Basketball Organizational Handbook*: Leisure Press, Champaign, IL, 1983.
187. **Brown, Gene**: *New York Times Scrapbook Encyclopedia of Sports History*; Bobbs-Merrill, New York, NY, 1980.
188. **Brown, Gene**: *Sports as Reported by the New York Times*; Arno, New York, NY, 1976.
189. **Brown, Glen**: *Secrets of the Zone Press*; School Aid, Danville, IL, 1962.
190. **Brown, Lyle**: *Offensive and Defensive Drills for Winning Basketball*; Prentice-Hall, Englewood Cliffs, NJ, 1965.
191. **Brown, Ron**: *Basketball's Modern Shuffle Offense*; Furbush-Roberts, Bangor, ME, 1985.
192. **Brown, Ron**: *Teaching Basketball's Passing Game*; Forbush-Roberts, Bangor, ME, 1978.
193. **Browning, Clifford Lee**: *Basketball for Girls and Women*; McGraw-Hill, New York, NY, 1954.
194. **Browning, O.**: *How to Get the Most out of Basketball*; Phillips Petroleum, Bartlesville, OK, 1949.
195. **Browning, W.**: *Basketball: Fundamentals, Defense, Offense, Officiating, Coaching, Rules*; Pitman, London, 1949.
196. **Bruce, Robert M.**: *Annotated Bibliography of Basketball Literature*; National Association of Basketball Coaches, West Point, NY, 1947.
197. **Buchanan, L.**: *The Story of Basketball in Text and Pictures*; Stephen-Paul, New York, NY, 1948.
198. **Buck, Robert**: *The Shuffle and Press Offense for High School Basketball*; Parker, New York, NY, 1969.
199. **Buck, Robert J.**: *Shuffle and Press Offense for Winning Basketball*; Prentice-Hall, Englewood Cliffs, NJ, 1969.
200. **Bukata, Jim**: *One on One*; Stadia Sports, New York, NY, 1973.

201. **Bukata, Jim, Poretz, Art, and Croke, Ed:** *Illustrated Digest of Pro Basketball, 1972–73*; Stadia Sports, New York, NY, 1972.
202. **Bunn, John:** *The Art of Basketball Officiating*; Pond-Ekbers, Springfield, MA, 1948.
203. **Bunn, John:** *The Basketball Coach*; Prentice-Hall, Englewood Cliffs, NJ, 1961.
204. **Bunn, John:** *Basketball Methods*; Macmillan, New York, NY, 1939.
205. **Bunn, John:** *Basketball Techniques and Team Play*; Prentice-Hall, Englewood Cliffs, NJ, 1964.
206. **Bunn, John:** *Scientific Principles of Coaching*; Prentice-Hall, Englewood Cliffs, NJ, 1955.
207. **Burchard, Marshall:** *Sports Hero: Bill Walton*; G.P. Putnam's Sons, New York, NY, 1978.
208. **Burchard, Marshall:** *Sports Hero: Dr. J: The Story of Julius Erving*; G.P. Putnam's Sons, New York, NY, 1978.
209. **Burchard, Marshall:** *Sports Hero: Magic Johnson*; G.P. Putnam's Sons, New York, NY, 1981.
210. **Burchard, Marshall:** *Sports Hero: Rick Barry*; G.P. Putnam's Sons, New York, NY, 1977.
211. **Burchard, S.H.:** *Sports Star: Elvin Hayes*; Harcourt, Brace, Jovanovich, New York, NY, 1980.
212. **Bouchard, S.H.:** *Sports Star: Larry Bird*; Harcourt, Brace, Jovanovich, New York, NY, 1983.
213. **Burchard, S.H.:** *Sports Star: Walt Frazier*; Harcourt, Brace, Jovanovich, New York, NY, 1975.
214. **Burdette, Dick:** *The Fabulous Waterloo Wonders*; Lawhead Press, Athens, OH, 1975.
215. **Burgoyne, Leon E.:** *Jack Davis, Forward*; Winston, Philadelphia, PA, 1953.
216. **Burgoyne, Leon E.:** *State Champs*; Winston, Philadelphia, PA, 1951.
217. **Burton, Bill:** *The Sportsman's Encyclopedia*; Grosset, New York, NY, 1971.
218. **Burton, Roger G. and Boyden, Douglas E.:** *Staging Successful Tournaments*; Creative Sports Books, Hollywood, CA, 1969.
219. **Byrd, Ben:** *The Basketball Volumes: University of Tennessee Basketball*; Strode, Huntsville, AL, 1974.
220. **Camelli, Allen:** *Basketball: Great Teams, Great Men, Great Moments*; Bantam Books, New York, NY, 1972.
221. **Cameron, David, Wood, William R. and Bacon, Francis L.:** *Just for Sport*; Lippincott, New York, NY, 1943.
222. **Campbell, Darrell and Maravich, Pete:** *Heir to a Dream*; Nelson, Nashville, TN, 1987.
223. **Campbell, Nelson (Ed.):** *Grass Roots and Schoolyards: A High School Basketball Anthology*; Stephen Greene Press, Lexington, MA, 1988.
224. **Card, Orson S.:** *Ainge*; Signature, 1982.
225. **Carey, Steven:** *Steven Carey's Invention Book*; Workman, New York, NY, 1985.
226. **Carlson, Henry Clifford:** *Basketball, the American Game*; Funk and Wagnalls, New York, NY, 1939.
227. **Carlson, Henry Clifford:** *You and Basketball*; Brown, Braddock, PA, 1929.
228. **Carnesecca, Lou and Pepe, Phil:** *Louie: In Season*; McGraw-Hill, New York, NY, 1988.
229. **Carr, M.L. and Schron, Bob:** *Don't Be Denied*; Quinlan, Boston, MA, 1987.
230. **Carroll, Jock:** *The Summer Olympic Games From 1896 to 1968*; Simon and Schuster, Toronto, ON, 1972.
231. **Carson, John F.:** *The Coach That Nobody Liked: A Basketball Story*; Ariel Books, New York, NY, 1960.

232. **Carson, John F.:** *Floorburns*; Ariel Books, New York, NY, 1957.
233. **Carson, John F.:** *Hotshot: A Basketball Story*; Ariel Books, New York, NY, 1959.
234. **Carson, John F.:** *The Twenty-Third Street Crusaders*; Ariel Books, New York, NY, 1958.
235. **Carter, J. Ted:** *Patterned Fast-Break Basketball*; Parker, New York, NY, 1971.
236. **Case, Everett, N.:** *New Pressure Game in Basketball*; Technical Press, Raleigh, NC, 1948.
237. **Cathcart, James:** *A Multiple-Continuous Offense for High School Basketball*; Parker, New York, NY, 1968.
238. **Caudle, Edwin C.:** *Collegiate Basketball: Facts and Figures on Cage Sport*; J.F. Blair, Winston-Salem, NC, 1960.
239. **Caulkins, E. Dana:** *School Athletics in Modern Education*; Wingate Memorial Foundation, New York, NY, 1931.
240. **Cebulash, Mel:** *Basketball Players Do Amazing Things*; Random House, New York, NY, 1976.
241. **Cebulash, Mel:** *The Spring Street Boys Settle a Score*; Scholastic, New York, NY, 1981.
242. **Cella, George A:** *The Young Sportsmen's Guide to Basketball*; T. Nelson and Sons, New York, NY, 1962.
243. **Ceravolo, Joseph H.:** *The Modern 1-4 Basketball Offense—An Attack for All Defenses*; Parker, New York, NY, 1970.
244. **Chamberlain, Wilton and Shaw, David:** *Wilt, Just Like Any Other 7-Foot Black Millionaire Who Lives Next Door*; Macmillan, New York, NY, 1973.
245. *Championship Drills for Basketball: Volume 1. Offensive Drills*; Championship Books, Ames, IA, 1980.
246. *Championship Drills for Basketball: Volume 2. Defensive Drills*; Championship Books, Ames, IA, 1980.
247. *Championship Drills for Basketball: Volume 3. Conditioning Drills*; Championship Books, Ames, IA, 1980.
248. *Championship Drills for Basketball: Volume 4. General Drills*; Championship Books, Ames, IA, 1980.
249. **Chandler, Don and Halton, Vernon:** *Rupp From Both Ends of the Bench*; Houghton Mifflin, Boston, MA, 1973.
250. **Chandler, W.A. and Miller, G.F.:** *Basketball Technique*; Dunn County News, Menomonie, WI, 1922.
251. **Chansky, Art:** *March to the Top*; Four Corners Press, Chapel Hill, NC, 1982.
252. **Chapin, Dwight and Prugh, Jeff:** *The Wizard of Westwood: Coach John Wooden and His UCLA Bruins*; Houghton Mifflin, Boston, MA, 1973.
253. **Cheney, Bob:** *Basketball: 65 Programmed Principles*; Bear, Cambridge, NY, 1972.
254. **Chicago Park District:** *Basketball Fundamentals Freely Illustrated*; Chicago Park District, Chicago, IL, 1938.
255. **Christopher, Matt:** *Basketball Sparkplug*; Little Brown, Boston, MA, 1957.
256. **Christopher, Matt:** *The Basket Counts*; Little Brown, Boston, MA, 1968.
257. **Christopher, Matt:** *Break for the Basket*; Scholastic, New York, NY, 1960.
258. **Christopher, Matt:** *Shadow Over the Backcourt*; Franklin Watts, New York, NY, 1959.
259. **Christopher, Matt:** *Tall Man in the Pivot*; Little Brown, Boston, MA, 1961.
260. **Ciciora, Dale and Sweet, Virgil:** *Specific Drills for Basketball Fundamentals*; Ciciora and Sweet, Valparaiso, IN, 1966.
261. **Cimbollek, Robert:** *Basketball's Percentage Offense*; Parker, New York, NY, 1972.

262. **Clagg, Sam:** *The Cam Henderson Story: His Life and Times*; McClain, Parsons, WV, 1981.
263. **Clapp, A.B. and Pound, L. (Eds.):** *Collegiate Basketball Rules for Women*; University of Nebraska Press, Lincoln, NE, 1908.
264. **Clark, G.P. and Griffith, J.L.:** *Basketball Plays and Attack*; Wilson-Weston Sporting Goods, Chicago, IL, 1925.
265. **Clark, G.P. and Griffith, J.L.:** *Fundamentals of Basketball*; Wilson-Weston Sporting Goods, Chicago, IL, 1925.
266. **Clark, G.P. and Griffith, J.L.:** *Training the Basketball Team*; Wilson-Weston Sporting Goods, Chicago, IL, 1925.
267. **Clark, Patrick:** *Sports First*; Facts on File, New York, NY, 1981.
268. **Clark, Steve:** *Illustrated Basketball Dictionary for Young People*; Prentice-Hall, Englewood Cliffs, NJ, 1977.
269. **Clarkston, Rich and Hammell, Bob:** *Knight With the Hoosiers*; Josten's Publications, Topeka, KS, 1975.
270. **Clayton-Jones, H.:** *Basketball*; Arno, New York, NY, 1962.
271. *Coaching Basketball*; Contemporary, New York, NY, 1984.
272. **Coaching Clinic:** *The Best of Basketball From the Coaching Clinic*; Parker, New York, NY, 1970.
273. **Coaching Clinic:** *Handbook of Basketball Drills*; Parker, New York, NY, 1972.
274. **Coaching Youth League Sports Service:** *Coaching Youth League Basketball*; Athletic Institute, Chicago, IL, 1975.
275. **Coffey, Frank and Binacee, Tom:** *The Pride of Portland: The Story of the Trailblazers*; Everest House, New York, NY, 1980.
276. **Coffey, Wayne and Young, Faye:** *Winning Basketball for Girls*; Facts on File, New York, NY, 1984.
277. **Cohen, Joel:** *Big A: The Story of Lew Alcindor*; Scholastic Book Service, New York, NY, 1971.
278. **Cohen, Richard M., Neft, David S., Johnson, Roland T., and Deutsch, Jordan A.:** *All-Sports World Record Book*; Grosset, New York, NY, 1976.
279. **Cohen, Richard M., Neft, David S., Johnson, Roland T., and Deutsch, Jordan A.:** *The Sports Encyclopedia: Pro Basketball*; Grosset, New York, NY, 1975.
280. **Cohen, Stanley:** *The Game They Played*; Farrar, Straus, and Giroux, New York, NY, 1977.
281. **Cole, Lewis:** *Dream Team: The Candid Story of the Champion 1969–70 Knicks*; Morrow, New York, NY, 1981.
282. **Cole, Lewis:** *A Loose Game: The Sport and Business of Basketball*; Bobbs-Merrill, Indianapolis, IN, 1978.
283. **Coleman, Brian and Ray, Peter:** *Basketball*; Charles River Books, Boston, MA, 1977.
284. **Coleman, Brian E.:** *Basketball: Techniques, Teaching, and Training*; A.S. Barnes, San Diego, CA, 1978.
285. **Coleman, Brian E.:** *Better Basketball*; International Publication Service, New York, NY, 1979.
286. **Coleman, Ken:** *So You Want to Be a Sportscaster: The Techniques and Skills of Sports Announcing by One of the Country's Most Experienced Broadcasters*; Hawthorne, New York, NY, 1973.
287. **Colton, Larry and Meschery, Tom:** *Idol Time: Profile in Blazermania*; Timber Press, Forest Grove, OR, 1978.
288. *Compu-Scout System: Computerized Pro-Rated NBA-ABA Player's Guide*; Stadia Sports, New York, NY, 1973.
289. **Cooke, David C.:** *Better Basketball for Boys*; Dodd-Mead, New York, NY, 1960.

290. **Coombs, Charles:** *Be a Winner in Basketball*; William Morrow, New York, NY, 1975.
291. **Coombs, Charles:** *Young Readers Basketball Stories*; Latern Press, New York, NY, 1951.
292. **Coombs, Charles and Geer, Charles:** *Basketball Stories*; Grosset, New York, NY, 1951.
293. **Coombs, Charles and Geer, Charles:** *Indoor Sports Stories*; Grosset, New York, NY, 1952.
294. **Coombs, Charles I.:** *Teen-age Champion Sports Stories*; Latern, New York, NY, 1950.
295. **Coombs, Charles I.:** *Teen-age Treasure Chest of Sports Stories*; Latern, New York, NY, 1948.
296. **Cooper, John and Seidentop, Daryl:** *The Theory and Science of Basketball*; Lea and Febiger, Philadelphia, PA, 1969.
297. **Cooper, Michael and Lynn, Theodore J.:** *No Slack*; CompuPress, Albuquerque, NM, 1988.
298. **Cordell, Christopher:** *Basketball Assemblies*; Platform News, Portland, ME, 1942.
299. **Corn, Frederick L.:** *Basketball's Magnificent Bird: The Larry Bird Story*; Random House, New York, NY, 1982.
300. **Cousy, Bob:** *The Killer Instinct*; Random House, New York, NY, 1975.
301. **Cousy, Bob and Hirshberg, Al:** *Basketball Concepts and Techniques*; Allyn and Bacon, Boston, MA, 1970.
302. **Cousy, Bob and Linn, Ed:** *The Last Loud Roar*; Prentice-Hall, Englewood Cliffs, NJ, 1964.
303. **Cousy, Bob and Power, Frank, Jr.:** *Basketball Concepts and Techniques*; Allyn and Bacon, Boston, MA, 1970.
304. **Cousy, Bob and Ryan, Bob:** *Cousy on the Celtic Mystique*; McGraw-Hill, New York, NY, 1988.
305. **Couzens, Gerald Secor and Gandolfi, Giorgio:** *Hoops! The Official NBA Players Association Guide to Playing Basketball*; McGraw-Hill, New York, NY, 1987.
306. **Cox, William R.:** *Five Were Chosen: A Basketball Story*; Dodd-Mead, New York, NY, 1956.
307. **Cox, William R.:** *Tall on the Court*; Dodd-Mead, New York, NY, 1964.
308. **Craine, H.C.:** *Teaching Athletic Skills in Physical Education*; Inor, New York, NY, 1942.
309. **Cramer, Gary:** *Cavaliers: A Pictorial History of UVA Basketball*; Spring House, Charlottesville, VA, 1983.
310. **Crewell, Larry and Hammell, Bob (Eds.):** *NCAA: Indiana All the Way!*; Indiana University Press, Bloomington, IN, 1976.
311. **Croke, Ed, Poretz, Art, and Bukata, Jim:** *Illustrated Digest of Pro Basketball, 1972–73*; Stadia Sports, New York, NY, 1972.
312. **Crowell, Fred:** *Meet My Head Coach*; Moody Press, Chicago, IL, 1973.
313. **Cummins, Gloria and Cummins, Jim:** *Basketball by the Pros*; Litton Educational, New York, NY, 1976.
314. **Cummins, Jim and Cummins, Gloria:** *Basketball by the Pros*; Litton Educational, New York, NY, 1976.
315. **Curran, Jack:** *New York City High School Basketball*; Parker, New York, NY, 1972.
316. **Daher, J.G. and Bee, C.F.:** *Fundamentals of Basketball*; Crowder, Cheylyan, WV, 1940.
317. **Dahl, Richard:** *Stan Watts: The Man and His Game*; Horizon, Bountiful, UT, 1976.

318. **Daniels, Belinda S. and Davis, Lenwood G.:** *Black Athletes in the United States*; Greenwood, Westport, CT, 1981.
319. **Davies, John:** *The Legend of Hobey Baker*; Little Brown, Boston, MA, 1966.
320. **Davis, Gwenolyn C.:** *An Annotated Bibliography on the Construction and the Development of a Basketball Skill Test*; University of North Carolina Press, Chapel Hill, NC, 1978.
321. **Davis, Lenwood G. and Daniels, Belinda S.:** *Black Athletes in the United States*; Greenwood, Westport, CT, 1981.
322. **Davis, Mac:** *Basketball Unforgettables*; Bantam Books, New York, NY, 1972.
323. **Davis, Robert:** *Aggressive Basketball*; Parker, New York, NY, 1969.
324. **Davis, Tom:** *Zone Offense* (2nd ed.); KST, Stanford, CA, 1979.
325. **Davis, Tom and Winsor, Chuck:** *Garage-Door Basketball*; School Aid Co., Danville, IL, 1970.
326. **Dawkins, Darryl and Wirt, George:** *Chocolate Thunder*; Contemporary Books, Chicago, IL, 1986.
327. **Dawson, Buck and Jones, Thomas (Eds.):** *The Halls of Fame: Specialized Museums of Sports, Agronomy, Entertainment and the Humanities*; Ferguson, Chicago, IL, 1977.
328. **Dawson, Jack C.:** *Encyclopedia of Sport Thrills*; Hart, New York, NY, 1951.
329. **Dean, E.S.:** *Indiana Basketball*; E.S. Dean, Bloomington, IN, 1929.
330. **Dean, E.S.:** *Progressive Basketball*; Stanford University Press, Palo Alto, CA, 1942.
331. **Dean, Everett:** *Progressive Basketball Methods and Philosophy*; Prentice-Hall, Englewood Cliffs, NJ, 1950.
332. **DeBusschere, Dave, Zimmerman, Paul, and Schapp, Dick:** *The Open Man: A Championship Diary*; Grove Press, New York, NY, 1971.
333. **Deegan, Paul:** *The Jump Shot and the Lay-Up*; Creative Education, Minneapolis, MN, 1975.
334. **Deegan, Paul:** *Kareem Abdul-Jabbar*; Creative Education, Minneapolis, MN, 1973.
335. **Deegan, Paul:** *The Set Shot*; Creative Education, Minneapolis, MN, 1975.
336. **Deegan, Paul:** *Shooting in a Game*; Creative Education, Minneapolis, MN, 1975.
337. **Delsohen, Gary and English, Alex:** *English Language*; Contemporary Books, Chicago, IL, 1986.
338. **DeMarco, Mario:** *Great American Athletes*; Pacific Coast, Menlo Park, CA, 1962.
339. **Denlinger, Kenneth and Shapiro, Leonard:** *Athletes for Sale*; Thomas Y. Crowell, New York, NY, 1975.
340. **Deschner, Ramy B.:** *The Evolution of Sports and the Cultural Implications of Physical Education*; Fred Medart, St. Louis, MO, 1946.
341. **Deutsch, Jordan A., Neft, David S., Johnson, Roland T., and Cohen, Richard M.:** *All-Sports World Record Book*; Grosset, New York, NY, 1976.
342. **Deutsch, Jordan A., Neft, David S., Johnson, Roland T., and Cohen, Richard, M.:** *The Sports Encyclopedia: Pro Basketball*; Grosset, New York, NY, 1975.
343. **Devancey, John:** *The Champion Bucks*; Lancer, New York, NY, 1971.
344. **Devancey, John:** *The Story of Basketball*; Random House, New York, NY, 1976.
345. **Devancey, John:** *Tiny: The Story of Nate Archibald*; G.P. Putnam's Sons, New York, NY, 1977.

346. **DeVenzio, Dick:** *Stuff! Good Players Should Know*; Fool Court Press, Charlotte, NC, 1982.
347. **DeVette, Russell B. and Vanderbilt, William R.:** *Coaching Basketball: The Complete Book From Beginning to Championship Play*; American Press, Boston, MA, 1986.
348. **DeWitt, R.T.:** *Teaching Individual and Team Sports*; Prentice-Hall, New York, NY, 1953.
349. **Dickey, Glenn:** *The History of Professional Basketball Since 1896*; Stein and Day, New York, NY, 1982.
350. **Doane, Gene:** *Basketball's Explosive Inside Power Game*; Parker, New York, NY, 1979.
351. **Dobbs, Wayne and Pinholster, Garland, F.:** *Basketball's Stunting Defenses*; Prentice-Hall, Englewood Cliffs, NJ, 1964.
352. **Dodd, Gareth:** *Magic Johnson*; Halloway House, Los Angeles, CA, 1980.
353. **Doggett, Laurence Locke:** *Man and a School: Pioneering in Higher Education at Springfield College*; Association Press, New York, NY, 1943.
354. **Donohue, Jack and Walker, A.L.:** *The New Option Offense for Winning Basketball*; Leisure Press, Champaign, IL, 1988.
355. **Douglas, Amanda M.:** *The Girls of Mount Morris*; Donahue, Chicago, IL, 1914.
356. **Douglas, Gilbert:** *The Bulldog Attitude*; Crowell, New York, NY, 1957.
357. **Driesel, Lefty:** *Secrets of Offensive Basketball*; Meteor, Charlotte, NC, 1966.
358. **Dromo, John and Olsen, Bill:** *University of Louisville Basketball Playbook*; Louisville, KY, 1965.
359. **Dudley, G. and Kellor, F.A.:** *Athletic Games in the Education of Women*; Henry Holt, New York, NY, 1909.
360. **Dunhaime, Gary:** *You Gotta Love It: A Coach's Guide to Championship Basketball*; Interstate, Danville, IL, 1972.
361. **Dunn, William H.:** *Strength Training and Conditioning for Basketball*; Contemporary Books, Chicago, IL, 1984.
362. **Durant, John (Ed.):** *Yesterday in Sports: Memorable Glimpses of the Past as Selected from the Pages of Sports Illustrated*; Barnes, New York, NY, 1956.
363. **Durbin, Brice:** *How to Create a Winning Attitude*; Portrait, Columbus, KS, 1964.
364. **Durbin, Brice:** *Portrait of a Basketball Player*; Portrait, Columbus, KS, 1947.
365. **Durbin, Brice:** *Portrait of a Basketball Player*; Portrait, Columbus, KS, 1979.
366. **Durso, Joseph:** *Madison Square Garden: 100 Years of History*; Simon and Schuster, New York, NY, 1979.
367. **Dwyer, Bob:** *How to Coach and Attack the Zone Defenses*; Prentice-Hall, Englewood Cliffs, NJ, 1963.
368. **Dygard, Thomas:** *Rebound Caper*; William Morrow, New York, NY, 1983.
369. **Dygard, Thomas J.:** *Outside Shooter*; William Morrow, New York, NY, 1972.
370. **Dypwick, Otis and Loken, Newt:** *Cheerleading and Marching Bands*; Barnes, New York, NY, 1945.
371. **Earle, Jimmy:** *Coaching Basketball's Red-Dog Defenses*; Parker, New York, NY, 1971.
372. **Earle, Jimmy:** *Coaching the Flip-Flop Basketball Offense*; Parker, New York, NY, 1971.
373. **Earle, Jimmy:** *Complete Book of 1-3-1 Basketball*; Parker, New York, NY, 1976.
374. **Eaves, Joel:** *Basketball's Shuffle Offenses*; Prentice-Hall, Englewood Cliffs, NJ, 1960.

375. **Ebert, Frances:** *Basketball—Five Player*; Saunders, Philadelphia, PA, 1972.
376. **Ebert, Frances and Cheatum, Billye A.:** *Basketball*; Saunders, Philadelphia, PA, 1977.
377. **Ecker, Tom and King, Don:** *Athletic Journal's Encyclopedia of Basketball*; Parker, New York, NY, 1983.
378. **Eckes, Dennis and Beckett, James:** *Sport American Football and Basketball Card Price Guide*; William Collins, Cleveland, OH, 1979.
379. **Ecksl, Norb and MacLean, Norman:** *The Basketball Quizbook*; Drake, New York, NY, 1976.
380. **Edmundson, Clarence and Morris, Robert:** *Basketball for Players, Officials, and Spectators*; Frayne Printing Co., Seattle, WA, 1931.
381. **Educational Research Council of America:** *Pro Basketball Player*; Changing Times Education Services, St. Paul, MN, 1976.
382. **Egli, John S.:** *The Sliding Zone Defense for Winning Basketball*; Parker, New York, NY, 1970.
383. **Ehre, Edward and Marsh, Irving T.:** *Best Sports Stories of 1944*; Dutton, New York, NY, 1944.
384. **Ehre, Edward and Marsh, Irving T.:** *Best Sports Stories of 1945*; Dutton, New York, NY, 1945.
385. **Ehre, Edward and Marsh, Irving T.:** *Best Sports Stories of 1951*; Dutton, New York, NY, 1951.
386. **Ehre, Edward and Marsh, Irving T.:** *Best Sports Stories of 1953*; Dutton, New York, NY, 1953.
387. **Ehre, Edward and Marsh, Irving T.:** *Best Sports Stories of 1958*; Dutton, New York, NY, 1958.
388. **Ehre, Edward and Marsh, Irving T.:** *Best Sports Stories of 1960*; Dutton, New York, NY, 1960.
389. **Ehre, Edward and Marsh, Irving T.:** *Best Sports Stories of 1963*; Dutton, New York, NY, 1963.
390. **Ehre, Edward and Marsh, Irving T.:** *Best Sports Stories of 1967*; Dutton, New York, NY, 1967.
391. **Ehre, Edward and *The Sporting News*: *Best Sport Stories, 1982;* Dutton, New York, NY, 1982.
392. **Elbeetian Legion:** Celebrating the 25th anniversary of the Lone Scouts of America. In *Elbeetian Book of Memories*; Huron, Chicago, IL, 1941.
393. **Elbeetian Legion:** In commemoration of the Lone Scouts of America, 1915–1924. In *Elbeetian Book of Memories, Volume II*; Merlin, Hudson Heights, NJ, 1963.
394. **Elbeetian Legion:** *Elbeetian Book of Memories, Volume III*; Merlin, Hudson Heights, NJ, 1969.
395. **Ellis, Cliff:** *Complete Fast-Break Basketball*; Prentice-Hall, Englewood Cliffs, NJ, 1979.
396. **Ellis, Cliff:** *Zone Press Variations for Winning Basketball*; Parker, New York, NY, 1975.
397. **Embry, Mike:** *Basketball in the Blue Grass State: The Championship Teams*; Scribner's, New York, NY 1983.
398. **Embry, Mike:** *March Madness: The Kentucky High School Basketball Tournament*; Icarus, South Bend, IN, 1984.
399. **Emery, Donald:** *Court Decision*; David McKay, New York, NY, 1967.
400. **Emery, R.G.:** *Rebound*; Macrae Smith, Philadelphia, PA, 1955.
401. **Emery, R.G.:** *Warren of West Point*; Macrae Smith, Philadelphia, PA, 1950.
402. **English, Alex and Delsohen, Gary:** *English Language*; Contemporary Books, Chicago, IL, 1986.

403. **Enright, Jim:** *March Madness: The Story of High School Basketball in Illinois*; Bloomington High School Association, Bloomington, IL, 1977.
404. **Enright, Jim:** *Only in Iowa: Where the High School Girl Athlete is Queen*; Iowa Girl's High School Athletic Union, Des Moines, IA, 1976.
405. **Enright, Jim:** *Ray Meyer, America's #1 Basketball Coach*; Follet, Chicago, IL, 1980.
406. **Epstein, Buddy and Sandbrook, John:** *The 25 Wooden Years*; UCLA Communications Board, Los Angeles, CA, 1972.
407. **Erickson, Ted and Severson, Red:** *Build a Winning Tradition as a Master Teacher-Coach of Winning Basketball*; Severson and Erickson, St. Cloud, MN, 1978.
408. **Erickson, Ted and Severson, Red:** *Let's Shatter the Zones*; Severson and Erickson, St. Cloud, MN, 1978.
409. **Erickson, Ted and Severson, Red:** *Let's Teach Defense—Read the Offense*; Severson and Erickson, St. Cloud, MN, 1976.
410. **Erickson, Ted and Severson, Red:** *Let's Teach Defense—Read the Zone*; Severson and Erickson, St. Cloud, MN, 1976.
411. **Erickson, Ted and Severson, Red:** *Let's Teach Offense—Read the Defense*; Severson and Erickson, St. Cloud, MN, 1976.
412. **Erickson, Ted and Severson, Red:** *Position, Stance, Move and Play Defense*; Severson and Erickson, St. Cloud, MN, 1978.
413. **Erickson, Ted and Severson, Red:** *Run, Jump, Pass and Score: Offensive Tips for the Entire Family*; Severson and Erickson, St. Cloud, MN, 1978.
414. **Esposito, Michael:** *Game Situation in Basketball*; School Aid and Text Book, Danville, IL, 1966.
415. **Esposito, Michael:** *How to Coach Fast Break Basketball*; Prentice-Hall, Englewood Cliffs, NJ, 1959.
416. *Esquire's* **Editors:** *Esquire's Great Men and Moments in Sports*; Harper, New York, NY, 1962.
417. **Fankhauser, Henry:** *The Wacky World of Sports*; Barnes, New York, NY, 1968.
418. **Feinstein, John:** *A Season Inside: One Year in College Basketball*; Random House, New York, NY, 1988.
419. **Feinstein, John:** *A Season on the Brink: A Year with Bob Knight and the Indiana Hoosiers*; Macmillan, New York, NY, 1986.
420. **Fengler, Hank:** *Winning Basketball with One-Guard Offense*; Parker, New York, NY, 1976.
421. **Fenner, Phyllis R.:** *Quick Pivot: Stories of Basketball*; Alfred Knopf, New York, NY, 1965.
422. **FIBA International Amateur Basketball Federation:** *A Basketball World*; FIBA, Munich, West Germany, 1982.
423. **FIBA International Amateur Basketball Federation:** *International Basketball Results*; FIBA, Munich, West Germany, 1982.
424. **Finney, Peter:** *Pistol Pete: The Story of College Basketball's Greatest Star*; Levee Press, Baton Rouge, LA, 1969.
425. **Finney, Shan:** *Basketball* (Easy-Read Sports Book series); Watts, 1982.
426. **Fish, Marjorie:** *The Theory and Technique of Women's Basketball*; Heath, New York, NY, 1929.
427. **Fishel, Richard and Hare, Clair:** *Terry and Bunky Play Basketball*; Putnam, New York, NY, 1948.
428. **Fitzgerald, Joe:** *The Championship Feeling: The Story of the Boston Celtics*; Scribner and Sons, New York, NY, 1975.
429. **Fitzgerald, Joe and Heinsohn, Tom:** *Give 'Em the Hook*; Prentice-Hall, New York, NY, 1988.

430. **Flath, Arnold William, Ph.D.:** *A History of Relations Between the National Collegiate Athletic Association and the Amateur Athletic Union of the United States, 1902–1963;* Stipes, Champaign, IL, 1964.
431. **Fleischer, Nat:** *Black Dynamite;* Impress House, Bridgeport, CT, 1978.
432. **Fleming, Rhonda and Ingraham, Jo:** *NAGWS Basketball-Volleyball Guide: Tips and Techniques for Teachers and Coaches;* AAHPERD, Washington, DC, 1977.
433. **Flynn, George L. and Vandeweghe, Dr. Ernest M.:** *Growing with Sports: A Parent's Guide to the Young Athlete;* Prentice-Hall, Englewood Cliffs, NJ, 1979.
434. **Ford, Duane:** *The Area Key Offense: A New Multiple Attack for Basketball;* Parker, New York, NY, 1975.
435. **Foster, Bill:** *Conditioning for Basketball: A Guide for Coaches and Athletes;* Leisure Press, West Point, NY, 1983.
436. **Fox, Grace I. and Lawrence, Helen B.:** *Basketball for Girls and Women;* McGraw-Hill, New York, NY, 1954.
437. **Fox, Larry:** *Illustrated History of Basketball;* Grosset and Dunlap, New York, NY, 1974.
438. **Fox, Larry:** *Willis Reed: The Knicks' Comeback Captain;* Grosset, New York, NY, 1973.
439. **Fox, Larry:** *Willis Reed: Take-Charge Man of the Knicks;* Grosset, New York, NY, 1970.
440. **Fox, Stephen R. and Swan, Robert A., Jr.:** *The Kansas Betas, 1873–1973: A Centennial History of the Alpha Nu Chapter of Beta Theta Pi;* University of Kansas Press, Lawrence, KS, 1976.
441. **Fraley, Oscar:** *Basketball in Action;* A.A. Wynn, New York, NY, 1954.
442. **France, Michele Adler:** *Sportsfashion;* Avon, New York, NY, 1980.
443. **Francis, Helen Danneter:** *Basketball Bones;* Hastings House, New York, NY, 1962.
444. **Franks, Ray:** *What's In a Nickname? Exploring the Jungle of College Athletic Mascots;* Ray Franks Publishing Ranch, Amarillo, TX, 1982.
445. **Frazier, Walt and Berkow, Iraz;** *Rockin' Steady: A Guide to Basketball and Cool;* Prentice-Hall, Englewood Cliffs, NJ, 1974.
446. **Frazier, Walt and Jares, Joe:** *Clyde: The Walt Frazier Story;* Grosset and Dunlap, New York, NY, 1974.
447. **Frazier, Walt and Offen, Neil:** *Walt Frazier: One Magic Season and a Basketball Life;* Times Books, New York, NY, 1988.
448. **Fremon, David:** *Secrets of the Super Athletic: Basketball;* Dell, New York, NY, 1982.
449. **Frick, Constance H.:** *Tourney Team;* Harcourt, New York, NY, 1954.
450. **Frieder, Bill and Mortimer, Jeff:** *Basket Case: The Frenetic Life of Michigan Coach Bill Frieder;* Bonus Books, Chicago, IL, 1988.
451. **Friedman, A.J.:** *Basketball—Picking Winners Against the Spread;* GBC Press, Glenview, IL, 1978.
452. **Friendlich, Dick:** *Full Court Press;* Westminster, Philadelphia, PA, 1962.
453. **Friendlich, Dick:** *Panorama of Sports in America;* Funk and Wagnalls, New York, NY, 1970.
454. **Friendlich, Dick:** *Pivot Man;* Scholastic, New York, NY, 1949.
455. **Friendlich, Dick:** *Play Maker;* Westminster, Philadelphia, PA, 1953.
456. **Friendlich, Dick:** *Warrior Forward;* Westminster, Philadelphia, PA, 1950.
457. **Frommer, Harvey and Lieberman, Nancy:** *Basketball, My Way;* Charles Scribner and Sons, New York, NY, 1982.
458. **Frost, Helen and Wordlaw, Charles Digby:** *Basketball and Indoor Baseball for Women;* Scribner and Sons, New York, NY, 1920.

459. **Frymir, Alice W.:** *Basketball for Women: How to Coach and Play the Game*: A.S. Barnes, San Diego, CA, 1930.
460. **Fuller, Bob:** *Basketball's Man-Zone Defense*; Parker, New York, NY, 1977.
461. **Fuller, Bob:** *Basketball's Wishbone Offense*; Parker, New York, NY, 1973.
462. **Fulton, Reed:** *Rookie Coach*; Doubleday, Garden City, NJ, 1955.
463. **Furman, Josh:** *Teen-age Basketball Stories*; Grosset, New York, NY, 1949.
464. **Gallon, Arthur J.:** *Coaching Ideas and Ideals*; Houghton Mifflin, Boston, MA, 1974.
465. **Galotta, Hank and Wootten, Morgan:** *Dematha High School Blitz Defense*; Galotta and Wootten, Baltimore, MD, 1971.
466. **Gandolfi, Giorgi and Couzens, Gerald Secor:** *Hoops! The Official NBA Players Association Guide to Playing Basketball*; McGraw-Hill, New York, NY, 1987.
467. **Gardner, Jack:** *Championship Basketball*; Prentice-Hall, Englewood Cliffs, NJ, 1961.
468. **Garfinkel, Howard (Ed.):** *Five-Star Basketball Drills*; Masters Press, Grand Rapids, MI, 1987.
469. **Garstang, Jack G.:** *Basketball the Modern Way*; Sterling, New York, NY, 1967.
470. **Gault, Clare and Gault, Frank:** *How to Be a Good Basketball Player*; Scholastic Book Services, New York, NY, 1977.
471. **Gault, Frank and Gault, Clare:** *How to Be a Good Basketball Player*; Scholastic Book Services, New York, NY, 1977.
472. **Geer, Charles and Coombs, Charles:** *Indoor Sport Stories*; Grosset, New York, NY, 1952.
473. **Geline, Robert and Turner, Priscilla:** *Forward Rick Barry*; Raintree, Milwaukee, WI, 1978.
474. **Gelman, Steve:** *Bob Cousy, Magician of Pro Basketball*; Bartholomew House, New York, NY, 1961.
475. **Gelman, Steve and Stainback, Barry:** *Basketball Stars of 1966*; Pyramid, New York, NY, 1965.
476. **Gemme, Leila B.:** *Basketball Hall of Fame*; Childrens Press, Chicago, IL, 1978.
477. **Gergen, Joe:** *Final Four: An Illustrated History*; Sporting News Publications, St. Louis, MO, 1987.
478. **Geyer, Dick:** *Full Court Basketball: A Flexible Offense to Exploit Opponents' Weaknesses*; Parker, New York, NY, 1977.
479. **Gilbert, Bill and Hayes, Elvin:** *They Call Me ''The Big E''*; Prentice-Hall, Englewood Cliffs, NJ, 1978.
480. **Gilbert, Bill and Wootten, Morgan:** *From Orphans to Champions: The Story of Dematha's Morgan Wootten*; Atheneum, New York, NY, 1979.
481. **Gill, Amory T.:** *Basic Basketball*; Ronald Press, New York, NY, 1962.
482. **Gipe, George:** *The Great American Sports Book*; Hall of Fame Press, Geneva, IL, 1982.
483. **Glashagel, Jerry (Ed.):** *Young Winner's Basketball*; Youth Sports Press, LaGrange, IL, date unknown.
484. **Glickman, Harry:** *Promoter Ain't a Dirty Word*; Timber Press, Forest Grove, OR, 1978.
485. **Goldaper, Sam:** *Great Moments in Pro Basketball*; Grosset and Dunlap, New York, NY, 1977.
486. **Goldaper, Sam and Pincus, Arthur:** *How to Talk Basketball*; Dembner Books, New York, NY, 1983.
487. **Goldaper, Sam and Searcy, Jay:** *Rick Barry, Golden State Superstar*; Grosset, New York, NY, 1976.
488. **Goldaper, Sam et al.:** *Hot Shots*; Grosset and Dunlap, New York, NY, 1975.

489. **Gonzalez, Billy:** *Championship Basketball Pre-Season to Post-Season*; Creative Sports Books, Hollywood, CA, 1971.

490. **Goodrich, Gail and Levin, Rich:** *Gail Goodrich's Winning Basketball*; Contemporary Books, Chicago, IL, 1976.

491. **Gooter, Joe:** *Bullpen, Bullring, and Bull*; Colt, Patterson, NJ, 1961.

492. **Gooter, Joe:** *Sports Before Your Eyes*; Colt, Patterson, NJ, 1956.

493. **Graffis, Herbert (Ed.):** *Esquire's First Sports Reader*; Barnes, New York, NY, 1945.

494. **Graham, Frank, Jr. and Allen, Mel:** *It Takes Heart*; Harper, New York, NY, 1959.

495. **Grawer, Richard:** *Secrets of Winning Post Play Basketball*; Parker, New York, NY, 1980.

496. **Green, Bill:** *Bill Green's Match-Up Zone Defense*; Let's Teach Basketball, St. Cloud, MN, 1978.

497. **Greenfield, Jeff:** *World's Greatest Team: A Portrait of the Boston Celtics*; Random House, New York, NY, 1976.

498. **Greenstein, Mike:** *Syracuse University Basketball Trivia*; Quinlan Press, Boston, MA, 1988.

499. **Gregg, A.J. (Ed.):** *Basketball and Character*; Association Press, New York, NY, 1976.

500. **Grenier, Mike:** *Don't They Ever Stop Running?*; Book Production Services, Danvers, MA, 1973.

501. **Griffen, J.:** *Teamwork Between Coach and Scholastic Administrator*; School Aid and Text Book, Toronto, ON, 1965.

502. **Griffith, J.L. and Clark, G.P.:** *Basketball Plays and Attack*; Wilson-Weston Sporting Goods, Chicago, IL, 1925.

503. **Griffith, J.L. and Clark, G.P.:** *Fundamentals of Basketball*; Wilson-Weston Sporting Goods, Chicago, IL, 1925.

504. **Griffith, J.L. and Clark, G.P.:** *Training the Basketball Team*; Wilson-Weston Sporting Goods, Chicago, IL, 1925.

505. **Grimsley, Will and the Sports Staff at the Associated Press (Eds.):** *A Century of Sports*; Plimpton Press, New York, NY, 1971.

506. **Gromback, John V.:** *The 1972 Olympic Guide*; Coronet Communications, New York, NY, 1972.

507. **Gromback, John V.:** *The 1976 Olympic Guide*; Rand McNally, New York, NY, 1975.

508. **Gromback, John V.:** *The 1980 Olympic Guide*; Times Books, New York, NY, 1980.

509. **Guiliani, Dorothy A.:** *A Complete Guide to Coaching Women's Basketball*; Parker, West Nyack, NY, 1982.

510. **Gulick, Luther A. and Naismith, James A.:** *Basketball*; American Sports, New York, NY, 1896.

511. **Gullion, Blair:** *Basketball Offensive Fundamentals Analyzed*; Universal Printing, St. Louis, MO, 1936.

512. **Gullion, Blair:** *100 Drills for Teaching Basketball Fundamentals*; Nicholas Press, Richmond, VA, 1933.

513. **Gullion, Blair:** *Techniques and Tactics of Basketball Defense*; Bardgett Printing, St. Louis, MO, 1951.

514. **Guthrie, Bill:** *Hall of Famers*; Stadia Sports, New York, NY, 1973.

515. **Gutman, Bill:** *Chairmen of the Boards*; Tempo, New York, NY, 1980.

516. **Gutman, Bill:** *The Harlem Globetrotters: Basketball's Funniest Team*; Garrard, New Canaan, CT, 1977.

517. **Gutman, Bill:** *The Making of a Basketball Superstar: Pistol Pete Maravich*; Grosset, New York, NY, 1972.

518. **Haarlow, Bill:** *Basketball Diary*; Ronald Press, New York, NY, 1960.
519. **Hager, Robert:** *Percentage Basketball*; Oregon State College, Corvallis, OR, 1926.
520. **Hahn, James and Hahn, Lynn:** *Bill Walton: Maverick Cager*; EMC, St. Paul, MN, 1978.
521. **Hahn, Lynn and Hahn, James:** *Bill Walton: Maverick Cager*; EMC, St. Paul, MN, 1978.
522. **Halberstam, David:** *The Breaks of the Game*; Knopf, New York, NY, 1981.
523. **Hall, Joe B. and Dean, Joe:** *Kentucky Offensive Basketball*; Championship Books, Ames, IA, 1983.
524. **Halter, Jon C.:** *Bill Bradley: One to Remember*; Putnam, New York, NY, 1975.
525. **Halton, Vernon and Chandler, Dan:** *Rupp From Both Ends of the Bench*; Houghton Mifflin, Boston, MA, 1973.
526. **Hammel, Bob:** *Beyond the Brink With Indiana*; Indiana University Press, Bloomington, IN, 1987.
527. **Hammel, Bob:** *The Champs 1981: Indiana Basketball*; Indiana University Press, Bloomington, IN, 1981.
528. **Hammell, Bob and Clarkson, Rich:** *Knight With the Hoosiers*; Josten's Publications, Topeka, KS, 1975.
529. **Hammell, Bob and Crewell, Larry (Eds.):** *NCAA: Indiana All the Way!*; Indiana University Press, Bloomington, IN, 1976.
530. **Handler, Fred and Satalin, Jim:** *Coaching Winning Basketball in the Offensive Zone*; Parker, West Nyack, NY, 1985.
531. **Hankinson, Mel:** *Bench Coaching—Offensive Strategy*; Championship Books, Ames, IA, 1983.
532. **Hankinson, Mel:** *Progressions for Teaching Basketball*; Mel Hankinson, Cleveland, MS, 1979.
533. **Hankinson, Mel and Wade, Margaret:** *Basketball*; Delta State University, Cleveland, MS, 1980.
534. **Hanson, Dale:** *Basketball*; Prentice-Hall, Englewood Cliffs, NJ, 1972.
535. **Hare, Clair and Fishel, Richard:** *Terry and Bunky Play Basketball*; Putnam, New York, NY, 1948.
536. **Harkins, Harry L.:** *Basketball's Pro-Set Playbook: The Complete Offensive Arsenal*; Parker, New York, NY, 1982.
537. **Harkins, Harry L.:** *Coach's Guide to Basketball's 1-4 Offense*; Parker, New York, NY, 1980.
538. **Harkins, Harry L.:** *Complete Book of Zone Game Basketball*; Parker, West Nyack, NY, 1981.
539. **Harkins, Harry L.:** *The Flex-Continuity Basketball Offense*; Parker, West Nyack, NY, 1983.
540. **Harkins, Harry L.:** *Seven Championship-Tested Basketball Offenses*; Parker, New York, NY, 1976.
541. **Harkins, Harry L.:** *Successful Team Techniques in Basketball*; Parker, West Nyack, NY, 1966.
542. **Harkins, Harry L.:** *Win With Pressure Game Basketball*; Parker, New York, NY, 1978.
543. **Harkins, Mike:** *Basketball's Stack Offense*; Prentice-Hall, West Nyack, NY, 1984.
544. **Harkins, Mike:** *Successful Team Techniques in Basketball*; Parker, New York, NY, 1967.
545. **Harkins, Mike:** *Tempo-Control Basketball*; Parker, New York, NY, 1970.
546. **Harp, Richard and McCullough, Joseph:** *Tarkanian: Countdown of a Rebel*; Leisure Press, West Point, NY, 1984.

547. **Harrell, Bill D.:** *Championship-Tested Offensive and Defensive Basketball Strategies*; Parker, New York, NY, 1970.
548. **Harris, D.:** *Coaching Basketball's Zones Defenses*; Prentice-Hall, Englewood Cliffs, NJ, 1976.
549. **Harris, Del:** *Playing the Game, A Guide to Positive Living, Illustrated in a Sports Novel for Teenagers*; Harco, Houston, TX, 1981.
550. **Harris, Delmer:** *Multiple Defenses for Winning Basketball*; Parker, New York, NY, 1971.
551. **Harris, Marv:** *The Fabulous Lakers*; Lancer, New York, NY, 1972.
552. **Harris, Marv:** *On Court With Superstars of the NBA*; Viking Press, New York, NY, 1973.
553. **Harris, Richard:** *I Can Read about Basketball*; Troll Association, Mahwah, NJ, 1976.
554. **Harrison, Don:** *25 Years Plus One: Recounting the Meteoric Rise of Fairfield Basketball*; Donald F. Harrison, Fairfield, CT, 1974.
555. **Hartley, Joseph W. and Healey, William A.:** *Basketball's Greatest Defenses*; Prentice-Hall, Englewood Cliffs, NJ, 1973.
556. **Hartley, Joseph W. and Healey, William A.:** *Basketball's 10 Greatest Offenses*; Prentice-Hall, Englewood Cliffs, NJ, 1970.
557. **Hartley, Joseph W. and Healey, William A.:** *Twelve Great Basketball Offenses*; AAHPERD, Reston, VA, 1982.
558. **Hartley, Joseph W. and Healey, William A.:** *Winning Edge in Basketball: How to Coach Special Situation Plays*; Parker, New York, NY, 1973.
559. **Harvey, Charles (Ed.):** *Sport International, With Full XVII Olympiad Results*; Barnes, New York, NY, 1960.
560. **Harvey, Richard:** *Coaching Basketball's Multiple Set Zone Offense*; Parker, New York, NY, 1973.
561. **Harvey, Richard W.:** *Situation-Reaction Drills for Offensive Basketball*; Parker, New York, NY, 1983.
562. **Hashagen, Kenneth A. and Jourdet, Lon Walter:** *Modern Basketball*; W.B. Saunders, Philadelphia, PA, 1939.
563. **Haskins, James:** *Doctor J: A Biography of Julius Erving*; Doubleday, Garden City, NY, 1978.
564. **Haskins, James:** *From Lew Alcindor to Kareem Abdul-Jabbar*; Lee Lothrop and Shepard Books, New York, NY, 1978.
565. **Haskins, James:** *George McGinnis: Basketball Superstar*; Hastings House, New York, NY, 1978.
566. **Haskins, James:** *The Magic Johnson Story*; Enslow, Hillside, NJ, 1980.
567. **Haun, Roger (Ed.):** *Portfolio of Basketball Drills from College Coaches*; Parker, West Nyack, NY, 1985.
568. **Havlicek, John:** *Hondo: Celtic Man in Motion*; Prentice-Hall, Englewood Cliffs, NJ, 1977.
569. **Hayes, Elvin and Gilbert, Bill:** *They Call Me ''The Big E''*; Prentice-Hall, Englewood Cliffs, NJ, 1978.
570. **Haywood, Spencer and Libby, Bill:** *Stand Up for Something: The Spencer Haywood Story*; Grosset, New York, NY, 1973.
571. **Healey, W.A.:** *Basketball's Rotation Offense*; Interstate Printers, Danville, IL, 1964.
572. **Healey, William:** *Coaching and Managing High School Basketball*; Interstate Printing, Danville, IL, 1942.
573. **Healey, William:** *High School Basketball: Coaching, Managing, and Administering*; Burgess, Minneapolis, MN, 1940.
574. **Healey, William A. and Hartley, Joseph W.:** *Basketball's Greatest Defenses*; Prentice-Hall, Englewood Cliffs, NJ, 1973.

575. **Healey, William A. and Hartley, Joseph W.**: *Basketball's 10 Greatest Offenses*; Prentice-Hall, Englewood Cliffs, NJ, 1970.

576. **Healey, William A. and Hartley, Joseph W.**: *Twelve Great Basketball Offenses*; AAHPERD, Reston, VA, 1982.

577. **Healey, William A. and Hartley, Joseph W.**: *Winning Edge in Basketball: How to Coach Special Situation Plays*; Parker, New York, NY, 1973.

578. **Heard, Robert:** *You Scored One More Point Than a Dead Man*; Lemons-Heard, TX, 1978.

579. **Heartwell, James C.**: *The History of Oregon State College Basketball, 1901–02, 1952–53;* Cascade, Corvallis, OR, 1953.

580. **Heinsohn, Tom and Fitzgerald, Joe:** *Give 'Em the Hook*; Prentice-Hall, New York, NY, 1988.

581. **Heitzmann, William Ray:** *Opportunities in Sports and Athletics;* VMG Career Horizons, Skokie, IL, 1980.

582. **Henderson, Edwin Bancroft:** *The Negro in Sports*; Associated, Washington, DC, 1939.

583. **Herb, George T.**: *How to Play Basketball*; American Sports, New York, NY, 1904.

584. **Herkimer, L.R. and Hollander, Phyllis (Eds.):** *The Complete Book of Cheerleading*; Doubleday, New York, NY, 1975.

585. **Herschlag, Jack:** *Halfcourt Basketball: The Official Book of Three-on-Three Basketball*; Parker, New York, NY, 1984.

586. **Heuman, William:** *Backcourt Man*; Dodd-Mead, New York, NY, 1960.

587. **Heuman, William:** *City High Five*; Dodd-Mead, New York, NY, 1964.

588. **Heuman, William:** *Famous Pro Basketball Stars*; Dodd-Mead, New York, NY, 1970.

589. **Heuman, William:** *Fighting Five*; Morrow, New York, NY, 1950.

590. **Heuman, William:** *Powerhouse Five*; Dodd-Mead, New York, NY, 1963.

591. **Hickey, Eddie:** *Basketball Drills*; Coaches Press, New York, NY, 1955.

592. **Higdon, Hal:** *Find the Key Man*; Putnam, New York, NY, 1974.

593. **Hill, Bob and Baron, Randall:** *The Amazing Basketball Book*; Devya Press, Louisville, KY, 1987.

594. **Hill, Danny and Richards, Jack:** *Complete Handbook of Sports Scoring and Record Keeping*; Parker, New York, NY, 1971.

595. **Hill, Ray:** *Pro Basketball's Little Men*; Random House, New York, NY, 1974.

596. **Hill, Ray:** *Unsung Heroes of Pro Basketball*; Random House, New York, NY, 1973.

597. **Hirshberg, Al:** *Basketball's Greatest Stars*; G.P. Putnam's Sons, New York, NY, 1963.

598. **Hirshberg, Al:** *Basketball's Greatest Teams*; G.P. Putnam's Sons, New York, NY, 1966.

599. **Hirshberg, Al:** *Bill Russell of the Boston Celtics*; Messner, New York, NY, 1963.

600. **Hirshberg, Al and Cousy, Bob:** *Basketball Is My Life*; Prentice-Hall, Englewood Cliffs, NJ, 1957.

601. **Hobson, Howard:** *Basic Basketball Shots*; Seamless Rubber, New Haven, CT, 1952.

602. **Hobson, Howard:** *Basketball Illustrated*; Ronald Press, New York, NY, 1948.

603. **Hobson, Howard A.**: *Scientific Basketball: For Coaches, Players, Officials, Spectators, and Sports Writers*; Prentice-Hall, Englewood Cliffs, NJ, 1949.

604. **Hobson, Howard A.**: *Shooting Ducks: A History of University of Oregon Basketball*; Oregon Historical Society, Eugene, OR, 1984.

605. **Hoenig, Gary and Shaughnessy, Dan:** *Courtside: The Fan's Guide to Pro Basketball*; Vanderbilt Press, Miami, FL, 1984.

606. **Hoffman, Anne Byrne:** *Echoes from the Schoolyard: Informal Portraits of NBA Greats*; Hawthorne Books, New York, NY, 1977.
607. **Hoffman, Vern B. and Hulton, Joe:** *Basketball*; Creative Education, Minneapolis, MN, 1966.
608. **Hollander, Phyllis and Herkimer, L.R. (Eds.):** *The Complete Book of Cheerleading*; Doubleday, New York, NY, 1975.
609. **Hollander, Zander:** *Basketball's Greatest Games*; Prentice-Hall, Englewood Cliffs, NJ, 1971.
610. **Hollander, Zander:** *Complete Handbook of College Basketball*; New American Library, 1979, 1980, 1981.
611. **Hollander, Zander (Ed.):** *The Complete Handbook of the Olympic Games, 1984, Los Angeles*; Signet, New York, NY, 1984.
612. **Hollander, Zander:** *The Complete Handbook of Pro Basketball* (1974 edition to 1987 edition); Signet, New York, NY, 1987.
613. **Hollander, Zander (Ed.):** *Great American Athletes of the 20th Century*; Random House, New York, NY, 1966.
614. **Hollander, Zander:** *Great Rookies of Pro Basketball*; Random House, New York, NY, 1969.
615. **Hollander, Zander (Ed.):** *Madison Square Garden: A Century of Sport and Spectacle on the World's Most Versatile Stage*; Hawthorn, New York, NY, 1973.
616. **Hollander, Zander:** *The Modern Encyclopedia of Basketball*; Dolphin Books, Garden City, NY, 1979.
617. **Hollander, Zander (Ed.):** *The Pro Basketball Encyclopedia*; Corwin Books, Los Angeles, CA, 1979.
618. **Hollander, Zander (Ed.):** *Pro Basketball: Its Superstars and History*; Scholastic Book Service, New York, NY, 1971.
619. **Hollander, Zander and Pawde, Sandy:** *Basketball Lingo*; Grosset and Dunlap, New York, NY, 1971.
620. **Hollander, Zander and Pepe, Phil:** *The Book of Sports Lists*; Pinnade Books, Los Angeles, CA, 1979.
621. **Holman, Nat:** *Holman on Basketball*; Crown, New York, NY, 1950.
622. **Holman, Nathan:** *Championship Basketball*; Ziff-Davis, Chicago, IL, 1942.
623. **Holman, Nathan:** *Scientific Basketball*; Incra, New York, NY, 1922.
624. **Holman, Nathan:** *Winning Basketball*; Scribner and Sons, New York, NY, 1932.
625. **Holme, Christopher (Ed.):** *German Mosaic: An Album for Today*; Suhrkamp Verlag, Frankfurt, West Germany, 1972.
626. **Holzman, Red:** *Defense, Defense*; Warner Communications, New York, NY, 1974.
627. **Holzman, Red and Lewin, Leonard:** *Holzman's Basketball: Winning Strategy and Tactics*; Macmillan, New York, NY, 1973.
628. **Holzman, Red and Lewin, Leonard:** *A View from the Bench*; Suhrkamp Verlag, Frankfurt, West Germany, 1972.
629. **Hoose, Phillip M.:** *Hoosiers: The Fabulous Basketball Life of Indiana*; Vintage, New York, NY, 1986.
630. **Hoover, Jay:** *Blueprint for Ballhandling*; Central Florida YMCA, Gainesville, FL, 1976.
631. **Horky, Rita and Miller, Kenneth:** *Modern Basketball for Women*; Merrill, Columbus, OH, 1970.
632. **Horyza, Len:** *The Pick and Screen Offense for Winning Basketball*; Parker, New York, NY, 1984.
633. **Hosey, Tim and Perceval, Bob:** *Bobby Knight: Countdown to Perfection*; Leisure Press, Champaign, IL, 1983.

634. **Hoyt, Dan and Oliver, Newt:** *One Basketball and Glory;* Oliver, Springfield, OH, 1969.
635. **Hudson River Basketball League of New York:** *Official Constitution, Rules, and Regulations;* American Sports, New York, NY, 1910.
636. **Hughes, W.L.:** *Book of Major Sports;* A.S. Barnes, San Diego, CA, 1938.
637. **Hulton, Joe and Hoffman, Vern B.:** *Basketball;* Creative Education, Minneapolis, MN, 1966.
638. **Hulton, Joseph W.:** *Learning How to Play Basketball;* Creative Education, Minneapolis, MN, 1964.
639. **Hundley, Rod "Hot-Rod":** *Basketball—Individual Offense;* Gainsford, Delray Beach, FL, 1959.
640. **Hunter, Bob:** *Buckeye Basketball: Ohio State Basketball;* Strode, Huntsville, AL, 1980.
641. **Hurt, Marcia:** *Inside Basketball for Women;* Contemporary Books, Chicago, IL, 1979.
642. **Ibach, Bob and Locke, Tates:** *Caught in the Net;* Leisure Press, West Point, NY, 1982.
643. **Ingraham, Jo and Fleming, Rhonda:** *NAGWS Basketball-Volleyball Guide: Tips and Techniques for Teachers and Coaches;* AAHPERD, Washington, DC, 1977.
644. **Isaacs, Neil David:** *All the Moves: A History of College Basketball;* Lippincott, Philadelphia, PA, 1973.
645. **Isaacs, Neil David and Motta, Dick:** *Sports Illustrated Basketball;* Harper and Row, New York, NY, 1981.
646. **Issel, Dan and Martin, Buddy:** *Parting Shots;* Contemporary Books, Chicago, IL, 1985.
647. **Jackson, C.P. and Jackson, O.B.:** *Basketball Clown;* McGraw-Hill, New York, NY, 1956.
648. **Jackson, C.P. and Jackson, O.B.:** *Freshman Forward;* McGraw-Hill, New York, NY, 1959.
649. **Jackson, C.P. and Jackson, O.B.:** *The Short Guard;* McGraw-Hill, New York, NY, 1961.
650. **Jackson, C. Paul:** *Bud Plays Junior High Basketball;* Hastings House, New York, NY, 1959.
651. **Jackson, C. Paul:** *Bud Plays Senior High Basketball;* Hastings House, New York, NY, 1964.
652. **Jackson, C. Paul:** *How to Play Better Basketball;* Crowell, New York, NY, 1968.
653. **Jackson, Cary:** *The Jamesville Jets;* Follett, Chicago, IL, 1959.
654. **Jackson, Cary Paul:** *Shorty at the State Tournament;* Follett, New York, NY, 1955.
655. **Jackson, Cary Paul:** *Shorty Makes the First Team;* Follett, Chicago, IL, 1950.
656. **Jackson, O.B.:** *Basketball Comes to North Island;* McGraw-Hill, New York, NY, 1963.
657. **Jackson, O.B. and Jackson, C.P.:** *Basketball Clown;* McGraw-Hill, New York, NY, 1956.
658. **Jackson, Phil:** *Take It All;* Macmillan, New York, NY, 1970.
659. **Jackson, Phil and Rosen, Charles:** *More Trouble Than a Game;* Playboy Press, Chicago, IL, 1976.
660. **Jackson, Robert B.:** *Earl the Pearl: The Story of Earl Monroe;* Walch, New York, NY, 1971.
661. **Jacobs, A. (Ed.):** *Basketball Rules in Pictures;* Grosset and Dunlap, New York, NY, 1966.
662. **Jacobs, Barry and Morris, Ron:** *ACC Basketball: A Fan's Guide;* Carolina Academic Press, Chapel Hill, NC, 1985.

663. **Jacobs, Linda:** *Julius Erving: Dr. J and Julius*; EMC, St. Paul, MN, 1976.
664. **Jagger, B.:** *Basketball: Coaching and Playing*; Transatlantic Arts, New York, NY, 1971.
665. **Jagger, B.:** *Your Book of Basketball*; Faber, London, 1961.
666. **Jakes, John:** *Famous Firsts in Sports*; Putnam, New York, NY, 1967.
667. **Janoff, Murray:** *Inside Pro Basketball*; Stadia Sports, New York, NY, 1973.
668. **Jares, Joe:** *Basketball: The American Game*; Follet, Chicago, IL, 1971.
669. **Jares, Joe and Frazier, Walt:** *Clyde, The Walt Frazier Story*: Grosset and Dunlap, New York, NY, 1974.
670. **Jenkins, Jerry and Motta, Dick:** *Stuff It: The Story of Dick Motta*; Chilton, Radnor, PA, 1975.
671. **Jenkins, Jerry B. and Lemon, Meadowlark:** *Meadowlark*; Thomas Nelson, Nashville, TN, 1987.
672. **Jeremiah, Maryalyce:** *Basketball: The Woman's Game*; The Athletic Institution, North Palm Beach, FL, 1983.
673. **Jeremiah, Maryalyce:** *Coaching Basketball: Ten Winning Concepts*; Wiley and Sons, New York, NY, 1979.
674. **John, Maurice:** *Drake's Belly Button Defense*; Drake University Press, Des Moines, IA, 1970.
675. **Johnson, Blaine:** *What's Happenin'?*; Prentice-Hall, Englewood Cliffs, NJ, 1978.
676. **Johnson, Dewayne and Tolson, Homer:** *Basketball*; American Press, Boston, MA, 1980.
677. **Johnson, Earvin and Levin, Richard:** *Magic*; Viking, 1983.
678. **Johnson, Ken:** *Coaching Winning Basketball With the Overplay-Pressure Defense*; Parker, New York, NY, 1982.
679. **Johnson, Roland T., Neft, David S., Cohen, Richard M. and Deutsch, Jordan A.:** *All-Sports World Record Book*; Grosset, New York, NY, 1976.
680. **Johnson, Roland T., Neft, David S., Cohen, Richard M. and Deutsch, Jordan A.:** *The Sports Encyclopedia: Pro Basketball*; Grosset, New York, NY, 1975.
681. **Jones, Betty:** *Nancy Lieberman, Basketball's Magic Lady*; Harvey House, New York, NY, 1980.
682. **Jones, K.C. and Warner, Jack:** *Rebound: The Autobiography of K.C. Jones and an Inside Look at the Champion Boston Celtics*; Quinlan, Boston, MA, 1986.
683. **Jones, R.R.:** *Basketball From a Coaching Standpoint*; University of Illinois Press, Champaign, IL, 1916.
684. **Jones, Ron:** *We Killed Them: Trials and Tribulations of a Special Olympic Basketball Team*; AAHPERD, Reston, VA, 1980.
685. **Jones, Thomas and Dawson, Buck (Eds.):** *The Halls of Fame, Featuring Specialized Museums of Sports, Agronomy, Entertainment, and the Humanities*; Ferguson, Chicago, IL, 1977.
686. **Jordan, Pat:** *Choose the Game*; Dodd-Mead, New York, NY, 1979.
687. **Jourdet, Lon Walter and Hashagen, Kenneth A.:** *Modern Basketball*; W.B. Saunders, Philadelphia, PA, 1939.
688. **Jucker, Ed:** *Cincinnati Power Basketball*; Prentice-Hall, Englewood Cliffs, NJ, 1962.
689. **Julian, Alvin F.:** *Bread and Butter Basketball*; Prentice-Hall, Englewood Cliffs, NJ, 1960.
690. **Justice, John B.:** *Duke Basketball*; Strode, Huntsville, AL, 1980.
691. **Kaegel, Dick (Ed.) and The Sporting News:** *Best Sport Stories, 1983*; The Sporting News, St. Louis, MO, 1983.
692. **Kaegel, Dick (Ed.) and The Sporting News:** *Best Sport Stories, 1984*; The Sporting News, St. Louis, MO, 1984.

693. **Kaegel, Dick (Ed.) and** *The Sporting News: Best Sport Stories, 1985*; The Sporting News, St. Louis, MO, 1985.
694. **Kaese, Harold:** *Famous American Athletes of Today*; L.L. Page, Boston, MA, 1942.
695. **Kamm, Herbert and Mullin, Willard (Eds.):** *The Junior Illustrated Encyclopedia of Sports*; Bobbs-Merrill, New York, NY, 1960.
696. **Kalich, R.A.:** *The Basketball Rating Handbook*; A.S. Barnes, San Diego, CA, 1970.
697. **Kapan, Arthur:** *Basketball: How to Improve Your Technique*; F. Watts, New York, NY, 1974.
698. **Keating, Lawrence A.:** *Ace Rebounder*; Westminster, Philadelphia, PA, 1964.
699. **Keidel, Robert W.:** *Game Plans: Sport Strategies for Business*; Dutton, New York, NY, 1985.
700. **Keith, Harold:** *A Pair of Captains*; Crowell, New York, NY, 1951.
701. **Keith, Harold:** *Sport and Games*; Crowell, New York, NY, 1953.
702. **Keith, Larry and Phelps, Richard:** *A Coach's World*; Crowell, New York, NY, 1974.
703. **Kellner, Stan:** *Taking It to the Limit With Basketball Cybernetics*; Durite, West Islip, NY, 1978.
704. **Kellor, F.A. and Dudley, G.:** *Athletic Games in the Education of Women*; Henry Holt, New York, NY, 1909.
705. **Kelly, Robert:** *Domino's: The Original Hockey/Basketball Trivia Puzzler*; Domino's, West Hemstead, NY, 1980.
706. **Kennard, A.B.:** *Tips on Girl's Basketball*; Sport Tips and Teaching Aids, Detroit, MI, 1941.
707. **Kennedy, Charles W.:** *College Athletics*; Princeton University Press, Princeton, NJ, 1925.
708. **Kessler, Kent:** *Hail West Virginians*; Kessler, Weston, WV, 1959.
709. **Kieran, Leonard:** *Championship NBA: NBA's Official Championship Playoff History*; Dial, New York, NY, 1970.
710. **Kindred, Dave:** *Basketball: The Dream Game in Kentucky*; Data Courier, Louisville, KY, 1976.
711. **King, Don and Ecker, Tom:** *Athletic Journal's Encyclopedia of Basketball*; Parker, New York, NY, 1983.
712. **King, George and Toney, David:** *Basketball*; Athletic Institute, Chicago, IL, 1973.
713. **Kirkland, Winifred:** *Introducing Corinna*; Revell, New York, NY, 1909.
714. **Kirkpatrick, Curry and Vitale, Dick:** *Vitale: Just Your Average Bald, One-Eyed Basketball Wacko Who Beat the Ziggy and Became a PTP'er*; Simon and Schuster, New York, NY, 1988.
715. **Klein, Dave:** *Playoff—24 Seconds to Glory: A Chronicle of NBA and ABA Title Series*; Stadia Sports, New York, NY, 1973.
716. **Klein, Dave:** *Pro Basketball's Big Men*; Random House, New York, NY, 1973.
717. **Klein, Dave:** *Rookie: The World of the NBA*; Grosset, New York, NY, 1971.
718. **Klein, Dave:** *A Thinking Person's Guide to Pro Basketball*; Grosset and Dunlap, New York, NY, 1978.
719. **Klein, Monica:** *The Backyard Basketball Superstar*, Knopf, New York, NY, 1981.
720. **Klores, Dan:** *Roundball Culture: South Carolina Basketball*; AM Press, Huntsville, AL, 1980.
721. **Knapp, Sally:** *Sink the Basket*; Crowell, New York, NY, 1953.
722. **Knight, Bob and Newell, Pete:** *Basketball According to Knight and Newell*; Knight and Newell, Graessle-Mercer, Seymour, IN, 1986.

723. **Knosher, Harley:** *Basic Basketball Strategy;* Garden City, NY, 1973.
724. **Knudson, R.R.:** *Zanbanger;* Dell, New York, NY, 1977.
725. **Koch, Tom:** *Tournament Trail;* Lothrop, New York, NY, 1950.
726. **Koppet, Leonard:** *Championship NBA;* Dial Press, New York, NY, 1970.
727. **Koppet, Leonard:** *The Essence of the Game is Deception: Thinking About Basketball;* Little Brown, Boston, MA, 1973.
728. **Koppet, Leonard:** *The New York Times Guide to Spectator Sports;* Quadrangle Books, New York, NY, 1971.
729. **Koppet, Leonard:** *Twenty-Four Seconds to Shoot;* Macmillan, New York, NY, 1980.
730. **Krajewski, Bob and Baralto, John:** *Coaching Junior High School Basketball;* Mr. Studios, East Chicago, IN, 1960.
731. **Krause, Jerry:** *The Basketball Bible;* Leisure Press, West Point, NY, 1982.
732. **Krause, Jerry:** *Better Basketball Basics: Before the X's and O's;* Leisure Press, West Point, NY, 1984.
733. **Krause, Jerry:** *The Boys Clubs' Guide to Youth Basketball;* Leisure Press, West Point, NY, 1983.
734. **Krugel, Mitchell:** *Michael Jordan;* St. Martin's Press, New York, NY, 1988.
735. **Krzyzewski, Mike:** *Duke's Team Man-to-Man Defense;* Krzyzewski, Duke University Press, Durham, NC, 1986.
736. **LaGrand, Louis:** *Coach's Complete Guide to Winning Basketball;* Parker, New York, NY, 1967.
737. **Lai, William T.:** *Winning Basketball;* Stadia Sports, New York, NY, 1973.
738. **Lai, William T.:** *Winning Basketball: Individual Play and Team Strategy;* Prentice-Hall, Englewood Cliffs, NJ, 1955.
739. **Lambert, Ward Lewis:** *Practical Basketball;* Athletic Journal, Chicago, IL, 1932.
740. **Lance, Kathryn:** *A Woman's Guide to Spectator Sports;* A and W, New York, NY, 1980.
741. **Langrock, Dave and Borcherding, Jim:** *Winning Basketball Drills;* Jim Borcherding, Rock Island, IL, 1971.
742. **Lapchick, Joe and Bee, Clair:** *Fifty Years of Basketball;* Prentice-Hall, Englewood Cliffs, NJ, 1968.
743. **Larrit, Barry,** *Pro Basketball 1976–77;* Ballantine Books, New York, NY, 1976.
744. **Laudeman, Tev:** *The Rupp Years: The University of Kentucky's Golden Era of Basketball;* Courier-Journal, Louisville, KY, 1972.
745. **Lawrence, Alfred C. and Bole, Robert D.:** *From Peachbaskets to Slamdunks;* B & L, Canaan, NH, 1988.
746. **Lawrence, Helen B. and Fox, Grace I.:** *Basketball for Girls and Women;* McGraw-Hill, New York, NY, 1954.
747. **Lawtner, John:** *Psychology of Coaching;* Prentice-Hall, Englewood Cliffs, NJ, 1951.
748. **Lay, Nancy E.:** *The Summitt Season: An Inside Look at Pat Head Summitt and the Lady Vols;* Leisure Press, Champaign, IL, 1989.
749. **Lazenby, Roland:** *Georgetown, the Championships and Thompson;* Full Court Press, Roanoke, VA, 1985.
750. **Lazenby, Roland:** *Sampson: A Life Above the Rim;* Full Court Press, Roanoke, VA, 1983.
751. **Lazenby, Roland:** *The Second Season: Virginia's Rise to the Final Four;* Full Court Press, Roanoke, VA, 1983.
752. **Lee, S.C.:** *Best Basketball Booster;* Strode, Huntsville, AL, 1974.
753. **LeGrand:** *How Basketball Began;* Abington Press, New York, NY, 1962.
754. **Lehane, Jack:** *Basketball Fundamentals: Teaching Techniques for Winning;* Allyn and Bacon, Newton, MA, 1980.

755. **Lemon, Meadowlark and Jenkins, Jerry B.:** *Meadowlark*; Thomas Nelson, Nashville, TN, 1987.

756. **Leonard, Burgess:** *Phantom of the Foul Lines*; Lippincott, New York, NY, 1952.

757. **Lerner, Mark:** *Careers in Basketball*; Lerner, 1983.

758. **Lester, Pauline:** *Marjorie Dean—High School Junior*; Burt, New York, NY, 1917.

759. **Lester, Pauline:** *Marjorie Dean—High School Senior*; Burt, New York, NY, 1917.

760. **Levin, Rich:** *Magic Johnson: Court Magician*; Childrens Press, Chicago, IL, 1981.

761. **Levin, Rich and Goodrich, Gail:** *Gail Goodrich's Winning Basketball*; Contemporary Books, Chicago, IL, 1976.

762. **Levin, Robert (Ed.):** *Y Basketball Dribblers Manual: For 5th–6th Grade Players*; Human Kinetics, Champaign, IL, 1984.

763. **Levin, Robert (Ed.):** *Y Basketball Passers Manual: For 3–4th Grade Players*; Human Kinetics, Champaign, IL, 1984.

764. **Levine, Lee Daniel:** *Bird: The Making of an American Sports Legend!*; McGraw-Hill, New York, NY, 1988.

765. **Levitt, Bunny:** *Basketball Handbook*; Bunny Levitt, Neptune, NJ, 1963.

766. **Levitt, Bunny:** *Basketball Player's Digest*; Bunny Levitt, Neptune, NJ, 1964.

767. **Lewin, Leonard and Holzman, Red:** *Holzman's Basketball: Winning Strategy and Tactics*; Macmillan, New York, NY, 1973.

768. **Lewin, Leonard and Holzman, Red:** *A View From the Bench*; Norton, New York, NY, 1980.

769. **Lewis, Guy and Redmond, Gerald:** *Sporting Heritage: A Guide to Halls of Fame, Special Collections and Museums in the United States and Canada*; Barnes, New York, NY, 1974.

770. **Ley, Katherine L. and Miller, Donna Mae:** *Individual and Team Sports for Women*; Prentice-Hall, Englewood Cliffs, NJ, 1955.

771. **Libby, Bill:** *Goliath: The Wilt Chamberlain Story*; Dodd-Mead, New York, NY, 1977.

772. **Libby, Bill:** *The Walton Gang*; Coward, New York, NY, 1974.

773. **Libby, Bill and Barry, Rick:** *Confessions of a Basketball Gypsy*; Dell, New York, NY, 1972.

774. **Libby, Bill and Haywood, Spencer:** *Stand Up for Something: The Spencer Haywood Story*; Grosset, New York, NY, 1975.

775. **Libby, Bill and West, Jerry:** *Mr. Clutch: The Jerry West Story*; Grosset, New York, NY, 1971.

776. **Liebendorfer, Don. E.:** *The Color of Life Is Red: A History of Stanford Athletics, 1892–1972*; Stanford University Press, Palo Alto, CA, 1972.

777. **Lieberman, Nancy and Frommer, Harvey:** *Basketball My Way*; Charles Scribner and Sons, New York, NY, 1982.

778. **Lindenburg, Franklin A.:** *How to Play and Teach Basketball*; Associated Press, New York, NY, 1963.

779. **Linehan, Don:** *Soft Touch: A Sport That Lets You Touch Life*; Acropolis Books, Washington, D.C., 1976.

780. **Lipe, C.C. and Ruby, James Craig:** *How to Coach and Play Basketball*; Bailey and Himes, Champaign, IL, 1926.

781. **Lipsky, Richard:** *How We Play the Game: Why Sports Dominate American Life*; Beacon, Boston, MA, 1981.

782. **Liss, Howard:** *Basketball Talk for Beginners*; Pocket Books, New York, NY, 1973.

783. **Liss, Howard:** *The Pocket Book of Pro Basketball '80–'81*; Pocket Books, New York, NY, 1980.

784. **Liss, Howard:** *Strange but True Basketball Stories*; Random House, New York, NY, 1972.

785. **Litsky, Frank, and Tyno, Steve (Comps.):** *The New York Times Sports Almanac*; J. Lowell Pratt, New York, NY, 1965.

786. **Litwiler:** *Basketball Coach's Guide to Drills and Skills*; Prentice-Hall, Englewood Cliffs, NJ, date unknown.

787. **Lochlons, Colin:** *Stretch Smith Makes a Basket*; Crowell, New York, NY, 1949.

788. **Locke, Tates and Ibach, Bob:** *Caught in the Net*; Leisure Press, West Point, NY, 1982.

789. **Loeffler, Kenneth and Berstein, Ralph:** *Ken Loeffler on Basketball*; Prentice-Hall, Englewood Cliffs, NJ, 1955.

790. **Logan, Robert:** *The Bulls and Chicago: A Stormy Affair*; Follet, Chicago, IL, 1975.

791. **Loken, Newt and Dypwick, Otis:** *Cheerleading and Marching Bands*; Barnes, New York, NY, 1945.

792. **Lord, Beman:** *Guards for Matt*; Walsh, New York, NY, 1961.

793. **Lowitt, Bruce and Rosenthal, Bert:** *Pro Basketball Superstars of 1975*; Pyramid, New York, NY, 1975.

794. **Lowry, Carla:** *Pictorial Basketball*; Creative Sports Books, Hollywood, CA, 1968.

795. *The LSU Basketball Organizational Handbook: The LSU Way*; Leisure Press, Champaign, IL, 1983.

796. **Lundgren, Hal:** *Calvin Murphy: The Giant Slayer*; Childrens Press, Chicago, IL, 1982.

797. **Lundgren, Hal:** *Moses Malone: Philadelphia's Peerless Center*; Childrens Press, Chicago, IL, 1982.

798. **Lynn, Theodore J. and Cooper, Michael:** *No Slack*; CompuPress, Albuquerque, NM, 1988.

799. **Lyon, Bill and Williams, Pat:** *We Owed You One! The Uphill Struggle of the Philadelphia 76'ers*; Trimark, New Castle, DE, 1983.

800. **Lyttle, Richard B.:** *Getting Into Pro Basketball*; Franklin Watts, New York, NY, 1979.

801. **MacDonald, Frank:** *Chicago Bulls*; Creative Education, Minneapolis, MN, 1984.

802. **MacDonald, Frank:** *Cleveland Cavaliers*; Creative Education, Minneapolis, MN, 1984.

803. **MacDonald, Frank:** *Golden State Warriors*; Creative Education, Minneapolis, MN, 1984.

804. *MacGregor Basketball Series: Volume 1. Zone Defense*; MacGregor Sports Education, Waukesha, WI, 1987.

805. *MacGregor Basketball Series: Volume 2. Zone Offense*; MacGregor Sports Education, Waukesha, WI, 1987.

806. *MacGregor Basketball Series: Volume 3. Man-to-Man Defense*; MacGregor Sports Education, Waukesha, WI, 1987.

807. *MacGregor Basketball Series: Volume 4. Match-up Zone*; MacGregor Sports Education, Waukesha, WI, 1987.

808. *MacGregor Basketball Series: Volume 5. The Fast Break*; MacGregor Sports Education, Waukesha, WI, 1987

809. *MacGregor Basketball Series: Volume 6. Team Organization*; MacGregor Sports Education, Waukesha, WI, 1987.

810. *MacGregor Basketball Series: Volume 7. Organizing Practice*; MacGregor Sports Education, Waukesha, WI, 1987.

811. *MacGregor Basketball Series: Volume 8. Player-Coach Relationship*; MacGregor Sports Education, Waukesha, WI, 1987.
812. *MacGregor Basketball Series: Volume 9. Developing the High School Program*; MacGregor Sports Education, Waukesha, WI, 1987.
813. *MacGregor Basketball Series: Volume 10. Motivating Your Athletes*; MacGregor Sports Education, Waukesha, WI, 1987.
814. *MacGregor Basketball Series: Volume 11. Special Game Situations*; MacGregor Sports Education, Waukesha, WI, 1987.
815. *MacGregor Basketball Series: Volume 12. Post Play*; MacGregor Sports Education, Waukesha, WI, 1987.
816. *MacGregor Basketball Series: Volume 13. Defensive Drills*; MacGregor Sports Education, Waukesha, WI, 1987.
817. *MacGregor Basketball Series: Volume 14. Post Offense*; MacGregor Sports Education, Waukesha, WI, 1987.
818. *MacGregor Basketball Series: Volume 15. Man-to-Man Offense*; MacGregor Sports Education, Waukesha, WI, 1988.
819. *MacGregor Basketball Series: Volume 16. Individual Fundamentals*; MacGregor Sports Education, Waukesha, WI, 1988.
820. *MacGregor Basketball Series: Volume 17. Pressure Offense*; MacGregor Sports Education, Waukesha, WI, 1988.
821. *MacGregor Flashback Notebook* (Vols. 10–14); MacGregor Medalist Sports Education, Waukesha, WI, 1984–1988.
822. **MacKellar, William:** *The Team That Wouldn't Quit*; McGraw-Hill, New York, NY, 1956.
823. **MacLean, Norman and Ecksl, Norb:** *The Basketball Quizbook*; Drake, New York, NY, 1976.
824. **MacWilliams, Don:** *Yours in Sports: A History of Baseball, Basketball, Boxing and Bowling in Maine*; Monmouth Press, Lewiston, ME, 1969.
825. **Madison, Paul and Randall, Chuck:** *Coach, God Loves You and So Do I*; Union, Bellingham, WA, 1976.
826. **Magula, Steve:** *Before the Big Moment*; Aristocratic, Fort Lauderdale, FL, 1982.
827. **Manley, Martin:** *Martin Manley's Basketball Heaven*; FACTS, Topeka, KS, 1987.
828. **Mann, Leslie:** *Basketball Notes*; publisher unknown, 1923.
829. **Maravich, Pete and Campbell, Darrell:** *Heir to a Dream*; Thomas Nelson, Nashville, TN, 1987.
830. **Marsh, Irving T. and Ehre, Edward:** *Best Sport Stories of 1944*; Dutton, New York, NY, 1945.
831. **Marsh, Irving T. and Ehre, Edward:** *Best Sport Stories of 1945*; Dutton, New York, NY, 1945.
832. **Marsh, Irving T. and Ehre, Edward:** *Best Sport Stories of 1951*; Dutton, New York, NY, 1951.
833. **Marsh, Irving T. and Ehre, Edward:** *Best Sport Stories of 1953*; Dutton, New York, NY, 1953.
834. **Marsh, Irving T. and Ehre, Edward:** *Best Sport Stories of 1958*; Dutton, New York, NY, 1958.
835. **Marsh, Irving T. and Ehre, Edward:** *Best Sport Stories of 1960*; Dutton, New York, NY, 1960.
836. **Marsh, Irving T. and Ehre, Edward:** *Best Sport Stories of 1963*; Dutton, New York, NY, 1963.
837. **Marsh, Irving T. and Ehre, Edward:** *Best Sport Stories of 1967*; Dutton, New York, NY, 1967.
838. **Marquette, Ray:** *Indiana Basketball*; Alpine Books, New York, NY, 1975.

839. **Martin, Molly:** *New York Knicks*; Creative Education, Minneapolis, MN, 1984.

840. **Martin, Molly:** *Portland Trailblazers*; Creative Education, Minneapolis, MN, 1984.

841. **Masin, Herman:** *The Best of Basketball From Scholastic Coach*; Prentice-Hall, Englewood Cliffs, NJ, 1962.

842. **Masin, Herman:** *How to Star in Basketball*; Scholastic Book Services, New York, NY, 1975.

843. **Masin, Herman L.:** *A New Treasury of Sports Humor*; Prentice-Hall, Englewood Cliffs, NJ, 1964.

844. **Masin, Herman L.:** *Speaker's Treasury of Sports Stories*; Prentice-Hall, Englewood Cliffs, NJ, 1954.

845. **Mather, Edwin J. and Mitchell, Elmer D.:** *Basketball*; C.W. Graham, Ann Arbor, MI, 1922.

846. **Mather, Edwin J. and Mitchell, Elmer D.:** *Basketball: How to Coach the Game*; A.S. Barnes, San Diego, CA, 1922.

847. **Mazer, Bill:** *The Sports Answer Book*; Grosset, New York, NY, 1972.

848. **McCall, Fred:** *McCall's Rebounder Book of Drills*; Sorenson, address unknown, 1969.

849. **McCallum, John:** *College Basketball USA, Since 1892*; Stein and Day, Briar Cliff Manor, New York, NY, 1978.

850. **McClary, Pat:** *Coaching Basketball's New Passing Game Offense*; Parker, West Nyack, NJ, 1981.

851. **McClelland, Marshall and Osborn, Chuck:** *Basketball for Boys*; Follett, Chicago, IL, 1960.

852. **McClendon, John B.:** *Fast Break Basketball: Fundamentals and Fine Points*; Parker, New York, NY, 1965.

853. **McCormick, Wilfred:** *The Five Man Break*; David McKay, New York, NY, 1962.

854. **McCormick, Wilfred:** *Too Many Forwards*; David McKay, New York, NY, 1960.

855. **McCracken, Branch:** *Indiana Basketball*; Prentice-Hall, Englewood Cliffs, NJ, 1955.

856. **McCreary, Jay:** *Winning High School Basketball*; Prentice-Hall, Englewood Cliffs, NJ, 1956.

857. **McCullough, Joseph and Harp, Richard:** *Tarkanian: Countdown of a Rebel*; Leisure Press, West Point, NY, 1984.

858. **McGregor, Jim and Rappaport, Ron:** *Called for Traveling*; Macmillan, New York, NY, 1978.

859. **McGuire, Frank:** *Defensive Basketball*; Prentice-Hall, Englewood Cliffs, NJ, 1959.

860. **McGuire, Frank:** *Offensive Basketball*; Prentice-Hall, Englewood Cliffs, NJ, 1958.

861. **McGuire, Frank:** *Team Basketball Offense and Defense*; Prentice-Hall, Englewood Cliffs, NJ, 1967.

862. **McLane, Hardin (Ed.):** *Championship Basketball by 12 Great Coaches*; Prentice-Hall, Englewood Cliffs, NJ, 1966.

863. **McLendon, John B., Sr.:** *Fast Break Basketball: Fundamentals and Fine Points*; Parker, West Nyack, NJ, 1971.

864. **McMahon, James D.:** *Pro-Am Basketball Scorebook*; Anthelion Press, Corte Madera, CA, 1976.

865. **McPhee, John:** *A Sense of Where You Are*; Bantam Pathfinders, New York, NY, 1967.

866. **McSweeny, William and Russell, Bill:** *Go Up for Glory*; Coward-McCann, New York, NY, 1966.

867. **McWhirter, Norris (Comp. and Ed.):** *Guiness 1983 Book of World Records*; Sterling, New York, NY, 1982.

868. **McWhirter, Norris and McWhirter, Ross (Comp. and Ed.):** *Guiness 1974–75 Book of World Records*; Sterling, New York, NY, 1974.

869. **Meader, Stephen:** *Sparkplug of the Hornets*; Harcourt, New York, NY, 1953.

870. **Meanwell, W.E. and Rockne, K.K.:** *Training, Conditioning and the Care of Injuries*; H.D. Gath, Madison, WI, 1930.

871. **Meanwell, Dr. Walter E.:** *Basketball for Men*; H.D. Gath, NY, 1922.

872. **Meanwell, Walter Ernest:** *The Science of Basketball for Men*; H.D. Gath, NY, 1924.

873. **Meany, Tom:** *There's Been Some Changes in the World of Sports*; Thomas Nelson, New York, NY, 1962.

874. **Mears, Ray:** *The Basketball Notebook of Coach Mears*; Ray Mears, Knoxville, TN, 1961.

875. **Mears, Ray:** *It's All in the State of Mind*; Ray Mears, Knoxville, TN, 1961.

876. **Medalist Flashback Notebook** *(Vols. 2–15)*: Medalist Sports Education, Waukesha, WI, 1976–1989.

877. **Meissner, Wilhelmine F. and Meyers, E.Y.:** *Modern Basketball for Girls*; Scholastic Coach Bookshop, New York, NY, 1935.

878. **Mellen, Joan:** *Bob Knight: His Own Man—The Man Behind the Myth On and Off the Court*; Donald I. Fine, New York, NY, 1988.

879. **Mellville, Chuck:** *The Harlem Globetrotters*; David McKay, New York, NY, 1978.

880. **Mendell, L.:** *Who's Who in Basketball*; Arlington House, New Rochelle, NY, 1973.

881. **Menke, Frank G.:** *Encyclopedia of Sports*; Menke, New York, NY, 1939.

882. **Menke, Frank G.:** *The New Encyclopedia of Sports*; Barnes, New York, NY, 1947.

883. **Meschery, Tom:** *Caught in the Pivot: The Diary of a Rookie Coach in the Exploding World of Pro Basketball*; Dell, New York, NY, 1973.

884. **Meschery, Tom:** *Over the Rim*; McCall, New York, NY, 1979.

885. **Meschery, Tom and Colton, Larry:** *Idol Time: Profile in Blazermania*; Timber Press, Forest Grove, OR, 1978.

886. **Messer, G.:** *How to Play Basketball*; American Sports, New York, NY, 1913.

887. **Meyer, Margaret and Schartz, Marguerite:** *Team Sports for Girls and Women*; W.B. Saunders, Philadelphia, PA, 1957.

888. **Meyer, Ray:** *Basketball as Coached by Ray Meyer*; Prentice-Hall, Englewood Cliffs, NJ, 1967.

889. **Meyer, Ray:** *How to Play Winning Basketball*; Wood Associates, Chicago, IL, 1987.

890. **Meyer, Ray and Sons:** *Coach*; Contemporary Books, Chicago, IL, 1987.

891. **Meyers, E.Y. and Meissner, Wilhelmine F.:** *Basketball for Girls*; Barnes, New York, NY, 1940.

892. **Michelson, Herb:** *Almost a Famous Person*; Harcourt, Brace, Jovanovich, New York, NY, 1980.

893. **Michener, James A.:** *Sports in America*; Random House, New York, NY, 1976.

894. **Micolean, Tyler and Anderson, Forest:** *Basketball Techniques Illustrated*; A.S. Barnes, San Diego, CA, 1952.

895. **Miers, Earl:** *Basketball: The Greatest Teams, Coaches, and Star Players of All Time*; Grosset and Dunlap, New York, NY, 1974.

896. **Mifflin, Lawrie and Rush, Cathy:** *Women's Basketball*; Hawthorn Books, New York, NY, 1976.
897. **Mikan, George:** *Mr. Basketball*; Greenbury, New York, NY, 1951.
898. **Mikes, Jay:** *Basketball FundaMENTALS: A Complete Mental Training Guide*; Leisure Press, Champaign, IL, 1987.
899. **Miller, Donna Mae and Ley, Katherine L.:** *Individual and Team Sports for Women*; Prentice-Hall, Englewood Cliffs, NJ, 1955.
900. **Miller, G.F. and Chandler, W.A.:** *Basketball Technique*; Dunn County News, Menomonie, WI, 1922.
901. **Miller, Gary:** *Official's Manual: Basketball*; Leisure Press, West Point, NY, 1979.
902. **Miller, Kenneth and Horky, Rita:** *Modern Basketball for Women*; Merrill, Columbus, OH, 1970.
903. **Miller, William H.:** *Basketball of Tomorrow*; Jordon, Tulsa, OK, 1938.
904. **Mills, John:** *Basketball Handbook*; Hancock House, Seattle, WA, 1980.
905. **Milner, Gene:** *The Indiana High School Basketball Book*; Indiana Basketball High School.
906. **Mitchell, E.D. and Bowen, W.P.:** *The Practice of Organized Play*; A.S. Barnes, San Diego, CA, 1929.
907. **Mitchell, Elmer D.:** *Intramural Athletics*; Barnes, New York, NY, 1928.
908. **Mitchell, Elmer D. (Ed.):** *Sports Officiating*; Barnes, New York, NY, 1949.
909. **Mitchell, Elmer D. and Mather, Edwin J.:** *Basketball*; C.W. Graham, Ann Arbor, MI, 1922.
910. **Mitchell, Elmer D. and Mather, Edwin J.:** *Basketball: How to Coach the Game*; A.S. Barnes, San Diego, CA, 1922.
911. **Mitchell, W.W.:** *Official Basketball Scorebook*; Burgess, Minneapolis, MN, 1941.
912. **Mlecka, Louis F. (Comp.):** *Famous People: Historical Biographical Books of Birthdays*; Mlecka, Brooksville, FL, 1973.
913. **Moen, Aaron N.:** *Basketball Performance Profiles*; Corner Brook Press, Lansing, NY, 1978.
914. **Mokray, Bill:** *Averages*; Potter Printing, Boston, MA, 1967.
915. **Mokray, Bill:** *Ronald Encyclopedia of Basketball*; Ronald Press, New York, NY, 1963.
916. **Mokray, William G.:** *Basketball Stars of 1961*; Pyramid, New York, NY, 1960.
917. **Mokray, William G.:** *Basketball Stars of 1962*; Pyramid, New York, NY, 1961.
918. **Mokray, William G.:** *Basketball Stars of 1963*; Pyramid, New York, NY, 1962.
919. **Mokray, William G.:** *Basketball Stars of 1964*; Pyramid, New York, NY, 1963.
920. **Monroe, Earl and Unseld, Wes:** *Basketball Skillbook*; Atheneum of Philadelphia, Philadelphia, PA, 1973.
921. **Montieth, Mark:** *Passion Play: A Season with the Purdue Boilermakers and Coach Gene Keady*; Bonus Books, Chicago, IL, 1988.
922. **Moore, Billie J. and White, John:** *Basketball: Theory and Practice*; William C. Brown, Dubuque, IA, 1980.
923. **Moore, Jim:** *Atlanta Hawks*; Creative Education, Minneapolis, MN, 1984.
924. **Moore, Jim:** *Dallas Mavericks*; Creative Education, Minneapolis, MN, 1984.
925. **Moore, Jim:** *Detroit Pistons*; Creative Education, Minneapolis, MN, 1984.
926. **Moore, Jim:** *Houston Rockets*; Creative Education, Minneapolis, MN, 1984.
927. **Moore, Jim:** *Indiana Pacers*; Creative Education, Minneapolis, MN, 1984.
928. **Moore, Jim:** *Kansas City Kings*; Creative Education, Minneapolis, MN, 1984.
929. **Moore, Jim:** *Los Angeles Lakers*; Creative Education, Minneapolis, MN, 1984.
930. **Moore, Jim:** *Milwaukee Bucks*; Creative Education, Minneapolis, MN, 1984.
931. **Moore, Jim:** *New Jersey Nets*; Creative Education, Minneapolis, MN, 1984.

932. **Moore, Jim:** *Phoenix Suns;* Creative Education, Minneapolis, MN, 1984.
933. **Moore, Jim:** *San Antonio Spurs;* Creative Education, Minneapolis, MN, 1984.
934. **Moore, Jim:** *San Diego Clippers;* Creative Education, Minneapolis, MN, 1984.
935. **Moore, Jim:** *Utah Jazz;* Creative Education, Minneapolis, MN, 1984.
936. **Moore, Jim:** *Washington Bullets;* Creative Education, Minneapolis, MN, 1984.
937. **Morley, Leroy et al.:** *Fundamentals and Techniques for Winning Basketball;* School Aid and Text Book, Toronto, ON, 1951.
938. **Morris, Donald:** *Kentucky High School Basketball;* Parker, New York, NY, 1969.
939. **Morris, Gregory:** *Basketball Basics;* Prentice-Hall, Englewood Cliffs, NJ, 1976.
940. **Morris, Robert and Edmundson, Clarence:** *Basketball for Players, Officials, and Spectators;* Frayne Printing, Seattle, WA, 1931.
941. **Morris, Ron:** *ACC Basketball: An Illustrated History;* Four Corners Press, Chapel Hill, NC, 1988.
942. **Morrison, Gertrude W.:** *The Girls of Central High at Basketball, or, The Great Gymnasium Mystery;* Goldsmith, Cleveland, OH, 1914.
943. **Morrison, W.P. and Wardlaw, C.D.:** *Basketball: A Handbook for Coaches and Players;* Scribner and Sons, New York, NY, 1921.
944. **Morrow, Douglas:** *Maurie: A True Story;* Grosset, New York, NY, 1973.
945. **Mortimer, Jeff and Frieder, Bill:** *Basket Case: The Frenetic Life of Michigan Coach Bill Frieder;* Bonus Books, Chicago, IL, 1988.
946. **Motta, Dick and Isaacs, Neil David:** *Sports Illustrated Basketball;* Harper and Row, New York, NY, 1981.
947. **Motta, Dick and Jenkins, Jerry:** *Stuff It: The Story of Dick Motta;* Chilton, Radnor, PA, 1975.
948. **Movius, Geoffrey H. (Ed.):** *The Second Handbook of Harvard Athletics, 1923-1963;* Harvard Varsity Club, Cambridge, MA, 1964.
949. **Mullin, Willard and Kamm, Herbert (Eds.):** *The Junior Illustrated Encyclopedia of Sports;* Bobbs-Merrill, New York, NY, 1960.
950. **Mulvoy, Mark and Powers, Richie:** *Overtime: An Uninhibited Account of a Referee's Life in the NBA;* Ballantine, New York, NY, 1975.
951. **Mumau, Todd:** *The Dean Smith Story: North Carolina Basketball;* Strode, Huntsville, AL, 1980.
952. **Mundell, Chuck:** *Triple Threat Basketball;* Parker, New York, NY, 1968.
953. **Murphy, Charles C.:** *Basketball;* Barnes, New York, NY, 1939.
954. **Mussleman, Bill:** *Basketball for the High School Coach and P.E. Teacher;* William C. Brown, Dubuque, IA, 1961.
955. **Myers, Walter Dean:** *Hoops;* Dell, New York, NY, 1981.
956. **Nagle, Jack:** *Power Pattern Offenses for Winning Basketball;* Parker, West Nyack, NY, 1986.
957. **Naismith, James:** *Basketball: Its Origin and Development;* Association Press, New York, NY, 1941.
958. **Naismith, James:** *Basketball's Origins: Creative Problem Solving in the Gilded Age;* Bear, Cambridge, NY, 1976.
959. **Naismith, James A. and Gulick, Luther A.:** *Basketball;* American Sports, New York, NY, 1896.
960. **Nash, Bruce and Zutto, Allan:** *The Sports Hall of Shame;* Parker, New York, NY, 1987.
961. **Nathan, Barbara:** *Gambling Times Guide to Basketball Handicapping;* Lyle Stuart, Secaucus, NJ, 1984.
962. **National Basketball Association:** *NBA Official Guide;* Sporting News, St. Louis, MO, annual.

963. **National Basketball Association:** *NBA Register*; Sporting News, St. Louis, MO, annual.

964. **National Biographical Society:** *Who's Who in American Sports*; National Biographical Society, Washington, DC, 1928.

965. **National Federation of State High School Athletic Associations:** *Basketball Play Situations*; A.S. Barnes, San Diego, CA, 1941.

966. **National Strength and Conditioning Association:** *Strength Training and Conditioning for Basketball: A Coaches Guide*; NSCA, Lincoln, NE, 1988.

967. *NBA Guide 1984*85*; Sporting News, St. Louis, MO, 1983.

968. **Neal, Patsy:** *Basketball Techniques for Women*; Ronald Press, New York, NY, 1966.

969. **Neel, Roy M.:** *Dynamite! 75 Years of Vanderbilt Basketball*; Burr-Oak, Nashville, TN, 1975.

970. **Neely, Tim:** *Hooping It Up: The Complete History of Notre Dame Basketball*; Diamond Communications, Notre Dame, IN, 1985.

971. **Neft, David S., Johnson, Roland T., Cohen, Richard M., and Deutsch, Jordan A.:** *All-Sports World Record Book*; Grosset, New York, NY, 1976.

972. **Neft, David S., Johnson, Roland T., Cohen, Richard M., and Deutsch, Jordan A.:** *The Sports Encyclopedia: Pro Basketball*; Grosset, New York, NY, 1975.

973. **Neil, Randy:** *The Official Handbook of School Spirit*; Simon and Schuster, New York, NY, 1981.

974. **Nelli, Bert:** *The Winning Tradition: A History of Kentucky Wildcat Basketball*; University of Kentucky Press, Lexington, KY, 1984.

975. **Neugeboren, Jay:** *Big Man*; Houghton, Boston, MA, 1966.

976. **Newell, Pete and Benington, John:** *Basketball Methods*; Ronald Press, New York, NY, 1962.

977. **Newell, Pete and Berger, Dan:** *Basketball: The Sports Playbook*; Doubleday, Garden City, NY, 1976.

978. **Newell, Pete and Knight, Bob:** *Basketball According to Knight and Newell*; Knight and Newell, Graaessle-Mercer, Seymour, IN, 1986.

979. **Newsom, Heber Allen:** *Basketball for the High School Coach and Physical Education Teacher*; William C. Brown, Dubuque, IA, 1952.

980. **Nichols, J.R.:** *Basketball Officiating*; J.R. Nichols, Minneapolis, MN, 1926.

981. **Nisenson, Sam:** *A Handy Illustrated Guide to Basketball*; Permabooks, New York, NY, 1948.

982. **Norton, Ken and Bee, Clair:** *Basketball Fundamentals and Techniques*; Ronald Press, New York, NY, 1959.

983. **Norton, Ken and Bee, Clair:** *The Bee-Norton Basketball Series*; Ronald Press, New York, NY, 1959.

984. **Norton, Ken and Bee, Clair:** *Individual and Team Basketball Drills*; Ronald Press, New York, NY, 1959.

985. **Norton, Ken and Bee, Clair:** *Man to Man Defense and Attack*; Ronald Press, New York, NY, 1959.

986. **Norton, Ken and Bee, Clair:** *The Science of Coaching*; Ronald Press, New York, NY, 1959.

987. **Norton, Ken and Bee, Clair:** *Zone Defense and Attack*; Ronald Press, New York, NY, 1959.

988. **Notre Dame Club of Chicago:** *The University of Notre Dame Club of Chicago Yearbook and Directory: Centenary 1942–43 on the Occasion of the 100th Anniversary of the Founding of the University of Notre Dame*; Clancy, Chicago, IL, 1943.

989. **Nucutola, John:** *Basketball Officiating*; Republic, New York, NY, 1959.

990. **O'Brien, Jim:** *ABA All-Stars*; Lancer, New York, NY, 1972.

991. **O'Brien, Jim:** *The Complete Handbook of Pro Basketball, 1972–73*; Lancer, New York, NY, 1972.
992. **O'Brien, Jim (Ed.):** *Hail to Pitt: A Sports History of the University of Pittsburgh*; Wolfson, Pittsburgh, PA, 1982.
993. **O'Bryan, M. and Beddoes, Dick:** *Basketball and Volleyball*; Coblam of Canada, Toronto, ON, 1976.
994. **O'Connor, John J.:** *Man Was Born to Play and Other Essays*; Springfield College, Springfield, MA, 1973.
995. **O'Donnell, Rev. Michael J. (Comp.):** *Villanova University Basketball: A Statistical History*; Villanova Press, Villanova, PA, 1962.
996. **Odle, Don J.:** *Basic Basketball*; A.D. Freese and Son, Upland, IN, 1950.
997. **Odle, Don J.:** *Basketball Around the World*; Economy Printing, Berne, IN, 1960.
998. **Odle, Don J.:** *Basketball for Young Dribblers*; Economy Printing, Berne, IN, 1962.
999. **Offen, Neil and Frazier, Walt:** *Walt Frazier: One Magic Season and A Basketball Life*; Times Books, New York, NY, 1988.
1000. *Official NBA Guide 1980–1981*; Sporting News, St. Louis, MO, 1979.
1001. **Ogawa, Hirohide:** *Enlightenment Through the Art of Basketball*; Oleander Press, New York, NY, 1979.
1002. **Olderman, Murray:** *The Warrior Way*; San Francisco Examiner, San Francisco, CA, 1976.
1003. **Olgin, Joseph:** *Backcourt Atom*; Houghton, Boston, MA, 1960.
1004. **Olgin, Joseph:** *Backcourt Rivals*; Dutton, New York, NY, 1955.
1005. **Olgin, Joseph and Archer, Jay:** *The Scoring Twins: A Story of Biddy Basketball*; Biddy Basketball, Scranton, PA, 1956.
1006. **Oliver, Newt and Hoyt, Dan:** *One Basketball and Glory*; Oliver, Springfield, OH, 1969.
1007. **Olney, Ross:** *Basketball*; Golden Press, Racine, WI, 1975.
1008. **Olsen, Bill and Dromo, John:** *University of Louisville Basketball Playbook*; Louisville, KY, 1965.
1009. **Olson, Gene:** *The Ballhawks*; Westminster, Philadelphia, PA, 1960.
1010. **Olson, Gene:** *The Tall One: A Basketball Story*; Dodd-Mead, New York, NY, 1957.
1011. **O'Reilly, Sean:** *Meet the Centers*; Creative Education, Minneapolis, MN, 1977.
1012. **O'Reilly, Sean:** *Meet the Coaches*; Creative Education, Minneapolis, MN, 1977.
1013. **O'Reilly, Sean:** *Meet the Forwards*; Creative Education, Minneapolis, MN, 1977.
1014. **O'Reilly, Sean:** *Meet the Guards*; Creative Education, Minneapolis, MN, 1977.
1015. **Orr, Jack (Ed.):** *Pro Basketball Factbook, 1971–72: Official Lifetime Records of NBA and ABA Players*; Sports Communication, Ridgewood, NJ, 1971.
1016. **Orr, Jack (Ed.):** *Pro Basketball Factbook, 1973–74: Official Lifetime Records of NBA and ABA Players*; Sports Communication, Ridgewood, NJ, 1973.
1017. **Orr, Jack (Ed.):** *Pro Basketball Factbook, 1974–75: Official Lifetime Records of NBA and ABA Players*; Sports Communication, Ridgewood, NJ, 1974.
1018. **Osborn, Chuck and McClelland, Marshall:** *Basketball for Boys*; Follett, Chicago, IL, 1960.
1019. **Osborn, Jesse and Riefling, Adeline:** *Cage Champion's Adventures With Numbers*; Webster, St. Louis, MO, 1948.
1020. **Osborne, Charles (Ed.):** *Yesterday in Sport*; Time-Life, New York, NY, 1968.

1021. **Ostler, Scott and Springer, Steve:** *Winnin' Times: The Magical Journey of the Los Angeles Lakers*; Macmillan, New York, NY, 1986.
1022. **Owen, Ed:** *Playing and Coaching Wheelchair Basketball*; University of Illinois Press, Champaign, IL, 1982.
1023. **Owen, Frank (Ed.):** *Teenage Sport Stories*; Latern, New York, NY, 1947.
1024. **Pachter, Marc:** *Champions of American Sport*; Abrams, New York, NY, 1981.
1025. **Packer, Billy and Lazenby, Roland:** *50 Years of the Final Four*; Taylor, Dallas, TX, 1987.
1026. **Packer, Billy and Lazenby, Roland:** *Hoops: Confessions of a College Basketball Analyst*; Contemporary Books, Chicago, IL, 1985.
1027. **Paige, David:** *A Day in the Life of a School Basketball Coach*; Troll Association, Mahwah, NJ, 1980.
1028. **Paige, David:** *Pro Basketball: An Almanac of Facts and Records*; Creative Education, Minneapolis, MN, 1977.
1029. **Pancretan Association of America:** *19th National Convention Yearbook*; Springfield, MA, 1977.
1030. **Pate, Steve:** *Dallas Mavericks, 1987–88*; Taylor, Dallas, TX, 1987.
1031. **Paterson, Ann (Ed.):** *Team Sports for Girls*; Ronald Press, New York, NY, 1958.
1032. **Paulson, Gary:** *Dribbling, Shooting, and Scoring Sometimes*; Raintree, Milwaukee, WI, 1976.
1033. **Pawde, Sandy:** *Basketball's Hall of Fame*; Grosset and Dunlap, New York, NY, 1973.
1034. **Pawde, Sandy and Hollander, Zander:** *Basketball Lingo*; Grosset and Dunlap, New York, NY, 1971.
1035. **Paxton, Harry and Zaharias, Babe Didrikson:** *This Life I've Led: My Autobiography*; Barnes, New York, NY, 1955.
1036. **Paye, Burrall:** *Basketball's Zone Presses: A Complete Coaching Guide*; Parker, New York, NY, 1983.
1037. **Paye, Burrall:** *Coaching the Full Court Man-to-Man Press*; Parker, New York, NY, 1978.
1038. **Paye, Burrall:** *Encyclopedia of Defensive Basketball Drills*; Parker, West Nyack, NY, 1986.
1039. **Paye, Burrall:** *Secrets of Passing-Dribbling Game Offense*; Parker, New York, NY, 1976.
1040. **Paye, Burrall:** *The Winning Power of Pressure Defense in Basketball*; Parker, New York, NY, 1974.
1041. **Paye, Burrall and Bonham, Aubrey R.:** *Secrets of Winning Fast-Break Basketball*; Prentice-Hall, West Nyack, NY, 1986.
1042. **Peale, Norman Vincent (Ed.):** *Faith Made Them Champions*; Guideposts, Carmel, NY, 1954.
1043. **Pepe, Phil:** *Greatest Stars of the NBA*; Prentice-Hall, Englewood Cliffs, NJ, 1970.
1044. **Pepe, Phil:** *The Incredible Knicks*; Popular Library, New York, NY, 1970.
1045. **Pepe, Phil:** *Kareem Abdul-Jabbar*; Grosset and Dunlap, New York, NY, 1970.
1046. **Pepe, Phil and Carnesecca, Lou:** *Louie: In Season*; McGraw-Hill, New York, NY, 1988.
1047. **Pepe, Phil and Hollander, Zander:** *The Book of Sports Lists*; Pinnade Books, Los Angeles, CA, 1979.
1048. **Pepe, Phil and Reed, Willis:** *View From the Rim: Willis Reed on Basketball*; J.B. Lippincott, New York, NY, 1972.
1049. **Perceval, Bob and Hosey, Tim:** *Bobby Knight: Countdown to Perfection*; Leisure Press, Champaign, IL, 1983.

1050. **Peterman, Mark A.**: *Secrets of Winning Basketball*; Interstate, Danville, IL, 1935.

1051. **Peterson, Bob**: *Basketball's High Powered Multiflex Offense*; Parker, West Nyack, NY, 1985.

1052. **Peterson, Bob**: *Three!*; Bob Peterson and MSOE Press, Milwaukee, WI, 1986.

1053. **Peterson, James A. and Stanley, Maryann**: *Conditioning for Women's Basketball: The Old Dominion Way*; Leisure Press, West Point, NY, 1982.

1054. **Pettit, Bob**: *The Drive Within Me*; Prentice-Hall, Englewood Cliffs, NJ, 1966.

1055. **Phelps, Digger**: *A Coach's World*; Thomas Crowell, New York, NY, 1974.

1056. **Phelps, Richard and Scanlon, Pat**: *Digger Phelps and Notre Dame Basketball*; Prentice-Hall, Englewood Cliffs, NJ, 1981.

1057. **Phillips, Betty Lou**: *Go! Fight! Win! The NCAA Guide for Cheerleaders*; Delacorte, New York, NY, 1981.

1058. *Physical Education 1892–1893: A Monthly Journal Edited by Luther Gulic and James Naismith*; Triangle, Springfield, MA, 1893.

1059. **Pincas, Arthur and Goldpaper, Sam**: *How to Talk Basketball*; Dembner Books, New York, NY, 1983.

1060. **Pinholster, Garland F.**: *Coach's Guide to Modern Basketball Defense*; Prentice-Hall, Englewood Cliffs, NJ, 1962.

1061. **Pinholster, Garland F.**: *Encyclopedia of Basketball Drills*; Prentice-Hall, Englewood Cliffs, NJ, 1958.

1062. **Pinholster, Garland F.**: *Illustrated Basketball Coaching Techniques*; Prentice-Hall, Englewood Cliffs, NJ, 1966.

1063. **Pinholster, Garland F.**: *Pinholster's Wheel of Offense for Basketball*; Prentice-Hall, Englewood Cliffs, NJ, 1966.

1064. **Pinholster, Garland F. and Dobbs, Wayne**: *Basketball's Stunting Defenses*; Prentice-Hall, Englewood Cliffs, NJ, 1964.

1065. **Pitino, Rick and Reynolds, Bill**: *Born to Coach: A Season With the New York Knicks*; New American Library, New York, NY, 1988.

1066. **Pitol, Frank R.**: *The Wonderful World of Collinsville Basketball, 1908–1976*; Herald, Collinsville, IL, 1976.

1067. **Platt, Kin**: *Frank and Stein and Me*; Scholastic, New York, NY, 1982.

1068. **Platt, Kin**: *The Giant Killer*; Random House, New York, NY, 1974.

1069. **Plott, William J.**: *State Champs*; Troy State University, Troy, NY, 1978.

1070. **Pluto, Terry and Ryan, Bob**: *Forty-Eight Minutes: A Night in the Life of the NBA*; Macmillan, New York, NY, 1988.

1071. **Pluto, Terry and Tarkanian, Jerry**: *Tark: College Basketball's Winningest Coach*; McGraw-Hill, New York, NY, 1988.

1072. **Poretz, Art, Croke, Ed and Bukata, James**: *Illustrated Digest of Pro Basketball, 1972–73*; Stadia Sports, New York, NY, 1972.

1073. **Porter, Archie**: *Complete Book of Man to Man Defense*; Parker, New York, NY, 1975.

1074. **Porter, Henry Van Arsdale (Comp.)**: *An Athletic Anthology*; Chicago, IL, 1930.

1075. **Porter, Mark**: *Overtime Upset*; Simon and Schuster, New York, NY, 1960.

1076. **Potter, Glenn**: *Basketball: A Simplified, Straightforward Approach to a Complex Game*; Burgess, Minneapolis, MN, 1982.

1077. **Poulin, Art**: *The One-Two-Two Jug Offense for Attacking Basketball's Zones*; Parker, New York, NY, 1983.

1078. **Pound, L. and Clapp, A.B. (Eds.)**: *Collegiate Basketball Rules for Women*; University of Nebraska Press, Lincoln, NE, 1908.

1079. **Power, Frank, Jr. and Cousy, Bob**: *Basketball Concepts and Techniques*; Allyn and Bacon, Boston, MA, 1970.

1080. **Powers, John:** *The Short Season: A Boston Celtics Diary: 1977–78:* Harper, New York, NY, 1979.

1081. **Powers, Richie and Mulvoy, Mark:** *Overtime: An Uninhibited Account of a Referee's Life in the NBA;* Ballantine, New York, NY, 1975.

1082. **Pratt, John Lowell and Benaugh, Jim:** *The Official Encyclopedia of Sports;* Franklin Watts, New York, NY, 1964.

1083. **Presley, Bud:** *Pressure Defense—West Coast Style;* D and G Sports, San Carlos, CA, 1962.

1084. **Pruden, Vic:** *Conceptual Approach to Basketball;* Leisure Press, Champaign, IL, 1987.

1085. **Prugh, Jeff and Chapin, Dwight:** *The Wizard of Westwood: Coach John Wooden and His UCLA Bruins;* Houghton Mifflin, Boston, MA, 1973.

1086. **Pruitt, Jim:** *Coaching Beginning Basketball;* Contemporary Books, Chicago, IL, 1980.

1087. **Pruitt, Jim:** *Play Better Basketball;* Contemporary Books, Chicago, IL, 1982.

1088. **Pugliese, D.J. and Rose, James V.:** *Basketball for the New Coach;* Canadian Association for Health, Physical Education, and Recreation, Ottawa, ON, date unknown.

1089. **Pulvermacher, W.D. and Bancroft, J.H.:** *Handbook of Athletic Games;* Macmillan, New York, NY, 1929.

1090. **Rainbolt, Richard:** *Basketball's Big Men;* Lerner, Minneapolis, MN, 1975.

1091. **Ralbovsky, Martin:** *Lords of the Locker Room: The American Way of Coaching and Its Effect on Youth;* Wyden, New York, NY, 1974.

1092. **Ramsay, Jack:** *Basketball Coaching;* Prentice-Hall, Englewood Cliffs, NJ, 1963.

1093. **Ramsay, Jack:** *Pressure Basketball;* Prentice-Hall, Englewood Cliffs, NJ, 1963.

1094. **Ramsay, Jack and Strawn, John:** *The Coach's Art;* Timber Press, Forest Grove, OR, 1978.

1095. **Randall, Chuck and Madison, Paul:** *Coach, God Loves You and So Do I;* Union, Bellingham, WA, 1976.

1096. **Rappaport, Ken:** *The Classic: The History of the NCAA Basketball Championship;* Lowell Press, Kansas City, MO, 1979.

1097. **Rappaport, Ken:** *Tarheel, North Carolina Basketball;* Strode, Huntsville, AL, 1976.

1098. **Rappaport, Ron and McGregor, Jim:** *Called for Traveling;* Macmillan, New York, NY, 1978.

1099. **Raveling, George:** *Rebounder's Workshop;* Leisure Press, West Point, NY, 1982.

1100. **Raveling, George:** *War on the Boards;* Leisure Press, West Point, NY, 1982.

1101. **Ray, Peter and Coleman, Brian:** *Basketball;* Charles River Books, Boston, MA, 1977.

1102. **Read, Herbert W.:** *Fast Break Basketball* (information unavailable)

1103. **Redin, Harley:** *Basketball Guide for Girls;* Wayland College, Plainview, TX, 1961.

1104. **Redin, Harley:** *The Queens Fly High;* 1958.

1105. **Redmond, Gerald and Lewis, Guy:** *Sporting Heritage: A Guide to Halls of Fame, Special Collections and Museums in the United States and Canada;* Barnes, New York, NY, 1974.

1106. **Reed, Billy:** *The Final Four: Reliving America's Basketball Classic;* Host Communications, Lexington, KY, 1988.

1107. **Reed, Willis:** *A Will to Win;* Prentice-Hall, Englewood Cliffs, NJ, 1973.

1108. **Reed, Willis and Pepe, Phil:** *View From the Rim: Willis Reed on Basketball;* J.B. Lippincott, New York, NY, 1972.

1109. **Reeves, Fred:** *Basketball Play;* Impress House, Bridgeport, CT, date unknown.

1110. **Reeves, Fred:** *A Modern Basketball Program*; Strode, Huntsville, AL, date unknown.

1111. **Reiff, Joe:** *Basketball Fundamentals*; Chicago Park District, Chicago, IL, 1938.

1112. **Reinhart, Bob:** *Free Throw Shooting: Psychological and Physiological Techniques*; Chicago Review, Chicago, IL, 1982.

1113. **Renick, Marion:** *The Big Basketball Prize*; Scribner's, New York, NY, 1963.

1114. **Renick, Marion:** *Jimmy's Own Basketball*; Scribner's, New York, NY, 1952.

1115. **Reynolds, Bill and Pitino, Rick:** *Born to Coach: A Season with the New York Knicks*; New American Library, New York, NY, 1988.

1116. **Reynolds, H.A.:** *The Games Way to Sports*; A.S. Barnes, New York, NY, 1937.

1117. **Ribalow, Harold V.:** *The Jew in American Sports*; Bloch, New York, NY, 1966.

1118. **Rice, Russ:** *Kentucky Basketball*; Strode, Huntsville, AL, 1978.

1119. **Rice, Russell:** *Joe B. Hall: My Own Kentucky Home*; Strode, Huntsville, AL, 1981.

1120. **Rice, Russell:** *Kentucky Basketball's Big Blue Machine*; Strode, Huntsville, AL, 1980.

1121. **Rice, Russell and Baron, Randall:** *The Official University of Kentucky Basketball Book*; Devyn Press, Louisville, KY, 1987.

1122. **Rich, Michael and West, Jan:** *A Wife's Guide to Pro Basketball*; Viking, New York, NY, 1970.

1123. **Richards, Jack:** *Attacking Zone Defenses in Basketball*; Parker, New York, NY, 1977.

1124. **Richards, Jack (Ed. and Comp.):** *New Treasury of Basketball Drills From Top Coaches*; Parker, West Nyack, NY, 1982.

1125. **Richards, Jack:** *Scramble Attack for Winning Basketball*; Prentice-Hall, Englewood Cliffs, NJ, 1968.

1126. **Richards, Jack:** *Treasury of Basketball Drills From Top Coaches*; Parker, New York, NY, 1971.

1127. **Richards, Jack and Hill, Danny:** *Complete Handbook of Sports Scoring and Record Keeping*; Parker, New York, NY, 1971.

1128. **Ridl, Charles:** *How to Develop a Deliberate Basketball Offense*; Parker, New York, NY, 1966.

1129. **Riefling, Adeline and Osborn, Jesse:** *Cage Champions Adventures With Numbers*; Webster, St. Louis, MO, 1948.

1130. **Riemcke, Cal:** *Guard Freedom Offense for Winning Basketball*; Prentice-Hall, Englewood Cliffs, NJ, 1974.

1131. **Righter, Ron:** *Flex: The Total Offense*; Championship Books, Ames, Iowa, 1988.

1132. **Robertson, Oscar:** *Play Better Basketball*; Oscar Robertson and Michael O'Daniel, Cincinnati, OH, 1964.

1133. **Robertson, Oscar:** *Winning Basketball*; Grow Ahead Press, Columbus, OH, 1968.

1134. **Robinson, Bob:** *Bill Walton: Star of the Blazers*; School Book Services, New York, NY, 1978.

1135. **Rockne, K.K. and Meanwell, W.E.:** *Training, Conditioning and the Care of Injuries*; H.D. Gath, Madison, WI, 1930.

1136. **Rogers, A. Glenn:** *Forgotten Stories of the Finger Lakes: Dramatic Tales of Fact and Legend*; W.R. Carpenter, Geneva, NY, 1953.

1137. **Rohman, D. Gordon and Basloe, Frank J.:** *I Grew Up With Basketball*; Greenburg, New York, NY, 1952.

1138. **Romney, E.L.:** *The "Dick" Romney Story*; Deseret, Salt Lake City, UT, 1965.

1139. **Rooney, John F.:** *The Recruiting Game: Toward a New System of Intercollegiate Sports*; University of Nebraska Press, Lincoln, NE, 1980.

1140. **Rose, James V. and Pugliese, D.J.:** *Basketball for the New Coach*; Canadian Association for Health, Physical Education, and Recreation, Ottawa, ON, date unknown.

1141. **Rosen, Charles:** *God, Man and Basketball: The Thinking Fan's Guide to Professional Basketball*; Holt, Rinehart, and Winston, New York, NY, 1979.

1142. **Rosen, Charles:** *Players and Pretenders: The Basketball Team That Couldn't Shoot Straight*; Holt, Rinehart, and Winston, New York, NY, 1981.

1143. **Rosen, Charles:** *Scandals of '51: How the Gamblers Almost Killed Basketball*; Holt, Rinehart, and Winston, New York, NY, 1978.

1144. **Rosen, Charles and Jackson, Phil:** *More Trouble Than a Game*; Playboy Press, Chicago, IL, 1976.

1145. **Rosenberg, John M.:** *Basic Basketball*; Oceana Publications, Dobbs Ferry, NY, 1962.

1146. **Rosenthal, Bert:** *Basketball*; Childrens Press, Chicago, IL, 1983.

1147. **Rosenthal, Bert:** *Darryl Dawkins: The Master of Disaster*; Childrens Press, Chicago, IL, 1982.

1148. **Rosenthal, Bert:** *Larry Bird: Cool Man on the Court*; Childrens Press, Chicago, IL, 1982.

1149. **Rosenthal, Bert:** *Ralph Sampson: The Center for the 1980's*; Childrens Press, Chicago, IL, 1984.

1150. **Rosenthal, Bert and Lowitt, Bruce:** *Pro Basketball Superstars of 1975*; Pyramid, New York, NY, 1975.

1151. **Rubin, Bob:** *Basketball's Big Men: Supergiants and Superstars*; School Book Services, New York, NY, 1975.

1152. **Rubin, Bob:** *Great Centers of Pro Basketball*; Random House, New York, NY, 1975.

1153. **Rubin, Roy:** *Attacking Basketball's Pressure Defenses*; Prentice-Hall, Englewood Cliffs, NJ, 1966.

1154. **Ruby, J.C.:** *Basketball*; Bailey and Himes, Champaign, IL, 1926.

1155. **Ruby, James Craig:** *Coaching Basketball*; Basketball Book Company, Champaign, IL, 1931.

1156. **Ruby, James Craig:** *Team Play in Basketball*; Basketball Book Company, Champaign, IL, 1931.

1157. **Rudy, James Craig and Lipe, C.C.:** *How to Coach and Play Basketball*; Bailey and Himes, Champaign, IL, 1926.

1158. **Rudman, Daniel (Ed.):** *Take It to the Hoop: A Basketball Anthology*; North Atlantic Books, Richmond, CA, 1980.

1159. *Rules for Coeducational Activities and Sports*; AAHPERD, Reston, VA, 1980.

1160. **Rupp, Adolph:** *An Outline of Basketball*; University of Kentucky, Lexington, KY, 1938.

1161. **Rupp, Adolph F.:** *Championship Basketball*; Prentice-Hall, Englewood Cliffs, NJ, 1957.

1162. **Rupp, Adolph F.:** *Championship Basketball for Player, Coach, and Fan*; Prentice-Hall, Englewood Cliffs, NJ, 1958.

1163. **Rupp, Adolph F.:** *Rupp's Basketball Guide Book*; McGraw-Hill, New York, NY, 1967.

1164. **Rush, Cathy and Mifflin, Laurie:** *Women's Basketball*; Hawthorn Books, New York, NY, 1976.

1165. **Russell, Bill:** *Go Up for Glory*; Berkley, New York, NY, 1980.

1166. **Russell, Bill and McSweeny, William:** *Go Up for Glory*; Coward-McCann, New York, NY, 1966.

1167. **Russell, William and Taylor, Branch:** *Second Wind: The Memoirs of an Opinionated Man*; Random House, New York, NY, 1979.

1168. **Ruxin, Robert H.:** *An Athlete's Guide to Agents*; Indiana University Press, Bloomington, IN, 1982.
1169. **Ryan, Bob:** *Celtic Pride*; Little Brown, Boston, MA, 1975.
1170. **Ryan, Bob:** *The Pro Game: The World of Professional Basketball*; McGraw-Hill, New York, NY, 1975.
1171. **Ryan, Bob and Cousy, Bob:** *Cousy on the Celtic Mystique*; McGraw-Hill, New York, NY, 1988.
1172. **Ryan, Bob and Havlicek, John:** *Hondo: Celtic Man in Motion*; Prentice-Hall, Englewood Cliffs, NJ, 1977.
1173. **Ryan, Bob and Pluto, Terry:** *Forty-Eight Minutes: A Night in the Life of the NBA*; Macmillan, New York, NY, 1988.
1174. **Rydell, Wendell:** *Basketball*; Abelard-Schumn, New York, NY, 1971.
1175. **Sabin, Lou:** *Hot Shots of Pro Basketball*; Random House, New York, NY, 1974.
1176. **Sabin, Lou and Sendler, Dave:** *Stars of Pro Basketball*; Random House, New York, NY, 1970.
1177. **Sabin, Louis:** *Basketball Stars of 1970*; Pyramid, New York, NY, 1969.
1178. **Sabin, Louis:** *Basketball Stars of 1971*; Pyramid, New York, NY, 1970.
1179. **Sabin, Louis:** *Basketball Stars of 1972*; Pyramid, New York, NY, 1971.
1180. **Sabin, Louis:** *Basketball Stars of 1973*; Pyramid, New York, NY, 1972.
1181. **Sabin, Louis:** *The Famous Dr. J: All-Time All Star*; G.P. Putnam's Sons, New York, NY, 1976.
1182. **Sahadi, Lou:** *All-Time Basketball Stars*; Scholastic Services, New York, NY, 1979.
1183. **Sahadi, Lou:** *Basketball's Fastest Hands*; Scholastic Services, New York, NY, 1977.
1184. **Sainsbury, Noel, Jr.:** *The Fighting Five*; Copples, New York, NY, 1934.
1185. **Saladino, Tom:** *Pistol Pete Maravich: The Louisiana Purchase*; Strode, Huntsville, AL, 1974.
1186. **Salzberg, Charles:** *From Set Shot to Slamdunk: The Glory Days of Basketball in the Words of Those Who Played It*; E.P. Dutton, New York, NY, 1987.
1187. **Samaras, Robert:** *Cut and Slash Basketball*; Prentice-Hall, Englewood Cliffs, NY, 1974.
1188. **Samaras, Robert T.:** *Blitz Basketball: A Winning System of Pressure Play*; Parker, New York, NY, 1966.
1189. **Samaras, Robert T.:** *A Treasury of Winning Basketball Tips*; Parker, West Nyack, NY, 1984.
1190. **Sandbrook, John and Epstein, Buddy:** *The 25 Wooden Years*; UCLA Communications Board, Los Angeles, CA, 1972.
1191. **Santos, Harry G.:** *How to Attack and Defeat Zone Defenses in Basketball*; Parker, New York, NY, 1966.
1192. **Sarra, LaMar and Barbour, R.H.:** *How To Play Better Basketball*; Appleton-Century, New York, NY, 1941.
1193. **Satalin, Jim and Handler, Fred:** *Coaching Winning Basketball in the Offensive Zone*; Parker, West Nyack, NY, 1985.
1194. **Sather, Sally:** *Images of Excellence: Carolina Basketball*; Mennasah Ridge Press, Birmingham, AL, 1988.
1195. **Savitz, Harriet May:** *On the Move*; Avon, New York, NY, 1973.
1196. **Scanlon, Pat and Phelps, Richard:** *Digger Phelps and Notre Dame Basketball*; Prentice-Hall, Englewood Cliffs, NJ, 1981.
1197. **Schaafsma, Frances:** *Women's Basketball*; William C. Brown, Dubuque, IA, 1977.
1198. **Schapp, Dick, DeBusschere, Dave, and Zimmerman, Paul:** *The Open Man: A Championship Diary*; Grove Press, New York, NY, 1971.

1199. **Schapp, Richard:** *An Illustrated History of the Olympics;* Knopf, New York, NY, 1963.

1200. **Schartz, Marguerite and Meyer, Margaret:** *Team Sports for Girls and Women;* W.B. Saunders, Philadelphia, PA, 1957.

1201. **Schiffer, Don:** *The First Book of Basketball;* Franklin Watts, New York, NY, 1959.

1202. **Schofield, Jay:** *How to Coach Basketball's Two-Two-One Penetrating Offense;* Parker, New York, NY, 1982.

1203. *Scholastic Coach* **(Ed.):** *The Best of Basketball From Scholastic Coach;* Prentice-Hall, Englewood Cliffs, NJ, 1962.

1204. **Schron, Bob and Carr, M.L.:** *Don't Be Denied;* Quinlan, Boston, MA, 1987.

1205. **Schron, Bob and Stevens, Kevin:** *Bird Era: History of the Boston Celtics, 1978–88;* Quinlan Press, Boston, MA, 1988.

1206. **Schwomeyer, Herb:** *Hoosier Hysteria: A History of Indiana High School Basketball* (1st ed.); Mitchell-Fleming, Greenfield, IN, 1970.

1207. **Schwomeyer, Herb:** *Hoosier Hysteria: A History of Indiana High School Basketball* (3rd ed.); Mitchell-Fleming, Greenfield, IN, 1975.

1208. **Schwomeyer, Herb:** *Hoosier Hysteria: A History of Indiana High School Basketball* (5th ed.); Mitchell-Fleming, Greenfield, IN, 1982.

1209. **Schwomeyer, Herb:** *Hoosier Hysteria: A History of Indiana High School Basketball* (6th ed.); Mitchell-Fleming, Greenfield, IN, 1985.

1210. **Schwomeyer, Herb:** *Hoosier Hysteria: A History of Indiana High School Girl's Basketball;* Mitchell-Fleming, Greenfield, IN, 1985.

1211. **Scott, Jack:** *Bill Walton: On the Road With the Portland Trailblazers;* Crowell, New York, NY, 1978.

1212. **Scott, John W.:** *Step-by-Step Basketball Fundamentals for the Player and Coach;* Randall, Salt Lake City, UT, 1985.

1213. **Sealy, Adrienne V.:** *Little Tommy and the Basketball;* Association for the Study of Family Living, New York, NY, 1980.

1214. **Searcy, Jay and Goldaper, Sam:** *Rick Barry: Golden State Superstar;* Grosset, New York, NY, 1976.

1215. **Seidentop, Daryl and Cooper, John:** *The Theory and Science of Basketball;* Lea and Febiger, Philadelphia, PA, 1969.

1216. **Sendler, Dave and Sabin, Lou:** *Stars of Pro Basketball;* Random House, New York, NY, 1970.

1217. **Severson, Red and Erickson, Ted:** *Build a Winning Tradition as a Master Teacher-Coach of Winning Basketball;* Severson and Erickson, St. Cloud, MN, 1978.

1218. **Severson, Red and Erickson, Ted:** *Let's Shatter the Zones;* Severson and Erickson, St. Cloud, MN, 1978.

1219. **Severson, Red and Erickson, Ted:** *Let's Teach Defense—Read the Offense;* Severson and Erickson, St. Cloud, MN, 1976.

1220. **Severson, Red and Erickson, Ted:** *Let's Teach Defense—Read the Zone;* Severson and Erickson, St. Cloud, MN, 1976.

1221. **Severson, Red and Erickson, Ted:** *Let's Teach Offense—Read the Defense;* Severson and Erickson, St. Cloud, MN, 1976.

1222. **Severson, Red and Erickson, Ted:** *Position, Stance, Move and Play Defense;* Severson and Erickson, St. Cloud, MN, 1978.

1223. **Severson, Red and Erickson, Ted:** *Run, Jump, Pass and Score: Offensive Tips for the Entire Family;* Severson and Erickson, St. Cloud, MN, 1978.

1224. **Shapiro, Leonard and Denlinger, Kenneth:** *Athletes for Sale;* Thomas Y. Crowell, New York, NY, 1975.

1225. **Sharman, Bill:** *Sharman on Basketball Shooting;* Prentice-Hall, Englewood Cliffs, NJ, 1965.

1226. **Sharman, Bill and Wooden, John:** *The Wooden-Sharman Method: A Guide to Winning Basketball*; Macmillan, New York, NY, 1975.
1227. **Shaughnessy, Dan and Hoenig, Gary:** *Courtside: The Fan's Guide to Pro Basketball*; Vanderbilt Press, Miami, FL, 1984.
1228. **Shaw, David and Chamberlain, Wilton:** *Wilt, Just Like Any Other 7-Foot Black Millionaire Who Lives Next Door*; Macmillan, New York, NY, 1973.
1229. **Sherman, Harold M.:** *Shoot That Ball and Other Basketball Stories*; Grosset, New York, NY, 1930.
1230. **Sherman, Harold M.:** *Under the Basket and Other Basketball Stories*; Goldsmith, Chicago, IL, 1932.
1231. **Sherman, Pat:** *NAGWS Basketball Guide (July 1978–July 1979): Official Rules and Interpretations, Including Officiating*; AAHPERD, Washington, DC, 1978.
1232. **Shilts, Dick:** *Teaching Basketball Fundamentals*; New Issues Press, Tallahassee, FL, 1977.
1233. **Shublom, Walter R.:** *Tips to Titles*; Walter Shublom, Kansas City, KS, 1964.
1234. **Shublom, Walter R.:** *The Ways of a Champion*; Walter Shublom, Kansas City, KS, 1964.
1235. **Simon, Tony (Ed.):** *Arrow Book of Sport Stories*; Scholastic, New York, NY, 1969.
1236. **Slaughter, Reid and Webb, Spud:** *Spud Webb, Flying High*; Harper and Row, New York, NY, 1986.
1237. **Smith, Carroll:** *The One-Two-Two Offense for Winning Basketball*; Parker, New York, NY, 1976.
1238. **Smith, Chet and Wolfson, Marty:** *Greater Pittsburgh History of Sports, 1800–1970's*; Wolfson, Pittsburgh, PA, 1969.
1239. **Smith, Chuck and Bartlow, Gene:** *Winning Basketball*; Forum Press, St. Louis, MO, 1978.
1240. **Smith, Dean and Spear, Bob:** *Basketball—Multiple Offense and Defense*; Parker, New York, NY, 1982.
1241. **Smith, Kent:** *Winning Basketball with the Multiple Motion Offense*; Parker, New York, NY, 1982.
1242. **Smith, L. Virginia:** *Larry Bird: From Country Hick to Boston Celtic*; L. Virginia Smith, Holland, IN, 1982.
1243. **Smith, Michael D.:** *Violence and Sport*; Butterworths, Toronto, ON, 1983.
1244. **Smith, T.H.:** *Official Basketball Guide and Association Rules for 1908–09*; R.K. Fox, New York, NY.
1245. **Smith, Walter W.:** *Strawberries in the Wintertime: The Sporting World of Red Smith*; Quadrangle, New York, NY, 1974.
1246. **Smith, Walter W.:** *Views of Sport*; Knopf, New York, NY, 1954.
1247. **Smithson, Gene:** *The Fun in Basketball Is Winning: A Fundamental Basketball Program Assured to Produce the Right Results*; Smithson, Wichita, KS, 1971.
1248. **Smithson, Gene:** *The Mixed Dictator Defense*; Smithson, Wichita, KS, 1972.
1249. **Soderberg, Paul, and Washington, Helen:** *The Big Book of Halls of Fame in the United States and Canada: Sports*; Bowker, New York, NY, 1977.
1250. **Sons, Ray and Meyer, Ray:** *Coach*; Contemporary Books, Chicago, IL, 1987.
1251. **Southern Conference:** *Sports Annual, 1965–1972*; presented by the Southern Conference at its annual tournament.
1252. **Spaulding, Dayton:** *Basketball's Destroyer Offense*; Parker, New York, NY, 1972.
1253. **Spaulding's Athletic Library:** *Official Basketball Guide*; American Sports, New York, NY, annually in 1930s.
1254. **Spaulding's Athletic Library:** *Spaulding's Women's Basketball Guide*; American Sports, New York, NY, 1971.

1255. **Spear, Bob and Smith, Dean:** *Basketball—Multiple Offense and Defense*; Parker, New York, NY, 1982.
1256. **Sperling, Dan:** *A Spectator's Guide to Basketball: The Action, Rules and Beauty of the Game*; Avon, New York, NY, 1983.
1257. *The Sporting News Official NBA Guides: 1979-1980 to 1987-1988*; The Sporting News, St. Louis, MO., annual.
1258. *The Sporting News Official NBA Registers: 1980-81 to 1987-88*; The Sporting News, St. Louis, MO, annual.
1259. *Sports Illustrated* **(Ed.):** *Sports Illustrated Book of Basketball*; Lippincott, New York, NY, 1962.
1260. *Sports Illustrated* **(Ed.):** *The Olympic Games: A Book of Records and Reminiscing, 1896-1964*; Time-Life, New York, NY, 1967.
1261. *Sports Illustrated* **(Ed.):** *Sports Illustrated Book of Basketball*; J.B. Lippincott, New York, NY, 1971.
1262. **Springfield College:** *Massasoit 1967* (annual yearbook).
1263. **Springer, Steve and Ostler, Scott:** *Winnin' Times: The Magical Journey of the Los Angeles Lakers*; Macmillan, New York, NY, 1986.
1264. **Stainback, Barry:** *Basketball Stars of 1967*; Pyramid, New York, NY, 1966.
1265. **Stainback, Barry:** *Basketball Stars of 1968*; Pyramid, New York, NY, 1967.
1266. **Stainback, Barry:** *Basketball Stars of 1969*; Pyramid, New York, NY, 1968.
1267. **Stainback, Barry and Gelman, Steve:** *Basketball Stars of 1966*; Pyramid, New York, NY, 1965.
1268. **Stambler, Irwin:** *Bill Walton: Super Center*; G.P. Putnam's Sons, New York, NY, 1976.
1269. **Stanley, Maryann and Peterson, James A.:** *Conditioning for Women's Basketball: The Old Dominion Way*; Leisure Press, West Point, NY, 1982.
1270. **Steitz, Edward S.:** *Fundamentals, Officiating, Interpretations, and Scientific Techniques in Basketball*; United States Information Service, New Delhi, India, 1972.
1271. **Steitz, Edward S.:** *Illustrated Basketball Rules*; Doubleday, Garden City, NJ, 1976.
1272. **Stephens, Steve and Versace, Richard:** *Trident Attack for Winning Basketball*; Parker, New York, NY, 1969.
1273. **Stern, Robert:** *They Were Number One: A History of the NCAA Basketball Tournament*; Leisure Press, Champaign, IL, 1983.
1274. **Stern, Theodore:** *The Rubber-Ball Games of the Americans*; Augustin, New York, NY, 1948.
1275. **Stevens, Kevin and Schron, Bob:** *Bird Era: History of the Boston Celtics, 1978-88*; Quinlan Press, Boston, MA, 1988.
1276. **Stiver, John:** *Double Post Basketball: Offensive Power and Fundamentals*; Parker, New York, NY, 1982.
1277. **Stockton, J. Roy:** *The Gashouse Gang and a Couple of Other Guys*; Barnes, New York, NY, 1945.
1278. **Stone, Eddie:** *Julius Erving*; Holloway House, Los Angeles, CA, 1980.
1279. **Stoutenburg, Adrien:** *In This Corner*; Westminster, Philadelphia, PA, 1957.
1280. **Strack, David H.:** *Basketball*; Parker, New York, NY, 1968.
1281. **Strawn, John and Ramsay, Jack:** *The Coach's Art*; Timber Press, Forest Grove, OR, 1978.
1282. **Studer, A.G.:** *One Hundred Years With Youth: The Story of the Detroit Y.M.C.A. 1852-1952*; no information available.
1283. **Stutts, Ann:** *Women's Basketball*; Goodyear, Palisades, CA, 1969.
1284. **Sugar, Bert Randolph:** *The Book of Sports Quotes*; Quick Fox, New York, NY, 1979.

1285. **Sullivan, Gene:** *A Frame of Mind: A Story of Notre Dame Basketball*; Sullivan, Chicago, IL, 1971.

1286. **Sullivan, George:** *Amazing Sports Facts*; Scholastic, New York, NY, 1978.

1287. **Sullivan, George:** *Better Basketball for Boys*; Dodd-Mead, New York, NY, 1980.

1288. **Sullivan, George:** *Better Basketball for Girls*; Dodd-Mead, New York, NY, 1978.

1289. **Sullivan, George:** *Dave Cowens: A Bibliography*; G.P. Putnam's Sons, New York, NY, 1976.

1290. **Sullivan, George:** *How to Play Winning Basketball*; Cornerstone Library, New York, NY, 1977.

1291. **Sullivan, George:** *The Picture History of the Boston Celtics*; Bobbs-Merrill, Indianapolis, IN, 1981.

1292. **Sullivan, George:** *This Is Pro Basketball*; Dodd-Mead, New York, NY, 1977.

1293. **Sullivan, George:** *Wilt Chamberlain*; Grosset and Dunlap, New York, NY, 1966.

1294. **Sullivan, George:** *Winning Basketball*; David McKay Co., New York, NY, 1976.

1295. **Swan, Robert A. and Fox, Stephen R.:** *The Kansas Betas, 1873–1973: A Centennial History of the Alpha Nu Chapter of Beta Theta Pi*; University of Kansas Press, Lawrence, KS, 1976.

1296. **Sweet, Virgil:** *Series of Specifics: Free Throw Shooting, Offense, Basketball Fundamentals, Drills for Fundamentals*; Virgil Sweet, Valparaiso, IN, 1966.

1297. **Sweet, Virgil and Ciciora, Dale:** *Specific Drills for Basketball Fundamentals*; Ciciora and Sweet, Valparaiso, IN, 1966.

1298. **Talisman Books (Ed.):** *Pro Basketball 1977–78*; Ballantine, New York, NY, 1977.

1299. **Tarkanian, Jerry:** *Winning Basketball Systems*; Allyn and Bacon, Boston, MA, 1980.

1300. **Tarkanian, Jerry and Pluto, Terry:** *Tark: College Basketball's Winningest Coach*; McGraw-Hill, New York, NY, 1988.

1301. **Tarkanian, Jerry and Warren, William E.:** *Winning Basketball Drills and Fundamentals*; Allyn and Bacon, Boston, MA, 1983.

1302. **Tarleton, Tom:** *Tips and Ideas for Winning Basketball*; Prentice-Hall, Englewood Cliffs, NJ, 1965.

1303. **Taylor, Branch and Russell, William:** *Second Wind: The Memoirs of an Opinionated Man*; Random House, New York, NY, 1979.

1304. **Taylor, Chuck:** *Basketball Finesse*; Sayger Sports Syndicate, Tiffin, OH, 1933.

1305. **Taylor, Joe (Ed.):** *How to Be an Effective Coach: The Manulife Manual*; Manulife/C.A.L., Toronto, ON, 1975.

1306. **Taylor, Paula:** *Basketball's Finest Center, Kareem Abdul-Jabbar*; Creative Education Society, Mankato, MN, 1977.

1307. **Teague, Bertha Frank:** *Basketball for Girls*; Ronald Press, New York, NY, 1962.

1308. **Telander, Rick:** *Heaven Is a Playground*; St. Martin's Press, New York, NY, 1976.

1309. **Thomas, Donzell:** *Doctor J*; Holloway House, Los Angeles, CA, 1980.

1310. **Thomas, Ronald L.:** *Walt Bellamy: The Saturnine Center*; Anaeus, NY, 1985.

1311. **Thomas, Vaughan:** *Basketball: Techniques and Tactics*; Merrimack Book Service, Lawrence, MA, 1972.

1312. **Thompson, John A.:** *Numerical Basketball Scorebook*; Interstate, Danville, IL, 1964.

1313. **Thorndike, Dr. Augustus:** *Athletic Injuries: Prevention, Diagnosis, and Treatment*; Lea and Febiger, Philadelphia, PA, 1956.
1314. *Time and Tigers: Reading Basic Skills Text*; Harper and Row, New York, NY, 1980 (basketball on pp. 119–129).
1315. **Tobey, Dave:** *Basketball Officiating*; A.S. Barnes, New York, NY, 1943.
1316. **Tolson, Homer and Johnson, Dewayne:** *Basketball*; American Press, Boston, MA, 1980.
1317. **Toney, David and King, George:** *Basketball*; Athletic Institute, Chicago, IL, 1973.
1318. **Toomasian, John:** *Developing a Winning Offense for High School Basketball*; Prentice-Hall, Englewood Cliffs, NJ, 1964.
1319. **Truax, Terry and Wootten, Morgan:** *Dematha High School Basketball Notebook*; Truax and Wootten, Baltimore, MD, 1970.
1320. **Tulane University:** *Newcomb College Basketball Guide for Women*; Tulane University, New Orleans, LA, 1914.
1321. **Tunis, John R.:** *Go, Team, Go!*; Scholastic, New York, NY, 1954.
1322. **Tunis, John R.:** *Yea! Wildcats!*; Harcourt, New York, NY, 1944.
1323. **Turnbull, Anne:** *Basketball for Women*; Addison-Wesley, Reading, MA, 1973.
1324. **Turnbull, J.E.:** *The Iowa Conference Story: Forty Years of Intercollegiate Sports, 1922–1961*; State Historical Society, Iowa City, IA, 1961.
1325. **Turner, Priscilla and Geline, Robert:** *Forward Rick Barry*; Raintree, Milwaukee, WI, 1978.
1326. **Tuttle, Anthony:** *Bob McAdoo*; Creative Education, Minneapolis, MN, 1976.
1327. *Twelve Great Basketball Offenses*; AAHPERD, Reston, VA, 1982.
1328. **Tyno, Steve, and Litsky, Frank (Comps.):** *The New York Times Sports Almanac*; J. Lowell Pratt, New York, NY, 1965.
1329. **Underwood, John:** *Spoiled Sport: A Fan's Notes on the Troubles of Spectator Sports*; Little Brown, Boston, MA, 1984.
1330. **United States Navy Bureau of Aeronautics:** *Basketball*; United States Naval Institute, Annapolis, MD, 1943.
1331. **United States Office of Naval Operations:** *Basketball*; United States Naval Institute, Annapolis, MD, 1950.
1332. **United States Olympic Committee:** *Olympic Sports: A Handbook of Recognized Olympic Sports*; U.S. Olympic Committee, New York, NY, 1964.
1333. **United States Senate Committee on the Judiciary, Subcommittee on Antitrust and Monopoly:** *A Bill to Allow the Merger of Two or More Professional Basketball Leagues.* Hearing, Ninety-second Congress, first session. September 21-23, 1971. Government Printing Office, Washington, DC, 1972.
1334. **United States Senate, Committee on the Judiciary, Subcommittee on Antitrust and Monopoly:** *A Bill to Allow the Merger of Two or More Professional Basketball Leagues.* Hearing, Ninety-second Congress, second session. November 15, 1971, and January 25, March 6, May 3 and 9, 1972. Government Printing Office, Washington, DC, 1972.
1335. *University of Indiana Trivia Book*; Quinlan, Bloomington, IN, 1986.
1336. *University of Virginia Basketball Handbook*; Full Court Press, Roanoke, VA, 1983.
1337. **Unseld, Wes and Monroe, Earl:** *Basketball Skillbook*; Atheneum of Philadelphia, Philadelphia, PA, 1973.
1338. **Utect, Bob:** *This is Gold Country*; Piper, Blue Earth, MN, 1977.
1339. **Valvano, Jim:** *Too Soon to Quit: The Story of N.C. State's National Championship Season*; Coman, Raleigh, NC, 1983.
1340. **Van Arsdale, Tom and Dick:** *Our Basketball Lives*; G.P. Putnam's Sons, New York, NY, 1973.

1341. **Vanatta, Bob:** *Coaching Pattern Play Basketball;* Prentice-Hall, Englewood Cliffs, NJ, 1959.

1342. **Vanderbilt, William R. and DeVette, Russell B.:** *Coaching Basketball: The Complete Book from Beginning to Championship Play;* American Press, Boston, MA, 1986.

1343. **Vandeweghe, Dr. Ernest M. and Flynn, George L.:** *Growing With Sports: A Parent's Guide to the Young Athlete;* Prentice-Hall, Englewood Cliffs, NJ, 1979.

1344. **Van Riper, Guernsey, Jr.:** *Game of Basketball;* Garrard, New Canaan, CT, 1968.

1345. **Van Ryswyk, Ron:** *Ball Control Offense and Disciplined Defense in Basketball;* Parker, New York, NY, 1967.

1346. **Veenker, George Fred:** *Basketball for Coaches and Players;* A.S. Barnes, San Diego, CA, 1938.

1347. **Verderame, Sal:** *Organization for Championship High School Basketball;* Prentice-Hall, Englewood Cliffs, NJ, 1963.

1348. **Verral, Charles Spain:** *Champion of the Court;* Crowell, New York, NY, 1954.

1349. **Versace, Dick:** *The Wit and Wisdom of Dick Versace;* St. George, Des Moines, IA, 1981.

1350. **Versace, Richard and Stephens, Steve:** *Trident Attack for Winning Basketball;* Parker, New York, NY, 1969.

1351. **Versey, George:** *Harlem Globetrotters;* Scholastic, New York, NY, 1970.

1352. **Versey, George:** *Pro Basketball Champions;* Scholastic, New York, NY, 1970.

1353. **Vitale, Dick and Kirkpatrick, Curry:** *Vitale: Just Your Average Bald, One-Eyed Basketball Wacko Who Beat the Ziggy and Became a PTP'er;* Simon and Schuster, New York, NY, 1988.

1354. **Von Borries, E. (Ed.):** *Official Basketball Guide for Women and Girls;* American Sports, 1934.

1355. **Voth, Roberg:** *Basketball's Continuity Pattern Offenses;* Parker, New York, NY, 1979.

1356. **Wachs, Bob:** *A Patterned Shuffle Attack: A New Approach to Individual Excellence and Balanced Team Play;* Parker, New York, NY, 1974.

1357. **Wade, Margaret and Hankinson, Mel:** *Basketball;* Delta State University, Cleveland, MS, 1980.

1358. **Walden, A.E.:** *Basketball Girl of the Year;* McGraw-Hill, New York, NY, date unknown.

1359. **Walden, Amelia Elizabeth:** *A Boy to Remember;* Berkley, New York, NY, 1960.

1360. **Walden, Amelia:** *A Girl Called Hank;* Morrow, New York, NY, 1951.

1361. **Walden, Amelia:** *My Sister Mike;* Whittlesey House, New York, NY, 1956.

1362. **Waldman, F.:** *Basketball Scandal;* Ariel, New York, NY, 1953.

1363. **Waldman, Frank:** *Famous American Athletes of Today;* Page, Boston, MA, 1949.

1364. **Walker, A.L. and Donahue, Jack:** *The New Option Offense for Winning Basketball;* Leisure Press, Champaign, IL, 1988.

1365. **Walker, A. Lee:** *The Option Offense for Winning Basketball;* Parker, New York, NY, 1977.

1366. **Walter, Claire:** *Winners: The Blue Ribbon Encyclopedia of Awards;* Facts on File, New York, NY, 1978.

1367. **Walton, Luke:** *Basketball's Fabulous Five;* Greenberg, New York, NY, 1950.

1368. **Ward, Charles R.:** *Basketball's Matchup Defense;* Prentice-Hall, Englewood Cliffs, NJ, 1964.

1369. **Ward, Don:** *Seattle Supersonics;* Creative Education, Minneapolis, MN, 1984.

1370. **Wardlaw, C.D. and Morrison, W.R.:** *Basketball: A Handbook for Coaches and Players*; Scribner and Sons, New York, NY, 1921 (2nd ed. 1923, 3rd ed. 1926).

1371. **Warner, G.S. and Wright, L.:** *Pop Warner's Book for Boys*; Dodd-Mead, New York, NY, 1945.

1372. **Warner, Jack and Jones, K.C.:** *Rebound: The Autobiography of K.C. Jones and an Inside Look at the Champion Boston Celtics*; Quinlan, Boston, MA, 1986.

1373. **Warren, William:** *Zone Offenses for Women's Basketball*; Allyn and Bacon, Boston, MA, 1980.

1374. **Warren, William E.:** *Team Patterns in Girls's and Women's Basketball*; A.S. Barnes, San Diego, CA, 1976.

1375. **Warren, William E. and Tarkanian, Jerry:** *Winning Basketball Drills and Fundamentals*; Allyn and Bacon, Boston, MA, 1983.

1376. **Washington, Helen and Soderberg, Paul:** *The Big Book of Halls of Fame in the United States and Canada: Sports*; Bowker, New York, NY, 1977.

1377. **Watts, Stan:** *Developing an Offensive Attack in Basketball*; Prentice-Hall, Englewood Cliffs, NJ, 1959.

1378. **Webb, Bernice Larson:** *The Basketball Man: James Naismith*; University Press of Kansas, Wichita, KS, 1973.

1379. **Webb, Spud and Slaughter, Reid:** *Spud Webb, Flying High*; Harper and Row, New York, NY, 1986.

1380. **Weber, Bruce:** *All-Pro Basketball Stars, 1977*; Scholastic, New York , NY, 1976.

1381. **Weber, Bruce:** *All-Pro Basketball Stars, 1978*; Scholastic, New York, NY, 1977.

1382. **Weber, Bruce:** *All-Pro Basketball Stars, 1979*; Scholastic, New York, NY, 1978.

1383. **Weber, Bruce:** *All-Pro Basketball Stars, 1981*; Scholastic, New York, NY, 1980.

1384. **Weber, Bruce:** *All-Pro Basketball Stars, 1982*; Scholastic, New York, NY, 1981.

1385. **Webster, Fran:** *Basketball's Amoeba Defense: A Complete Multiple System*; Parker, New York, NY, 1984.

1386. **Webster, Jean:** *Daddy-Long-Legs*; Century, New York, NY, 1913.

1387. *Webster's Sport Dictionary*; Merriam-Webster, Springfield, MA, 1976.

1388. **Wells, Clifford:** *The National Association of Basketball Coaches of the United States Guide and Procedures*; NABC, Branford, CT, 1967.

1389. **Welsh, Ray (Ed.):** *Basketball Coaches and Players Scrapbook*; Sports Tips and Teaching Aids, Detroit, MI, 1941.

1390. **Welsh, Ray:** *Winning Basketball: Successful Offenses and Defenses*; Burgess, Minneapolis, MN, 1947.

1391. **West, Jan and Rich, Michael:** *A Wife's Guide to Pro Basketball*; Viking, New York, NY, 1970.

1392. **West, Jerry:** *Basketball My Way*; Prentice-Hall, Englewood Cliffs, NJ, 1973.

1393. **West, Jerry and Libby, Bill:** *Mr. Clutch: The Jerry West Story*; Prentice-Hall, Englewood Cliffs, NJ, 1971.

1394. **Weyland, Alexander M.:** *The Cavalcade of Basketball*; Macmillan, New York, NY, 1960.

1395. **Weyland, Alexander M.:** *The Olympic Pageant*; Macmillan, New York, NY, 1952.

1396. **White, Dean:** *Play to Win: A Profile of Princeton Basketball Coach Pete Carril*; Prentice-Hall, Englewood Cliffs, NJ, 1978.

1397. **White, John and Moore, Billie J.:** *Basketball: Theory and Practice*; William C. Brown, Dubuque, IA, 1980.

1398. **White, Nathan W.:** *Fifty Years of Basketball Playing in Aroostook County, Maine, 1900–1950*; Aroostook Broadcasting Corporation, Augusta, ME, 1950.

1399. **Whitelaw, Reed Morrison and Wardlaw, Charles Digby:** *Basketball: A Handbook for Coaches and Players*; Scribner and Sons, New York, NY, 1923.

1400. **Whittingham, Richard:** *The Final Four: A Pictorial History of the NCAA Basketball Classic*; Contemporary Books, Chicago, IL, 1983.

1401. **Whittingham, Richard:** *Rand McNally Sports Places Rated: Ranking America's Best Places to Enjoy Sports;* Rand McNally, New York, NY, 1986.
1402. **Wielgus, Chuck and Wolff, Alexander:** *The Back-in-Your-Face Guide to Pickup Basketball;* Dodd-Mead, New York, NY, 1986.
1403. **Wielgus, Chuck, Jr. and Wolff, Alexander:** *The In-Your-Face Basketball Book;* Everest House, New York, NY, 1980.
1404. **Wilcox, D.:** *Basketball Star;* Little Brown, Boston, MA, 1956.
1405. **Wilkens, Lenny:** *The Lenny Wilkens Story;* Eriksson, New York, NY, 1974.
1406. **Wilkes, Glenn:** *Basketball* (Exploring Sports Series); William C. Brown, Dubuque, IA, 1984.
1407. **Wilkes, Glenn:** *Basketball* (P.E. Activities Series); William C. Brown, Dubuque, IA, 1984.
1408. **Wilkes, Glenn:** *Basketball Coach's Complete Handbook;* Prentice-Hall, Englewood Cliffs, NJ, 1963.
1409. **Wilkes, Glenn:** *Basketball for Men;* William C. Brown, Dubuque, IA, 1977.
1410. **Wilkes, Glenn:** *Winning Basketball Strategy;* Prentice-Hall, Englewood Cliffs, NJ, 1959.
1411. **Williams, Bob:** *Hoosier Hysteria! Indiana High School Basketball;* Icarus, South Bend, IN, 1982.
1412. **Williams, Carol L.:** *Coaches Guide to Basketball's Simplified Shuffle;* Parker, New York, NY, 1971.
1413. **Williams, E. and Zinkoff, David:** *Around the World with the Harlem Globetrotters;* McRae Smith, Philadelphia, PA, 1953.
1414. **Williams, Edgar and Zinkoff, Dave:** *Go Mango;* Pyramid Willow Books, New York, NY, 1971.
1415. **Williams, Joe:** *Better Basketball: A Guide to the Serious Coach and Player;* Sterling, New York, NY, 1983.
1416. **Williams, Pat and Lyon, Bill:** *We Owed You One! The Uphill Struggle of the Philadelphia 76'ers;* Trimark, New Castle, DE, 1983
1417. **Wilson, Mary and Blackwell, Lee:** *To Benji With Love;* Independent, Chicago, IL, 1986.
1418. **Wimick, Milt:** *National Basketball Association Official Guide;* Sporting News, St. Louis, MO, 1980.
1419. **Winsor, Chuck and Davis, Tom:** *Garage Door Basketball;* School Aid, Danville, IL, 1970.
1420. **Winter, Fred:** *The Triple Post Offense;* Prentice-Hall, Englewood Cliffs, NJ, 1962.
1421. **Wirt, George and Dawkins, Darryl:** *Chocolate Thunder;* Contemporary Books, Chicago, IL, 1986.
1422. **Wolf, Dave and Bruns, Bill:** *Great Moments in Pro Basketball;* Random House, New York, NY, 1968.
1423. **Wolf, David:** *Foul! The Connie Hawkins Story;* Warner Books, New York, NY, 1972.
1424. **Wolfe, Herman:** *From the Tryouts to Championship;* Prentice-Hall, Englewood Cliffs, NJ, 1964.
1425. **Wolff, Alexander and Wielgus, Chuck:** *The Back-in-your-Face Guide to Pickup Basketball;* Dodd-Mead, New York, NY, 1986.
1426. **Wolff, Alexander and Wielgus, Chuck, Jr.:** *The In-Your-Face Basketball Book;* Everest House, New York, NY, 1980.
1427. **Wolfson, Marty (Ed.):** *How to Watch Sports on TV and Enjoy It;* Wolfson, Pittsburgh, PA, 1972.
1428. **Wolfson, Marty and Smith, Chet:** *Greater Pittsburgh History of Sports, 1800–1970's;* Wolfson, Pittsburgh, PA, 1969.

1429. **Wood, William R., Bacon, Francis L., and Cameron, David (Eds.):** *Just for Sport*; Lippincott, Chicago, IL, 1943.
1430. **Wooden, John:** *Practical Modern Basketball*; Ronald Press, New York, NY, 1966.
1431. **Wooden, John:** *Practical Modern Basketball* (2nd ed.); John Wiley and Sons, New York, NY, 1980.
1432. **Wooden, John:** *They Call Me Coach*; Word, Waco, TX, 1972.
1433. **Wooden, John and Sharman, Bill:** *The Wooden-Sharman Method: A Guide to Winning Basketball*; Macmillan, New York, NY, 1975.
1434. **Woodling, Chuck:** *Against All Odds*; University of Kansas Press, Lawrence, KS, 1988.
1435. **Wootten, Morgan and Galotta, Hank:** *Dematha High School Blitz Defense*; Wooten and Galotta, Baltimore, MD, 1971.
1436. **Wootten, Morgan and Gilbert, Bill:** *From Orphans to Champions: The Story of Dematha's Morgan Wootten*; Atheneum, New York, NY, 1979.
1437. **Wootten, Morgan and Truax, Terry:** *Dematha High School Basketball Notebook*; Wootten and Truax, Baltimore, MD, 1970.
1438. **Wordlaw, Charles Digby and Frost, Helen:** *Basketball and Indoor Baseball for Women*; Scribner and Sons, New York, NY, 1920.
1439. **Wordlaw, Charles Digby and Whitelaw, Reed Morrison:** *Basketball: A Handbook for Coaches and Players*; Scribner and Sons, New York, NY, 1923.
1440. **Wright, L. and Warner, G.S.:** *Pop Warner's Book for Boys*; Dodd-Mead, New York, NY, 1945.
1441. **Yaksick, Rudy:** *Winning Basketball With the Freelance System*; Parker, New York, NY, 1968.
1442. **Yarnell, Duane:** *The Winning Basket*; World, Cleveland, OH, 1940.
1443. **Young, Faye and Coffey, Wayne:** *Winning Basketball for Girls*; Facts on File, New York, NY, 1984.
1444. **Youngman, Randy:** *Officiating Basketball*; Contemporary Books, Chicago, IL, 1978.
1445. **Young Men's Christian Association:** *YMCA Basketball Rules*; YMCA Press, New York, NY, 1911.
1446. **Zadra, Dan:** *Boston Celtics*; Creative Education, Minneapolis, MN, 1984.
1447. **Zaharias, Babe Didrikson and Paxton, Harry:** *This Life I've Led: My Autobiography*; Barnes, New York, NY, 1955.
1448. **Zampardi, Frank:** *Multiple Penetrating Attacks for Winning Basketball*; Parker, New York, NY, 1980.
1449. **Zingg, Bob:** *Pride of the Palestra: Ninety Years of Pennsylvania Basketball*; University of Pennsylvania Athletic Department, Philadelphia, PA, 1988.
1450. **Zimmerman, Paul, DeBusschere, Dave, and Schapp, Dick:** *The Open Man: A Championship Diary*; Grove Press, New York, NY, 1971.
1451. **Zinkoff, Dave and Williams, Edgar:** *Go Mango*; Pyramid Willow Books, New York, NY, 1971.
1452. **Zinkoff, David and Williams, E.:** *Around the World With the Harlem Globetrotters*; McRae Smith, Philadelphia, PA, 1953.

Chapter 2

Periodicals and Journal Articles

This chapter is divided into three parts: (1) a listing of the most relevant periodicals in which basketball-related articles frequently appear, (2) a listing by volume of the basketball articles that have appeared in the *Athletic Journal*, and (3) a listing by volume of the basketball articles that have been published in *Scholastic Coach*.

Note: Scholastic Coach and the *Athletic Journal* merged in June 1987. Therefore, Volume 67, 1986–87, of the *Athletic Journal* is the final volume listed under that title.

Listing of Periodicals

1453. *Basketball Clinic*
Princeton Educational Publishers
CN 5245
Princeton, NJ 08540

1454. *Basketball Digest*
Century Publishing Company
1020 Church St.
Evanston, IL 60201

1455. *Basketball Weekly*
c/o The Football News Company
17820 East Warren Avenue
Detroit, MI 48224

1456. *The Bulletin*
c/o National Association of Basketball Coaches
12 Pine Orchard Road, Box 307
Bradford, CT 05405

1457. *Coaching Clinic*
c/o Parker Publishing Company, Inc.
West Nyack, NY 10994

1458. *International Basketball*
c/o Promextour, s. v. 1
20123 Milano, Via Panzeri 4, Italy

1459. *Journal of Physical Education, Recreation and Dance* (JOPERD)
c/o American Alliance for Health, Physical Education, Recreation and Dance
1900 Association Drive
Reston, VA 22091

1460. *Juco Review, the Official NJCAA Magazine*
c/o National Junior College Athletic Association
P.O. Box 1586
Hutchinson, KS 67501

1461. *NAIA News*
c/o National Association of Intercollegiate Athletics
1205 Baltimore Street
Kansas City, MO 64105

1462. *National Wheelchair Basketball Association Newsletter*
110 Seaton Building
University of Kentucky
Lexington, KY 40506

1463. *P.G. Basketball Newsletters*
P.G. Sports Service, Inc.
Box 405, Main Post Office
Niagara Falls, NY 14302

1464. *Physical Educator*
c/o Phi Epsilon Kappa, School of Health, Physical Education, and Recreation
Indiana University
Bloomington, IN 47405

1465. *Referee Magazine*
P.O. Box 161
Franksville, WI 53126

1466. *Research Quarterly*
c/o American Alliance for Health, Physical Education, Recreation and Dance
1900 Association Drive
Reston, VA 22091

1467. *Scholastic Coach*
Scholastic, Inc.
730 Broadway
New York, NY 10003

1468. *Sports Weekly Newsletter— Basketball*
R. W. Livingston, Editor and Publisher
Box 5332
North Charleston, SC 29406

1469. *Strategies Magazine*
c/o American Alliance for Health, Physical Eduction, Recreation and Dance
1900 Association Drive
Reston, VA 22091

1470. *Women's Coaching Clinic*
P.O. Box 14
West Nyack, NY 10036

1471. *Women's Varsity Sports Magazine*
P.O. Box 4511
Portland, OR 97208

Athletic Journal *Articles, 1925–1987*

Volume 6, 1925–26

1472. **Ashmore, James N.:** *The Eighth Annual National Interscholastic*; May, p. 3.

1473. **Case, Everett N.:** *Basketball Offense in Indiana*; Mar., p. 32.

1474. **Coleman, J.W.:** *The Five Man Defense*; Feb., p. 38.

1475. **De Silva, Lionel:** *The Interscholastic Inter-Island Basketball Tournament of Hawaii*; May, p. 22.

1476. **Griffith, John L.:** *Basketball*, Editorial; Apr., p. 18.

1477. **Griffith, John L.:** *Popularity of Basketball*, Editorial; Apr., p. 18; *Basketball*, Editorial; Apr., p. 18.

1478. **Lippert, Jack K.:** *Foul Shooting*; Nov., p. 12.

1479. *Analysis of Basketball Plays*; Feb., p. 5.

1480. *An Analysis of the Basketball Plays of the February Issue*; Mar., p. 26.

1481. *Basketball Plays (Contest Plays)*; Dec., p. 16; Jan., p. 14; Feb., p. 3.

1482. *How to Coach a High School Basketball Team*; Feb., p. 17.

1483. *Types of Basketball Plays*; Feb., p. 6.

Volume 7, 1926–27

1484. **Allen, Dr. Forrest C.:** *Zone or Man-to-Man Defense*; Dec., p. 12; *Stalling or Hot-Shooting Against a Set or Zone Defense*; Jan., p. 17; *Making the Routine of Practice of Drills Competitive in Spirit*; Feb., p. 3.

1485. **Barry, Sam:** *New Basketball Rules*; May, p. 17.
1486. **Crisler, H.O.:** *Ninth Annual Basketball Tournament*; May, p. 18.
1487. **Dean, E.S.:** *New Basketball Rules*; May, p. 24.
1488. **Godfrey, Percy:** *Drills for Teaching Basketball Fundamentals*; Dec., p. 17.
1489. **Griffith, John L.:** *Basketball Rules*, Editorial; May, p. 22.
1490. **Grover, B.T.:** *Offensive Side of Basketball*; Nov., p. 26.
1491. **Hager, R.H.:** *New Basketball Rules*; May, p. 16.
1492. **Kent, M.A.:** *New Basketball Rules*; May, p. 24.
1493. **Lambert, Ward:** *New Basketball Rules*; May, p. 26.
1494. **Long, H.K.:** *How Morton Won the Basketball Tournament*; May, p. 20.
1495. **Mann, Leslie J.:** *Suggestions to Basketball Coaches*; Jan., p. 10.
1496. **Mather, E.J.:** *A Summary of Western Conference Basketball*; Apr., p. 14.
1497. **Meanwell, Walter E.:** *New Basketball Rules*; May, p. 28.
1498. **Mendenhall, L.L.:** *A Discussion of Basketball Rules for the Young Official*; Feb., p. 7.
1499. **Nichols, James A.:** *Basketball Officiating*; Nov., p. 22.
1500. **Olson, H.G.:** *New Basketball Rules*; May, p. 30.
1501. **Page, H.O.:** *Handling Basketball Material*; Jan., p. 15.
1502. **Ruby, Craig J.:** *Mental Conditioning of Basketball Teams*; Nov., p. 18; *Strategy of Basketball Substitutions*; Dec., p. 14; *Goal Throwing*; Jan., p. 3; *Importance and Pedagogy of Correct Basketball Playing Habits*; Feb., p. 6; *New Basketball Rules*; May, p. 24.
1503. *Basketball Contest Plays*; Mar., p. 19; Apr., p. 15.

Volume 8, 1927–28

1504. **Allen, Forrest C.:** *Winning Basketball Games by Making Fewer Fouls*; Jan., p. 21.
1505. **Ashmore, J.N.:** *Possession and Control in Basketball*; Mar., p. 39; *Basketball in the Southern Conference*; Mar., p. 42.
1506. **Calland, Leo:** *Basketball in Southern California*; Jan., p. 5.
1507. **Carlson, Dr. H.C.:** *Basketball in the Middle-Atlantic States*; Mar., p. 12.
1508. **Chandler, W.S.:** *Basketball in the Missouri Valley Conference*; Mar., p. 44.
1509. **Clark, S.M.:** *Rocky Mountain Conference*; Mar., p. 12.
1510. **Dean, Everett S.:** *Offensive Basketball in the Big Ten Conference*; Apr., p. 14.
1511. **Edmundson, C.S.:** *Basketball in the Pacific Northwest*; Jan., p. 6; *Basketball Defense*; Jan., p. 20.
1512. **Fletcher, W.D.:** *Basketball as Played Today in the Northern Pacific Conference*; Mar., p. 11.
1513. **Greene, R.H.:** *Suggested Plan to Eliminate Stalling in Basketball*; Mar., p. 38.
1514. **Hinkle, Paul D.:** *Indiana Basketball Tournament*; Apr., p. 18.
1515. **Kline, W.G.:** *Five-Man Defense*; Oct., p. 20; *Basketball Systems*; Nov., p. 14; *Basketball Objectives*; Jan., p. 16; *Dribble Should Be Retained*; Feb., p. 5.
1516. **Lambert, Ward:** *Evolutionary Stages in Basketball*; Apr., p. 13.
1517. **Messer, G.N.:** *Basketball in the East*; Feb., p. 3.
1518. **Morgenstern, W.V.:** *National Basketball Tournament*; Apr., p. 20.
1519. **Naismith, Dr. James:** *Is Basketball Injurious?*; Oct., p. 18.
1520. **Norgen, N.H.:** *National Interscholastic Basketball Tournament*; May, p. 11.
1521. **Olson, Harold G.:** *System in Basketball*; Dec., p. 13.
1522. **Ruby, J. Craig:** *Basketball in the Western Conference*: Mar., p. 44.
1523. **Schmidt, Frances A.:** *Basketball in the Southwest Conference*; Mar., p. 42; *A Few Basketball Suggestions*; Apr., p. 26.
1524. **Schommer, John J.:** *The 1928 Rules in Basketball*; Jan., p. 18.

1525. **Stafford, George T.:** *Prevention of Injuries in Basketball;* Nov., p. 20.
1526. **Tower, Oswald:** *College Basketball in the East;* Jan., p. 6; *Blocking and the Screen Play in Basketball;* Jan., p. 15; *College Basketball in the East;* Mar., p. 13.
1527. **Walker, Fred M.:** *Basketball in the Southwest Conference;* Mar., p. 42.

Volume 9, 1928–29

1528. **Allen, Dr. Forrest C.:** *Versatility in Defense and Balance in Offense in the Present Basketball Situation;* Feb., p. 5.
1529. **Allen, F.C.:** *International Growth of Basketball;* Mar., p. 36.
1530. **Ballard, Roy:** *A Proposed Change in the Basketball Rules;* Feb., p. 8.
1531. **Betz, Lester C.:** *Basketball on the Small Floor;* Feb., p. 7.
1532. **Carlson, Dr. H.C.:** *Basketball Fundamentals;* Sept., p. 18; Oct., p. 20; *Team Offense;* Nov., p. 15.
1533. **Carlson, H.C.:** *Man-Ahead-of-the-Ball Offensive;* Jan., p. 7.
1534. **Dunbar, Ralph E.:** *A Unique Code of Sportsmanship for Basketball;* Dec., p. 12.
1535. **Freezle, Stanley S.:** *Basketball Officiating;* Jan., p. 34.
1536. **Fletcher, W.O.:** *Basketball in the Northwest;* May, p. 24.
1537. **Griffith, Coleman R.:** *Basketball Tactics from the Point of View of Psychology;* Apr., p. 42.
1538. **Henderson, Roy B.:** *More About the Stall;* May, p. 46.
1539. **Huffman, P.E.:** *The So-Called Stall;* Dec., p. 26.
1540. **Keogan, George:** *Delayed Offensive in Basketball;* Sept., p. 26; *Lessons From the Basketball Tournament of 1927-28;* Nov., p. 40; *The Requisites of a Good Basketball Player;* Dec., p. 17.
1541. **McMillan, David:** *The Short Passing Game;* Jan., p. 17.
1542. **Morrison, W. Coy:** *Professional Basketball;* Feb., p. 37.
1543. **Norgen, N.H.:** *High School Basketball Tournaments;* May, p. 18.
1544. **Page, H.O.:** *Basketball Energy;* Feb., p. 3; *Indiana State Basketball Tournament;* May, p. 20.
1545. **Porter, H.V.:** *Basketball Game Preparations and Management;* Jan., p. 13.
1546. **Tower, Oswald:** *Basketball Rules for 1928-29;* Dec., p. 11.
1547. *Massachussetts Agricultural College Basketball Tournament;* Aug., p. 37.

Volume 10, 1929–30

1548. **Bassett, Charles F.:** *Southwest Conference;* May, p. 20.
1549. **Bearg, Ernest E.:** *Basketball Training and Preparation;* Sept., p. 30.
1550. **Beresford, H.C.:** *Rocky Mountain Conference;* May, p. 20.
1551. **Bingham, Glenn A.:** *Iowa Intercollegiate Conference;* May, p. 22.
1552. **Bohler, J. Fred:** *Basketball on the Pacific Coast;* Dec., p. 5.
1553. **Carlson, Dr. H.C.:** *System in Basketball;* Sept., p. 34; *Basketball in the Grades;* Nov., p. 20; *Basketball of Nineteen Twenty-Eight and Nine;* Dec., p. 5; *High School Offensive System;* Dec., p. 16; *Figure Eight Offensive;* Jan., p. 17; *Report of Atlantic Section;* May, p. 24.
1554. **Cooper, George E.:** *Report of Coaching Ethics Committee;* May, p. 14.
1555. **Daugherty, R.R. and Novak, L.V.:** *Modern Types of Offensive and Defensive Basketball;* Jan., p. 7.
1556. **Detrick, R.O.:** *Basketball in Ohio;* Dec., p. 42.
1557. **Dyche, Shubert R.:** *Rocky Mountain Intercollegiate Basketball;* Dec., p. 6.
1558. **Edwards, G.R.:** *Basketball in the Missouri Valley;* Dec., p. 7.
1559. **Griffith, Coleman R., Ph.D.:** *Experiments in Basketball;* June, p. 9.
1560. **Grover, B.F.:** *Buckeye Conference;* May, p. 22.

1561. **Hager, R.H.:** *Early Training in Basketball;* Oct., p. 46; *Dribbling;* Nov., p. 24; *Basketball Scouting;* Jan., p. 22.
1562. **Hunt, E.P.:** *Pacific Coast Conference;* May, p. 18.
1563. **Kitts, James:** *Championship High School Basketball;* Jan., p. 16.
1564. **MacMillan, David:** *Big Ten Conference;* May, p. 22.
1565. **Menze, Louis:** *Big Six Conference;* May, p. 20.
1566. **Mundorff, Roy:** *Southern Conference—Southern Section;* May, p. 20.
1567. **Novak, L.V. and Daugherty, R.R.:** *Modern Types of Offensive and Defensive Basketball;* Jan., p. 7.
1568. **Ortner, Howard B.:** *Eastern Collegiate Basketball;* Dec., p. 8.
1569. **Page, H.O.:** *Indiana State High School Basketball Tournament of 1930;* Apr., p. 42.
1570. **Powell, Arthur L.:** *New York State Conference;* May, p. 26.
1571. **Roosma, Lt. John S.:** *Shooting Baskets;* Nov., p. 6.
1572. **Schmidt, Francis A.:** *Basketball in the Southwest Conference;* Dec., p. 44.
1573. **Smith, R.A.:** *Southern Conference—Northern Section;* May, p. 24.
1574. **Swetland, J.E.:** *Building Up Basketball With Intramural Competition;* Apr., p. 34.
1575. **Tebell, G.K.:** *Basketball in Southeast;* Dec., p. 38.
1576. **Tower, Oswald:** *Basketball Rules for 1929–30;* Sept., p. 24; *Basketball Rules for 1930–31;* June, p. 21.
1577. **Truesdale, J.C.:** *Missouri Valley Conference;* May, p. 22.
1578. **Watson, Thomas A.:** *Blindfold Test for Free Throw Accuracy;* Apr., p. 38.

Volume 11, 1930–31

1579. **Allen, Dr. F.C.:** *Report of Terminology Committee;* May, p. 18; *Report of the Nomination Committee;* May, p. 22.
1580. **Barry, J.M. (Sam):** *Twelve Diagrams of Pacific Coast Basketball Plays;* Jan., p. 10.
1581. **Bassett, Charles:** *Offensive and Defensive Basketball;* Dec., p. 8.
1582. **Benz, Lester G.:** *Developing the High School Team;* Nov., p. 24.
1583. **Edwards, George R.:** *Basketball in the Missouri Valley;* Dec., p. 10.
1584. **Fletcher, Dr. W.D.:** *Importance of Defense in Basketball;* Oct., p. 18.
1585. **Griffith, Coleman R., Ph.D.:** *Types of Errors in Throwing Free Throws;* Sept., p. 22.
1586. **Hager, R.H.:** *Early Plans for Basketball;* Nov., p. 30; *Defense Against Stalling;* Dec., p. 7; *Road Teams in Basketball;* Jan., p. 6.
1587. **Kitts, James:** *Stalling;* Oct., p. 50.
1588. **Lambert, Ward:** *Basketball Styles in the Big Ten;* Dec., p. 16.
1589. **Lonborg, Arthur C.:** *Preparation for a Basketball Squad;* Jan., p. 8.
1590. **Ortner, H.B.:** *Report of Officers;* May, p. 13.
1591. **Pfeiffer, E.A.:** *Offensive Basketball;* Dec., p. 53; *Passing, Catching and Pivoting in Basketball;* Jan., p. 7.
1592. **Ruby, J.C.:** *Reports of Rules Committee;* May, p. 18.
1593. **Schabinger, A.A.:** *Types of Play in the Missouri Valley;* Dec., p. 20; *Address of the President-Elect of the National Basketball Coaches Association;* May, p. 22.
1594. **Tower, Oswald:** *Stalling in Basketball;* Oct., p. 11.
1595. **Trythall, Donald:** *Diagnostic Basketball;* Jan., p. 22.

Volume 12, 1931–32

1596. **Adams, J. Arthur:** *Basketball Practice Formations;* Nov., p. 43.
1597. **Adams, Oliver J.:** *Conditioning the Basketball Squad;* Nov., p. 12.
1598. **Ashmore, James N.:** *Defense Keeps Pace;* Jan., p. 7.

1599. **Baller, Stewart:** *Miniature Golf Basketball*; Sept., p. 44.
1600. **Beck, Leslie F.:** *New York Championship Basketball*; May, p. 43.
1601. **Beresford, H.C.:** *Rocky Mountain Basketball*; June, p. 30.
1602. **Bohnhoff, Edward:** *Game Condition Drills in Basketball*; Apr., p. 43.
1603. **Bollerman, Howard M.:** *Mind in Basketball*; Nov., p. 44.
1604. **Buehler, J.B.:** *Control and Possession of the Ball*; Dec., p. 30.
1605. **Bunn, John W.:** *Pacific Coast Basketball*; June, p. 26,
1606. **Case, Everett:** *Delayed Offense in Indiana High Schools*; Nov., p. 34.
1607. **Correy, Stephen M. and Messersmith, Lloyd L.:** *Activity in Basketball*; Oct., p. 32.
1608. **Dean, Everett:** *Is Basketball Too Strenuous?*; May, p. 15,
1609. **Dooley, Roger W.:** *Minnesota State Championship Basketball*; May, p. 20.
1610. **Draper, Walter L.:** *Breaking in Basketball*; Dec., p. 17.
1611. **Dunmire, J.R.:** *Basketball Training for the Younger Boys*; Apr., p. 17.
1612. **Fisher, Harold:** *Handling a Basketball Team on the Road*; Jan., p. 14.
1613. **Forehand, George:** *Texas Championship Basketball*; May, p. 45.
1614. **Freeman, Chester:** *Florida Championship Basketball*; May, p. 34.
1615. **Friddle, Burl:** *Pivot Play*; Dec., p. 8.
1616. **Halpin, Edward F.:** *Missouri Championship Basketball*; May, p. 42.
1617. **Hanna, Glen A.:** *Hints on the Dribble*; Apr., p. 19.
1618. **Hanscom, William A.:** *Maine Championship Basketball*; May, p. 40.
1619. **Harris, Carl G.:** *Iowa Championship Basketball*; May, p. 30.
1620. **Harrison, R.A.:** *Meeting Varied Basketball Defenses*; Apr., p. 17.
1621. **Hooker, Orville J.:** *Ball Possession in Basketball*; Jan., p. 44; *Indiana Championship Basketball*; May, p. 22.
1622. **Houck, D.A.:** *Deliberate and Fast Break Basketball*; Dec., p. 28.
1623. **Jackson, C.O.:** *Basket Shooting Tournaments*; p. 52.
1624. **Jones, W.L.:** *Wisconsin Championship Basketball*; May, p. 18.
1625. **Klein, L.F.:** *Nebraska Championship Basketball*; May, p. 46.
1626. **Livingstone, Alfred:** *Teaching Basketball Fundamentals Early*; Oct., p. 38.
1627. **Lumley, Raymond A.:** *Knowing the Rules*; Nov., p. 45.
1628. **McCormick, Frank:** *Junior Basketball*; May, p. 50.
1629. **McGuinnes, Charles:** *Outline of Basketball Fundamentals*; Sept., p. 34.
1630. **McMahon, Leonard C.:** *Individual Defense in Basketball*; Apr., p. 44.
1631. **Messersmith, Lloyd L. and Correy, Stephen M.:** *Activity in Basketball*; Oct., p. 32.
1632. **Miller, Claude:** *Conserving Energy in Basketball*; Apr., p. 16.
1633. **Nevins, Joseph G.:** *Breaking Through the Five Man Defense*; Nov., p. 45.
1634. **Pfeiffer, E.A.:** *Team Defense in Basketball*; Oct., p. 26.
1635. **Purdy, E.R.:** *Technique of the Free Throw*; Oct., p. 38.
1636. **Quintal, A.A.:** *South Dakota Championship Basketball*; May, p. 42.
1637. **Ransdell, Sam R.:** *Shifting Zone in Basketball*; Jan., p. 38.
1638. **Rice, Henry L.:** *North Dakota Championship Basketball*; May, p. 36.
1639. **Roels, H.J.:** *Set Play Offense Versus Five-Man Defense*; Dec., p. 42.
1640. **Ruby, J. Craig:** *Fall Basketball Practice*; Sept., p. 22: *Dribble Practice*; Oct., p. 24; *Basketball System Strategy*; Dec., p. 6.
1641. **Rupert, Arch:** *Shots Under the Basket*; Oct., p. 38.
1642. **Rupp, A.F.:** *Southern Conference Basketball*; June, p. 30.
1643. **Rushton, C.C.:** *Self-Made Systems*; Jan., p. 40.
1644. **St. John, L.W.:** *Basketball Rules Changes for 1932–1933*; June, p. 6.
1645. **Sangster, Earl Y.:** *Checking on Basketball Fundamentals*; Jan., p. 42.
1646. **Smith, Willard:** *Basketball Teamwork*; Nov., p. 46; *Moving Zone Defense*; Jan., p. 25.

1647. **Swain, John W.:** *Drills for Basketball Defense;* Dec., p. 17.
1648. **Thomas, Eugene S.:** *Teaching Basketball Defense;* Apr., p. 18; *Michigan Championship Basketball;* May, p. 36.
1649. **Trythall, Donald:** *Relative Merits of Basketball Defense;* Sept., p. 45.
1650. **Turner, Ralph R.:** *Pattern of Play in the Coaching of Basketball;* Oct., p. 28.
1651. **Varnes, Blair L.:** *National Tournament Play;* May, p. 22.
1652. **Wakefield, Mark:** *Wise Schedule Making;* Dec., p. 16.
1653. **Warncke, Winfield:** *Delaware Championship Basketball;* May, p. 32.
1654. **Warren, John A.:** *Oregon Championship Basketball;* May, p. 40.
1655. **Weaver, E.B.:** *Kansas Championship Basketball;* May, p. 32.
1656. **Wells, Clifford:** *Indiana High School Block Plays;* Oct., p. 20.
1657. **Woodbury, Lawrence C.:** *Changing the Defense in Basketball;* Nov., p. 13.
1658. **Ziebell, Norman A.:** *Illinois Championship Basketball;* May, p. 20.
1659. *Sixth Annual Meeting of the National Association of Basketball Coaches;* June, p. 8.

Volume 13, 1932–33

1660. **Anderson, William H.:** *Pennsylvania Championship Basketball;* May, p. 28.
1661. **Asher, Howard:** *Rhode Island Basketball Championship;* May, p. 32.
1662. **Baker, H. Cecil:** *Utah Championship Basketball;* May, p. 32.
1663. **Barclay, James:** *Michigan Championship Basketball;* Feb., p. 12.
1664. **Beck, Leslie E.:** *Handling the Team During a Tournament;* Feb., p. 12.
1665. **Beer, Frank A.:** *Teach Two Defenses;* Sept., p. 19.
1666. **Bell, Farley W.:** *West Virginia Basketball;* May, p. 36.
1667. **Bowers, W.L.:** *Set Shots in Basketball;* Feb., p. 14; *Extended Type of Tournament;* Mar., p. 15; *Maryland Championship Basketball;* May, p. 17.
1668. **Buck, Selby H.:** *Georgia Championship Basketball;* May, p. 14.
1669. **Bunn, John W.:** *An Investigation of the Center Jump in Basketball;* Dec., p. 8; *Study of Baskets at Different Heights;* Feb., p. 6.
1670. **Burbage, Major J.S.:** *Basketball in a Military School;* Jan., p. 17.
1671. **Carlson, Dr. H.C.:** *Evolution of Offensive Maneuvers;* Jan., p. 6.
1672. **Case, Everett N.:** *Test Games Under the New Rules in Basketball;* Dec., p. 22.
1673. **Coutchie, S.A.:** *Arizona Championship Basketball;* May, p. 11.
1674. **Curtin, Lee L.:** *Free Throwing;* Dec., p. 44.
1675. **Davison, Glenn E.:** *Basketball for Girls;* Sept., p. 18.
1676. **Dickey, Levi:** *Adjustable Basketball Offense;* Oct., p. 16.
1677. **Diebold, Marshall J.:** *Operation of the Ten-Second and Three-Second Rules;* Feb., p. 7.
1678. **Dienhart, Joe:** *National Tournament Play;* Apr., p. 14.
1679. **Dooley, Roger M.:** *Suggestions on Tournament Play;* Feb., p. 11.
1680. **Dunaway, W.A.:** *Arkansas Championship Basketball;* May, p. 11.
1681. **Edwards, George R.:** *Operation of the So-Called Double-Referee System;* Nov., p. 24.
1682. **Foreman, F.B.:** *Wyoming Championship Basketball;* May, p. 38.
1683. **Freeman, Chester:** *"Pointing" for the Tournament;* Jan., p. 15.
1684. **Garrett, R.J.:** *New Hampshire Basketball Championship;* May, p. 24.
1685. **Godwin, Frank M.:** *Nevada Championship Basketball;* May, p. 23.
1686. **Gullion, Blair:** *Free Throw Technique in Basketball;* Mar., p. 38.
1687. **Halpin, Edward F.:** *Why the Best Team Does Not Always Win;* Feb., p. 13.
1688. **Hanscom, William A.:** *Rest and Food in the Tournament;* Mar., p. 32.
1689. **Harris, Carol G.:** *Tournament Strategy;* Mar., p. 15.
1690. **Hartman, W. Harold:** *Iowa Basketball Championship;* May, p. 15.
1691. **Hays, George L.:** *North Dakota Championship Basketball;* May, p. 26.

1692. **Henry, Harold B.**: *Sportsmanship in Basketball*; Dec., p. 38.
1693. **Holgate, C.**: *South Dakota Championship Basketball*; May, p. 32.
1694. **Jacobson, H.L.**: *Wisconsin Championship Basketball*; May, p. 37.
1695. **Jenkins, Paul**: *Kentucky Championship Basketball*; May, p. 16.
1696. **Johnson, R.H.**: *Mississippi Championship Basketball*; May, p. 21.
1697. **Johnson, Ray C.**: *Michigan Championship Basketball*; May, p. 19.
1698. **Knight, Clay**: *Alabama Championship Basketball*; May, p. 8.
1699. **Lambert, Ward L.**: *Will the New Rules Speed Up Basketball?*; Oct., p. 22.
1700. **Larson, Emil L. and Young, G.T.**: *Increasing Consistency in Basketball Officiating*; Jan., p. 40.
1701. **Lipe, Jack**: *Illinois Basketball Championship*; May, p. 15.
1702. **Mielenz, Frank E.**: *Nebraska Championship Basketball*; May, p. 23.
1703. **Miller, William L.**: *Colorado Championship Basketball*; May, p. 12.
1704. **Mix, Gale L.**: *Idaho Championship Basketball*; May, p. 14.
1705. **Monaham, Thomas M.**: *Connecticut Championship Basketball*; May, p. 13.
1706. **Mundorff, Roy**: *Basketball in the Southwest*; Dec., p. 12.
1707. **Osborne, William**: *New Basketball Officiating*; Mar., p. 40.
1708. **Peters, I.L.**: *Intramural Basketball League*; Oct., p. 42.
1709. **Polster, Raymond G.**: *Missouri Championship Basketball*; May, p. 22.
1710. **Prudhom, Harold C.**: *Individual Zone Defense*; Feb., p. 8.
1711. **Purdy, E.R.**: *Vermont Championship Basketball*; May, p. 36.
1712. **Rearick, Herman**: *Ohio Championship Basketball*; May, p. 26.
1713. **Romney, G. Ott**: *So-Called Fast Break System*; Nov., p. 20.
1714. **Schneider, N.O.**: *Standardizing the Playing Court*; Jan., p. 43.
1715. **Skidmore, Walter D.**: *North Carolina Championship Basketball*; May, p. 14.
1716. **Smith, L. Jack**: *Basketball for All*; Jan., p. 16.
1717. **Stewart, Fred K.**: *Florida Championship Basketball*; May, p. 13.
1718. **Tannery, Fladger**: *Making Basketball Pay*; Dec., p. 14.
1719. **Thomas, Eugene**: *Leading Up to the Tournament*; Mar., p. 16.
1720. **Warncke, Winfield A.**: *Building for the Tournament*; Jan., p. 15.
1721. **Weaver, E.B.**: *Training Hints for the Tournament*; Mar., p. 32.
1722. **Wilkinson, Perry**: *Balancing Offense and Defense*; Feb., p. 15.
1723. **Wilson, W.S.**: *New Mexico Basketball Championship*; May, p. 24.
1724. **Young, G.T. and Larson, Emil L.**: *Increasing Consistency in Basketball Officiating*; Jan., p. 40.
1725. **Ziebell, Norman A.**: *Learning From Tournament Play*; Jan., p. 13.
1726. *Proceedings of the Seventh Annual Meeting of the National Association of Basketball Coaches*; June, p. 13.

Volume 14, 1933–34

1727. **Allen, Forrest C.**: *Standardized Nomenclature in Basketball*; Nov., p. 36.
1728. **Baker, H. Cecil**: *Utah Championship Basketball*; June, p. 36.
1729. **Baller, Stuart**: *Nebraska Championship Basketball*; May, p. 23.
1730. **Bowers, W.L.**: *Maryland Championship Basketball*; May, p. 18.
1731. **Buck, Selby H., Jr.**: *Georgia Championship Basketball*; June, p. 12.
1732. **Bunn, John W.**: *Defensive Play and How to Meet It*; Feb., p. 16.
1733. **Chandler, W.S.**: *Overcoaching Basketball Fundamentals*; Dec., p. 7.
1734. **Clark, Forrest G.**: *West Virginia Championship Basketball*; June, p. 40.
1735. **Dahl, Edwin J.**: *Basketball Rules and Officiating*; Mar., p. 16.
1736. **Davis, Leslie H.**: *Iowa Championship Basketball*; June, p. 14.
1737. **Dimick, Harold A.**: *Washington Championship Basketball*; June, p. 36.
1738. **Dunaway, W.A.**: *Arkansas Championship Basketball*; June, p. 10.

1739. **Evans, Jack:** *Colorado Championship Basketball*; May, p. 14.
1740. **Foreman, F.B.:** *Wyoming Championship Basketball*; June, p. 42.
1741. **Geremonty, Francis H.:** *New Hampshire Championship Basketball*; June, p. 30.
1742. **Graff, Walter A.:** *Michigan Championship Basketball*; June, p. 22.
1743. **Gridley, Rollin T.:** *Arizona Championship Basketball*; June, p. 10.
1744. **Hug, Procter R.:** *Nevada Championship Basketball*; June, p. 19.
1745. **Jacobson, H.L.:** *Wisconsin Championship Basketball*; June, p. 42.
1746. **Lambert, Ward L.:** *Offensive Footwork Drills*; Dec., p. 17.
1747. **Long, H.K.:** *Basketball Problems for the High School Coach*; Dec., p. 25.
1748. **Mansfield, W.L.:** *Maine Championship Basketball*; June, p. 10.
1749. **Miller, Harold T.:** *Oklahoma Championship Basketball*; June, p. 28.
1750. **Milner, Ryland H.:** *Missouri Championship Basketball*; May, p. 20.
1751. **Mix, Gale L.:** *Idaho Championship Basketball*; June, p. 12.
1752. **Money, C.V.:** *Test for Evaluating the Abilities of Basketball Players*; Nov., p. 32; Dec., p. 18.
1753. **Morris, R.B.:** *Rhode Island Championship Basketball*; June, p. 34.
1754. **Nelson, Paul M.:** *Ohio Championship Basketball*; May, p. 32.
1755. **Olsen, H.G.:** *Individual Defensive Play in Basketball*; Jan., p. 5; *Coaching the Pivot*; Feb., p. 5.
1756. **O'Neill, Leo:** *Basketball on a Small Floor*; Mar., p. 15.
1757. **Parnell, Ed.:** *Florida Championship Basketball*; June, p. 11.
1758. **Rearick, Herman:** *Strict Man-for-Man Defensive Basketball*; Feb., p. 9.
1759. **Robertson, H.L.:** *North Dakota Championship Basketball*; June p. 16.
1760. **Roels, Harvey J.:** *Minnesota Championship Basketball*; June, p. 16.
1761. **Ruby, J. Craig:** *Crowding Around the Center Jump*; Oct., p. 17; *Legal and Illegal Maneuvers in Basketball*; Dec., p. 10.
1762. **Schabinger, A.A.:** *Questions That Coaches Ask Concerning Basketball*; Sept., p. 44.
1763. **Seibert, A.H.:** *Montana Championship Basketball*; June, p. 17.
1764. **Smith, Alfred D.:** *Kansas Championship Basketball*; May, p. 17.
1765. **Stahl, Floyd S.:** *Offensive and Defensive Drills on Basketball Fundamentals*; Dec., p. 27.
1766. **Storby, S.O.:** *Illinois Championship Basketball*; June, p. 13.
1767. **Tower, Oswald:** *Interpretations Made on the 1933–1934 Basketball Rules*; Feb., p. 11.
1768. **Warren, John A.:** *Oregon Championship Basketball*; June, p. 30.
1769. **Washabaugh, Grover C.:** *Pennsylvania Championship Basketball*; June, p. 30.
1770. **Wells, Clifford:** *Indiana Championship Basketball*; May, p. 15.
1771. **Wilbur, William M.:** *Vermont Championship Basketball*; May, p. 34.
1772. **Wood, Howard:** *South Dakota Championship Basketball*; June, p. 34.
1773. *Basketball Rule Changes—1933–34*; Dec., p. 8.
1774. *Offensive Basketball (Thirteen Plays)*; Jan., p. 8.

Volume 15, 1934–35

1775. **Arney, Richard:** *Minnesota Championship Basketball*; June, p. 18.
1776. **Baker, H. Cecil:** *Tournament Strategy*; Mar., p. 14.
1777. **Baller, Stuart:** *Screen Offense*; Dec., p. 16.
1778. **Blanchard, C.H.:** *Wyoming Championship Basketball*; June, p. 29.
1779. **Braucher, William E.:** *One More Way of Coaching a Basketball Team*; Feb., p. 40.
1780. **Buck, Selby H., Jr.:** *Seasons's Play on the Tournament*; Feb., p. 13.
1781. **Bursey, Lester G.:** *Drills on Basketball Fundamentals for High School Players*; Jan., p. 26.

1782. **Carlson, Dr. H.C.:** *Five Man Figure 8 Continuities;* Nov., p. 24; *Tonic and Phasic Actions of the Muscles in Basket Shooting;* Dec., p. 24.
1783. **Cavanaugh, John J.:** *Maryland Championship Basketball;* June, p. 17.
1784. **Chadd, A.R.:** *Indiana Championship Basketball;* June, p. 14.
1785. **Cheyne, Arthur:** *Washington Championship Basketball;* June, p. 27.
1786. **Chinske, Edward:** *Montana Championship Basketball;* June, p. 18.
1787. **Clark, Forrest G.:** *Developing Fundamental Skills of Basketball Under Competitive Conditions;* Nov., p. 20.
1788. **Coane, Gray:** *Vermont Championship Basketball;* June, p. 26.
1789. **Cottrell, Jack:** *Maine Championship Basketball;* June, p. 16.
1790. **Crabtree, Clyde:** *Florida Championship Basketball;* May, p. 30.
1791. **Crum, J. Birney:** *Pennsylvania Championship Basketball;* June, p. 23.
1792. **Dimick, H.A.:** *Individuality in Basketball Offense;* Jan., p. 30.
1793. **Dunaway, W.A.:** *Mental Attitude of Tournament Players;* Mar., p. 14; *Arkansas Championship Basketball;* May, p. 20.
1794. **Edgren, H.D.:** *Study of Basketball Scoring;* Mar., p. 35.
1795. **Erps, Joseph W.:** *Colorado Championship Basketball;* May, p. 21.
1796. **Freman, F.B.:** *Reducing the Strain of Tournament Play;* Feb., p. 14.
1797. **Foti, John C.:** *Does the 10-Second Rule Achieve Its Purpose?;* Mar., p. 15.
1798. **Grimsley, J.A.:** *Iowa Championship Basketball;* May, p. 34.
1799. **Haller, William:** *Oklahoma Championship Basketball;* June, p. 22.
1800. **Hetzner, E.A.:** *Combination Crisscross and Side Line Attack;* Feb., p. 16.
1801. **How, John D.:** *Suggested Change in Basketball Rules;* Feb., p. 39.
1802. **Hug, Procter R.:** *Nevada Championship Basketball;* June, p. 21.
1803. **Jacobsen, H.L.:** *Keying Only for Final Tournament Games;* Feb., p. 15.
1804. **Keogan, George E.:** *Defense for the Figure 8 Offense;* Dec., p. 15; *Is the Zone Defense Hurting Basketball?;* Feb., p. 10.
1805. **Lake, Michael M.:** *Pressing Defense and the 10-Second Rule;* Feb., p. 28.
1806. **Lonborg, Arthur C.:** *Possibilities of the Fast-Break Offense;* Nov., p. 36; *Pivot Play Offense and a Defense for It;* Jan., p. 12; *Push Shot and the Free Throw in Basketball;* Feb., p. 5.
1807. **Milner, Ryland H.:** *Basketball System Adaptable to Both Large and Small Courts;* Jan., p. 11.
1808. **Palrang, Maurice H.:** *Nebraska Championship Basketball;* June, p. 19.
1809. **Read, Herbert W.:** *Integrating Fundamentals and System in Basketball;* Jan., p. 7.
1810. **Robinson, R.R.:** *Arizona Championship Basketball;* June, p. 14.
1811. **Ruby, J. Craig:** *Positions in Passing and Shooting a Basketball;* Dec., p. 10.
1812. **Schuhmann, Robert:** *National Catholic Championship;* June, p. 36.
1813. **Schweinfurt, Leo:** *North Dakota Championship Basketball;* Jan., p. 22.
1814. **Skelton, J. Dale:** *Kansas Championship Basketball;* June, p. 15.
1815. **Taylor, Dunn L.:** *Utah Championship Basketball;* June, p. 26.
1816. **Tower, Oswald:** *Basketball Rules for 1934-1935;* Sept., p. 30.
1817. **Twitchell, Paul:** *Care of the Feet of Basketball Players;* Jan., p. 38.
1818. **Warren, John A.:** *Physical Fitness and Mental Attitude in the Tournament;* Feb., p. 12; *Oregon Championship Basketball;* May, p. 36.
1819. **Wells, Clifford:** *Defense for the Screen;* Dec., p. 18.
1820. **Wimer, Frank C.:** *West Virginia Championship Basketball;* June, p. 28.

Volume 16, 1935–36

1821. **Allen, Peter C. and Bunn, John W.:** *Should the Center Jump Be Banned?;* Dec., p. 6.

1822. **Beechner, Ralph W.**: *Zone Defense and Methods of Attacking It*; Dec., p. 28.
1823. **Buehler, J.B.**: *Association of Basketball Officials in Southern California*; Jan., p. 38.
1824. **Bunn, John W. and Allen, Peter C.**: *Should the Center Jump Be Banned?*; Dec., p. 6.
1825. **Bunnell, George L. and Buriff, Gilbert B.**: *Shifting Defense for Basketball Teams*; Jan., p. 10.
1826. **Buriff, Gilbert B. and Bunnell, George L.**: *Shifting Defense for Basketball Teams*; Jan., p. 10.
1827. **Bush, Clarence A.**: *Pointing for Olympic Basketball*; Mar., p. 30.
1828. **Conley, Harry T.**: *Adapting the System to the Material*; June, p. 33.
1829. **Dill, W. A.**: *Useful Plan for Scoring Basketball*; Feb., p. 31.
1830. **Edwards, George**: *Coaches' Creed*; Dec., p. 40; *Field Goals and Free Throws*; Dec., p. 40; Mar., p. 42.
1831. **Hines, Clarence**: *An Efficiency Rating Chart for Basketball Players*; Nov., p. 24.
1832. **Kahler, Arthur**: *"Fire Ball" Style of Play*; Feb., p. 5.
1833. **Kelly, James D. and Lonborg, Arthur C.**: *Offenses and Defenses of Olympic Tryout Tournament Teams*; May, p. 18.
1834. **Knapp, Clyde**: *Man-to-Man Defense and Methods of Attacking It*; Dec., p. 31.
1835. **Lonborg, Arthur C.**: *Special Basketball Defenses*; Jan., p. 5.
1836. **Lonborg, Arthur C. and Kelly, James D.**: *Offenses and Defenses of Olympic Tryout Tournament Teams*; May, p. 18.
1837. **Lorton, Frank**: *Are We Penalizing the Small Teams?*; Jan., p. 41.
1838. **McEwen, T.R.**: *Intramural Basketball Program for High Schools*; Feb., p. 10.
1839. **Money, C.V.**: *Three-Second Rule in Basketball*; Jan., p. 35.
1840. **Palrang, M.H.**: *Quick-Break Attack the Defense to Be Used With It*; Dec., p. 26; *Relying on Reserves in Tournament Play*; June, p. 30.
1841. **Payseur, Ted**: *Offenses for Use Against the Man-to-Man Defense*; Feb., p. 9.
1842. **Petree, W.L.**: *Basketball Official's Job*; Jan., p. 6.
1843. **Robbins, H.M.**: *Stressing Defensive Basketball*; June, p. 28.
1844. **Root, Dan O.**: *Reduce Contact in Basketball*; Jan., p. 37.
1845. **Ruby, J. Craig**: *Effect of the 1935–1936 Rules on Coaching of Basketball*; Oct., p. 25.
1846. **Rupp, A.F.**: *Offensive and Defensive Footwork in Basketball*; Feb., p. 11.
1847. **Schneider, Fred B.**: *Successful Basketball Defense for Use on a Small Floor*; Dec., p. 14.
1848. **Weinstein, Alex**: *Basketball Scouting*; May, p. 26.
1849. **Wells, Clifford**: *Basketball Strategy Under the 1935–36 Rules*; Sept., p. 32; *Combination for Man-to-Man and Zone Defense*; Nov., p. 26; *For the Good of Basketball*; Jan., p. 34; *Game Tactics in Basketball*; June, p. 26.
1850. **Wright, Robert D.**: *Suggested Change in the Basketball Center Jump Rule*; Jan., p. 34.
1851. *Evaluation of Offensive and Defensive Basketball Systems*; Dec., p. 26.
1852. *State Championship Basketball*; June, p. 26.

Volume 17, 1936–37

1853. **Baller, Stuart**: *Basketball Coaching Practices Involving Fundamentals*; Feb., p. 7.
1854. **Barry, J.M.**: *Basketball Fundamentals—Footwork, Balance and Passing*; Dec., p. 10; *Offensive Basketball With the Elimination of the Tip-Off*; Jan., p. 9; *Defenses Used by Basketball Teams on the Pacific Coast*; Feb., p. 5.
1855. **Browne, W.H.**: *Fast-Break Offense in Basketball*; Nov., p. 14; *Five-Man Interchanging System of Offense*; Dec., p. 15.

1856. **Case, Everett N.**: *Fundamental Drills and Their Value*; Dec., p. 16; *Offensive Set Plays in Basketball*; Jan., p. 10; *High School Basketball Tournament Play*; Feb., p. 13.
1857. **Clarno, L.M.**: *Mechanics of Basketball Officiating*; Nov., p. 30.
1858. **Edwards, George R.**: *Administrative Difficulties in Basketball*; Feb., p. 31.
1859. **Hall, Hal O.**: *Game Drill for the High School Basketball Squad*; Feb., p. 30.
1860. **Hanson, Raymond W.**: *Basketball Ethics*; Jan., p. 26.
1861. **Hickox, Edward J.**: *Springfield Figure 8 Offensive*; Jan., p. 5.
1862. **Kelly, James D.**: *Early Practice Work With the Basketball Squad*; Dec., p. 8.
1863. **Lambert, Eugene**: *Double Pivot Offensive in Basketball*; Feb., p. 9.
1864. **Lambert, Ward L.**: *Offsetting the Restrictions of the Three-Second Rule*; Dec., p. 12; *Possibilities of Single and Double Pivot Plays*; Jan., p. 8.
1865. **Lindley, Frank**: *Basketball Theory, System and Style*; Jan., p. 16.
1866. **May, C. R.**: *Self-Analysis Charts for the High School Basketball Players*; Mar., p. 24.
1867. **Neff, Ben**: *Continuity Screen Play in Basketball*; Jan., p. 15.
1868. **Noble, Virgil J.**: *Basketball Training Program for Junior High School Boys*; May, p. 26.
1869. **Storey, Edward J.**: *Junior High School Basketball*; Jan., p. 34.
1870. **Tower, Oswald**: *Basketball Rules for 1936–37*; Dec., p. 7; *Basketball Rules for 1937–38*; May, p. 17.
1871. **Wells, Clifford**: *Center Jump Formations Under the 1936–37 Basketball Code*; Sept., p. 22; *One Type of Figure 8 Offense*; Oct., p. 32.
1872. **Works, Pierce**: *Various Types of Defensive Play in Basketball*; Nov., p. 22.

Volume 18, 1937–38

1873. **Baker, Floyd H.**: *Co-ordinating Offense and Defense in Basketball*; Oct., p. 30; *Development of Reserve Basketball Teams*; Nov., p. 47.
1874. **Baker, H. Cecil**: *Utah Championship Basketball*; June, p. 34.
1875. **Brickley, Frank**: *Arizona Championship Basketball*; June, p. 14.
1876. **Brickman, V. Everett**: *West Virginia Championship Basketball*; June, p. 35.
1877. **Brockmeyer, Win**: *Wisconsin Championship Basketball*; June, p. 36.
1878. **Browne, W.H.**: *Early Season Basketball Hints*; Sept., p. 26; *Principles of Defensive Basketball*; Oct., p. 20; *Individual Defensive Play in Basketball*; Nov., p. 8.
1879. **Buck Selby H., Jr.**: *Georgia Championship Basketball Class A*; June, p. 16.
1880. **Burns, G.L.**: *Unorthodox Defensive Play*; Feb., p. 11.
1881. **Conn, Julius**: *Virginia Championship Basketball*; June, p. 35.
1882. **De Lacy, Eugene**: *Illinois Championship Basketball*; June, p. 16.
1883. **Eberhart, Harold**: *Missouri Championship Basketball*; June, p. 19.
1884. **Edmundson, C.S.**: *One-Hand Shot*; Jan., p. 7.
1885. **Fay, Paul J. and Messersmith, Floyd L.**: *Distance Traversed by College and High School Basketball Players and Effect of Rule Changes Upon Distance Traversed in College Games*; May, p. 37.
1886. **Flint, Ed**: *Colorado Championship Basketball*; June, p. 14.
1887. **Friddle, Burl**: *Indiana Championship Basketball*; June, p. 17.
1888. **Hampton, R.C.**: *Pictorial Review of Basketball Fundamentals*; Dec., p. 16.
1889. **Hauser, Mike**: *Florida Championship Basketball*; June, p. 14.
1890. **Healey, William A.**: *Play in the Back Court*; Feb., p. 7.
1891. **Kitchen, Howard R.**: *Texas Championship Basketball*; June, p. 33.
1892. **Lee, George E.**: *Minnesota Championship Baksetball*; June, p. 18.
1893. **Mansfield, W.L.**: *Maine Championship Basketball*; June, p. 18.
1894. **Masters, Arthur B.**: *Fast-Break Offense*; Jan., p. 9.

1895. **May, C.R.:** *Shot Analysis;* Dec., p. 32; *Deception in Basketball;* Jan., p. 37.
1896. **McElroy, George A.:** *Championship Basketball in the Small High School;* Jan., p. 34; *Nevada Championship Basketball;* June, p. 21.
1897. **McLendon, Dana C.:** *Georgia Championship Basketball Class B;* June, p. 16.
1898. **Messersmith, Floyd L. and Fay, Paul J.:** *Distance Traversed by College and High School Basketball Players and Effect of Rule Changes Upon Distance Traversed in College Games;* May, p. 37.
1899. **Morris, Robert B.:** *Rhode Island Championship Basketball;* June, p. 33.
1900. **O'Brien, W.G.:** *Alabama Championship Basketball;* June, p. 13.
1901. **Orr, Clifford E.:** *Ohio Championship Basketball;* June, p. 21.
1902. **Rice, Henry L.:** *North Dakota Championship Basketball;* June, p. 20.
1903. **Sachs, Len:** *Modern Adaptation of the Professional;* Dec., p. 39.
1904. **Skillern, Grady:** *Oklahoma Championship Basketball;* June, p. 32.
1905. **Sykes, Paul K.:** *North Carolina Championship Basketball;* June, p. 20.
1906. **Torney, John A., Jr.:** *Games, Drills and Teaching Devices for Basketball;* Nov., p. 18.
1907. **Varner, O.C.:** *Iowa Championship Basketball;* June, p. 18.
1908. **Wakefield, Mark C.:** *Backboard Play;* Jan., p. 8.
1909. **Wells, Clifford:** *Rushing Back-Court Defense;* Feb., p. 8.
1910. **Wright, Robert D.:** *Should Basketball Teams Be Rated?;* May, p. 42.
1911. *Away from the Center Jump;* Dec., p. 7.
1912. *A Few Scoring Basketball Plays of 1938;* Feb., p. 10.
1913. *First National Intercollegiate Basketball Tournament;* Feb., p. 26.
1914. *Graphic Study of Important Basketball Rules;* Dec., p. 14.
1915. *What They're Saying About Basketball Without the Center Jump;* Feb., p. 5.

Volume 19, 1938–39

1916. **Allen, Forrest C.:** *Versatile Offense Against Changing Defenses;* Jan., p. 7.
1917. **Alley, Lyles:** *South Carolina Basketball Championship Class B;* May, p. 52.
1918. **Baker, Floyd H.:** *Defenses in High School Tournament Play;* Dec., p. 12.
1919. **Baker, Henry:** *Michigan Lower Peninsula Basketball Championship Class D;* June, p. 16.
1920. **Barclay, James:** *Michigan Lower Peninsula Basketball Championship Class;* June, p. 14.
1921. **Barnard, Chester S.:** *Deciding a Conference Three-Way Tie in Basketball;* Apr., p. 38.
1922. **Beane, Syd:** *South Dakota Basketball Championship;* June, p. 10.
1923. **Beechner, R.W.:** *Basketball Offense Without Set Plays;* Dec., p. 14.
1924. **Blanchard, C.H.:** *Wyoming Basketball Championship;* June, p. 12.
1925. **Bower, Harold E.:** *Sanitation in Basketball;* Feb., p. 12.
1926. **Breuer, W.R.:** *Missouri Basketball Championship Class B;* June, p. 18.
1927. **Brickey, Frank:** *Co-ordinating Basketball Program;* Oct., p. 44; *Arizona Basketball Championship;* May, p. 15.
1928. **Buck, Selby H.:** *Set Plays in Basketball;* Jan., p. 12.
1929. **Cavanaugh, John J.:** *Maryland Basketball Championship;* June, p. 30.
1930. **Carlson H.C., M.D.:** *West is West—East is East;* Feb., p. 5.
1931. **Chambers, Eddie:** *Michigan Upper Peninsula Basketball Championship Class C;* June, p. 17.
1932. **Collins, Wilson:** *Tennessee Basketball Championship;* June, p. 10.
1933. **Cooper, J. Ray:** *South Carolina Basketball Championship Class C;* June, p. 9.
1934. **Cox, Dewey:** *Alabama Basketball Championship;* May, p. 15.
1935. **Daher, Joseph G.:** *The 2-1-2 Defense;* Dec., p. 13.

1936. **Dawson, Paul:** *Virginia Basketball Championship*; June, p. 11.
1937. **De Lacey, Eugene:** *Part Played by Intramurals in the Development of a State Championship Team*; Oct., p. 22.
1938. **Des Combes, Don:** *Colorado Basketball Championship*; May, p. 16.
1939. **Dorland, Floyd:** *Michigan Basketball Championship Class B*; June, p. 15.
1940. **Flint, Ed:** *Why We Use a Man-to-Man Defense*; Jan., p. 40.
1941. **Gallagher, John J.:** *Suggestions for Promoting Good Sportsmanship in Basketball*; Dec., p. 5.
1942. **Gates, Ernst:** *North Dakota Basketball Championship*; May, p. 26.
1943. **Gernard, Clarence:** *Texas Basketball Championship*; June, p. 10.
1944. **Gibble, Alfred T.:** *An Individual Basketball Rating Chart*; Oct., p. 26.
1945. **Hale, Herman:** *Kentucky Basketball Championship*; May, p. 19.
1946. **Hashingen, Kenneth A.:** *Scoring Charts*; Dec., p. 20.
1947. **Hauk, Harold:** *Oregon Basketball Championship*; June, p. 10.
1948. **Himsi, A.V.:** *Montana Basketball Championship Class B*; May, p. 21.
1949. **Hopkins, W. Harold:** *Iowa Basketball Championship*; June, p. 30.
1950. **Hosfield, Luther:** *Ohio Basketball Championship*; May, p. 47.
1951. **Houser, Mike:** *Combination Fast-Break and a Set-Play Offense*; Feb., p. 10.
1952. **Hunta, Elmer:** *Washington Basketball Championship*; May, p. 53.
1953. **Jenkins, Ray:** *Nebraska Basketball Championship Class C*; May, p. 24.
1954. **Johnson, G. C.:** *Michigan Upper Peninsula Basketball Championship Class D*; June, p. 17.
1955. **Kemmer, Harry G.:** *Florida Basketball Championship*; May, p. 16.
1956. **Kirste, Virgil A.:** *Novelty Defenses for Special Situations*; Feb., p. 10.
1957. **Kitchen, Howard:** *Team and Coach Co-operation in Basketball*; Nov., p. 10.
1958. **Laude, James A.:** *Illinois Basketball Championship*; May, p. 18.
1959. **Liston, Lee:** *Nevada Basketball Championship*; May, p. 24.
1960. **Lizio, Ralph:** *Ten-Man Team*; Feb., p. 12; *New Hampshire Basketball Championship*; June, p. 22.
1961. **Mansfield, W.L.:** *Maine Basketball Championship*; May, p. 19.
1962. **Martindale, A.:** *Idaho Basketball Championship*; May, p. 18.
1963. **Mason, George T.:** *Michigan Upper Peninsula Basketball Championship Class B*; June, p. 17.
1964. **May, Cecil R.:** *Basketball Poster for Your Dressing Room*; Oct., p. 34.
1965. **McElroy, George:** *Review of the Fundamentals That Contribute to Championship Basketball*; Nov., p. 10.
1966. **Mikkelsen, Claude:** *Missouri Basketball Championship Class A*; May, p. 20.
1967. **Monahan, Thomas:** *Connecticut Basketball Championship*; June, p. 13.
1968. **O'Brien, W.G.:** *Shifting Zone Defense*; Dec., p. 13.
1969. **Orr, Clifford E.:** *Beating a Zone Defense*; Jan., p. 11.
1970. **Pierce, Robert:** *New Mexico Basketball Championship*; May, p. 26.
1971. **Pierla, Stanley:** *New Jersey Basketball Championship Group III*; June, p. 24.
1972. **Reiff, Joe:** *Defensive Footwork in Basketball*; Jan., p. 9; *Defense Maneuvers*; Feb., p. 7.
1973. **Rice, Henry L.:** *Fast Break Offense*; Dec., p. 14.
1974. **Saunders, Horace:** *Virginia Basketball Championship*; June, p. 26.
1975. **Skillern, Grady:** *Importance of Fundamentals and How to Teach Them to High School Boys*; Oct., p. 17; *Oklahoma Basketball Championship*; May, p. 49.
1976. **Sullivan, V.A.:** *Nebraska Basketball Championship Class B*; May, p. 24.
1977. **Taylor, Charles:** *Arkansas Basketball Championship*; June, p. 13.
1978. **Thomas, Ollie C.:** *Kansas Basketball Championship*; May, p. 19.
1979. **Thompson, J.A.:** *Montana Basketball Championship Class A*; May, p. 20.
1980. **Tracy, John B.:** *Physical Condition of Basketball Players*; Nov., p. 30.

1981. **Wells, Clifford:** *Comments on the Changes in the 1938 Basketball Rules;* Sept., p. 19; *Fundamental Training;* Nov., p. 6; Dec., p. 7.
1982. **Whelan, Tom:** *Massachusetts Basketball Championship;* June, p. 14.
1983. **Wingard, Lester L.:** *Alaska Basketball Championship;* June, p. 31.
1984. **Wright, Frank W.:** *Utah Basketball Championship;* June, p. 26.
1985. *Basketball Ethics for Coaches;* Sept., p. 30.
1986. *Comments on Changes for 1939–1940 Basketball Rules;* June, p. 37.
1987. *Is Basketball Too Strenuous?;* Nov., p. 36.
1988. *Newly Organized Basketball Association in Texas;* Sept., p. 133.

Volume 20, 1939–40

1989. **Alley, Lyles:** *Values of Winning a Championship;* Feb., p. 13.
1990. **Antonides, Robert C.:** *Class Basketball;* Dec., p. 34.
1991. **Baker, Floyd H.:** *Offensive Basketball Trends;* Oct., p. 21.
1992. **Barclay, James:** *What to Look for in a Basketball Player;* Dec., p. 8; *Michigan Championship Basketball Lower Peninsula;* Apr., p. 24.
1993. **Binford, Harold:** *Kansas Championship Basketball Class B;* May, p. 29.
1994. **Birkett, Louis D.:** *Indiana Championship Basketball;* June, p. 17.
1995. **Bowers, W.L.:** *Maryland Championship Basketball;* June, p. 21.
1996. **Bradley, Grover:** *Oklahoma Championship Basketball;* June, p. 24.
1997. **Braly, Buddy:** *Alabama Championship Basketball;* May, p. 18.
1998. **Brickey, Frank:** *Arizona Championship Basketball;* Apr., p. 24.
1999. **Brinkman, V. Everett:** *West Virginia Championship Basketball;* June, p. 36.
2000. **Carte, Walter:** *Idaho Championship Basketball Class A;* May, p. 24.
2001. **Cavanaugh, John J.:** *Fast-Break Offense;* Jan., p. 38.
2002. **Chambers, Eddie:** *Michigan Championship Basketball Upper Peninsula Class C;* June, p. 22.
2003. **Cooper, Gilbert and Lerda, Louis:** *Planning the Players' Manual for Coaching Basketball Fundamentals;* Nov., p. 12.
2004. **Cooper, J. Roy:** *Team Play Versus Individual Play;* Jan., p. 38.
2005. **Cox, Dewey:** *Man-to-Man Defense;* Dec., p. 12.
2006. **Cox, J.D.:** *Louisiana Championship Basketball;* June, p. 20.
2007. **Dawson, Paul B.:** *How to Develop Team Morale;* Dec., p. 12.
2008. **Dean, Everett S.:** *Basketball Vitamins;* Dec., p. 5.
2009. **Dell, Robert G.:** *Fundamental Passing Judgement;* Jan., p. 36.
2010. **DesCombes, Don:** *Use of Self-Rating Chart for Basketball;* Dec., p. 11.
2011. **Dodge, Winston S.:** *Massachusetts Championship Basketball;* May, p. 30.
2012. **Dorland, Floyd:** *Individual Offense in Basketball;* Jan., p. 40.
2013. **Eby, Floyd:** *Michigan Championship Basketball Lower Peninsula;* May, p. 32.
2014. **England, Forrest W.:** *Eliminate Jump Balls from Basketball;* Oct., p. 45.
2015. **Ennis, James:** *Washington Championship Basketball;* June, p. 36.
2016. **Furr, Jack:** *Oklahoma Championship Basketball Class C;* June, p. 29.
2017. **Garrett, R.J.:** *New Hampshire Championship Basketball;* May, p. 40.
2018. **Gates, Ernest H.:** *Trends in Defense;* Feb., p. 14.
2019. **Geis, Clarence H.:** *Arkansas Championship Basketball;* May, p. 18.
2020. **Gibble, Alfred T.:** *Hitting Averages in Basketball;* Nov., p. 46.
2021. **Grimsley, J.A.:** *Iowa Championship Basketball;* Apr., p. 36.
2022. **Grosvener, George:** *Colorado Championship Basketball Class A;* May, p. 19.
2023. **Grunenfelder, F.A.:** *North Dakota Championship Basketball;* May, p. 43.
2024. **Hauk, Harold:** *Oregon Championship Basketball;* June, p. 29.
2025. **Hay, Lester L.:** *Colorado Championship Basketball;* May, p. 21.
2026. **Hoernemann, Paul:** *Ohio Championship Basketball;* June, p. 22.

2027. **Hogarty, Dr. Alexander J.:** *The Changing Game;* Sept., p. 38.
2028. **Hosfield, Luther:** *Practice Tips;* Jan., p. 7.
2029. **Jowers, Milton:** *Texas Championship Basketball;* June, p. 34.
2030. **Kamp, C.O.:** *Missouri Championship Basketball;* May, p. 38.
2031. **Keast, Roger:** *Michigan Championship Basketball Upper Peninsula Class B:* May, p. 36.
2032. **Keegan, William G.:** *Analyzing Screens for High School Players;* Dec., p. 18.
2033. **Kemmer, Harry G.:** *Combined Zone and Shifting Man-to-Man Defense;* Dec., p. 9.
2034. **Kerner, Frank A.:** *South Dakota Championship Basketball Class B;* June, p. 32.
2035. **Kleimola, J.W.:** *Michigan Championship Basketball Upper Peninsula;* May, p. 37.
2036. **Lerda, Louis and Cooper, Gilbert:** *Planning the Players' Manual for Coaching Basketball Fundamentals;* Nov., p. 12.
2037. **Liston, Lee:** *Team Spirit and Morale in Basketball;* Feb., p. 15.
2038. **Littrell, G. W.:** *Nebraska Championship Basketball Class B;* June, p. 22.
2039. **Lizio, Ralph A.:** *More About the Ten-Man Basketball Team;* Dec., p. 7.
2040. **Lyon, Harry S.:** *Connecticut Championship Basketball;* June, p. 17.
2041. **Malley, Mike C.:** *New Jersey Championship Basketball Group II;* June, p. 23.
2042. **May, C. R.:** *Some Hints on the Psychology of Coaching Basketball;* Dec., p. 44.
2043. **Mikkelsen, Claude E.:** *Continuity in the Offense;* Feb., p. 14.
2044. **Mikulich, Walter M.:** *Minnesota Championship Basketball;* May, p. 38.
2045. **Morris, Robert A.:** *Rhode Island Championship Basketball;* June, p. 29.
2046. **Newell, Russell A.:** *Michigan Championship Basketball Lower Peninsula Class D;* Apr., p. 34.
2047. **Noble, Virgil J.:** *Getting Results from Your Shooting Practice;* Oct., p. 24.; *An Unusual Play;* Dec., p. 28.
2048. **Orr, Lester D.:** *Michigan Championship Basketball Lower Peninsula Class B;* May, p. 32.
2049. **Perez, Salvador:** *New Mexico Championship Basketball;* May, p. 42.
2050. **Piela, Stanley:** *Developing Players for Future Teams;* Dec., p. 10.
2051. **Quintal, A.A.:** *South Dakota Championship Basketball;* June, p. 30.
2052. **Skillern, Grady:** *Developing a Basketball Team for Tournament Play;* Feb., p. 13.
2053. **Smith, Tip:** *Tennessee Championship Basketball;* June, p. 32.
2054. **Stone, R.M.:** *South Carolina Championship Basketball Class B;* June, p. 30.
2055. **Taliaferro, Paul:** *High School Basketball Schedule;* Sept., p. 36.
2056. **Taylor, R. W.:** *Montana Championship Basketball;* May, p. 40.
2057. **Thomas, Ollie:** *Kansas Championship Basketball;* May, p. 29.
2058. **Thompson, J. A.:** *Where Do Basketball Players Come From?;* Feb., p. 46.
2059. **Warren, Hugh:** *Oklahoma Championship Basketball;* June, p. 23.
2060. **Wells, Clifford:** *Methods and Training in Free Throwing;* Sept., p. 16.
2061. **Whelan, Tom:** *Preparing a Team for a Championship Campaign;* Jan., p. 8.
2062. **Whitehead, Edwin:** *Nevada Championship Basketball;* May, p. 43.
2063. **Whitmore, Richard L.:** *Maine Championship Basketball;* June, p. 20.
2064. **Williams, L.L.:** *Arkansas Championship Basketball;* May, p. 19.
2065. **Worley, Paul:** *Florida Championship Basketball Class B;* May, p. 22.
2066. **Wyatt, C.H.:** *Kentucky Championship Basketball;* June, p. 18.
2067. *Basketball Clinic;* Dec., p. 26.
2068. *New Game Developed by a Noted Basketball Authority: Goal-Hi;* Dec., p. 36.
2069. *The Pivot—Its Applications;* Jan., p. 16.
2070. *Second Annual N.C.A.A. Basketball Tournament;* Mar., p. 38.
2071. *Team Play at Its Best;* Feb., p. 16.

Volume 21, 1940–41

2072. **Allen, Forrest C.:** *Twenty Years of Gains and Changes in Basketball*; Mar., p. 20.
2073. **Baker, Floyd H.:** *Early Development of High School Basketball*; Oct., p. 42; *Military Value of Games, Basketball in Particular*; Mar., p. 14.
2074. **Birkett, Lou:** *Style of Play Used in Winning the 1940 Indiana High School State Basketball Tournament*; Jan., p. 12.
2075. **Blake, Ray:** *Distance Traversed by Basketball Players in Different Types of Defense*; Jan., p. 18.
2076. **Caine, A.B.:** *Selecting the High School Basketball Squad*; Dec., p. 37.
2077. **Cochran, Arthur M.:** *Tufts Set Offense*; Nov., p. 42; *Alternatives for the Tufts Set Offense*; Dec., p. 6.
2078. **Cooper, John M.:** *More Shots Mean More Points*; June, p. 28.
2079. **Daher, Joseph G.:** *Screening Offense as Used With the Double Pivot*; Dec., p. 10; *Conditioning and Training Basketball*; Jan., p. 26.
2080. **Eblen, R.H.:** *Basketball as Played in the Southeastern Junior College Conference*; May, p. 21.
2081. **Gibble, Alfred T.:** *Notes From the Diary of a Basketball Coach*; Jan., p. 35.
2082. **Kerner, Frank A.:** *Basketball Defenses*; Feb., p. 28.
2083. **Larson, Emil L.:** *Mechanics of Officiation in Basketball*; Jan., p. 13.
2084. **Lenser, Kurt W.:** *Shoot Free Throws by Mail*; Dec., p. 36.
2085. **Lester, Howard:** *Team Co-operation*; Jan., p. 34.
2086. **Ligon, D.L.:** *Free Basketball Clinic*; May, p. 22.
2087. **Lonborg, Arthur C.:** *Offensive Play in the All-Stars/Globe-trotters Basketball Game*; Jan., p. 7.
2088. **Malarek, John:** *Building the Basketball Team*; Oct., p. 38.
2089. **Mundt, Howard L.:** *Coaching Basketball in Junior High School*; Feb., p. 18.
2090. **Noble, Virgil:** *Passport to Better Basketball*; Oct., p. 32.; *Basketball Fundamentals on a Dime*; Feb., p. 12.
2091. **Porter, H.V.:** *1940–1941 Basketball*; Sept., p. 32; *Modernized Basketball Equipment*; June, p. 26.
2092. **Presthus, R. Vance:** *Technique of the One-Hand Push Shot*; Feb., p. 12.
2093. **Rood, W. Harold:** *Landscaping Basketball*; Dec., p. 20.
2094. **Scofield, W. Listman:** *Speed Up Your Offense*; Dec., p. 34.
2095. **Taliaferro, Paul:** *Developing the High School Basketball Passer*; Dec., p. 40.
2096. **Whitney, Franklyn:** *A Drill the Boys Will Like*; Dec., p. 10.
2097. **Williams, L.L.:** *Building Team Morale*; Nov., p. 36.
2098. *Illustrated Basketball Rules*; Sept., p. 20; Oct., p. 16.
2099. *Basketball Officiating, Editorial*; Feb., p. 15.

Volume 22, 1941–42

2100. **Alexander, Hiram:** *Combination Zone and Man-for-Man Defense*; Jan., p. 30.
2101. **Anderson, M.G.:** *Keeping a Basketball Team in Condition Throughout the Season*; Jan., p. 42.
2102. **Baumgartner, Albert:** *Special Exercises for Basketball Players*; Nov., p. 46.
2103. **Bohm, Wilbur:** *Modern Basketball as Viewed from the Training Standpoint*; Mar., p. 32.; *Training and Conditioning Practices of College and University Basketball Coaches and Trainers*; May, p. 30.
2104. **Budge, Rulon:** *Deliberate Set Style Plus a Fast Break*; Jan., p. 16.
2105. **Carlson, H.C., M.D.:** *Eight to Eighty-Eight in Continuity*; Dec., p. 10.
2106. **Cook, Max B.:** *Basketball Meet by Mail*; May, p. 22.

2107. **Crawley, Marion:** *Combination Slow Set Offense and the Fast Break*; Jan., p. 22.
2108. **Daher, Joseph G.:** *Methods and Techniques of Coaching Basketball*; Oct., p. 22.
2109. **Foster, H.E.:** *Old-Fashioned Basketball at the University of Wisconsin*; Dec., p. 8.
2110. **Friel, John B.:** *Basketball Offenses of Interest—Washington State College*; Feb., p. 6.
2111. **Gilkeson, Glenn:** *Easiest Basket in Basketball*; May, p. 29.
2112. **Hall, Edward D.:** *An Offensive Defense*; Dec., p. 14.
2113. **Ketchum, Ellison E.:** *Fundamentals of Inside Screening*; Dec., p. 6.
2114. **Littman, Herman:** *Mastery of Fundamentals*; Dec., p. 12.
2115. **Neff, Ben:** *System Play Versus Free Play*; Feb., p. 6.
2116. **Shelton, Everett:** *Single Post and the Five-Man Weave at the University of Wyoming*; Dec., p. 9.
2117. **Willett, A.E.:** *Question of the Modified Bankboard*; Dec., p. 18.
2118. **Wills, George:** *Mass and Duo Basketball*; June, p. 26.
2119. **Zara, Louis A.:** *Basketball Clinic for Spectators*; Oct., p. 44.
2120. *Golden Jubilee of Basketball*; Dec., p. 5.

Volume 23, 1942–43

2121. **Abramoski, E.R.:** *New Plan—For Scoring*; Apr., p. 26;
2122. *Basketball Exercise for the Victory Corps*; May, p. 27.
2123. **Allen, Forrest C.:** *Rapid Rolling Offensive Triangle Merging a Set and a Moving Screen*; Feb., p. 22.
2124. **Bescos, Julie, Lt., U.S.N.R.:** *Basketball Wins Its Wings*; Oct., p. 20.
2125. **Brownlee, Joseph:** *Method of Developing Intramural Basketball Officials*; Mar., p. 18.
2126. **Clarno, Lyle:** *Using the Double Referee System*; Jan., p. 13.
2127. **Daher, Joseph G.:** *Individual Basketball Play*; Sept., p. 18; *End Play: Offensive and Defensive Suggestions*; Oct., p. 15; *Basketball Plus*; Jan., p. 12.
2128. **Dean, Everett S.:** *Technique of the Basketball Bulletin Board*; Oct., p. 13; *Defense—The Stabilizer*; Nov., p. 9; *Passing Pointers*; Dec., p. 7; *An Over-All Review of Tournament Offenses*; Feb., p. 16.
2129. **Decker, James H., Lt. (j.g.), U.S.N.R.:** *They Have to Be Tough to Win*; Nov., p. 21.
2130. **Durbin, Brice:** *So You Are Trying Out for the Basketball Team*; Oct., p. 30.
2131. **Eveland, E.W.:** *Cross-Country Running as a Conditioner in Basketball*; May, p. 18.
2132. **Hartley, Joseph W.:** *Fast Break Coaching Philosophy for the High School Basketball Team*; Jan., p. 14.
2133. **Lawther, John:** *Scissors Plays of Penn State*; Feb., p. 18.
2134. **May, Cecil P.:** *Change of Pace in Basketball*; Dec., p. 24.
2135. **McBride, Clyde:** *Western Play-Offs of the National Collegiate Athletic Association a Thriller!*; May, p. 14.
2136. **Mendenhall, Murray:** *Fast Break Prevailed in the Indiana Tournament*; May, p. 18.
2137. **Mills, Douglas R.:** *Making Use of the Players' Initiative*; Feb., p. 20.
2138. **Nitchman, Nelson, Lt. (j.g.), U.S.C.G.R.:** *Final Game of the National Game of the National Collegiate Athletic Association Tournament from a Technical Viewpoint*; May, p. 16.
2139. **Rupp, A.F.:** *Kentucky's Pivot Play*; Feb., p. 18.
2140. **Saltis, L.R.:** *Accuracy in Basketball*; Jan., p. 33.
2141. *Keep Them Playing Basketball*; Nov., p. 20.
2142. *High School Basketball and Transportation*; Jan., p. 16.

Volume 24, 1943–44

2143. **Abramoski, Edward R.:** *Improving Intramural Basketball by Use of the Single Dribble;* Dec., p. 40.
2144. **Allen, Forrest C.:** *Double Trouble for Poor Fundamentalists;* Feb., p. 8.
2145. **Baker, Floyd H.:** *Shooting of Free Throws;* Dec., p. 10.
2146. **Carlson, Roy L.:** *Five Fouls or Four?;* Feb., p. 9.
2147. **Dean, Everett S.:** *Footwork Cleverness;* Nov., p. 8; *Building Morale Through Basketball;* Dec., p. 9; *Basketball and Physical Fitness;* Mar., p. 22.
2148. **Eveland, E.W.:** *Defensive Change of Pace;* Mar., p. 32.
2149. **Hartley, Joseph:** *"Gunning" For Jump Balls;* Nov., p. 20.
2150. **Lawther, John:** *A Few Maneuvers in Offense Basketball;* Feb., p. 5.
2151. **Lonborg, Arthur C.:** *All-Star Basketball Game;* Jan., p. 20.
2152. **May, Cecil R.:** *Teaching Basketball Defense by the Question and Answer Method;* Dec., p. 41; Jan., p. 22.
2153. **Mundt, Howard G.:** *Basketball With Civilian Talent;* Nov., p. 34; *Speeded-Up Basketball Program;* Jan., p. 16.
2154. **Nitchman, Nelson W., Lt., Q.S.C.G.R.:** *Basketball of 1944;* Apr., p. 18.
2155. **Porter, H.V.:** *1943–44 Basketball Rules;* Nov., p. 13; *Basketball Trends;* Apr., p. 5.
2156. **Shelton, Everett F.:** *Fine Points of Scouting in Basketball;* Oct., p. 30.
2157. **Wells, Clifford:** *Fundamental Training in Basketball;* Sept., p. 20; *Basketball Continuities;* Oct., p. 10; *Out-of-Bounds Plays;* Nov., p. 10; *Meeting a Pressing Defense in the Back Court;* Dec., p. 12.
2158. *Story of Wat Misaka and a Basketball Crowd, Editorial;* Apr., p. 12.

Volume 25, 1944–45

2159. **Allen, Forrest C.:** *Watchdog of the Basket;* Dec., p. 11; *Devitalizing the Razzle-Dazzle Game;* Jan., p. 14.
2160. **Baker, Floyd:** *Selecting Basketball Drills That Teach the Skills You Prefer;* Sept., p. 34.
2161. **Christensen, R., C.Sp. (A) U.S.N.R.:** *Developing a Basketball Offense;* Nov., p. 12; *Development and Strategy of Team Defense in Basketball;* Dec., p. 22.
2162. **Dean, Everett S.:** *It's Fundamental Time!;* Nov., p. 16; *Three Practical Uses of the Inside Screen;* Dec., p. 14.
2163. **Drenckpohl, Vernon W.:** *New Method of Determining a Conference Champion;* Dec., p. 50.
2164. **Dromo, John:** *Attacking the Zone;* Feb., p. 34.
2165. **Hartley, Joseph:** *Basketball Game Somewhere in France;* Nov., p. 48.
2166. **Keaney, Frank W.:** *Fire-Horse Basketball;* Dec., p. 18.
2167. **Krafft, Hoh. A.:** *How to Combat a Pressing Defense;* Nov., p. 32.
2168. **Lawther, John D.:** *Winning Through Ball Control;* Dec., p. 7; *Problems in Teaching Basketball;* Jan., p. 7.
2169. **May, Cecil R.:** *Objectives in Basketball;* Oct., p. 43.
2170. **Moren, Roy W.:** *Man-to-Man Defense Employing Rushing, Switching and Floating Tactics;* Jan., p. 30.
2171. **Nitchman, Lt. Nelson W., U.S.C.G.R.:** *Early Season Basketball Practice;* Sept., p. 30; *Suggestions on Basketball Practice Routine;* Oct., p. 18.
2172. **Peterson, Vadal:** *Conditioning to Win;* Sept., p. 51.
2173. **Rupp, Adolph F.:** *Guard Play;* Dec., p. 20; *Zone Defense;* Feb., p. 12.
2174. **Thomas, Stanley:** *Texas State Basketball Tournament;* Apr., p. 36.
2175. **Wakefield, Mark:** *Can the Youngster Take It?;* Dec., p. 29.

2176. **Wells, Clifford:** *Question and Answer Period;* Nov., p. 20; *Zone Defense—Pro and Con;* Dec., p. 42; *Solving a Zone Defense;* Jan., p. 20; *A Few Basketball Plays of the 1945 Season;* Mar., p. 7.
2177. *First-hand Information from the State Basketball Tournaments;* Apr., p. 36.
2178. *Fundamentals of Shooting Analyzed;* Jan., p. 12.
2179. *Basketball in the Pacific Coast Junior Colleges;* Apr., p. 44.

Volume 26, 1945–46

2180. **Baker, Floyd H.:** *Styles of Forcing Offense;* Oct., p. 14; *Basic Defensive Play;* Feb., p. 13.
2181. **Biechly, R.J.:** *An Offense Against a Zone;* Nov., p. 17.
2182. **Case, Ford L.:** *Moving Offense Against Zones;* Feb., p. 15.
2183. **Christensen, Richard:** *Offensive Tactics of Basketball;* Nov., p. 30; *Out-of-Bounds Plays;* Feb., p. 14.
2184. **Davis, Joe W.:** *How We Teach Shooting;* Nov., p. 16.
2185. **Drake, Bruce:** *Optional Sequence in Basketball;* Dec., p. 16.
2186. **Harrison, Lawrence:** *Quick-Break Basketball;* Nov., p. 18; *Slow Break in Basketball;* Jan., p. 9.
2187. **Hobson, Howard A.:** *Plea for Better Basketball Defense;* Dec., p. 7; *Team Defense;* Jan., p. 7.
2188. **Iba, Henry P.:** *Present-Day Basketball;* Jan., p. 22.
2189. **Johns, Wilbur C.:** *Defense Against the Tall Pivot Man;* Dec., p. 10.
2190. **Jones, E.D.:** *Guard-Around Offensive Continuity;* Sept., p. 34; *Spot Plays and Pinch Baskets;* Nov., p. 22.
2191. **Keaney, Frank W.:** *College Basketball, Its History;* Mar., p. 44.
2192. **Lawther, John D.:** *Fundamentals of Basketball;* Sept., p. 16; Oct., p. 10; *Zone Defense;* Nov., p. 5.
2193. **Nitchman, Nelson:** *National Invitation Tournament;* May, p. 20; *National Collegiate Athletic Association Eastern Finals;* May, p. 34.
2194. **Porter, H.V.:** *Basketball;* Mar., p. 38.
2195. **Skelton, L.C.:** *Building a Basketball Offense;* Jan., p. 35.
2196. **Thomas, Stanley:** *Texas Tournament Plays;* Jan., p. 20.
2197. **Turner, Charlie:** *Pre-Tournament Training Procedure;* Feb., p. 8.
2198. **Wells, Clifford:** *Team Harmony in Basketball;* Jan., p. 32; *Daily Dozen in Fundamental Drills;* Jan., p. 10; *Combination Offense;* Feb., p. 7; *Basketball Offense in the South;* Apr., p. 28.
2199. *Basketball Takes to the Air;* Feb., p. 49.
2200. *College Prospects;* Nov., p. 24.

Volume 27, 1946–47

2201. **Baker, Floyd H.:** *Defense Against the Fast Break;* Oct., p. 18; *Advancing the Ball Against a Pressing Defense;* Jan., p. 20.
2202. **Boles, Leo L.:** *Dangerous Zone Ahead;* Dec., p. 13; *Fast Break Basketball;* Jan., p. 15.
2203. **Christensen, Richard:** *Practice Suggestions;* Oct., p. 26; *Defensive Rebounding;* Jan., p. 30.
2204. **Crum, J. Birney:** *Drills in Building Your Offense;* Nov., p. 46.
2205. **Cummings, Charles L.:** *Fast Break;* Oct., p. 15.
2206. **Dean, Everett S.:** *Basketball Testing;* Nov., p. 15.
2207. **Ellis, Loren E.:** *Basketball's Tandem Pivot;* Dec., p. 8.
2208. **Esposito, Michael:** *Three-On-Two Fast Break;* Dec., p. 10.

2209. **Fein, Lester S.:** *Tall and Short of It*; Dec., p. 42.
2210. **Hasser, George V.:** *Which Defense and How to Meet It?*; Dec., p. 12; *Feinting the Defensive Man*; Feb., p. 12.
2211. **Hubbard, Glenn S.:** *Handle That Ball*; Sept., p. 16.
2212. **Jones, E.D.:** *Shooting Percentages in the Kentucky State High School Basketball Tournament*; Jan., p. 42.
2213. **Nitchman, Nelson:** *1947 Basketball Technique*; May, p. 14.
2214. **Nooney, Arthur J.:** *Adaptability—The Keynote in High School Basketball*; Nov., p. 18.
2215. **Parsons, Beck:** *Shooting Accurately*; Feb., p. 32.
2216. **Ravenscroft, John M.:** *Stopping a Zone*; Nov., p. 22.
2217. **Wells, Cliff:** *Solving a Zone Defense*; Dec., p. 38.
2218. **Weyand, Lyle:** *An Unused Offense*; Jan., p. 32.
2219. **Wilson, Gilbert:** *Rebounding*; Sept., p. 20.
2220. *Basketball Technique as Demonstrated by Anderson, Indiana, Champions*; Dec., p. 18.
2221. *Films: Play Championship Basketball*; Nov. p. 43.
2222. *1947 Basketball Champions*; Apr., p. 38.

Volume 28, 1947–48

2223. **Anderson, Forrest G.:** *Free-Lance Play*; Jan., p. 10.
2224. **Baker, Floyd:** *Offensive-Defensive Set-Ups From Out of Bounds*; Nov., p. 16; *Basic Defensive Techniques*; Dec., p. 32.
2225. **Borcher, William:** *First Pass Counts in the Fast Break*; Dec., p. 24.
2226. **Christensen, Richard:** *Straight-Rush Fast Break*; Dec., p. 34; *Basketball in the Southern Division Pacific Coast Conference*; Apr., p. 38.
2227. **Dean, Everett S.:** *How to Coach Defense*; Dec., p. 8.
2228. **Ehrbright, Less:** *Ball-Handling*; Sept., p. 46.
2229. **Fein, Lester S.:** *Third Quarter, One to Go*; Dec., p. 40.
2230. **Floyd, John:** *Coaching the Passer and Receiver*; Dec., p. 30.
2231. **Foti, John C.:** *What the Tabulators Report on Basketball Offense*; Nov., p. 48.
2232. **Givens, Aubrey J.:** *Important Factors in Choosing a Defense*; Nov., p. 44.
2233. **Gray, Jack:** *Composite Offense*; Feb., p. 42.
2234. **Grayson, John A.:** *Roving Single-Pivot Offense*; Nov., p. 20; *Preparation Is the Thing When It's State Tournament Time*; Feb., p. 30.
2235. **Hobson, Howard:** *What to Look for in Scouting*; Dec., p. 16.
2236. **Hubbard, Glenn:** *Fundamentals of Individual Defense*; Nov., p. 32.
2237. **Jones, E.D.:** *Is Defense Worth the Effort?*; Nov., p. 28.
2238. **Julian, Alvin F.:** *"Doggie": Fast Break with a Purpose*; Nov., p. 11.
2239. **Keefe, Leo F.:** *Drilling to Be a Pass-Master*; Nov., p. 36.
2240. **Lawther, John D.:** *Footwork*; Nov., p. 8; *Screening—Interpretations and Types*; Dec., p. 11.
2241. **MacMillan, Dave:** *Play of the Tall Pivot-Man*; Jan., p. 20.
2242. **McMillin, A.N.:** *Defense for the Individual*; Oct., p. 13.
2243. **Messersmith, Murl:** *Small-Floor Defense*; Sept., p. 44.
2244. **Nitchman, Nelson W.:** *National Collegiate 1948 Basketball Finals*; May, p. 20.
2245. **Porter, H.V.:** *Basketball—A Chain Reaction*; Jan., p. 47.
2246. **Rarick, G. Lawrence:** *Ball Possession in Basketball*; June, p. 26.
2247. **Read, Herbert W.:** *Center Play and the Tall Pivot-Man*; Oct., p. 11; *Early Training of the Big Pivot-Man*; Dec., p. 17.
2248. **Rourke, Roland:** *Man-for-Man Defense*; Nov., p. 12.
2249. **Staton, Wesley M.:** *Ball Possession in Basketball*; June, p. 26.

2250. **Ward, Paul:** *Free Throwing;* Feb., p. 63.
2251. **Wells, Cliff:** *Inside Screens I've Seen;* Dec., p. 10.
2252. **Williams, Lee:** *Inside Screen;* Dec., p. 20.
2253. **Wilson, Gilbert:** *Overbalanced Attack;* Oct., p. 56.
2254. *American Scholastic Game Basketball;* Jan., p. 18.
2255. *Meet the Man-for-Man Basketball;* Jan., p. 24.
2256. *Meet the Zone;* Jan., p. 26.
2257. *1948 State High School Basketball Tournaments;* Apr., p. 46.

Volume 29, 1948–49

2258. **Adkisson, James:** *Pivot Post Play;* Nov., p. 58.
2259. **Allen, Forrest C.:** *Zone Defense and Rebounding;* Dec., p. 22.
2260. **Bachman, Carl:** *Adapting the Style of Play to the Personnel;* Oct., p. 32.
2261. **Baker, Floyd:** *Fundamentals and Drills;* Oct., p. 26.
2262. **Barnette, Quentin:** *Man-to-Man Defense and Drills;* Jan., p. 20.
2263. **Bender, Sam:** *Variations of the Zone Defense;* Jan., p. 22.
2264. **Brown, Delmer:** *Conditioning for Basketball;* Nov., p. 6.
2265. **Brumblay, Robert:** *Double-Post Attack;* Nov., p. 30.
2266. **Bunn, John W.:** *Offense for Pressing Defenses;* Nov., p. 9.
2267. **Burgoyne, Leon E.:** *Ball-Handling Fundamentals;* Sept., p. 42.
2268. **Carlson, Dr. H.C.:** *Pressing Defense;* Jan., p. 11.
2269. **Corcoran, William:** *Don't Neglect the Freeze;* Jan., p. 9.
2270. **Crawley, Marion:** *Offensive Screens Against the Man-for-Man;* Nov., p. 14.
2271. **Curran, William:** *The T in Basketball;* Dec., p. 32.
2272. **Doolen, B.C.:** *Back to Defense;* Jan., p. 11.
2273. **Drake, Bruce:** *Shifting Man-to-Man Defense;* Jan., p. 11.
2274. **Dromo, John:** *S.E.C. Tournament;* Apr., p. 12.
2275. **Dye, W.H.H.:** *Combination Defenses;* Jan., p. 10.
2276. **Esposito, Michael:** *Fast Break Principles;* Feb., p. 26.
2277. **Foster, H.E.:** *Offense Against Varying Defenses;* Dec., p. 26.
2278. **Friel, John B.:** *Variations of the Zone Defense;* Jan., p. 10; *National Collegiate 1949 Basketball Finals;* May, p. 38.
2279. **Gardner, Jack:** *Offensive Screens;* Jan., p. 26.
2280. **Grayson, John:** *Teaching Split Vision;* Oct., p. 30.
2281. **Henderson, Bill:** *Guard Play in Offense;* Nov., p. 42.
2282. **Hobson, Howard A.:** *Western Versus Eastern Basketball;* Dec., p. 9.
2283. **Krause, Edward:** *Fast Break From the Shifting Zone;* Dec., p. 11.
2284. **Osborn, Fred P.:** *Offenses Against Various Defenses;* Nov., p. 13.
2285. **Reyner, E.V.:** *Coaching the B-Team;* Jan., p. 46.
2286. **Rupp, Adolph:** *Out-of-Bounds Plays;* Dec., p. 12.
2287. **Sailer, H. Carl:** *Offense Against Set Defenses;* Dec., p. 13.
2288. **Slater, Floyd:** *Shifting Man-to-Man Defense;* Jan., p. 30.
2289. **Smelser, Carroll:** *Offense Used at Classen Against Set and Zone Defenses;* Nov., p. 24.
2290. **Stalcup, Wilbur:** *Possession Basketball;* Dec., p. 17.
2291. **Steneker, C.W.:** *Short Shots to Beat a Zone;* Nov., p. 10.
2292. **Stokenberry, Glenn S.:** *Revolving Offense With a Pivot;* Nov., p. 18.
2293. **Tarry, McCoy:** *Philosophy of Coaching Basketball in a Small High School;* Nov., p. 50.
2294. **Weaver, Willard:** *Zone Defenses;* Feb., p. 42.
2295. **Wells, Cliff:** *Figure-Eight Offense;* Nov., p. 20.
2296. **Woodard, Chalmer:** *Combination Defenses;* Feb., p. 34.

2297. *Basketball Literature, Editorial;* Oct., p. 16.
2298. *King Basketball, Editorial;* Feb., p. 20.

Volume 30, 1949–50

2299. **Angelich, James D.:** *Revolving Offense;* Oct., p. 30.
2300. **Belpuliti, Boris and Maravich, Press:** *Does the Visiting Team Have a Chance?;* Dec., p. 32.
2301. **Billett, Ralph E.:** *Basketball Drills With Game Opportunities;* Nov., p. 36.
2302. **Blikre, Clair:** *Pre-Game Warm-Up;* Nov., p. 40.
2303. **Brooks, Charles W.:** *Country Fair Basketball;* Oct., p. 40.
2304. **Bunn, John W.:** *Standard Basketball for 1950–51;* Nov., p. 32; *Why Give Conditioning Exercises for Basketball?;* Dec., p. 6.; *Special Defensive Maneuvers;* Jan., p. 9.
2305. **Christensen, Richard:** *Double Post;* Nov., p. 22.
2306. **Combes, Harry and Knapp, Clyde:** *Basketball for Elementary School Boys;* Jan., p. 51.
2307. **Corcoran, William:** *Stop the Fast Break;* Jan., p. 40.
2308. **Cronin, Vincent R.:** *There's More Fun in the Screen Offense;* Oct., p. 38.
2309. **Dawson, Paul B.:** *Developing an Offense;* Oct., p. 28.
2310. **DeShazo, W.H.:** *Offense Against Set and Zone Defenses;* Feb., p. 13.
2311. **Diskin, Pat:** *Fast Break;* Dec., p. 24.
2312. **Doolen, B.C.:** *Winning by Good Defense and Ball Control;* Jan., p. 15.
2313. **Foster, H.E. "Bud":** *Basketball Fundamentals—Passing;* Sept., p. 40; *Basketball Fundamentals—Dribbling;* Oct., p. 14; *Basketball Fundamentals—Pivot;* Nov., p. 18; *Basketball Fundamentals—Shooting;* Dec., p. 18.
2314. **Gardner, Jack:** *Kansas State Guard Play in Offense;* Nov., p. 9.
2315. **Harrison, Lawrence:** *Individual Defense;* Dec., p. 11.
2316. **Hobson, Howard:** *Two Against One and Three Against Two;* Dec., p. 8.
2317. **Jordan, Elmer:** *Double Post;* Jan., p. 10.
2318. **Knapp, Clyde and Combes, Harry:** *Basketball for Elementary School Boys;* Jan., p. 51.
2319. **Liegerot, Giles:** *Eliminating the Tall Man's Advantage;* Feb., p. 50.
2320. **Maasdam, Fred:** *Offensive Screens;* Nov., p. 46.
2321. **Maravich, Press and Belpuliti, Boris:** *Does the Visiting Team Have a Chance?;* Dec., p. 32.
2322. **Matthews, Eddie:** *Fundamentals and Drills;* Sept., p. 54.
2323. **May, Cecil:** *Passing Illustrated;* Nov., p. 10.
2324. **Michael, Les:** *Floor Position for Short Lay-Ups;* Nov., p. 56.
2325. **Neipp, Ernest:** *Basketball Fundamentals and Drills;* Sept., p. 54.
2326. **Nitchman, Nelson W.:** *NCAA 1950 Basketball Finals;* May, p. 28.
2327. **O'Neill, Leo:** *Fast Break From the Shifting Zone;* Jan., p. 13.
2328. **Peterson, Art:** *Preparation for Tournament Play;* Feb., p. 30.
2329. **Petrich, Peter:** *Practice Suggestions;* Nov., p. 28.
2330. **Quiring, Robert:** *Ball-Handling;* Nov., p. 44.
2331. **Stokenberry, Glenn:** *Composite Offense Against a Man-to-Man Defense;* Jan., p. 24.
2332. **Tuma, John:** *More on the Revolving Offense;* Nov., p. 44.
2333. **Turner, Charles:** *Ball-Handling and Passing in the Double Post Attack;* Oct., p. 12.
2334. **Vergamini, Carl:** *Free-Lance Basketball;* Feb., p. 44.
2335. **Wells, Cliff:** *Out-of-Bounds Plays;* Dec., p. 26.
2336. *1950 State Basketball Championships;* Apr., p. 44.
2337. *Our Basketball Offense, Editorial;* Feb., p. 62.

Volume 31, 1950–51

2338. **Anderson, Forrest:** *Play of the Small Pivot Man;* Apr., p. 24.
2339. **Bennett, L.S.:** *Basketball Photography with a Motion Picture Camera;* Jan., p. 16.
2340. **Box, James P.:** *Position Shooting Wins Games;* Nov., p. 38.
2341. **Brown, J.A.:** *Variable Single Post Attack;* Jan., p. 14.
2342. **Bunn, John W.:** *Effective Ball Control Tactics;* Dec., p. 28.
2343. **Campagnolo, Theodore J.:** *Scouts Out;* Nov., p. 50.
2344. **Cassell, Stafford H.:** *Twilight of the Zone;* Oct., p. 22; *Offense Against the Zone;* Nov., p. 7; *Sliding Zone Defense;* Dec., p. 35.
2345. **Corcoran, William J.:** *End Line Out-of-Bounds Play;* Dec., p. 20.
2346. **Eckert, Thomas:** *Fast Break from the Pressing Man-to-Man;* Nov., p. 28.
2347. **Eddy, Ray:** *Preparation for Tournament Play;* Feb., p. 10.
2348. **Erdman, Bernard:** *Basketball Practice Tips;* Jan., p. 28.
2349. **Henderson, George L.:** *Modifying the 1-3-1 Zone;* Jan., p. 15.
2350. **Johnson, Eddie:** *Man-to-Man Defense;* Jan., p. 42.
2351. **Kaminsky, Russ:** *Pre-Season Planning;* Oct., p. 16.
2352. **McCluskey, Edward:** *Drills and the Pattern Play;* Dec., p. 22.
2353. **McWilliams, Jay:** *Three-Phase Basketball Offense;* Dec., p. 26.
2354. **Moon, Paul C.:** *Fast Break Principles;* Oct., p. 13.
2355. **Morland, Richard B.:** *Basketball Enigma: The Free Throw;* Jan., p. 17.
2356. **Neipp, Ernest G.:** *Adapting the Style of Play to the Personnel;* Nov., p. 26.
2357. **Peyton, Mack:** *Developing the Fast Break;* Nov., p. 32.
2358. **Quiring, Robert:** *Out-of-Bounds Plays;* Nov., p. 36.
2359. **Rourke, Roland:** *Attacking the Zone;* Nov., p. 40.
2360. **Rupp, Adolph:** *Kentucky Continuity;* Dec., p. 6.
2361. **Saltis, Larry:** *Pressing Zone in Junior High School;* Jan., p. 38.
2362. **Sempeles, George:** *Independent Basketball;* Jan., p. 11.
2363. **Smith, Willard:** *Mass Basketball;* Sept., p. 46.
2364. **Straub, Paul F.:** *Screens;* Nov., p. 22.
2365. **Sullivan, James L.:** *Basketball Organizations;* Sept., p. 52.
2366. **Verdell, Thomas:** *Why Not Time Out for Held Ball?;* Jan., p. 34.
2367. **Ward, Stan:** *Fast Break with the Weakside Trailer;* Dec., p. 24.
2368. **Wells, Cliff:** *Stopping the Pivot;* Dec., p. 16.
2369. **Wilson, F.M.:** *Fouling Can Be Reduced;* Nov., p. 34.
2370. *1951 State Basketball Championships;* Apr., p. 14.

Volume 32, 1951–52

2371. **Anderson, Charles E.:** *Raise Those Shooting Percentages;* Nov., p. 26.
2372. **Beckman, Edwin J.:** *Good Defense for More Wins;* Jan., p. 26.
2373. **Buck, Selby:** *Lanier's Winning Offense;* Nov., p. 24.
2374. **Bunn, John W.:** *Zone Hysteria;* Jan., p. 11.
2375. **Chuck, Edward M.:** *Zone Variation;* Jan., p. 28.
2376. **Conn, Julius:** *Psychological Aspects of High School Basketball;* Feb., p. 13.
2377. **Day, Kenner S.:** *Back to Defense;* Oct., p. 22.
2378. **Foley, John:** *An Offense From the Free Throw Line;* Nov., p. 18.
2379. **Gaylord, Curtiss:** *Basket Is Big;* Oct., p. 50.
2380. **Hauk, Harold:** *Basketball Drills;* Oct., p. 30.
2381. **Humphrey, Fred:** *Offense or Defense Responsible?;* Feb., p. 12.
2382. **Jameson, D.W.:** *Revolving Offense;* Dec., p. 16.
2383. **Katchmer, George A.:** *Pressing Sliding Zone;* Dec., p. 33.
2384. **Kinert, Harry:** *Kinert Press;* Dec., p. 14.

2385. **Lande, Leon:** *Basketball Trends in North Dakota;* Dec., p. 24.
2386. **Longcope, Don:** *End Line Options;* Nov., p. 30.
2387. **McWilliams, Jay:** *The 2-3 Sliding Zone Defense;* Jan., p. 13.
2388. **Moon, Paul C.:** *We Beat Ourselves;* Nov., p. 36.
2389. **Newsom, Herbert A.:** *Basketball Fundamentals for the Physical Education Classes;* Jan., p. 12.
2390. **Quiring, Robert:** *Basketball Organization;* Oct., p. 20.
2391. **Russell, John "Honey":** *Seton Hall's Set Offense;* Nov., p. 7.
2392. **Sipos, John E.:** *Winning Attacks;* Dec., p. 13.
2393. **Smith, C.Q.:** *Tournament Preparation;* Jan., p. 34.
2394. **Trowbridge, William:** *Guard Play;* Nov., p. 28.
2395. **Ward, Stan:** *Applying the Full Court Press;* Dec., p. 20.
2396. **Wells, Cliff:** *Tulane's Pivot Continuity;* Dec., p. 6.
2397. *1952 State Basketball Championship;* Apr., p. 8.

Volume 33, 1952–53

2398. **Ahearn, Russ:** *Building a Championship Team With Limited Material;* Nov., p. 26.
2399. **Anderson, Charles E.:** *Statistics in Basketball;* Nov., p. 20.
2400. **Belichick, Steve:** *Varsity Play and Test Results in Basketball;* Nov., p. 22.
2401. **Bender, Sam:** *Defense Against the Fast Break;* Dec., p. 26.
2402. **Blanchard, C.H.:** *Defense Against a Stall;* Nov., p. 15.
2403. **Brannon, Byron S.:** *TCU's Switching Defense;* Dec., p. 6.
2404. **Chambers, Bob:** *Free Throw Shooting Drill Under Game Conditions;* Oct., p. 25.
2405. **Clark, Francis:** *Some Fundamental Drills of Basketball;* Sept., p. 18.
2406. **Crowe, Leo J.:** *Assigned Man-to-Man Defense;* Dec., p. 11.
2407. **Engel, Frederic C.:** *Set Attack;* Nov., p. 40.
2408. **Foster, H.E.:** *Jump Shooting;* Nov., p. 7.
2409. **Guillory, Joe H.:** *Are You Wasting Your Time on the Screen?;* Nov., p. 12.
2410. **Hopper, Eugene:** *Figure Eight Offense;* Oct., p. 26.
2411. **Jansky, Larry:** *Attacking the Two-Three Zone;* Nov., p. 28.
2412. **Keefe, Leo Francis:** *Defense Basketball Drills;* Sept., p. 42.
2413. **King, Carroll:** *Tournament Preparation;* Dec., p. 12.
2414. **Loveless, George K.:** *Fast Break;* Nov., p. 13.
2415. **McCreary, Jay:** *Half-Court Press;* Dec., p. 28.
2416. **McFarland, Jerry:** *Out-of-Bounds Plays;* Oct., p. 22.
2417. **Moon, Paul:** *Modified Zone Defense;* Dec., p. 14.
2418. **Neff, Ben:** *Sideline Pass Variations;* Jan., p. 14.
2419. **Pfitsch, John A.:** *What to Do Against the Press;* Nov., p. 11.
2420. **Ravenscroft, John:** *Psychology of the Full Court Press;* Dec., p. 30.
2421. **Raymonds, Henry C.:** *Single Pivot;* Nov., p. 8.
2422. **Richmond, Link:** *Possession Basketball;* Nov., p. 24.
2423. **Rowlett, Roy:** *Free Lance Game With Rules;* Nov., p. 34.
2424. **Saake, Alvin C.:** *In Defense of a Zone;* Dec., p. 20.
2425. **Van Metar, J.R.:** *Fundamental Drills;* Nov., p. 17.
2426. **Walker, Paul:** *Double Pivot;* Nov., p. 9.
2427. **Wink, James M.:** *Teaching Individual Defense;* Sept., p. 52.
2428. **Witt, Van Wayne:** *Sinking Man-to-Man;* Dec., p. 13.
2429. **Wooten, Richard M.:** *Fluid Zone Defense;* Dec., p. 16.
2430. *Basketball Hall of Fame, Editorial;* Dec., p. 18.
2431. *1953 State Basketball Tournaments;* Apr., p. 12.

Volume 34, 1953–54

2432. **Anderson, Forrest:** *It's the Change-Up That Counts;* Dec., p. 6.
2433. **Auwater, T.K.:** *Improve Your Rebounding;* Nov., p. 24.
2434. **Baker, Roy T.:** *Only the Ball Can Score!;* Dec., p. 14.
2435. **Beckman, Edwin J.:** *Playing the Offense;* Nov., p. 30.
2436. **Bonham, Aubrey R.:** *Stunting Defenses;* Dec., p. 4.
2437. **Bunn, John W.:** *Why the Underhand Free Throw?;* Nov., p. 12.
2438. **Burger, Bud:** *Fast Break Drills;* Oct., p. 20.
2439. **Cartier, Warren L.:** *Basketball Holder;* Apr., p. 45.
2440. **Foley, John C.:** *Teaching the Man-for-Man;* Dec., p. 28.
2441. **Francis, Clarence "Bevo" and Oliver, Newton:** *Shooting Illustrated;* Nov., p. 6.
2442. **Greer, Hugh and Ward, Stan:** *Drills for Better Fundamentals;* Oct., p. 34; *Penetrating the Zone With the 1-3-1;* Nov., p. 26.
2443. **Grieve, Andrew W.:** *Inside Weave;* Nov., p. 17.
2444. **Humphrey, Fred:** *Analysis of Team Efficiency;* Nov., p. 42.
2445. **King, Eddie and Levitt, Bunny:** *Underhand Free Throw;* Nov., p. 10.
2446. **Levitt, Bunny and King, Eddie:** *Underhand Free Throw;* Nov., p. 10.
2447. **Morland, Richard B.:** *Free-Throws—Frozen Assets or Redeemable Dividends?;* Nov., p. 9.
2448. **Morris, Mortimer H.:** *Zoned Basketball;* Dec., p. 26.
2449. **Nagle, Jack:** *Approved Shotgetter;* Dec., p. 16.
2450. **Oliver, Newton and Francis, Clarene "Bevo":** *Shooting Illustrated;* Nov., p. 6.
2451. **Patrick, John:** *Analysis of Defense Footwork;* Dec., p. 20.
2452. **Pegram, W.D.:** *Position Shooting;* Sept., p. 36.
2453. **Pfitsch, John A.:** *Concentration in Shooting;* Dec., p. 22.
2454. **Potter, Marsh:** *Triple Post;* Nov., p. 14.
2455. **Schlundt, Don and Wells, Cliff:** *One Hand Free Throw;* Nov., p. 11.
2456. **Van Buren, Gordan:** *Simple Man-for-Man Scissors;* Nov., p. 20.
2457. **Walters, Bill:** *Pressing Defense;* Nov., p. 28.
2458. **Ward, Stan and Green, Hugh:** *Drills for Better Fundamentals;* Oct., p. 34; *Penetrating the Zone With the 1-3-1;* Nov., p. 26.
2459. **Watson, Bob C.:** *Composite Offense Against a Man-for-Man Defense;* Nov., p. 22; *Plus-Minus Chart;* Jan., p. 32.
2460. **Wells, Cliff and Schlundt, Don:** *One Hand Free Throw;* Nov., p. 11.
2461. **Wisher, P.R.:** *Defense Against the Tall Pivot;* Dec., p. 13.
2462. *1954 State Basketball Tournaments;* May, p. 42.

Volume 35, 1954–55

2463. **Ahlbom, Harold:** *Try a Competitive Practice;* Nov., p. 26.
2464. **Baker, Roy T.:** *Vertical Post Offense;* Sept., p. 68.
2465. **Foley, John C.:** *Pure Give-and-Go;* Nov., p. 32.
2466. **Fuoss, Donald E.:** *The Theory of Defense Play;* Dec., p. 30.
2467. **Gross, Elmer A.:** *Offenses Against Zone Defenses;* Nov., p. 22.
2468. **Herron, Blair L.:** *New Life for Cold Statistics;* Dec., p. 12.
2469. **Hickey, E.S.:** *St. Louis' Set Offense;* Nov., p. 40.
2470. **Hill, Elam R.:** *Passing to Win;* Nov., p. 38.
2471. **Kloppenburg, Bob:** *Put the Defense Back in Basketball;* Dec., p. 31.
2472. **Levy, Marv:** *Scoring With the Fast Break;* Dec., p. 22.

2473. **Lindeburg, Franklin A.:** *Basketball Manager;* Oct., p. 22; *1-3-1 All-Purpose Zone Offense;* Dec., p. 16.
2474. **Noll, Philip D.:** *Comparative Rating Scale for Basketball;* Oct., p. 30.
2475. **Saltis, Larry R.:** *Teaching Free Throwing;* Nov., p. 24.
2476. **Stalcup, Wilbur "Sparky":** *Defensive Maneuvers;* Dec., p. 6.
2477. **Tansey, James A.:** *Play Patterns Can Work in Junior High School Basketball;* Dec., p. 11.
2478. **Van Buren, Gordon:** *Pass-and-Go-Away Pattern;* Nov., p. 20.
2479. **Watson, Bobby C.:** *Fun Drills in Basketball;* Nov., p. 18.
2480. **Wells, Cliff:** *End Line Out-of-Bounds Plays;* Dec., p. 26.
2481. **Winter, Fred "Tex":** *Offensive Maneuvers and Footwork;* Nov., p. 6.
2482. **Woods, Edward L.:** *Planning the Offense;* Oct., p. 26.
2483. *1955 State Basketball Tournaments;* May, p. 62.

Volume 36, 1955–56

2484. **Abrahamson, Bob:** *An Early Season Offense for a Beginning Coach;* Nov., p. 18.
2485. **Adkisson, Hershel C.:** *Training Young Candidates for Post Play;* Oct., p. 30; *Teaching the Jump Shot in Junior High School;* Nov., p. 25.
2486. **Baker, Roy T.:** *Your First Season?;* Oct., p. 28.
2487. **Bonnickson, Jack and Hagler, Bob:** *Developing a Set Play Type of Offense;* Nov., p. 24.
2488. **Corcoran, Mike:** *Developing the Fast Break;* Sept., p. 30.
2489. **Eidens, Clyde O.:** *Saratoga's Flanking Attack;* Nov., p. 12.
2490. **Gill, Amory T.:** *Squaring the Offense;* Dec., p. 16.
2491. **Grieve, Andrew W.:** *3-2 Sliding Zone;* Nov., p. 20; *Shift to the Zone;* Nov., p. 34.
2492. **Hagler, Bob and Bonnickson, Jack:** *Developing a Set Play Type of Offense;* Nov., p. 24.
2493. **Martin, William H.:** *Attacks Against Zones;* Dec., p. 14.
2494. **McWilliams, Jay:** *Fast Breaking From the 2-1-2;* Dec., p. 18.
2495. **Myers, Ward L.:** *Guarding the Jump Shooter;* Dec., p. 20.
2496. **Nagle, Jack:** *Marquette's Tandem Post;* Nov., p. 6.
2497. **Nixon, John E. and Vroom, Gerald A.:** *Fundamental Basketball Skills of College Freshmen;* Mar., p. 16.
2498. **O'Connor, Frank "Bucky" and Sills, Frank, Ph.D.:** *Heavy Resistance Exercises for Basketball Players;* June, p. 6.
2499. **Patrick, John:** *Analyzing the Drive Shot;* Oct., p. 13.
2500. **Pennington, John:** *Continuity Freeze Offense;* Nov., p. 28.
2501. **Porter, Archie:** *Held Ball Situations;* Dec., p. 32.
2502. **Seymour, Emery W.:** *The Use of Rating for Basketball Officials;* Nov., p. 34.
2503. **Sills, Frank, Ph.D. and O'Connor, Frank "Bucky":** *Heavy Resistance Exercises for Basketball Players;* June, p. 6.
2504. **Tansey, James A.:** *Fundamental Basketball Drills for the Junior High School;* Nov., p. 30.
2505. **Thompson, Ronald B.:** *Give-and-Go;* Nov., p. 16.
2506. **Vroom, Gerald A. and Nixon, John E.:** *Fundamental Basketball Skills of College Freshmen;* Mar., p. 16.
2507. **Wells, Cliff:** *Will the New Twelve-Foot Lane Ruling Affect the Style of Play?;* Oct., p. 7.
2508. **Woolpert, Phil:** *San Francisco's Single Post;* Dec., p. 8.
2509. *1956 State Basketball Tournaments;* May, p. 22.

Volume 37, 1956–57

2510. **Adkisson, Hershel C.:** *Maneuvering for the Jump Shot;* Nov., p. 12.
2511. **Adkisson, James W.:** *Guard: Basketball's Quarterback;* Oct., p. 8.
2512. **Boerger, Willard:** *Get Those Jump Balls;* Dec., p. 37.
2513. **Bonnickson, Jack:** *Teaching the Set Play;* Dec., p. 20.
2514. **Bottom, Raymond:** *Don't Forget the Close Ones;* Dec., p. 34.
2515. **Case, Everett N.:** *Controlled Fast Break;* Dec., p. 6.
2516. **Clark, John:** *Thinking Free Lance Offense;* Oct., p. 18.
2517. **Croyle, Robert C.:** *Combined Changing Defense;* Dec., p. 26.
2518. **Dell, Robert G.:** *Follow-up Game;* Oct., p. 9.
2519. **Graupman, Lee:** *Basketball in Three-Quarter Time;* Oct., p. 22.
2520. **Grieve, Andrew W.:** *Zone Under Attack;* Nov., p. 14.
2521. **Gullion, Blair:** *Individual Defensive Footwork;* Oct., p. 27.
2522. **Kloppenburg, Bob:** *Defense Is a Two-Way Street;* Dec., p. 30.
2523. **Lindeburg, Franklin A.:** *Basketball Curriculum;* Oct., p. 12.
2524. **McWilliams, Jay:** *Twelve Foot Lane Pivot Play;* Dec., p. 28.
2525. **Nagle, Jack:** *Secondary Fast Break;* Oct., p. 38.
2526. **O'Connor, Bucky:** *Fundamental Double Pass Drill;* Nov., p. 7.
2527. **Picariello, S.J.:** *Coaches Tender Traps Zany Zones;* Nov., p. 22.
2528. **Tansey, James A.:** *An Offensive Pattern for Junior High Schools;* Nov., p. 32.
2529. **Toomasian, John:** *Defensive Counters for Standard Offenses;* May, p. 24.
2530. **Watson, Bobby C.:** *Breaking the Zone Barrier;* Nov., p. 18.
2531. **Wells, Cliff:** *Umbrella Zone;* Dec., p. 13.
2532. **Whitney, George P.:** *The 1-Man Zone Breaker;* Nov., p. 24.
2533. **Wilbert, Warren:** *Screening the Zone;* Nov., p. 26.
2534. *Facilities and Equipment: Basketball Stadium;* Jan., p. 6.
2535. *For Your Bulletin Board: Dribble in Basketball;* Oct., p. 34.
2536. *1957 State Basketball Tournaments;* May, p. 38.
2537. *Shooting in Basketball;* Nov., p. 34.
2538. *Twelve Foot Lane,* Oct., p. 37.

Volume 38, 1957–58

2539. **Buckley, Chester:** *Build Your Own Basketball Weights;* Oct., p. 16.
2540. **Bush, Jerry:** *Rebounding;* Oct., p. 6.
2541. **Cabutti, Leedio:** *Four Topnotch Defensive Drills;* Nov., p. 6.
2542. **Damore, Patrick R.:** *Freeze to Win the Close Ones;* Dec., p. 9.
2543. **Esposito, Michael:** *Fast Break Offense;* Dec., p. 9.
2544. **Fitzhenry, Bob:** *Four Men Under;* Nov., p. 42.
2545. **Foster, William E.:** *The Basketball Player's Notebook;* Sept., p. 76.
2546. **Fox, A. Leo:** *A Positive Approach to Free Throw Practice;* Oct., p. 26.
2547. **Goodwin, Leslie K.:** *Basketball Drills;* Oct., p. 54.
2548. **Grieve, Andrew W.:** *Set to Score;* Dec., p. 7.
2549. **Hart, William R.:** *A New Light on Fast Break off the Free Throw;* Oct., p. 42.
2550. **Howell, Fred E.:** *Basketball Drills—Make Them Competitive;* June, p. 26.
2551. **Iba, Hank:** *Defensing the Fast Breaks and the Delayed Game;* Dec., p. 11.
2552. **Lindeburg, Franklin A.:** *The Jump Shot, Basketball's Potent Weapon;* Oct., p. 18; *The Screen—Use It Two Ways;* Nov., p. 18.
2553. **Morris, Mortimer H.:** *Basketball Yardstick;* Nov., p. 64.
2554. **Morris, Stanley:** *Evolution Through Alternate-Variation Patterns;* Nov., p. 37.
2555. **Mullaney, Dave:** *Free Throw Technique;* Nov., p. 53.
2556. **Nagle, Jack:** *The Alternating Post Continuity;* Nov., p. 26.

2557. **Picariello, S.J.:** *Defeating the Pressing Zone*; Dec., p. 22.
2558. **Price, Fred:** *An Anti-Press Pattern*; Dec., p. 16.
2559. **Richardson, Deane E.:** *The Shuttle Run as a Basketball Conditioner*; Oct., p. 52.
2560. **Rosentswieg, Joel:** *Score With the Jump*; Dec., p. 6.
2561. **Tucci, Ruben J.:** *Mass Line Basketball*; Sept., p. 54.
2562. **Wells, Cliff:** *Scouting: Why?*; Oct., p. 32.
2563. **Whitney, George P.:** *The Five-Man Weave*; Dec., p. 18.
2564. **Wilbert, Warren:** *Pre-Game Drill*; Nov., p. 32.
2565. **Wilkes, Glenn N.:** *The Screen and Roll for Out-of-Bounds Plays*; Nov., p. 30.
2566. *1958 State Basketball Tournaments*; May, p. 48.

Volume 39, 1958–59

2567. **Blackburn, Tom:** *Dayton's No. 4 Play*; Dec., p. 6.
2568. **Boesen, Marv:** *A Combination Zone for All Offenses*; Dec., p. 24.
2569. **Bottom, Raymond:** *The Box Weave Versus a Man-for-Man Offense*; Nov., p. 46.
2570. **Esposito, Michael:** *Fast Break Fundamentals*; Oct., p. 26.
2571. **Fears, Edward D., Jr.:** *The Revolving 1-3-1 Versus the 2-3 and the 3-1-2 Zones*; Oct., p. 15.
2572. **Filbert, Gary:** *Diversified Offense*; Nov., p. 24.
2573. **Foti, John C.:** *Let's Shoot the First Half*; June, p. 30.
2574. **Fowler, Charles L.:** *Stalling Offense*; Dec., p. 26.
2575. **Fox, A. Leo:** *Teaching a Milling Offense*; Oct., p. 16.
2576. **Grieve, Andrew W.:** *How's Your Defense*; Dec., p. 18.
2577. **Grunska, Jerry:** *Individual Guard Stunts—The Rock and Roll*; Sept., p. 32.
2578. **Hartle, James M.:** *Pyramid Offense*; Sept., p. 38.
2579. **Hill, Warren E.:** *A Semi-Control Offense for the Small High School*; Nov., p. 23.
2580. **Howell, Fred E.:** *Don't Neglect Managerial Organization*; Nov., p. 12.
2581. **Janick, Herbert and Monagan, George C.:** *A Stacked-Deck Offense*; Nov., p. 18.
2582. **Kalosh, Mike, Jr.:** *The Player Rating Scale*; Nov., p. 30.
2583. **Kloppenburg, Bob:** *Meet the Press*; Nov., p. 13.
2584. **Monagan, George C. and Janick, Herbert:** *A Stacked-Deck Offense*; Nov., p. 18.
2585. **Nelson, Jim:** *Improved Shooting*; Oct., p. 30.
2586. **Newell, Pete:** *Cal's Reverse Action and Double Post*; Oct., p. 6.
2587. **Rosentswieg, Joel:** *The Easy 2*; Nov., p. 6.
2588. **Sonstoem, Bob:** *An Examination of Defense*; Dec., p. 16.
2589. **Tener, Moe:** *Taking Advantage of Scoring Situations*; Nov., p. 9.
2590. **Toomasian, John:** *Cutting the Basketball Team*; June, p. 20.
2591. **Wall, William L.:** *The 1-2-2 Versus the Man-for-Man*; Nov., p. 14.
2592. **Wells, Cliff:** *An Offense Against a Zone Press*; Jan., p. 12.
2593. *1959 State Basketball Tournaments*; May, p. 14.

Volume 40, 1959–60

2594. **Anderson, Forrest A.:** *It's Mobility That Counts*; Nov., p. 8.
2595. **Basile, Louis A.:** *Two-Must System for Free Throws*; Oct., p. 30.
2596. **Benington, John:** *St. Louis' Freedom Weave*; Oct., p. 6.
2597. **Boesen, Marv:** *Patternize Your Zone Offense*; Dec., p. 18.
2598. **Bottom, Raymond:** *Simplified Defense for Junior Highs*; Dec., p. 34.
2599. **Davis, Bob:** *Georgetown's Half-Court Zone Press*; Oct., p. 10.

2600. **Filor, John:** *Simplifying the Multiple Defense for Basketball*; Nov., p. 26.
2601. **Fowler, Charles:** *Multiple Pressing Defense*; Nov., p. 37.
2602. **Green, Dr. Donald A.:** *The Triple Pivot Offense in Attacking the Zone*; Nov., p. 18.
2603. **Grieve, Andrew W.:** *The Three-Man Weave*; Oct., p. 24; *Overbalanced Zone Attack*; Nov., p. 31.
2604. **Hartle, James M.:** *Multiple Defense in Basketball*; Sept., p. 83.
2605. **Hill, George E.:** *A Ladder Tournament for Free Throw Accuracy*; Sept., p. 62.
2606. **Lambert, Paul M.:** *The Inclusive Fast Break Drill*; Oct., p. 18.
2607. **Lindeburg, Franklin A.:** *The Basics of Attacking Zones*; Nov., p. 15.
2608. **Lockhart, Paul D.:** *The Offense vs. All Defenses*; Nov., p. 38.
2609. **Peterson, Dr. H.D.:** *A Scientific Approach to Shooting in Basketball*; Oct., p. 32.
2610. **Picariello, S.J.:** *Basketball Patterns Pay Off*; Sept., p. 20; Oct., p. 26; Nov., p. 43.
2611. **Price, Fred:** *Simplified Set Offense*; Nov., p. 28.
2612. **Sauter, Waldo:** *Guiding Principles for the Beginning Basketball Coach*; Sept., p. 56.
2613. **Sells, Jim:** *A Zone Press Variation*; Nov., p. 32.
2614. **Tener, Moe:** *A Rotation Pattern Against Zones*; Dec., p. 16.
2615. **Van Buren, E. Gordon:** *Teaching Fast Break Tactics*; Nov., p. 42.
2616. **Ward, Charles R.:** *A Zone Man-for-Man*; Nov., p. 30.
2617. **Welch, Ron:** *In Behalf of the Man-for-Man*; Dec., p. 26.
2618. **Wells, Cliff:** *The Tulane Clear-Outs*; Oct., p. 28.
2619. **Woodward, David C.:** *60-Man Basketball*; Dec., p. 40.
2620. *1960 State Basketball Tournaments*; May, p. 22.

Volume 41, 1960–61

2621. **Arnold, Everett:** *High Low Post*; Nov., p. 26.
2622. **Bottom, Raymond:** *The Double Post for Double Effectiveness*; Oct., p. 18.
2623. **Braun, Howard J.:** *The Slashing Offense*; Dec., p. 23.
2624. **Chiappy, John E.:** *The Free Throw Shooting Story*; Nov., p. 38.
2625. **Fein, Lester S.:** *Zone Offense Philosophy*; Sept., p. 42.
2626. **Filbert, Gary:** *Covering the Outside Man*; Nov., p. 22.
2627. **Hager, Ed:** *Combination of Full Presses*; Dec., p. 28.
2628. **Hanson, Dale L.:** *An Organized Attack Against Pressing Defenses*; Dec., p. 26.
2629. **Harkins, Mike:** *The Blitz*; Nov., p. 28; *A Multi-Option Man-for-Man Offense*; June, p. 26.
2630. **Joor, Robert H.:** *Analysis of Basic Fakes*; Dec., p. 30.
2631. **Keller, Ronald C.:** *The Dribble and Drive Series*; Oct., p. 20.
2632. **Key, Billy A.:** *Strong and Weak Side Continuity Offense*; Nov., p. 7.
2633. **Lay, Floyd E.:** *Basketball Rules Experiments*; Nov., p. 18.
2634. **Lindeburg, Franklin:** *That Last-Minute Play*; Dec., p. 18.
2635. **McWilliams, Jay:** *A Combination Offense for Man-for-Man and Zone Defenses*; Jan., p. 36.
2636. **Meadows, Dr. Paul E.:** *Valpo's Shuttle Freeze*; Dec., p. 21.
2637. **Nitardy, Walter:** *Fundamentals for a Man-for-Man Defense*; Nov., p. 29.
2638. **Rogers, Gordon R.:** *Useful Basketball Charts*; Sept., p. 38.
2639. **Rupp, Adolph:** *Offensive Maneuvers*; Oct., p. 8.
2640. **Scott, Charles H., Jr.:** *Pre-Season Basketball Training*; Sept., p. 28.
2641. **Sells, Jim:** *Half-Court Squeeze*; Nov., p. 30.
2642. **Wall, William L.:** *Use Competition for Free Throw Practice*; Nov., p. 60.
2643. **Ward, Charles R.:** *Charting and Scouting Basketball*; Oct., p. 28.

2644. **Welch, Ronald R.:** *Planned Variations Within the Man-for Man*; Dec., p. 31.
2645. **Wickstrom, Ralph L.:** *The One-Hand Jumper*; Oct., p. 30.
2646. **Winsor, Charles:** *Variations for Two-Out Offensive Patterns*; Oct., p. 34.
2647. *1961 State Basketall Tournaments*; May, p. 20.

Volume 42, 1961–62

2648. **Alley, Dr. Louis B.:** *To Improve Shooting Accuracy Practice at Small Baskets*; Sept., p. 34.
2649. **Baden, Robert:** *The Roaming Stall*; Dec., p. 20.
2650. **Bottom, Raymond:** *Basketball Offense: The "Lonesome End"*; Sept., p. 72; *Don't Overlook the 2-1-2*; Nov., p. 20.
2651. **Farley, William E.:** *Basketball Pressure Drill*; Dec., p. 14.
2652. **Filor, John:** *A Squeeze Press*; Oct., p. 30.
2653. **Gardner, Jack:** *Feeding the Post at Utah*; Nov., p. 48.
2654. **Gourdouze, Frank:** *The Horseshoe Offense*; Nov., p. 48.
2655. **Hager, Edward C.:** *Pattern Play for High Schools*; Oct., p. 24.
2656. **Hanson, B.J.:** *Key to Successful Zone Offense, Movement, Men, and Ball*; Dec., p. 22.
2657. **Harkins, Mike:** *Rub 'Em and Weave 'Em*; Nov., p. 25.
2658. **Hartley, Joseph W.:** *Teaching Defense*; Oct., p. 8; *Presses and Pressure Defenses*; Nov., p. 18.
2659. **Jolley, Gerald E.:** *The Split Offense*; Nov., p. 16.
2660. **Luce, Charles R.:** *Basic Fundamentals of Basketball*; Dec., p. 34.
2661. **McDonald, George M.:** *Team Defense Wins Championships*; Jan., p. 38.
2662. **Nettles, Barry:** *Teaching Defensive Footwork to Junior High School Players*; Oct., p. 21; *A Tandem Post for Junior Highs*; Dec., p. 16.
2663. **Nitchman, Nelson.:** *1962 Basketball Trends*; June, p. 32.
2664. **Price, Fred A.:** *Man-to-Man Defense—The Stabilizer*; Oct., p. 50.
2665. **Sage, George H.:** *Specific Drills for the Switching Man-for-Man*; Sept., p. 42.
2666. **Shearburn, V.V.:** *A Proven Attack Against the 1-3-1*; Nov., p. 22.
2667. **Shults, Robert E.:** *The Rolling Pivot Offense*; Oct., p. 48.
2668. **Vokes, Sam:** *Some Notes on Zone Offense*; Oct., p. 46.
2669. **Wells, Cliff:** *The Tulane Tandem*; Oct., p. 32.
2670. *1962 State Basketball Tournaments*; May, p. 30.

Volume 43, 1962–63

2671. **Arnold, Everett:** *High Low Post Versus Man-for-Man*; Nov., p. 18.
2672. **Baldwin, Richard E.:** *Defensive Basketball*; Dec., p. 8.
2673. **Batway, Charles:** *Eight Two-Point Out-of-Bounds Plays*; Dec., p. 31.
2674. **Blount, Jim:** *Basketball Scouting*; Oct., p. 30.
2675. **Buckley, Chester W.:** *Mechanical Analysis of the Jump Shot*; Oct., p. 8.
2676. **Chiappy, John E.:** *Why Not the Left Hand on Defense?*; Nov., p. 58.
2677. **Davis, Bob:** *Full Court Zone Press*; Dec., p. 16.
2678. **Davis, Tom:** *Keeping in Touch With Basketball Players During the Summer*; May, p. 66.
2679. **Dickerson, William E.:** *Fundamentals and Drills in Junior High School Basketball*; Sept., p. 82.
2680. **Dromo, John:** *Building an Offense in High School*; June, p. 24.
2681. **Farley, William E.:** *How and When to Teach the Jump Shot*; Oct., p. 22.
2682. **Hager, Ed:** *Fundamentals of the Quick Break*; Nov., p. 46.
2683. **Handler, Fred D.:** *Give-and-Go*; Nov., p. 41.
2684. **Harkins, Harry L.:** *Back-Cutter Stall*; Nov., p. 42.

2685. **Hunter, Kenneth A.:** *One-Two-One-One Zone Press*; Dec., p. 36.
2686. **Jackson, Jack P.:** *A Simplified Zone Attack for Junior High School*; Dec., p. 14.
2687. **Johnston, James N.:** *Using Continuity Offense as a Zone Breaker*; Dec., p. 17.
2688. **Kretschmar, Joe:** *Offensively Jamming a Zone*; Dec., p. 34.
2689. **Luce, Charles B.:** *A Rule of Action and Basic Move Offense*; Nov., p. 50.
2690. **Meadows, Dr. Paul E.:** *Rolling the Front Line*; Oct., p. 32.
2691. **Meckfessel, Richard and Smith, Chuck:** *The Shuffle With a Double Screen*; Nov., p. 9.
2692. **Murphy, C.T.:** *The Lay-In Shot*; Nov., p. 26.
2693. **Nitchman, Nelson:** *Some Diversified Basketball Approaches in 1963*; May, p. 32.
2694. **Sage, George H.:** *Station Drills*; Oct., p. 20.
2695. **Sauter, Dr. Waldo:** *The Place of the Set Play*; Sept., p. 35.
2696. **Schils, Jack:** *Man-for-Man Offense*; Jan., p. 20.
2697. **Sells, Jim:** *Weak-Side Play*; Nov., p. 24.
2698. **Severson, M.G.:** *St. Cloud State's Associated and Progressive Drill Theory*; Sept., p. 66.
2699. **Smith, Chuck and Meckfessel, Richard:** *The Shuffle With a Double Screen*; Nov., p. 9.
2700. **Stevens, Robert L.:** *Man-for-Man Versus Zone Defense*; Oct., p. 37.
2701. **Swegan, Dr. Donald B.:** *The Wall Offense*; Oct., p. 10; *The Pressure-Pinch Zone Defense*; Nov., p. 40.
2702. **Tener, Moe:** *Combination Defenses*; Nov., p. 23.
2703. **Vanatta, Bob:** *Box Weave Offense*; Nov., p. 16.
2704. **Wall, William L.:** *MacMurray's Offense*; Sept., p. 54.
2705. **Wells, Cliff:** *How to Beat a Zone Press*; Oct., p. 60.
2706. *Mechanical Basketball*; Oct., p. 46.
2707. *1963 State Basketball Tournaments*; May, p. 12.

Volume 44, 1963–64

2708. **Avery, Art:** *Front Court Out-of-Bounds Play*; Oct., p. 28.
2709. **Briner, Robert A. and Smith, Robert E.:** *Combating Basketball Staleness*; Jan., p. 70.
2710. **Campbell, Robbie and Porter, Archie:** *The Platoon System in Basketball*; Oct., p. 36.
2711. **Carson, Glenn:** *Combining the Shuffle and Single Post Offenses*; Oct., p. 10.
2712. **Corr, Jim:** *Inside-Outside Zone Offense*; Nov., p. 10.
2713. **Disler, Jack R.:** *The Davies Zone Offense*; Dec., p. 22.
2714. **Edmonds, Ed:** *Triple Feature Fast Break Drill*; Nov., p. 22.
2715. **Filor, John:** *Snowplow Offense vs. a Man-for-Man*; Dec., p. 20.
2716. **Grady, Rex L.:** *The Low Post*; Oct., p. 12.
2717. **Gries, Donald L.:** *A Switching Zone Defense*; Nov., p. 8.
2718. **Handler, Fred D.:** *Basketball Scouting*; Oct., p. 32.
2719. **Hartle, James M.:** *Attacking Man-for-Man and Zone Presses*; Nov., p. 26.
2720. **Hill, George E.:** *The Fast Break Following an Opponent's Successful Free Throw*; Jan., p. 44.
2721. **Johnston, James N.:** *Combination Drills for the Press*; Dec., p. 24.
2722. **Joor, Robert H.:** *An Effective Out-of-Bounds Play*; Nov., p. 59.
2723. **Julian, Louis:** *Fundamental Drills to Develop a Winning Team at a Small School*; Sept., p. 26.
2724. **Key, Billy A.:** *Organizing a Fast Break*; Dec., p. 30.
2725. **Landa, Howie:** *Individual Offensive Moves*; Nov., p. 11.
2726. **Lewis, Fred:** *A Theory of Shot Discipline*; Oct., p. 9.

2727. **Lindeburg, Franklin A.:** *Unique Basketball Drills*; Nov., p. 24.
2728. **Lindsley, Herbert C.:** *Moving 1-3-1 Offensive Pattern*; Oct., p. 20.
2729. **Luce, Charles:** *A Mechanical Analysis of Jumping in Basketball*; Sept., p. 44.
2730. **McWhirter, Jeffries J.:** *The Application of Sociometric Technique in Basketball*; Nov., p. 32.
2731. **Noch, George D.:** *Drills for Successful Rebounding*; Nov., p. 42.
2732. **Paradise, Dom:** *Key the Guards*; Nov., p. 20.
2733. **Phillips, Goodrich:** *The Vertical I*; Nov., p. 34.
2734. **Porter, Archie and Campbell, Robbie:** *The Platoon System in Basketball*; Oct., p. 36.
2735. **Sells, Jim:** *Cordon the Box*; Oct., p. 24.; *Shoot from the Wrong Foot*; Dec., p. 19.
2736. **Severson, M.G.:** *Chasing Zone Offense*; Oct., p. 46.
2737. **Shublom, Walt:** *Preparing for Tournament Play*; Dec., p. 36.
2738. **Smith, Robert E. and Briner, Robert A.:** *Combating Basketball Staleness*; Jan., p. 70.
2739. **Watman, Thomas J.:** *Triangle Plus Two*; Nov., p. 28.
2740. **Wells, Cliff:** *Special Setups*; Oct., p. 50.
2741. **Winsor, Charles:** *Simplified Combination Offense*; Dec., p. 23.
2742. *1964 State Basketball Tournaments*; May, p. 10.

Volume 45, 1964–65

2743. **Baker, Paul M.:** *Methods of High School Basketball Conditioning*; Oct., p. 42.
2744. **Batogowski, Ed, Jr.:** *Officiating Fees for Basketball*; May, p. 10.
2745. **Batway, Charles:** *A Zone Offense*; Jan., p. 58.
2746. **Boesen, Marv:** *Not Press—Presses!*; Nov., p. 25.
2747. **Blake, Bob:** *Reverse Action for Counter Options*; Dec., p. 10.
2748. **Burger, Al:** *The Disciplined Offense*; Nov., p. 26.
2749. **Case, Wayne F.:** *Statistical and Chart Data—Advantages and Disadvantages*; Oct., p. 12.
2750. **Darr, John:** *Scoring on the Zone Press*; Dec., p. 8.
2751. **Ekker, Ronald:** *Get High Percentage Shots Against the Zone*; Nov., p. 36.
2752. **Feldmann, John A.:** *Purposeful Practice for Accurate Shooting*; Oct., p. 30.
2753. **Filor, John:** *The Percentage Play*; Nov., p. 50.
2754. **Freund, Al:** *Four Options Off the Reserve Action Offense*; Oct., p. 66.
2755. **Gibbons, Earl Eugene:** *An Rx for Intramural Basketball*; Dec., p. 47.
2756. **Gleaton, Nat:** *Training Versatility*; Oct., p. 9.
2757. **Grady, Rex:** *The Mechanical Defensive Pattern*; Nov., p. 34.
2758. **Hager, Ed:** *Attacking the Zone Defenses*; Dec., p. 9.
2759. **Hunter, Kenneth A.:** *Single Post Attack*; Nov., p. 8.
2760. **Johnston, James N.:** *Overcoming Offensive Height With the Combination Defense*; Dec., p. 23.
2761. **Joor, Robert H.:** *The Pick and Roll—Components and Variations*; Oct., p. 24.
2762. **Kernan, Ed:** *An Emergency Offense*; Feb., p. 8.
2763. **Kliewe, Louis:** *Pattern Defense*; Dec., p. 16.
2764. **Kowalk, Clayton J.:** *Basketball Managers—A Key to Organization Success*; Sept., p. 28.
2765. **Laterza, Tony:** *Akron's "Basic 10" Defensive Drills*; Sept., p. 110.
2766. **Lawrey, John F.:** *Four Option Offense for High Schools*; Oct., p. 48.
2767. **Livsey, Herb:** *The 1-1-3 Zone Defense*; Oct., p. 56.
2768. **Nitchman, Nelson W.:** *Various Basketball Strategies in 1964*; Nov., p. 33.
2769. **Obye, Charles H.:** *Basketball's Diagonal Cut Offense*; Oct., p. 22.
2770. **Orsborn, Chuck:** *An Offset High Pivot Offense*; Nov., p. 28.

2771. **Ortwerth, John G.:** *Quincy College's Reaction Teaching Techniques;* Oct., p. 34.
2772. **Oxford, Harry J.:** *All Fundamentals the Thirty-Minute Way;* Dec., p. 40.
2773. **Parker, George:** *Different Defensive Principles;* Dec., p. 15.
2774. **Picariello, S.J.:** *Defenses Deter Defeats;* Jan., p. 20.
2775. **Price, Fred:** *Attacking Pressure Defenses;* Nov., p. 40.
2776. **Quandt, H.G.:** *Cut Through Zone Offense;* Oct., p. 52.
2777. **Sanborn, John:** *The T and 1;* Oct., p. 62.
2778. **Severson, M.G. "Red":** *Drills for the Tall Man;* Nov., p. 20.
2779. **Summers, Art:** *Correct Basketball Statistics Using a Tape Recorder;* Sept., p. 31.
2780. **Swan, Jerry:** *One Is Enough Defense;* Jan., p. 42.
2781. **Tansey, Jim:** *A Complete Junior High Offense;* Nov., p. 68.
2782. **Turchi, Oliver G.:** *The Stalling Offense;* Jan., p. 48.
2783. **Van Buren, E. Gordon:** *Pre-Game Warm-Up Drills;* Nov., p. 16.
2784. **Wall, William L.:** *Single Post Variation Offense;* Oct., p. 20.
2785. **Winsor, Charles:** *Why the Half-Court Press;* Oct., p. 32; *Zone Attack With a Combination Offense;* Nov., p. 32.
2786. *1965 State Basketball Tournaments;* May, p. 48.

Volume 46, 1965–66

2787. **Bridges, Danny R.:** *The Shuffle Plus Interchanges;* Nov., p. 28.
2788. **Broaca, Peter:** *Attacking the Zone With Movement;* Nov., p. 26.
2789. **Carson, Glenn M.:** *Planned Variations Within the Shuffle;* Sept., p. 60.
2790. **Edwards, John, Jr.:** *Drills for the Development of Aggressiveness in Basketball;* Sept., p. 34.
2791. **Gourdouze, Frank:** *"T" Off on the Presses;* Nov., p. 15.
2792. **Hanson, Dr. Dale L.:** *Scientific Basis of Pre-Season and Early Season Training for Basketball;* Sept., p. 80.
2793. **Harris, Del:** *The A Offense;* Dec., p. 8.
2794. **Hobbs, Joe:** *An Analysis of Offensive Moves to Promote Better Defensive Preparation;* Nov., p. 54; *A Successful Multiple Man-for-Man Zone Continuity Attack;* Dec., p. 12.
2795. **Howell, Fred "Dixie":** *Duel-Purpose Freeze;* Oct., p. 54.
2796. **Huberty, Carl J.:** *It's the Little Things That Count;* Nov., p. 19.
2797. **Hunter, Kenneth A.:** *Basketball Scouting;* Nov., p. 18.
2798. **Jones, Norman:** *Organizing the Fast Break;* Sept., p. 90.
2799. **Keeling, Al:** *Attacking the Man-for-Man With a Tight Pattern;* Nov., p. 14.
2800. **King, Don:** *The Shortcut Rotation Zone Offense;* Oct., p. 18.
2801. **Kloppenburg, Bob:** *Two-in-One Offense;* Oct., p. 20.
2802. **Kowalk, Clayton J.:** *The Fundamental Outlook;* Sept., p. 18.
2803. **Lambert, Paul:** *Organization and Drilling for the Fast Break;* Nov., p. 17.
2804. **Landa, Howie:** *Training for Dribbling;* Nov., p. 10.
2805. **Leonard, Desmond:** *Attacking the UCLA Press With the Shifting 1-3-1;* Dec., p. 20.
2806. **Lockhart, Paul D.:** *Zone Offense by the Numbers;* Oct., p. 46.
2807. **Longfellow, Floyd, Jr.:** *Fast Break Analysis Chart;* Nov., p. 16.
2808. **McKay, Joseph D.:** *Developing the Pick-and-Roll Continuity Offense;* Sept., p. 92.
2809. **Miller, Bob:** *Tournament Time;* Mar., p. 82.
2810. **Mohr, Rich:** *The Quick Basket Against a Man-for-Man Defense;* Nov., p. 44.
2811. **Nettles, Barry:** *Attacking the Zone;* Oct., p. 19.
2812. **Nissalke, Tom:** *A Simple Press Offense;* Oct., p. 24.
2813. **Payton, John E.:** *Teaching Team Man-for-Man Defense;* Jan., p. 40.

2814. **Quenette, Bill:** *A Simple, Organized Free-Lane Offense*; Oct., p. 12.
2815. **Rocha, Red:** *Pass Reception in the Pivot*; Oct., p. 8.
2816. **Rogers, Dan S.:** *The Principles of Pressure Defense*; Dec., p. 18.
2817. **Severson, M.G. "Red":** *An All-Zone Offense*; Nov., p. 30.
2818. **Smith, Dr. Huron J.:** *A Wide-and-Open Basketball Offense*; Nov., p. 34.
2819. **Underwood, Don:** *One Version of the "Square"*; Dec., p. 13.
2820. **Van Buren, E. Gordon:** *Out-of-Bounds Plays Mean Baskets*; Nov., p. 41.
2821. **Van Ryswyk, Dr. Don:** *Weak Side Twin Post—An All-Purpose Attack*; Oct., p. 22.
2822. **Waters, Roy T.:** *An Offense for the 1-3-1 and 1-2-2 Zones*; Oct., p. 26.
2823. **Wells, Cliff:** *The NCAA Basketball Finals*; May, p. 14.
2824. *1966 State Basketball Tournaments*; May, p. 40.

Volume 47, 1966–67

2825. **Anderson, Eugene W.:** *Shuffle Specials*; Dec., p. 18.
2826. **Arnold, Frank H.:** *A Combination Set Pattern–Free Lance Offense*; Nov., p. 32.
2827. **Bennett, Carrol:** *Try the I*; Nov., p. 16.
2828. **Bennett, Jan:** *Revolving Offense*; Oct., p. 26.
2829. **Boudreaux, Roland:** *Setting Up the High Scorers*; Oct., p. 42.
2830. **Brown, Herb:** *Attacking the Various Zones*; Dec., p. 42.
2831. **Brown, Lyle:** *Low Budget Movies Can Help the Team Win*; Sept., p. 54.
2832. **Case, Wayne:** *The Rochester Fast Break*; Sept., p. 32.
2833. **Cotton, Richard:** *A Two-Two-One Zone Press With a Twist*; Oct., p. 52.
2834. **Dintiman, Dr. George B. and Hughes, Tom:** *Basketball Off-Season Training—The Development and Correction Period*; June, p. 28.
2835. **Disler, Jack R.:** *The Pro Offense*; Nov., p. 12.
2836. **Eskridge, Bill:** *Score When You Foul*; Nov., p. 8.
2837. **Forsythe, Larry:** *The Double Post Offense*; Oct., p. 8.
2838. **Fulton, Cliff:** *Attacking the Zone Press*; Oct., p. 10.
2839. **Grady, Rex:** *Defensive Transitions*; Nov., p. 14.
2840. **Hager, Ed:** *Pre-Season Basketball Conditioning*; Oct. p. 24.
2841. **Harmond, Bill:** *Supplementing the 3-2 Zone With the Tri-Lane Fast Break*; Nov., p. 18.
2842. **Hughes, Tom and Dintiman, Dr. George B.:** *Basketball Off-Season Training—The Development and Correction Period*; June, p. 28.
2843. **Johnston, James N.:** *The Rip Series*; Oct., p. 44.
2844. **Karabetsos, John:** *A Junior High School Offense*; Oct., p. 62.
2845. **Kasmer, Donald C.:** *The Point Press*; Dec., p. 26.
2846. **Ledbetter, Virgil:** *A Zone Offense With Principles*; Nov., p. 71.
2847. **Lockhart, Paul D.:** *We Would Rather Fight Than Switch*; Nov., p. 38.
2848. **Nettles, Barry:** *Attacking the Zone Press*; Nov., p. 40.
2849. **Nitardy, Dr. Walter J.:** *Developing an Aggressive Team Defense*; Dec., p. 37.
2850. **Nitchman, Nelson W.:** *A Variety of 1966 Basketball Offensive Moves*; Sept., p. 40; *The Best of 1967 Basketball Offense*; May, p. 19.
2851. **Noch, George D.:** *Beating the Zones*; Oct., p. 36.
2852. **Sage, Dr. George H.:** *Offensive Moves From the Low Post*; Oct., p. 12.
2853. **Severson, M.G.:** *Offensive Drills*; Jan., p. 60.
2854. **Stockholm, Alan J.:** *Shuffle the Easy Way*; Nov., p. 30.
2855. **Van Wie, Alvin J.:** *Teaching a Man-for-Man Defense With Zone Principles*; Nov., p. 20.
2856. **Verducci, Frank:** *Mirror Offense in Basketball*; Nov., p. 36.
2857. **Weinberg, Harry C.:** *Basketball Checklist*; Sept., p. 36.

2858. **Wissel, Harold R.:** *Interval Training for Basketball Players*; June, p. 22.
2859. **Wyllie, Lawrence A.:** *Attacking the Box-and-One*; Dec., p. 49.
2860. *1967 State Basketball Tournaments*; May, p. 88.

Volume 48, 1967–68

2861. **Allsen, Dr. Philip E.:** *The Rebound Area*; Sept., p. 34.
2862. **Anderson, Eugene W.:** *The Overload Principle in a Basketball Drill*; Sept., p. 20.
2863. **Baker, Willard G.:** *The Three-Up Zone Press*; Dec., p. 20.
2864. **Bash, Ron:** *Please Make the Free Throw*; Sept., p. 36.
2865. **Bataitis, George P.:** *"No Basket" Basketball: A Pre-Season Conditioner*; Sept., p. 52.
2866. **Breyfogle, Newell D.:** *Basketball Scouting Views*; Oct., p. 60.
2867. **Bryant, James E.:** *Percentage Rebounding*; Dec., p. 21.
2868. **Criss, Art:** *Principles and Variations of the 3-2 Zone*; Dec., p. 36.
2869. **Damore, Patrick R.:** *Last Shot to Win*; Nov., p. 43.
2870. **Ellis, R. "Buzz":** *Circuit Training for Basketball*; Oct., p. 14.
2871. **Eskidge, Bill:** *A Match-Up Half-Court Zone Press*; Nov., p. 46.
2872. **Esposito, Michael:** *Countering the Presses*; Oct., p. 46.
2873. **Ferrara, Dom:** *The Three-Two Trap*; Oct., p. 56.
2874. **Fulton, Cliff and Meinhardt, Tom:** *Area Rules for a 1-1-2-1 Half-Court Press*; Nov., p. 52.
2875. **Gonzalez, Billy G.:** *Two-in-One Offense*; Nov., p. 28.
2876. **Gourdouze, Frank:** *Erase the Floater*; Nov., p. 32.
2877. **Harris, Brooks:** *Clear-Out Series*; Oct., p. 44.
2878. **Harvey, John H.:** *Challenge and Strategy of One-on-One Defense*; Oct., p. 16.
2879. **Held, Norman:** *ABC's of the Zone Defense*; Sept., p. 31.
2880. **Jones, Norm:** *The Outlet Pass Starts the Fast Break*; Oct., p. 12.
2881. **Landa, Howie:** *Molding a Corner Man*; Nov., p. 22.
2882. **Landry, Don:** *Pre-Practice Organization*; Sept., p. 71.
2883. **Marchio, Sam:** *Odd and Even Front Offense*; Oct., p. 42.
2884. **Mathiesen, Pete:** *Combining the Swing-and-Go and the Reverse Action*; Oct., p. 36.
2885. **McKie, Ernie:** *Teaching the Jump Shot*; Sept., p. 38.
2886. **Meinhardt, Tom and Fulton, Cliff:** *Area Rules for a 1-1-2-1 Half-Court Press*; Nov., p. 52.
2887. **Mohatt, E. Skip:** *Attacking the Zone Again!*; Nov., p. 48.
2888. **Morse, Bill:** *An Out-of-Bounds Play Which Works Against a Zone or Man-for-Man*; Nov., p. 9.
2889. **Nitchman, Nelson W.:** *Variety of Attacks to Meet Today's Multiplicity of Defenses*; May, p. 12.
2890. **Rinella, Joe:** *Strong-Side Offense for Beating the Zones*; Oct., p. 74.
2891. **Rosmarin, Ed M.:** *Try Telegraphic Free Throw Competition*; Oct., p. 64.
2892. **Sesbeau, Joseph:** *Control and Prevention of Injuries in Basketball*; Sept., p. 32.
2893. **Stier, William F., Jr.:** *The Triangular Continuity*; Nov., p. 13; *Pass-Inviting Press*; Dec., p. 30.
2894. **Weiskopf, Don:** *Jump Shooting*; Oct., p. 18.
2895. **Worrell, Paul:** *The Anatomy of the One-on-One*; Oct., p. 8.
2896. *1968 State Basketball Tournaments*; May, p. 52.

Volume 49, 1968–69

2897. **Baker, Willard:** *1-3-1 Zone Offense Options;* Nov., p. 16.
2898. **Bennett, Carrol:** *Beating the Man-for-Man With a Single Side Offense;* Nov., p. 31.
2899. **Bolton, Bill:** *An Economical Device for Developing Jumping Ability;* Sept., p. 58.
2900. **Curtiss, Tom and Gutierrez, Bud:** *Why the Wrist Flip?;* Sept., p. 28.
2901. **Deckrosh, Hazen D.:** *Give 'Em the Gate;* Oct., p. 30.
2902. **Esposito, Michael:** *Strategy Against a Strong Man-for-Man Defense;* Nov., p. 52.
2903. **Gonzalez, Billy G.:** *1-2-1-1 Half-Court Press;* Nov., p. 40.
2904. **Gourdouze, Frank:** *Interchangeable Pressure Offense;* Oct., p. 41.
2905. **Gutierrez, Bud and Curtiss, Tom:** *Why the Wrist Flip?;* Sept., p. 28.
2906. **Hager, Ed:** *Control the Tempo With the Offense;* Oct., p. 41.
2907. **Harris, Delmer:** *Playing the Running Game With a Small Team;* Oct., p. 56.
2908. **Key, Gary L.:** *Squeeze Dribble;* Sept., p. 46.
2909. **LaGrand, Louis A.:** *Cross-Rebounding Drills for Best Reactions;* Oct., p. 22.
2910. **Lindsley, Herbert C.:** *Scoring on Out-of-Bounds Situations;* Sept., p. 70; *The Wild Man Press;* Oct., p. 18.
2911. **Logue, Errol:** *The Simplified 2-2-1 Zone Press for Young Players;* Oct., p. 28.
2912. **McBee, Gene:** *Penetrating the Zone with Minimum Preparation;* Oct., p. 38.
2913. **McLaughlin, F.J. "Spike":** *Run the Circle;* Oct., p. 54.
2914. **McPhee, Len:** *Free Throw Fast Break;* Dec., p. 26.
2915. **Moran, Sonny and Waters, Bucky:** *Defending the Pivot Area;* Nov., p. 10.
2916. **Nitchman, Nelson W.:** *This Year's Basketball Offenses;* June, p. 22.
2917. **Oldham, John:** *Western's 2-3 Offense;* Oct., p. 25; *Four Box Out-of-Bounds Plays;* Nov., p. 36.
2918. **Paradise, Dom:** *Attacking All Types of Zones;* Dec., p. 42; *Key the Point Man;* Jan., p. 64.
2919. **Saccone, Lou:** *Basketball Practice Organization;* Sept., p. 80.
2920. **Smith, Chuck:** *Ball-Handling Pays Off;* Oct., p. 34.
2921. **Smith, Dennis L.:** *Score With the Dealing Diamond;* Dec., p. 56.
2922. **Smithson, Gene:** *A Multi-Press Offense;* Oct., p. 48.
2923. **Stier, William F., Jr.:** *Statistics Play by Play;* Sept., p. 34; *Screening—Today's Most Neglected Phase of Basketball;* Oct., p. 60; *Stopping the Even-Odd Zones By Matching-Up;* Nov., p. 42; *A Delayed Action Out-of-Bounds Series;* Dec., p. 32.
2924. **Tansey, James J.:** *Sound Approach to the Basketball Feeder Program;* Sept., p. 90.
2925. **Unice, John P.:** *Driving—A Fundamental Basketball Skill;* Nov., p. 68.
2926. **Waters, Bucky and Moran, Sonny:** *Defending the Pivot Area;* Nov., p. 10.
2927. **Wilson, John R., Jr.:** *The Reverse Continuity;* Dec., p. 44.
2928. *1969 Basketball Tournaments;* June, p. 54.

Volume 50, 1969–70

2929. **Allsen, P.E. and Ruffner, William:** *Relationship Between the Type of Pass and the Loss of the Ball in Basketball;* Sept., p. 94.
2930. **Ammann, Kenneth M.:** *Offensive Post Movement;* Sept., p. 51.
2931. **Anderson, Robert B.:** *Attack the Zone with a 1-2-2;* Oct., p. 30.
2932. **Bennett, Jan:** *Tight 1-2-2 Offense;* Nov., p. 16.
2933. **Chiappy, John E.:** *The I in Basketball;* Oct., p. 40.
2934. **Criss, Art:** *The Effectiveness of the Power Move Offense;* Oct., p. 18.
2935. **Dobbert, John:** *An Out-of-Bounds Play for All Defenses;* Nov., p. 22.

2936. **Ellmers, Edwin:** *Rebounding the Missed Offensive Free Throw*; Oct., p. 38.
2937. **Gaffey, Bill:** *To Tip or Not to Tip*; Oct., p. 20.
2938. **Gonzalez, Billy G.:** *Score With a Freeze Pattern*; Dec., p. 16.
2939. **Harkins, Mike:** *Bang-Bang Plays*; Oct., p. 60.
2940. **Harris, Del:** *Footwork—Key to Good Jump Shooting*; Oct., p. 13; *Footwork for the Outside and Inside Jump Shot*; Nov., p. 10.
2941. **Herring, Ralph W.:** *Importance of Well-Organized Pre-Game Drills*; Oct., p. 74.
2942. **Hill, George:** *The 1-2-2 Three-Quarter Court Zone Press*; Nov., p. 26.
2943. **Huntington, George:** *A Stack Offense Against the Box-and-One*; Dec., p. 24.
2944. **Hurst, Hugh:** *One-on-One*; Oct., p. 46.
2945. **Huston, Ronald F.:** *The Warrior Press*; Dec., p. 36.
2946. **Jackard, Charles Roy, Jr.:** *Shuffle Single Post Continuity Offense*; Nov., p. 24.
2947. **Longo, George:** *Pressure on the Out-of-Bounds Play*; Nov., p. 40.
2948. **MacLeod, John:** *Oklahoma's Defensive Gems*; Oct., p. 26.
2949. **McKie, Ernie:** *Is Your Defense Obsolete?*; Nov., p. 38.
2950. **Miller, Paul F.:** *Double-Up*; Dec., p. 27.
2951. **Nitchman, Nelson W.:** *Basketball Offenses*; June, p. 16.
2952. **Oldham, John:** *Defensive Basketball Situations*; Dec., p. 10.
2953. **Phillips, Goodrich K.:** *New Concept in the Fast Break*; Oct., p. 50.
2954. **Ruffner, William and Allsen, P.E.:** *Relationship Between the Type of Pass and the Loss of the Ball in Basketball*; Sept., p. 94.
2955. **Satalin, Frank, Jr.:** *The Box-and-One as an Element of Surprise*; Dec., p. 24.
2956. **Schakel, Doug:** *The Stack*; Oct., p. 56.
2957. **Schoepfer, Martin:** *The Gap and Rotate Zone Offense*; Oct., p. 42.
2958. **Smith, Dennis L.:** *Beat the Box-and-One With the Swinging Gate*; Nov., p. 54.
2959. **Snyder, Jack:** *The Head-Hunter Shuffle*; Oct., p. 44.
2960. **Stier, Wililam F., Jr.:** *The Sideline Control Fast Break*; Nov., p. 32; *Use Multi-Purpose Drills*; Oct., p. 10.
2961. **Sweet, Virgil:** *Free Throw Shooting Heresy*; Dec., p. 28.
2962. **William, Carroll L.:** *Two-Man Shooting Drills for the Shuffle*; Sept., p. 22.
2963. **Wilson, Larry L.:** *3 Rule Defense*; Dec., p. 30.
2964. *Basketball Makes the Rounds*; Nov., p. 52.
2965. *1970 State Basketball Tournaments*; June, p. 38.

Volume 51, 1970–71

2966. **Barnes, Bill G.:** *A 1-3-1 Rotation Offense*; Dec., p. 48.
2967. **Bennett, Carrol L.:** *Philosophy and Use of a 1-2-2 Press*; Nov., p. 12.
2968. **Bybee, Phil D. and Gonzalez, Billy G.:** *Wide Post Shuffle*; Oct., p. 28.
2969. **Darnall, David:** *The 1-2-2 Adjustable Zone*; Dec., p. 56.
2970. **Ellis, John:** *Offensive Moves Versus Denial Defense*; Nov., p. 42.
2971. **Estes, Jack:** *Triple Option Offense*; Dec., p. 54.
2972. **Field, Charles:** *A Good Press From All Areas*; Dec., p. 39.
2973. **Fulton, Cliff and Hartley, Joe W.:** *Mechanical Analysis of the Jump Shot*; Mar., p. 92.
2974. **Glover, Bruce L.:** *A Shuffle That Stops*; Oct., p. 14; *Preparing the Team for Meeting a Zone*; Nov., p. 8.
2975. **Gonzalez, Billy G. and Bybee, Phil D.:** *Wide Post Shuffle*; Oct., p. 28.
2976. **Hartley, Joe W. and Fulton, Cliff:** *Mechanical Analysis of the Jump Shot*; Mar., p. 92.
2977. **Hobson, Howard A.:** *Western and Eastern Basketball (50th Anniversary)*; Oct., p. 37.
2978. **Huberty, Dr. Carl J.:** *Where the Rebounds Fall*; Sept., p. 54.

2979. **King, George:** *Freeing the Jump Shooter*; Mar., p. 96.
2980. **LaGrand, Louis E.:** *Dual Purpose Zone Attack*; Oct., p. 12.
2981. **McBee, George:** *Strong-Side Offense*; Dec., p. 58.
2982. **Nitchman, Nelson W.:** *This Season's Offenses*; May, p. 10.
2983. **Pinkham, I.J.:** *Three-Part Continuity for the Small Team*; Nov., p. 34.
2984. **Schakel, Doug:** *The Stack Versus Man-for-Man Defense*; Nov., p. 19.
2985. **Schneider, Walter:** *Get Those Jump Balls*; Jan., p. 30.
2986. **Scholl, Wayne:** *Progressive Presssure Defensive Drills*; Nov., p. 26.
2987. **Smithson, Gene:** *The 0-1-4 Attack*; Nov., p. 22.
2988. **Stier, William F., Jr.:** *Inside Continuity Against the Zone*; Nov., p. 29.
2989. **Updike, Buddy:** *Fast Break After a Score*; Dec., p. 42.
2990. **Wasem, Jim:** *Pressure Defense*; Dec., p. 26.
2991. **Waters, Bucky:** *Liberating the Standing Guard*; Mar., p. 80.
2992. **Watkins, Dave:** *Dickinson's 31 Series*; Oct., p. 22.
2993. **Welch, Ronald E.:** *Single File Drill*; Oct., p. 54.
2994. **Wilson, Larry L.:** *Fundamentals in Thirteen Minutes*; Oct., p. 52; *Use the Stagger Against a Full Court Press*; Dec., p. 52.
2995. *1971 State Basketball Tournaments*; June, p. 38.

Volume 52, 1971–72

2996. **Aizina, Jack:** *To Hook or Not to Hook*; Oct., p. 44.
2997. **Arietta, Ralph:** *Defensive Rebounding for Free Throws*; Nov., p. 16.
2998. **Bamford, Stephen:** *The Zone Press Breaker*; Oct., p. 48.
2999. **Collins, Darrel:** *A Right and Left Movement Against Zone Pressure*; Oct., p. 28.
3000. **Darnall, David:** *Overload With the Double Low Post*; Jan., p. 46.
3001. **Dutcher, James:** *Building a Sound Defense*; Oct., p. 63.
3002. **Eskridge, Bill:** *Seven Combination Drills*; Oct., p. 54.
3003. **Field, Charles A.:** *Basics Against the Even-Out Defense*; Dec., p. 24.
3004. **Ford, Duane:** *One Play Offense*; Oct., p. 38.
3005. **Gooch, Stan:** *Break from the Free Throw*; Jan., p. 64.
3006. **Harnum, Don:** *The Crazy 8's*; Sept., p. 26.
3007. **Hester, Tom:** *Tight Stack Offense*; Jan., p. 38.
3008. **Kahler, Thomas and Wilson, Larry:** *Get That Jump Ball*; Nov., p. 8.
3009. **Kaminer, Jack:** *1-2-2 Half-Court Zone Press*; Jan., p. 68.
3010. **Kipnes, Barry D.:** *The 1-2-2 Offense vs. Various Zones*; Nov., p. 50.
3011. **Knauss, Don E.:** *In-Season Weight Training Program for Basketball*; Sept., p. 31.
3012. **Miller, C. Richard:** *Big Man Moves*; Oct., p. 8; *The 3-2 Half-Court Press*; Nov., p. 24.
3013. **Moormeier, Don:** *Percentage Rebounding*; Nov., p. 10.
3014. **Morgan, Bob:** *The Multiple Zone Defense*; Dec., p. 20.
3015. **Nickols, John M.:** *Teaching a Containment Pressure Back Court Defense*; Sept., p. 48.
3016. **Nitardy, Dr. Walter J.:** *Drills for Teaching Individual Pressure Defense*; Oct., p. 56; *Basketball Drills for Teaching Team Offense*; Nov., p. 40.
3017. **Nitchman, Nelson W.:** *1971–72 Basketball Offenses*; Nov., p. 40.
3018. **O'Neal, Bill:** *Combining the 1-3-1 and the 2-2-1 Zone Presses*; Nov., p. 54.
3019. **Potts, Charles A., Jr.:** *Attacking the Two-Guard Zones*; Nov., p. 56.
3020. **Richey, Gary L.:** *The Stretched I, an Out-of-Bounds Offense*; Oct., p. 46.
3021. **Shambarger, Jack:** *An Adjusting 1-2-2 Zone Defense*; Nov., p. 38.
3022. **Smith, Dennis L.:** *Beat the Zone With the 1-3-1 Inside-Outside Attack*; Dec., p. 7.
3023. **Smith, Sonny:** *Dribble Pick Zone Offense*; Oct., p. 37.

3024. **Sweeney, Thomas:** *Defensive Confusion*; Jan., p. 60.
3025. **Viasin, Ronald:** *Breaking the 3-1-1 Press*; Jan., p. 16.
3026. **Wasem, Jim:** *A Simplified Stunting Defense*; Nov., p. 36.
3027. **Williams, Carroll L.:** *An Offense That Wins While Teaching Fundamentals*; Oct., p. 32.
3028. **Wilson, Bob:** *Pressure Defense and Trapping Techniques*; Dec., p. 15.
3029. **Wilson, Larry and Kahler, Thomas:** *Get That Jump Ball*; Nov., p. 8.
3030. *1972 State Basketball Tournaments*; June, p. 46.

Volume 53, 1972–73

3031. **Aizina, Jack:** *Reflections on the Practice Session*; Sept., p. 56.
3032. **Beiz, Paul:** *Individual Defense*; Oct., p. 8.
3033. **Bennett, Carrol:** *Use a Poised Anti-Press*; Nov., p. 14.
3034. **Collins, Darrel:** *Offense Against the Zone*; Oct., p. 24.
3035. **Davies, Tom:** *1-4 Full Court Press Attack*; Dec., p. 17.
3036. **DeVoe, Donald E.:** *Virginia Tech Defense*; Nov., p. 26.
3037. **Dunaway, Larry:** *Beat the Man-for-Man with an Overload*; Oct., p. 14.
3038. **Edelman, Sonny:** *A Sliding, Trapping Defense*; Oct., p. 62; *The Constantly Changing Defense*; Dec., p. 43.
3039. **Field, Charles:** *A Variety of Practice Methods and Drills*; Oct., p. 12.
3040. **Ford, Duane:** *Stopping the Exceptional Scorer*; Dec., p. 12.
3041. **Ford, Jack S.:** *The Long Pass Drill*; Oct., p. 42.
3042. **Galley, Bill:** *Developing the Shuffle Offense Into Pre-Game Drills*; Sept., p. 82.
3043. **Gonzalez, Billy G.:** *The Passing 2-2-1 Zone*; Nov., p. 46.
3044. **Hallihan, Jim:** *Pressure Man-for-Man and the Overplay*; Dec., p. 8.
3045. **Henada, Roger:** *Five Basic Rules for Attacking the Full Court Press*; Oct., p. 28.
3046. **Hostetter, Carlisle:** *Man-for-Man Offense*; Nov., p. 50.
3047. **Majick, David A.:** *The Go-Down Offense*; Nov., p. 32.
3048. **Musselman, Bill:** *Minnesota's Match-Up Zone*; Nov., p. 40.
3049. **Nickols, John M.:** *Teaching Front Court Defense*; Oct., p. 38.
3050. **Nitardy, Dr. Walter J.:** *Rebounding Drills*; Oct., p. 60.
3051. **Nitchman, Nelson W.:** *The Season in Review*; June, p. 16.
3052. **Parr, Daniel J.:** *Inside Patterns and Variations*; Oct., p. 44.
3053. **Riley, Douglas:** *Conditioning and Agility Drills*; Dec., p. 23.
3054. **Rinaldi, Anthony S.:** *I Formation Zone Press*; Nov., p. 12.
3055. **Ruggiero, George:** *All-Purpose Offense*; Oct., p. 54.
3056. **Sands, Gary:** *Individually Rating Basketball Players*; May, p. 53.
3057. **Smith, Jerry:** *Offensive Plays*; Oct., p. 30.
3058. **Smith, Sonny:** *Phases of Offensive Post Play*; Oct., p. 32.
3059. **Stephens, Sherrill:** *Two-Man Press*; Nov., p. 48.
3060. **Sweeten, Elvin R.:** *Single Post Offense That Wins*; Oct., p. 46.
3061. **Tansey, Jim:** *Octopus Offense*; Nov., p. 20.
3062. **Wall, Carol:** *The 1-4 Offense for Low Post Play*; Oct., p. 56.
3063. **Walsack, Robert:** *Defending the Clear-Out*; Oct., p. 53.
3064. **Weinert, John:** *1-4 Offense—An Offense for All Seasons*; Nov., p. 8.
3065. **Wilson, Frank and Yaksick, Rudy:** *Agility and Reaction Program*; Nov., p. 22.
3066. **Wilson, Larry L.:** *Don't Dribble—Rotate*; Dec., p. 14.
3067. **Yaksick, Rudy and Wilson, Frank:** *Agility and Reaction Program*; Nov., p. 22.
3068. *1973 State Basketball Tournaments*; June, p. 54.

Volume 54, 1973–74

3069. **Boller, W. Curt:** *2-Minute Drill*; Sept., p. 22.
3070. **Breves, Ray:** *Four-Line Continuous Fast Break Conditioning Drills*; Nov., p. 58.
3071. **Britner, Eric:** *A Simplified Zone Offense for Junior High School*; Oct., p. 54.
3072. **Covelski, Donald J.:** *Options for the Full Court Press*; Oct., p. 42; *A Master Practice Outline*; Nov., p. 62.
3073. **Edelman, Sonny:** *The 30-Minute Drill*; Dec., p. 48.
3074. **Falls, Harry, Jr.:** *Out-of-Bounds Series*; Dec., p. 12.
3075. **Fengler, Hank:** *Developing Ball-Handling Skills*; Sept., p. 28; *Drills for Dribbling*; Oct., p. 19.
3076. **Gonzalez, Billy G.:** *Three Guard Shuffle*; Nov., p. 34.
3077. **Hancock, Thomas C. and Wyllie, Lawrence A.:** *The Triangle and Two*; Oct., p. 36.
3078. **Hankinson, Mel:** *1-2-2 Multiple Match-Up Press*; Nov., p. 56.
3079. **Hurst, Hugh:** *Free Throw Line Situations*; Oct., p. 32.
3080. **Irvin, Calvin:** *Developing a Low Post Attack*; Oct., p. 44; *An Effective Press*; Jan., p. 50.
3081. **Jenkins, F. Compton:** *Diversionary Tactics for Off-Season Basketball*; May, p. 20.
3082. **Kaminer, Jack:** *Movement Offense for the Small Team*; Nov., p. 32.
3083. **Karhu, Milo and Phillippi, Donald:** *Officiating by the Numbers*; May, p. 54.
3084. **Klein, George:** *Ohio University's Exchange Defense*; Dec., p. 40.
3085. **Knuckle, Bob:** *The Pinching Press*; Nov., p. 50.
3086. **Lien, Richard D.:** *Rebound Those Missed Free Throws*; Oct., p. 50; *Don't Let the Opponents Rebound Missed Free Throws*; Nov., p. 8.
3087. **Litzenberger, Fred and Meyer, Don:** *Hamline's Off-Season Basketball Program*; June, p. 38.
3088. **Lucas, Ron:** *The 1-4 Breakers*; Oct., p. 46.
3089. **MacPhee, Leonard:** *Drill Sequence for Basketball Conditioning*; Nov., p. 30.
3090. **Macres, Dick:** *The Ramrod Offense*; Nov., p. 54.
3091. **McCarthy, Neil:** *The Mixer Offense*; Nov., p.24.
3092. **Meyer, Don and Litzenberger, Fred:** *Hamline's Off-Season Basketball Program*; June, p. 38.
3093. **Miller, Ken:** *Basic Attack Versus Zones*; Nov., p. 16.
3094. **Mills, Sam:** *Nine Quickie Drills*; Jan., p. 36.
3095. **Nichols, Robert:** *Passing Fancy*; Oct., p. 8; *Forwards Take a Peek*; Nov., p. 18.
3096. **Nitchman, Nelson:** *1973–74 Basketball Offense*; June, p. 10.
3097. **Palladino, Gary A.:** *Scientific Approach to Successful Free Throwing*; Nov., p. 52.
3098. **Phillippi, Donald and Karhu, Milo:** *Officiating by the Numbers*; May, p. 54.
3099. **Richey, Gary L.:** *The Fluctuating 1-2-2 Zone*; Nov., p. 48.
3100. **Rodich, Sam:** *Rx for Basketball's Crooked Elbow*; Nov., p. 14.
3101. **Satalin, Frank:** *Put Continuity in Your 2-1-2 Offense*; Oct., p. 34.
3102. **Schakel, Doug:** *The Double Stack Delay Game*; Dec., p. 14.
3103. **Sieman, Ronald S.:** *Stack the Zones*; Jan., p. 28.
3104. **Sweeten, Elvin R.:** *Fundamental Drills for Girls' Basketball*; Oct., ·p. 56.
3105. **Updike, Buddy:** *Simplified Method of Teaching Jump Shooting*; Sept., p. 26.
3106. **VanGundy, Bill:** *Individual Defense Drill*; Dec., p. 18.
3107. **Walker, Lee:** *Putting the Word* Team *in Your Offense*; Dec., p. 44.
3108. **Wilson, Bob:** *Station Drills for Better Fundamentals*; Oct., p. 40.
3109. **Wyllie, Lawrence A. and Hancock, Thomas C.:** *The Triangle and Two*; Oct., p. 36.
3110. *1974 State Basketball Tournaments*; June, p. 56.

Volume 55, 1974–75

3111. **Bash, Dr. Ronald:** *Give Your Break an Angle;* Sept., p. 8.
3112. **Cotton, Richard:** *Press the Modern Way;* Nov., p. 22.
3113. **Daniel, Mike:** *Shuffle Steps in Post Play;* Oct., p. 54.
3114. **Daniels, Bob:** *A Unique 1-3-1 Offense;* Oct., p. 38.
3115. **Fengler, Hank:** *Countdown for Quickness: The Timed Practice;* Dec., p. 46.
3116. **Field, Charles A.:** *Rebounding;* Nov., p. 48; *Four Basic Zone Defenses;* Dec., p. 10.
3117. **Ford, Duane:** *Developing the Strong Inside Game;* Dec., p. 8.
3118. **Foss, Bill:** *A Running Pre-Set Offense;* Nov., p. 80.
3119. **Gonzalez, Billy G.:** *Breakdown Drills of the Three Guard Shuffle;* Oct., p. 36; *Post Moves off the Three Guard Shuffle;* Nov., p. 26.
3120. **Hanna, George A.:** *2-in-1 Drill;* Oct., p. 26.
3121. **Hill, Lewis:** *Positional Offense;* Sept., p. 28.
3122. **Jackson, Marcus:** *Rotate and Step Offense Versus 1-2-2 Zone Defense;* Oct., p. 22.
3123. **Johns, Mary Lou:** *Circuit Stations for Practice Warm-Up;* Sept., p. 64; *The Reverse and Cross-Over;* Oct., p. 8.
3124. **Kelly, James:** *Drilling the 2-2-1 Zone Press;* Jan., p. 38.
3125. **Knight, Bob:** *1-3-1 Man-for-Man Continuity;* Nov., p. 14.
3126. **Kolsky, Michael B.:** *The City Game;* Dec., p. 50.
3127. **Landa, Howie:** *Fast Break Continuity;* Oct., p. 40.
3128. **Littlepage, Craig K.:** *Individual Man-for-Man Defense;* Oct., p. 52.
3129. **Litzenberger, Fred and Meyer, Don:** *Make Those Free Throws;* Oct., p. 12; *Hamline's Shooting Drills;* Nov., p. 16.
3130. **Long, Albert:** *Another Attack on the Zone;* Jan., p. 8.
3131. **Marks, Alan:** *Develop the Fast Break With Drills;* Nov., p. 42.
3132. **Meyer, Don and Litzenberger, Fred:** *Make Those Free Throws;* Oct., p. 12; *Hamline's Shooting Drills;* Nov., p. 16.
3133. **Mills, Sam:** *The Series Offense to Challenge the Outstanding Player;* Jan., p. 30.
3134. **Nitchman, Nelson:** *1974–75 Basketball Offense;* June, p. 18.
3135. **Parr, Daniel J.:** *The Big Wheel Offense;* Nov., p. 18.
3136. **Sisson, Kenneth:** *Practice Planning;* Oct., p. 34.
3137. **Stoll, Jerry A.:** *Improve Defensive Play With a Defensive Tournament;* Dec., p. 58.
3138. **Voth, Robert:** *The Triple Stack for Inside Power;* Jan., p. 46.
3139. **Walker, Lee:** *Put the Word Team in Your Offense Against the Zone;* Nov., p. 62.
3140. **Wilson, Larry:** *Basketball Double Vision;* Nov., p. 87.
3141. **Winter, Tex:** *Developing the Big Man;* Dec., p. 62.
3142. **Winters, Bob:** *Rotating Full Court Match-Up Press;* Oct., p. 64.
3143. *1975 State Basketball Tournaments;* June, p. 48.

Volume 56, 1975–76

3144. **Bennett, Jan S.:** *Four Corners Delay Game;* Nov., p. 38.
3145. **Cain, James:** *Inside Moves for the Post Man;* Nov., p. 48.
3146. **Congdon, Robert E.:** *Drill for Reaction;* Oct., p. 67.
3147. **Covelski, Donald J.:** *Stacking Against a Zone;* Nov., p. 14.
3148. **Gonzalez, Billy G.:** *The 2-2-1 Man-for-Man and Zone Offense;* Oct., p. 30; *Box-and-One Overload Offense;* Nov., p. 16.
3149. **Hankinson, Mel:** *Six Methods of Counteracting Pressure from Changing Defenses;* Nov., p. 52.
3150. **Hecker, Barry:** *Coach the Basics;* Sept., p. 82.
3151. **Johns, Mary Lou:** *The Jump Shot in Women's Basketball;* Oct., p. 16.

3152. **Kalmer, Dewey:** *Score From Out-of-Bounds*; Nov., p. 22.
3153. **Kelly, James:** *Beating the Box-and-One*; Oct., p. 70.
3154. **Kershner, Ed:** *Domino or Match Your Man Defense*; Oct., p. 20.
3155. **Landa, Howie:** *Post Delay Offense*; Oct., p. 42.
3156. **Litzenberger, Fred and Meyer, Don:** *Take Charge on Defense*; Oct., p. 32; *Decision Lines Rules for Post and Help-Side Defense*; Nov., p. 40.
3157. **Meyer, Don and Litzenberger, Fred:** *Take Charge on Defense*; Oct., p. 32; *Decision Lines Rules for Post and Help-Side Defense*; Nov., p. 40.
3158. **Nancy, Lynn:** *The Kentucky Shell Drill*; Dec., p. 35.
3159. **Nichols, Sam:** *Guarding the Player Without the Ball*; Dec., p. 16.
3160. **Nitchman, Nelson:** *1975–76 Offense*; June, p. 18.
3161. **O'Connor, Terrance J.:** *1-4 Offense*; Oct., p. 52.
3162. **Oman, Dennis:** *Developing the Fast Break*; Sept., p. 79.
3163. **Schneider, Walt:** *Take the Wrinkles Out of the Press*; Dec., p. 58.
3164. **Sharpe, Howard L.:** *Improve Shooting With Small Goals*; Sept., p. 24.
3165. **Smith, Sonny:** *Stack Guard Offense*; Nov., p. 8.
3166. **Swan, Jerry:** *Where It Is*; Oct., p. 24.
3167. **Swepston, Gregory B.:** *10-Minute Program*; Oct., p. 22; *Perimeter Offense*; Nov., p. 60.
3168. **Underwood, Don:** *Defense Designated by Digits and Terms*; Sept., p. 14.
3169. **Vanderbilt, Dr. William R.:** *The Show and Go Half-Court Press*; Sept., p. 58.
3170. **Wasem, Jim:** *Fast Break Following the Successful Free Throw*; Nov., p. 58.
3171. **Winters, Bob:** *A Four Rule Passing Game for High School Players*; Sept., p. 38; *Match-Up Defense*; Oct., p. 62.
3172. **Wolfsohn, Edward T.:** *Two Simple Zone Offenses vs. Even and Odd Man Fronts*; Dec., p. 14.
3173. *1976 State Basketball Tournaments*; June, p. 32.

Volume 57, 1976–77

3174. **Adamowicz, Edward J.:** *Total Pressure Defense*; Dec., p. 35.
3175. **Ahern, Frank and Williams, Mel:** *High Percentage Shooting*; Nov., p. 14.
3176. **Andrews, Robert L.:** *Defensive Rebounding Program*; Oct., p. 24.
3177. **Bennice, Donn:** *Selecting the Basketball Team*; Sept., p. 36.
3178. **Bianchi, George L.:** *A Press for All Seasons*; Nov., p. 22.
3179. **Boozer, Bernard:** *Developing the Tall Center*; Sept., p. 24.
3180. **Cotton, Dick:** *Step, Split-Leg, Half-Step Jumper*; Sept., p. 14.
3181. **David, Steve:** *The Use of Football Air Dummies in Basketball Practice*; Oct., p. 44.
3182. **DeMarchi, Gordon:** *Down the Championship Trail Via Summer Basketball*; May, p. 14.
3183. **Dougherty, Jay and Stier, William F.:** *Shooting Dice With the Offensive Continuity*; Dec., p. 10.
3184. **Edelman, Sonny:** *31 Defense*; Dec., p. 26.
3185. **Fengler, Hank:** *Development of an Offense*; Oct., p. 8.
3186. **Fisk, Robert, Jr.:** *Developing the Big Man Offensively*; Nov., p. 38.
3187. **Gaffey, Bill:** *The Inside Game*; Dec., p. 14.
3188. **Gonzalez, Billy G.:** *The 2-1-2 Lopsided Full Court Zone Press*; Nov., p. 8.
3189. **Graham, Larry:** *Early Season Station Drills to Develop the Press*; Oct., p. 66.
3190. **Hoch, David:** *Pressure Man-for-Man Defense for Girls*; Oct., p. 46.
3191. **Johns, Mary Lou:** *The 1-3-1 Zone Defense for Women*; Nov., p. 62.
3192. **Kautzner, Ronald C.:** *The Skill of Basketball Substituting*; Sept., p. 16.
3193. **Korobov, Glen:** *The Passing Game*; Dec., p. 46.
3194. **Landa, Howie:** *Drills for the 1-4 Offense*; Oct., p. 64.

Volume 58, 1977–78

3236. **Schnabel, Al:** *1-3-1 Rotaional Offense*; Nov., p. 65.
3237. **Simpson, Alice:** *Skill Checks During Practice*; Nov., p. 34.
3238. **Stier, Wiliam F. and Dougherty, Jay:** *Shooting Dice With the Offensive Continuity*; Dec., p. 10.
3239. **Van Gundy, Bill:** *Come From Behind*; Oct., p. 52.
3240. **Vitale, Dick:** *Detroit's Delay Game*; Oct., p. 18; *Attacking Pressure Defenses*; Nov., p. 44.
3241. **Voth, Robert:** *Combating Sloughing Defenses*; Nov., p. 30.

Volume 59, 1978–79

3242. **Akin, Ron:** *Stop the Cutter*; Oct., p. 24.
3243. **Beecroft, John:** *Individual Practice Program*; Oct., p. 66.
3244. **Belz, Paul:** *Turn and Double Defense*; Sept., p. 50; *Basic Rotations in an Aggressive Man-for-Man Defense*; Oct., p. 62.
3245. **Bieder, Jeff:** *Four Corner Press Breaker With a Four Stack Option*; Oct., p. 47.
3246. **Boozer, Bernard:** *Big Man Out-of-Bounds Plays*; Nov., p. 20.
3247. **Brouse, Thomas:** *Beating the Man-for-Man Defense: "The Red Offense"*; Dec., p. 26.
3248. **Cregier, Ron and Mueller, Tom:** *The Four-on-Four Drill for Better Man-for-Man Defense*; Oct., p. 22.
3249. **Damon, Dr. Lyle:** *Double Low Post Offense*; Nov., p. 32.
3250. **Dougherty, Jay and Stier, Dr. William F.:** *Veer Cut Offense*; Nov., p. 28.
3251. **Eldred, Vince:** *Pre-Season Preparation, Scouting*; Oct., p. 50; *Pre-Game Procedures, Scouting*; Nov., p. 24.
3252. **Gonzalez, Billy:** *Beating the Full-Court Presses*; Oct., p. 14.
3253. **Hallihan, James:** *1-on-1 Defense*; Dec., p. 28.
3254. **Hansley, Richard:** *Shell Drill for Man-for-Man Defense*; Oct., p. 18.
3255. **Harkins, Mike:** *10 Ways to Get the Ball Inside vs. Pressure*; Nov., p. 48.
3256. **Hofer, Herbert, Jr.:** *Develop the Arch for Better Shooting*; Oct., p. 34.
3257. **Hughes, Dan:** *Teaching the Reverse Move*; Dec., p. 10.
3258. **Kalmer, Dewey:** *Fast Break Basketball*; Sept., p. 60.
3259. **Kuhlman, Randy:** *Delay Your Break!*; Oct., p. 38.
3260. **Lopez, William:** *1-2-1-1 Full-Court Zone Press*; Nov., p. 36.
3261. **McClain, Rusty and Meyer, Don:** *Improve That Shooting*; Oct., p. 8.
3262. **Meyer, Don and McClain, Rusty:** *Improve That Shooting*; Oct., p. 8.
3263. **Miller, David Jon:** *Domino Zone Offense*; Nov., p. 38.
3264. **Miller, Randy:** *The Shuffle and Drive*; Nov., p. 10.
3265. **Nitchman, Nelson:** *1978–79 Offense*; June, p. 12.
3266. **Poulin, Art:** *The Killer Driller*; Nov., p. 14.
3267. **Roickle, Mary:** *Individual Defensive Drills*; Nov., p. 16.
3268. **Schnable, Al:** *Pressure Releases and Options: The 1-3-1 Rotational Offense*; Sept., p. 54.
3269. **Schoepfer, Martin:** *Attacking the Full-Court Zone Press*; Oct., p. 42.
3270. **Standridge, Charles:** *Screening Techniques vs. Zone Defenses*; Dec., p. 20.
3271. **Stier, Dr. William F. and Dougherty, Jay:** *Veer Cut Offense*; Nov., p. 28
3272. **Stier, Dr. Wiliam F., Jr.:** *Razzle Dazzle Warm-Up Drill*; Oct., p. 30.
3273. **Stiver, John:** *Blitz and Rotate Zone Offense*; Nov., p. 26.
3274. **Tulio, Joe:** *Agility Station Drills*; Oct., p. 36.
3275. **Underwood, Don:** *Catch-Up Offense*; Oct., p. 32; *Defending Against the 4-Corner Offense*; Dec., p. 24.
3276. **Winters, Robert:** *Three Corner Offense*; Nov., p. 44.

Volume 60, 1979–80

3277. **Bartow, Tom:** *Incorporating One-on-One Guard Play in a Team Offense;* Sept., p. 44.
3278. **Battenberg, Terry:** *Discovering and Developing the Extra-Tall Player;* Dec., p. 34.
3279. **Baumgarten, Carole:** *Offensive Moves;* Oct., p. 56.
3280. **Beecroft, John:** *The 3-2 Zone Press Defense;* Oct., p. 48.
3281. **Brown, Bruce:** *Developing a Total Team Concept in Basketball;* Sept., p. 28.
3282. **Burkhalter, Al:** *Side Out-of-Bounds Play;* Oct., p. 14.
3283. **Damon, Dr. Lyle:** *Press Offense;* Sept., p. 48; *The Chaser Zone Defense;* Oct., p. 10.
3284. **Dialer, Jack:** *The Jam Scramble;* Nov., p. 10.
3285. **Fitzpatrick, Dennis:** *Breaking the Press;* Nov., p. 24.
3286. **Gappy, Bill and Moran, Mike:** *Defending the 4-Corner Delay;* Oct., p. 18.
3287. **Gonzalez, Billy:** *Baseline Offense With an Overload;* Dec., p. 26.
3288. **Gould, Kay:** *Post Perimeter Offense;* Oct., p. 28.
3289. **Gourdouze, Frank:** *The Double Shuffle Offense;* Nov., p. 20.
3290. **Graves, Eben:** *Defensive Jab Step Drill;* Oct., p. 46.
3291. **Harmon, James:** *A Back-Up Offense;* Nov., p. 38.
3292. **Hoch, David:** *Penetration;* Nov., p. 8.
3293. **Hudiburg, George and Key, Gary:** *Drills That Build Winners;* Oct., p. 26.
3294. **Key, Gary and Hudiburg, George:** *Drills That Build Winners;* Oct., p. 26.
3295. **Lehr, Robert:** *Combating the Odd Front Zone Defenses;* Oct., p. 38.
3296. **Lopez, William:** *1-2-2 Half-Court Zone Press;* Dec., p. 8.
3297. **Miller, David Jon:** *Pick the Zones to Pieces;* Dec., p. 12.
3298. **Moran, Mike and Gappy, Bill:** *Defending the 4-Corner Delay;* Oct., p. 18.
3299. **Nitchman, Nelson:** *1979–80 Basketball Offense;* June, p. 16.
3300. **Pelech, Jim and Sullins, Quitman:** *Beating the Press;* Nov., p. 32.
3301. **Rainey, Ron:** *Baseball Foul Shot;* Sept., p. 62.
3302. **Russo, Rich:** *Organizing the Consistent Fastbreak;* Oct., p. 8.
3303. **Scheppler, Doc:** *Convert Those Pressure Free Throws;* Oct., p. 44.
3304. **Schmid, James:** *Teaching the Equalizer—The Low Block;* Sept., p. 40.
3305. **Schnabel, Al:** *Situation Plays for the 1-3-1 Rotational Offense;* Oct., p. 30.
3306. **Stier, Dr. William:** *Penetrate to Score and Win;* Oct., p. 64.
3307. **Stiver, John:** *I Alignment for Center Jumps;* Sept., p. 72.
3308. **Sullins, Quitman and Pelech, Jim:** *Beating the Press;* Nov., p. 32.
3309. **Svenningson, Allen:** *The Alaska Passing Game;* Dec., p. 24.
3310. **Tarkanian, Jerry and Warren, William:** *The Role of Quickness in Basketball;* Nov., p. 30.
3311. **Underwood, Don:** *2-3-4-5 Man Motion Offense;* Nov., p. 28.
3312. **Walker, Lee:** *Open the Back Door;* Nov., p. 16.
3313. **Warren, William and Tarkanian, Jerry:** *The Role of Quickness in Basketball;* Nov., p. 30.
3314. **Wolfsohn, Edward:** *Pass Your Greatest Expectations;* Nov., p. 40.
3315. **Zigler, Ted:** *Big Men Drills;* Oct., p. 16.

Volume 61, 1980–81

3316. **Ahern, Frank and David, Ron:** *Basketball Flexibility Exercises;* Apr., p. 40.
3317. **Battenberg, Terry:** *Using the Low Post Player;* Nov., p. 24.
3318. **Bonnette, Allen:** *Rebounding;* Nov., p. 16.

3319. **Borkowicz, Ronald:** *Out-of-Bounds Scoring From Under Your Basket*; Oct., p. 44.
3320. **Brennan, Steve:** *Quick Drills*; Oct., p. 25; *Teaching the Concepts of Time and Space on the Court*; Nov., p. 46.
3321. **Brown, Ron:** *1-3-1 Offense Against Zones*; Nov., p. 28.
3322. **Brubacher, Don and Janzen, Dennis:** *Variable Perimeter Passing Game*; June, p. 46.
3323. **Capano, Vincent:** *3 Guard Inside/Outside Zone Defense*; Dec., p. 48; *Minimizing the Effects of Defensive Erros*; Mar., p. 48.
3324. **Cornoa, John and McCall, Jeff:** *Sideline Fast Break*; Oct., p. 48.
3325. **Cramblitt, Steve:** *Spread Offense*; Apr., p. 48.
3326. **David, Ron and Ahern, Frank:** *Basketball Flexibility Exercises*; Apr., p. 40.
3327. **Eldred, Vince:** *Scouting: Game Procedures*; Nov., p. 12; *Scouting: Analyzing Defenses*; Mar., p. 26; *Scouting: Can We Match Up?*; May, p. 30.
3328. **Fengler, Hank:** *Pressure Defense (Part 1): Developing the Individual*; Oct., p. 48; *Pressure Defense (Part 2): Putting the Defense Together*; Nov., p. 20.
3329. **Ford, Jack:** *The Best Things in Life Are Free (Throws)*; Oct., p. 14.
3330. **Gonzalez, Billy and Smith, Gary:** *The Shotgun Pressing Zone and Zone Press*; Nov., p. 18.
3331. **Gould, Kay:** *Extending the Post Perimeter Offense*; Oct., p. 8.
3332. **Graves, Eben:** *Defense Is the Name of the Game*; Nov., p. 10.
3333. **Hess, Charles:** *Analysis of the Jump Shot*; Nov., p. 30.
3334. **Hoch, David:** *Foul Shooting Drills*; Apr., p. 38.
3335. **Hudson, Steve:** *Beating the 1-3-1 With the Runner*; Sept., p. 42.
3336. **Jack, Stan:** *Fast Break With a Forward in the Middle Lane*; Oct., p. 28.
3337. **Jantzen, Dennis and Brubacher, Don:** *Variable Perimeter Passing Game*; June, p. 46.
3338. **Keady, Gene:** *Attacking the Match-Up Zone*; Dec., p. 36.
3339. **Kelbick, Don:** *Four Multi-Purpose Defensive Drills*; Oct., p. 42; *Transition: Fast Break Offense*; Dec., p. 35.
3340. **Lambert, Randy:** *The Slam Dunk Jumping Program*; Sept., p. 36.
3341. **LaPoint, James:** *Tips to Improve Your Shot*; Oct., p. 12.
3342. **Linehan, Dave:** *Quick Inside Scoop Shot*; Nov., p. 42.
3343. **MacPhee, Len:** *Two Successful Press Breakers*; Nov., p. 8.
3344. **McCall, Jeff and Corona, John:** *Sideline Fast Break*; Oct., p. 48.
3345. **Miller, David Jon:** *The Numbered Fast Break Game*; Dec., p. 28.
3346. **Nitchman, Nelson:** *1980–81 Offense*; June, p. 55.
3347. **Patterson, Paul:** *Transition: Teaching Defense*; Dec., p. 34.
3348. **Pike, John:** *Teaching Dribbling Skills*; Oct., p. 22; *Rotating Zone Defense*; May, p. 16.
3349. **Powers, John:** *Man-for-Man Defensive Drills*; Oct., p. 30.
3350. **Scarano, Michael:** *Off-Season Work-Out Program*; May, p. 20.
3351. **Schacht, Chuck:** *Pass and Go Through*; Oct., p. 32.
3352. **Scheppler, Doc:** *Passing Game and Its Special Options*; Dec., p. 52.
3353. **Shambarger, Jack and Vining, Bill:** *Developing the Winning Edge*; May, p. 48.
3354. **Smith, Gary and Gonzalez, Billy:** *The Shotgun Pressing Zone and Zone Press*; Nov., p. 18.
3355. **Smith, Jerry:** *Attack With the Break*; Oct., p. 26.
3356. **Stockholm, Alan:** *Passing Game With a Pattern*; Oct., p. 10.
3357. **Vining, Bill and Shambarger, Jack:** *Developing the Winning Edge*; May, p. 48.
3358. **Zigler, Ted:** *Options for the Offense*; Dec., p. 12; *The Offense for Any Zone Defense*; Mar., p. 62.

Volume 62, 1981–82

3359. **Adamowicz, Joe:** *Press Principles*; Oct., p. 34.
3360. **Akagun, Faruk:** *A Multi-Purpose Zone Offense*; Oct., p. 38.
3361. **Baird, Will:** *Developing a Pee Wee Basketball Program*; Nov., p. 36.
3362. **Baker, Jim:** *Defending the Post*; Mar., p. 46.
3363. **Burdette, Jeff:** *The Cobra Offense*; May, p. 32.
3364. **Brennan, Steve:** *Special Strategy Situations*; Nov., p. 66.
3365. **Burdett, Jeff:** *The Cobra Offense*; May, p. 32.
3366. **Byers, John:** *1-2-1-1 Half-Court Press*; Sept., p. 46.
3367. **Capano, Vincent:** *Backdoor Delay Offense*; Oct., p. 32.
3368. **Casciano, Jim:** *Defending the Four Corners*; May, p. 26.
3369. **Chatterton, Dale:** *The Fun and Run Continuity Offense*; Oct., p. 6.
3370. **Collins, Darrel:** *Preparing for Tournament Play*; Dec., p. 24.
3371. **Ford, Duane:** *Keeping Your Big Man Home With Free-Lance Defense*; Jan., p. 18.
3372. **Gonzalez, Billy:** *32 Special Zone Defenses With a Unique Twist*; Nov., p. 22.
3373. **Graves, Eben:** *Buck Five Lane Controlled Fastbreak*; Sept., p. 52.
3374. **Harmon, James:** *A Simple Press With Rules*; Dec., p. 40.
3375. **Hatlem, Roger:** *The 3-1-1 Defense*; Nov., p. 62.
3376. **Hoppenstedt, Bob:** *Central Zone Attack*; Dec., p. 66.
3377. **Kelbick, Don:** *Shooting Practice at Game Speed*; Oct., p. 10.
3378. **Kerlin, Bob:** *F.E.E.F.E. Shooting*; Oct., p. 30.
3379. **Kolb, Barry:** *Drills to Counter Full-Court Pressure*; Oct., p. 45.
3380. **Landa, Howie:** *Pivot Playmaker Offense vs. Man-for-Man*; Nov., p. 44.
3381. **Martin, Mona:** *1-2-1-1 Press*; Mar., p. 36.
3382. **Meek, Jeff:** *Double Stack Versus 2-3 Defense*; Feb., p. 54.
3383. **Miller, Larry:** *Double Post Offense*; Nov., p. 58.
3384. **Mineo, James:** *Pressure Man-for-Man Defense*; Apr., p. 32.
3385. **Morrison, Danny:** *The Tick Defense*; June, p. 42.
3386. **Murray, Patrick:** *The Bank Shot: Locating the Correct Carom Spot*; Oct., p. 14.
3387. **Muse, Bill:** *Jump Ball Situations*; Dec., p. 64.
3388. **Price, Eldon:** *Transition Offense: End-to-End Attack*; Dec., p. 46.
3389. **Rinaldo, Jim:** *The Run and Jump Press*; Apr., p. 68.
3390. **Sanderford, Paul:** *Press Breaker Into Delayed Break*; Dec., p. 54.
3391. **Sarver, Martha:** *A Simple Fastbreak That Works*; Apr., p. 18.
3392. **Schoepfer, Martin:** *The Two-on-the-Ball Press*; Dec., p. 21; *The Block and Go Play*; June, p. 41.
3393. **Schwartz, Steve:** *The Zig System*; Sept., p. 28.
3394. **Shogan, Debra:** *Defending the Offside Screen*; June, p. 22.
3395. **Smith, Jim:** *Spread Offense For Lead Control*; Oct., p. 18.
3396. **Taylor, Terry:** *Utah's 13-Move Zone Offense*; Nov., p. 50.
3397. **Thornley, Rodney:** *The Free Throw Gamble*; Nov., p. 60.
3398. **Weinstein, Paul:** *1-3-1 Combination Defense*; Feb., p. 44.
3399. **Wescott, Richard:** *Winning Out-of-Bounds Plays*; Oct., p. 40.
3400. **Whitney, Craig:** *13 Special Defense*; Dec., p. 62.
3401. **Young, Stephen:** *Off-Season Conditioning for Basketball*; May, p. 52.

Volume 63, 1982–83

3402. **Armstrong, Tony:** *Versatile Zone Passing Game*; Jan., p. 44.
3403. **Barry, Ray:** *Out-of-Bounds Offense*; Jan., p. 58.
3404. **Bennett, Frank:** *Perimeter Player Development*; Jan., p. 16.
3405. **Braun, Timothy and Price, Eldon:** *Wake the Sleeping Giants*; June, p. 42.

3406. **Bringe, Bob:** *More Effective Drill Work*; Nov., p. 20.
3407. **Callahan, Robert:** *Triangle Pattern Offense*; Nov., p. 46.
3408. **Fengler, Hank:** *Fastbreak and Transition Game*; Dec., p. 30.
3409. **Gaffey, Bill:** *Getting the Jump on Your Opponent*; Nov., p. 26.
3410. **Galbraith, David:** *An Offense to Beat the Half-Zone Trap*; Oct., p. 48.
3411. **Goffnett, Charles and Pim, Ralph:** *Post Play: Get Your Inside Game on Track*; Nov., p. 8.
3412. **Hill, Kelly:** *Circuit Training for Basketball*; Oct., p. 26.
3413. **Hoch, David:** *Drills for Developing a Player-for-Player Defense*; Nov., p. 32.
3414. **Hoppenstedt, Bob:** *Michigan Offense*; Oct., p. 42.
3415. **Janopoulos, Michael:** *1-2-2 Overload Offense*; Sept., p. 31.
3416. **Jones, Dianne:** *1-2-2 Player-for-Player Offense*; Nov., p. 25.
3417. **Lahodny, Janice:** *Developing the Guard and Forward Positions*; Feb., p. 28.
3418. **Maxson, Don:** *Straight Line Press*; Dec., p. 64.
3419. **Miller, David:** *Box Shuffle Revised*; Jan., p. 34.
3420. **Nitchman, Nelson:** *Basketball Trends '81*; Sept., p. 24.
3421. **Olson, Pete:** *Cross-Court Press*; May, p. 22.
3422. **Pim, Ralph and Goffnett, Charles:** *Post Play: Get Your Inside Game on Track*; Nov., p. 8.
3423. **Price, Eldon and Braun, Timothy:** *Wake the Sleeping Giants*; June, p. 42.
3424. **Robards, Larry:** *Zone Offense Made Simple*; Apr., p. 96.
3425. **Schoderbek, Charles:** *Continuous Fastbreak Drill*; Nov., p. 22.
3426. **Simpson, Alice:** *Essentials of Junior High Basketball*; May, p. 58.
3427. **Smith, Jim:** *Effective Team Defense*; June, p. 28.
3428. **Thaller, Barb:** *Playing the Patient Game*; Dec., p. 8.
3429. **Traywick, James:** *Pressing: Psychological Warfare*; Dec., p. 48.
3430. **Webb, Thomas:** *Aggressive Defense!*; Nov., p. 34.
3431. **Zigler, Ted:** *Getting Your Post Player Open*; Dec., p. 16.

Volume 64, 1983–84

3432. **Andrist, Ed:** *Push Button Practice*; Sept., p. 42.
3433. **Balestrieri, Mario:** *Diamond Breaker*; Nov., p. 36.
3434. **Boyd, R. David:** *1-2-2 Multiple Offense*; Dec., p. 38.
3435. **Braun, Ben:** *Side Out-of-Bounds: An Offensive Weapon*; Mar., p. 32.
3436. **Brown, Bruce:** *Finding Your Team's "Hot Button"*; Nov., p. 12.
3437. **Darnall, Dave:** *Eureeka! A Versatile Zone Offense*; Mar., p. 16.
3438. **Davies, Mike, Goodfriend, Jim, and Korson, Bill:** *Corner Offense vs. Zone Defense*; Oct., p. 44.
3439. **Doperalski, Vic:** *Versatile Spread Offense*; Jan., p. 18.
3440. **Drown, Kip:** *Put Some Heart in Your Program*; Dec., p. 32.
3441. **Fields, Marvin:** *Diamond Lone Star Defense*; Oct., p. 42.
3442. **Franks, Joe:** *Group Drills for Individual Skills*; Nov., p. 8.
3443. **Gooch, Stanley:** *Numbered Fastbreak*; Jan., p. 30.
3444. **Goodfriend, Jim, Korson, Bill, and Davies, Mike:** *Corner Offense vs. Zone Defense*; Oct., p. 44.
3445. **Hamlin, George:** *Double Stack Offense vs. Man-for-Man Defense*; Dec., p. 48.
3446. **Harris, Ed:** *Fire Drill!*; Nov., p. 26.
3447. **Hatch, Boyd:** *Simple Offenses Can Work*; Sept., p. 20.
3448. **Haubrich, Bill:** *Score From the Sidelines*; Jan., p. 38.
3449. **Higgs, Layne:** *Coast to Coast Fastbreak*; Sept., p. 10.
3450. **Hoch, David:** *Face Guarding: Use It in Your Press*; June, p. 44.
3451. **Jenkins, Bert:** *Two Stunts Off the Man-for-Man Press*; June, p. 44.

3452. **Jubeck, Bernard:** *Controlled Motion Game*; Oct., p. 46.
3453. **Kestner, Dave:** *Designated Fastbreak*; Dec., p. 16.
3454. **Korson, Bill, Davies, Mike and Goodfriend, Jim:** *Corner Offense vs. Zone Defense*; Oct., p. 44.
3455. **Luther, Dick:** *Quick Hitting Offense*; Dec., p. 24.
3456. **McDougle, Timothy:** *Winning With the Press*; Jan., p. 36.
3457. **Meschery, Tom:** *Free Throw Shooting*; June, p. 14.
3458. **Muse, Bill:** *Free Throw Rebounding*; Dec., p. 36.
3459. **Nitchman, Nelson:** *Beating the Press in '83*; Jan., p. 8.
3460. **Nolan, Michael:** *The 1-4: A Starter Zone Offense*; Oct., p. 24.
3461. **Nolen, Rick:** *Triple Option Fastbreak*; Dec., p. 44.
3462. **Parkinson, Win:** *Why Press?*; Mar., p. 66.
3463. **Ribble, Larry:** *Off-Season Workout Program*; Apr., p. 16.
3464. **Ruwell, William:** *Simple Basketball vs. the Man-for-Man Press*; Dec., p. 8.
3465. **Shields, Tom:** *Go to the One and Run!*; Jan., p. 24.
3466. **Simpson, Alice:** *Teach the Clock . . . Then Beat the Clock*; Dec., p. 26.
3467. **Stein, Julian:** *Basketball Statistics the Microcomputer Way*; Mar., p. 52.
3468. **Strain, Joe:** *Position Fastbreak*; Nov., p. 42.
3469. **Walker, Lee:** *Basic Offensive Footwork*; Mar., p. 22.
3470. **Warkentien, Daniel:** *Continuous Trapping Defense*; Feb., p. 40.
3471. **Wolff, David:** *Flex Man-for-Man Offense*; Nov., p. 38.

Volume 65, 1984–1985

3472. **Andrist, Ed:** *Free Throw Fast Break*; Apr., p. 34.
3473. **Brennan, Stephen:** *Daily Dozen Shooting Drills*; Jan., p. 18.
3474. **Brown, Charles A.:** *Exploit the Inbounds Pass*; Jan., p. 30.
3475. **Fletcher, Neil:** *The 1-2-2 Matchup*; Mar., p. 34.
3476. **Hudson, Steve:** *Brand X*; Apr., p. 25.
3477. **Jones, Dianne and McKeown, Susan:** *A Total Player-to-Player Offense*; May, p. 16.
3478. **Kanaskie, Kurt and Morris, Robert C.:** *Scouting Basketball: Strategies for Winning*; Jan., p. 26.
3479. **Kelling, Mary Ann:** *Double Screen Offense*; Mar., p. 42.
3480. **McDonald, Tim:** *"Team Stats" Boost Morale*; Jan., p. 36.
3481. **McKeown, Susan and Jones, Dianne:** *A Total Player-to-Player Offense*; May, p. 16.
3482. **Morris, Robert C. and Kanaskie, Kurt:** *Scouting Basketball: Strategies for Winning*; Jan., p. 26.
3483. **Rush, Roger:** *Winning Guard Play*; Feb., p. 34.
3484. **Underwood, Don:** *By the Numbers*; Mar., p. 50.
3485. **Wilson, Russ:** *Varying Your Defensive Pressure*; Feb., p. 42.
3486. **Young, Stephen:** *The 1-2-1-1 Press: A Multiple Option Defense*; May, p. 34.

Volume 66, 1985–1986

3487. **Anderson, Bruce:** *Breaking the 1-2-1-1 Full Court Press*; Aug., p. 44.
3488. **Andrist, Eddie:** *Machine Gun Shooting*; Mar., p. 34.
3489. **Barnes, Marty:** *The Winning Edge*; Dec., p. 16.
3490. **Biancalana, Al:** *The "4-Across" Zone Offense*; Nov., p. 16.
3491. **Butterfield, Terry:** *Using Screener for the Screen Principles*; Mar., p. 42.
3492. **Cavallini, Felicia:** *Improving Basketball Fundamentals Through Aerobic Movements*; Jan., p. 10.

3493. **Chitwood, Ray:** *A Simple, Versatile Circuit Drill*; Sept., p. 26.
3494. **Dafler, Jim:** *Offensive Rebounding*; Dec., p. 42.
3495. **de Vaudrecourt, Billy:** *1-1-3 Tandem Zone Attack*; Sept., p. 34.
3496. **Fischer, Kevin:** *Using the 2-2-1 Zone Press*; Jan., p. 44.
3497. **Gonzalez, Billy:** *The 23 Blitz With Camouflage Maneuvers*; Oct., p. 38.
3498. **Haskell, Bill:** *Shooting Free Throws*; Aug., p. 30.
3499. **Henson, Lou:** *The Illini Defense*; Oct., p. 10.
3500. **Hill, George:** *A Lettering System for Zone Press Efficiency*; Dec., p. 32.
3501. **Hoch, David:** *Rover vs. Odd Front Zones*; Aug., p. 38.
3502. **Hoppenstedt, Bob:** *Gaining the Rebound Advantage While at the Line*; Nov., p. 34.
3503. **Hudson, Dr. Jackie:** *Shooting Techniques for Smaller Players*; Nov., p. 22.
3504. **Kenkel, Al:** *The Safe Press*; May, p. 48.
3505. **Kinningham, Russell:** *The Cutting Series Offense*; May, p. 14.
3506. **Link, Ron:** *Get an Edge by Mastering the Intangibles*; Oct., p. 44.
3507. **May, Joseph A.:** *Stopping a Fastbreak Offense*; Dec., p. 26.
3508. **May, Tom:** *Preparing for the Sideline Fastbreak*; May, p. 25.
3509. **McKinnie, Gil:** *Improving Defense with a Four Man Drill*; Nov., p. 10.
3510. **Mieure, Tim and Prohofsky, Ed:** *Attacking Pressure Defense*; Jan., p. 38.
3511. **Nitchman, Nelson:** *Winning on Transitions*; Sept., p. 16.
3512. **Prohofsky, Ed and Mieure, Tim:** *Attacking Pressure Defense*; Jan., p. 38.
3513. **Riley, Doug:** *St. Andrew's Passing Game*; Mar., p. 28.
3514. **Ryan, Karlin:** *PDPO*; Mar., p. 46.
3515. **Serio, Sal:** *Triple Option Entry Into the Flex*; Aug., p. 21.
3516. **Versace, Dick:** *Bradley's T-Game*; Feb., p. 12.
3517. **Walker, A.L.:** *Revisiting Option Defense*; Oct., p. 30.
3518. **Wilkes, Michael:** *Option Offense Against the Press*; Feb., p. 30.
3519. **Zigler, Ted:** *Drills to Stop the Flex Offense*; Feb., p. 18.
3520. **Zinn, David:** *Attacking the Half Court Trap*; Feb., p. 24.

Volume 67, 1986–1987

3521. **Anstett, Tom:** *The Value of Details*; Dec., p. 32.
3522. **Brown, Dennis:** *Post Offense*; Mar., p. 28.
3523. **Calhoun, Jim:** *Weakside Boxout*; Jan., p. 22.
3524. **Crawford, Ken:** *T-Town's Twin Titles Fundamental Defense*; Mar., p. 32.
3525. **Edelman, Bill:** *Rebounding the Viking Way*; Nov., p. 38.
3526. **Field, Terry:** *Routine Shooting Drills*; Sept., p. 32.
3527. **Foster, Frank:** *Breaking Into an Offense*; Nov., p. 46.
3528. **Gardner, Larry:** *Zone Breaker 1-3-1 Offense*; Apr., p. 14.
3529. **Gonzalez, Billy G.:** *The Unbeatable Five*; May, p. 26.
3530. **Graf, Bill:** *Changing Defenses*; Aug., p. 54.
3531. **Grimsley, Dr. Jimmie and Wallace, Michael:** *A Checklist for Efficiency in Practice*; Sept., p. 28.
3532. **Hamryka, Bonnie:** *The Smaller Ball and Women's Basketball*; Mar., p. 18.
3533. **Herrin, Beverly:** *Is the Inbounds Pass Destroying Your Team?*; Nov., p. 12.
3534. **Hoch, David:** *Isolating Your Best Shooters*; Oct., p. 20.
3535. **Kelly, Thomas:** *Corner Series Offense*; Feb., p. 30.
3536. **Koester, Dennis:** *How to Beat Zone Offense*; Mar., p. 33.
3537. **Lirgg, Cathy:** *Don't Lose the Game at the Line*; Nov., p. 20.
3538. **McQueen, Brian:** *11 Trap Defenses*; Nov., p. 26.
3539. **Rehrer, Randy:** *Full Court Zone Press*; Feb., p. 22.
3540. **Simpson, Alice:** *Six and Six Baseline Rebounding*; Oct., p. 46.

3541. **Simpson, Sanford:** *An Offensive and Defensive Rating System;* Aug., p. 48.
3542. **Smith, Melvin:** *A Dual Purpose for the 1-2-2;* Dec., p. 40.
3543. **Stanfield, Gary:** *"13" Spring;* Aug., p. 20.
3544. **Stanley, Dolph:** *A Beautiful Game Gone Awry?;* Mar., p. 36.
3545. **Travis, Russell:** *Passing Fundamentals;* Feb., p. 28.
3546. **Uhrig, Rick E.:** *Quick Hitters From the 1-2-2 Motion Offense;* Dec., p. 16.
3547. **Venuti, Frank:** *Man to Man Spot Offense;* Aug., p. 40.
3548. **Wallace, Michael and Grimsley, Dr. Jimmie:** *A Checklist for Efficiency in Practice;* Sept., p. 28.
3549. **Wells, Michael:** *The Tipping Zone;* Oct., p. 26.

Scholastic Coach *Articles 1931–88*

Volume 1, 1931–32

3550. **Anderson, James A.:** *A Scoring Formation;* Feb., p. 9.
3551. **Hager, R.H.:** *Basketball Inventory;* Apr., p. 7.
3552. **Holman, Nat:** *Basketball Training and Practice;* Nov., p. 7; *Every Player on Attack;* Jan., p. 7.
3553. **Lauderburn, Frederic C.:** *Basketball (A Poem);* Dec., p. 17.
3554. **Lindwall, Robert E.:** *Everybody in the Game;* Nov., p. 9.
3555. **Lippert, Jack:** *Catch the Ball: Run Toward It;* Jan., p. 10.
3556. **Meenan, Daniel F., Jr.:** *A Championship Attack;* Dec., p. 7.
3557. **Obey, Edward J.:** *Free Throw Technique;* Jan., p. 15.
3558. **Porter, H.V.:** *Full Comment on the Basketball Rules;* Oct., p. 9.
3559. **Zehfuss, Paul:** *The Best Shot Is the Easiest Shot;* Nov., p. 25.
3560. *Basketball Fundamentals at a Glance;* Oct., p. 25.
3561. *Basketball Rules Changes;* Apr., p. 30.
3562. *The Old Fight, the Old Pep;* Feb., p. 31.

Volume 2, 1932–33

3563. **Barclay, George:** *Coaching in a Large High School;* Jan., p. 10.
3564. **Case, Everett N.:** *"Fire Engine" Basketball;* Dec., p. 9.
3565. **Fishbein, Dr.:** *Diet for the Basketball Player;* Nov., p. 20.
3566. **Forehand, George W., Jr.:** *Suit the Action to the Players;* Feb., p. 14.
3567. **Frymir, Alice W.:** *In Favor of the Two-Court Girl's Game;* Nov., p. 12.
3568. **Holman, Nat:** *The Overhead and Other Passes;* Nov., p. 8; *The Bluff Crossover;* Dec., p. 8.
3569. **Lifschultz, Sam:** *Make the Best of the New Rules;* Dec., p. 7.
3570. **Porter, H.V.:** *Basketball Modern;* Sept., p. 11.
3571. **Price, C.M.:** *Circulation in the Front Court;* Feb., p. 5.
3572. **Ruby, Craig J.:** *New Defensive Tactics in Basketball;* Oct., p. 9.
3573. **Simpson, William H., Jr.:** *Shifting Crosscut Defense;* Jan., p. 24.
3574. **Tobey, David:** *Variations of the Pivot Play;* Jan., p. 5.
3575. **Wood, Wiliam R.:** *A Plan for Coaching Basketball;* Nov., p. 16.
3576. *Basketball Inventory;* Mar., p. 11.
3577. *Basketball Symposium;* Feb., p. 7.
3578. *Basketball Symposium;* Mar., p. 28.
3579. *New Basketball Rules;* Apr., p. 17.
3580. *The New Deal in Basketball: Rules in Committee Changes;* Apr., p. 5.

Volume 3, 1933–34

3581. **Allen, Forrest C.:** *Penetrating the Man-for-Man Defense;* Nov., p. 7; *Penetrating the Zone Defense;* Dec., p. 7.
3582. **Allen, James Pryor:** *Basketball: The Athletic Fad, 1897;* Mar., p. 14.
3583. **Burcky, Claine M.:** *Three Men at Work: Two at Rest;* Jan., p. 5.
3584. **Edwards, George R.:** *Keep Away Game in the Forward Court;* Feb., p. 5; *Basketball Coaches Meeting;* May, p. 28.
3585. **Johnson, C.S.:** *Shifting Zone Defense;* Jan., p. 24.
3586. **Jourdet, Lon:** *Play the Man, Not the Ball;* Feb., p. 9.
3587. **Kline, W.G.:** *Guarding the Thin Air;* Feb., p. 10.
3588. **Porter, H.V.:** *Some Fine Points in Basketball Rules;* Oct., p. 9.
3589. **Simpson, William H., Jr.:** *Bait for Your Jumpers;* Nov., p. 23.
3590. **Woodward, Stanley:** *Columbia Spinners in California;* Feb., p. 12.
3591. **Yeend, Elizabeth W.:** *Girls Basketball Fundamentals;* Jan., p. 7; Feb., p. 16.
3592. *Basketball Fundamentals in Moving Pictures;* Dec., p. 16.
3593. *Basketball Rules Changes;* May, p. 28.
3594. *Concerning the Pictures on Page 7;* Dec., p. 22.
3595. *Feigned High Pass and Dribble;* Feb., p. 3.
3596. *Here Below;* Mar., p. 5.
3597. *National High School Basketball Review;* May, p. 12.
3598. *Stop, Feint and Pass (Moving Pictures);* Dec., p. 7.

Volume 4, 1934–35

3599. **Anderson, William H.:** *The Detail of Passing and Shooting;* Dec., p. 10; *Building an Offense;* Jan., p. 7.
3600. **Carlson, H.C. Others:** *From Coaching School Notebooks;* Oct., p. 16; *The Mechanics of Basketball Shooting;* Dec., p. 18.
3601. **Day, Robert:** *The Pivot Play Can Be Guarded;* Feb., p. 4.
3602. **Edwards, George R.:** *Basketball Coaches Meeting;* May, p. 14.
3603. **Owen, W.B.:** *Straight-Away Basketball;* Jan., p. 12.
3604. **Porter, H.V.:** *Comment on the Basketball Rules;* Oct., p. 14; *Basketball Quiz;* Nov., p. 30.
3605. **Simes, Marie L.:** *Minor Changes in Girls Basketball Rules;* Nov., p. 32.
3606. **Wood, William H.:** *This Pivot-Post Play;* Nov., p. 17.
3607. *Corner Fadeaway Shot;* Feb., p. 31.
3608. *Cut, Stop, Reverse and Dribble;* Feb., p. 16.
3609. *Four Shots From One Angle;* Dec., p. 11.
3610. *Here Below [Column];* Jan., p. 5; Feb., p. 5; Mar., p. 5.
3611. *National High School Basketball Review;* May, p. 10.
3612. *Out-of-Bounds Play;* Dec., p. 16.
3613. *Pivot-Play Center-Jump Rules Altered;* May, p. 19.
3614. *Set "Dummy" Play;* Feb., p. 23.

Volume 5, 1935–36

3615. **Bergstrom, A.J.:** *Basketball in Relation to Floor Size;* Dec., p. 30.
3616. **Chadd, Archie R.:** *Building the Basketball Machine;* Dec., p. 16; *Picking the Players: Offense in Action;* Jan., p. 7.
3617. **Edwards, George R.:** *Basketball Strategy for 1935-36;* Nov., p. 7; Dec., p. 7.
3618. **Fishbein, Morris:** *Diet for the Basketball Player;* Feb., Inside the Back Cover.
3619. **Lippert, Jack:** *Basketball's Greatest Show;* May, p. 7.
3620. **Meissner, Wilhemine E.:** *Girls Basketball Rules—1935-36;* Dec., p. 20.

3621. *Basketball's Record Crowd*; Jan., p. 23.
3622. *Coaching School Review*; Oct., p. 7.
3623. *Here Below*; Feb., p. 5.
3624. *How to Throw 499 Fouls*; Feb., p. 30.
3625. *National High School Basketball Review*; May, p. 10.
3626. *Olympic Basketball Scenes, Photos at Madison Square Garden*; May, p. 9.
3627. *Photographs: Drag Dribble*; Dec., p. 16.
3628. *Photographs: Fake Pass to Confuse Guards*; Dec., p. 14.
3629. *Photographs: For Reverse to Setup Screen*; Jan., p. 12.
3630. *Photographs: Outside Feint, Inside Pass*; Jan., p. 14.
3631. *Several Changes in Basketball Rules*; May, p. 17.
3632. *Summary of State Basketball Tournaments*; May, p. 12.
3633. *What Have We, Screening or Blocking?*; Feb., p. 7.

Volume 6, 1936–37

3634. **Balter, Sam:** *Eleventh Olympiad Basketball*; Sept., p. 9; *Taking the Place of the Old Pivot*; Nov., p. 6.
3635. **Bee, Clair:** *The Two Pivot Attack and Variations*; Jan., p. 6.
3636. **Dahl, Edwin:** *The Whistle Blows*; Jan., p. 10.
3637. **Edwards, George:** *Screening-Blocking Interpretations*; Apr., p. 18.
3638. **Goldberg, Samuel:** *Notes on Holman's Coaching School*; Oct., p. 16.
3639. **Harman, J.A.:** *Handbook for Basketball Players*; Jan., p. 12.
3640. **Henderson, Marian E.M.:** *Girl's Basketball Beginners Drills*; Jan., p. 20.
3641. **Holman, Nat:** *60 Basketball Scouting Points*; Dec., p. 5.
3642. **Lippert, Jack:** *Your Choice of Basketball Rules*; Nov., p. 11.
3643. **Lustig, Arthur:** *A Basketball Practice Plan*; Nov., p. 18; *Basketball Diagrams*; Dec., p. 12.
3644. **Owen, W.B.:** *Do and Don't in Basketball*; Dec., p. 14.
3645. **Porter, H.V.:** *Test Yourself Basketball Rules Quiz*; Feb., p. 10; *Basketball Rules for 1937–38*; Apr., p. 18.
3646. **Prudhom, Harold C.:** *A Pass for Every Situation*; Jan., p. 14.
3647. **Trythall, D.L.:** *Defense the Fast Break*; Feb., p. 9.
3648. **Turner, Ralph R.:** *Whither Basketball?*; Oct., p. 16.
3649. **Wood, William R.:** *Individual Defensive Play*; Dec., p. 8.
3650. *Basketball Pictures*; Dec., p. 16; Jan., p. 16.
3651. *Common Dilemma*; Feb., p. 9.
3652. *Girl's Basketball Rules*; Dec., p. 29.
3653. *Here Below*; Mar., p. 5.
3654. *Is the Zone Defense Menacing Basketball?*; Mar., p. 7.
3655. *National High School Review*; May, p. 14.
3656. *Offensive Footwork*; Dec., p. 9.
3657. *Olympic Basketball Draw Chart*; Oct., p. 16.
3658. *Rhythm Rule*; Jan., p. 11.
3659. *Stealing a Dribble*; Feb., p. 11.

Volume 7, 1937–38

3660. **Adams, John L.:** *The Shifting Five-Man Defense*; Feb., p. 11.
3661. **Balter, Sam:** *Basketball Without the Center Jump*; Dec., p. 5.
3662. **Edwards, George R.:** *College Coaches Convention*; May, p. 36.

3663. **Gullion, Blair:** *Basketball Pre-Season Practice Plan;* Sept., p. 18.
3664. **Hein, F.V. and Randall, Dr. A.J.:** *Effects of the Center Jump Elimination;* Apr., p. 16.
3665. **Hirt, L.R.:** *Charting the Shooting Stars;* Nov., p. 14.
3666. **Kirste, Virgil:** *The Box-Type Defense;* Jan., p. 26.
3667. **Porter, H.V.:** *Basketball Brain Teasers;* Feb., p. 22.
3668. **Purdy, E.R.:** *The Unified All-Court Offense;* Dec., p. 8.
3669. **Randall, Dr. A.J. and Hein, F.V.:** *Effects of the Center Jump Elimination;* Apr., p. 16.
3670. **Schneidman, S.G.:** *Weapons for Individual Offense;* Nov., p. 7; *The 2-1-2 Shifting Zone;* Jan., p. 6.
3671. **Stenlies, Arthur:** *Sequence Play in Basketball;* Nov., p. 13.
3672. **Trythall, Donald L.:** *Play of the Offensive Guards;* Dec., p. 11.
3673. **Wood, William R.:** *The Figure Eight;* Dec., p. 7.
3674. *Changes in Basketball Rules;* Oct., p. 18.
3675. *490 Pages of Better Basketball;* Jan., p. 11.
3676. *From Coaching School Notebooks;* Nov., p. 10.
3677. *National High School Review;* May, p. 18.
3678. *Progressive Action Pictures: College Basketball in Madison Square Garden;* Feb., pp. 20, 21.
3679. *Progressive Action Pictures: Defensive Footwork;* Dec., pp. 10, 13.
3680. *Progressive Action Pictures: Defensive Tactics, Screen Plays;* Jan., pp. 8, 16, 17.
3681. *Progressive Action Pictures: Fakes and Pivots;* Nov., p. 8, 9, 20, 21.

Volume 8, 1938–39

3682. **Beaver, Preston:** *Against the Zone;* Dec., p. 8.
3683. **Chubb, G.T. and Lapp, V.W.:** *Spotting the Shooters;* Dec., p. 32.
3684. **Gullion, Blair:** *Another Weapon for the Offense;* Dec., p. 6.
3685. **Hanson, Ray:** *They Like the New Rules;* Nov., p. 40.
3686. **Healy, William A.:** *Know the Rules to Play the Game;* Mar., p. 16.
3687. **Hensley, Ralph:** *Standardizing Basketball Officiating;* Nov., p. 14; *The Drama of the Diagram;* Dec., p. 28.
3688. **Hirt, Lou:** *A General Practice Plan for Basketball;* Oct., p. 16.
3689. **Lapp, V.W and Chubb, G.T.:** *Spotting the Shooters;* Dec., p. 32.
3690. **McCarnes, Robert:** *Notes From Clair Bee's Coaching Course;* Nov., p. 7.
3691. **Owen, W.B.:** *Are Basketball Coaches Dumbbells?;* Nov., p. 12.
3692. **Porter, H.V.:** *If We Started From Scratch;* Nov., p. 28; *Basketball Brain Teasers;* Jan., p. 26; *Whistle Widow;* Apr., p. 30; *Basketball Rules Changes;* June, p. 26.
3693. **Purdy, Ellery R.:** *A Defense of the Zone Defense;* Dec., p. 12.
3694. **Ramsey, George E.:** *Rotation Basketball;* Nov., p. 10.
3695. **Selgelid, Oren C.:** *An Error Index as a Coaching Aid;* Jan., p. 32.
3696. **Trythall, Donald L.:** *Advice to Young Coaches;* Nov., p. 36.
3697. **Wood, William R.:** *Attacking From a Double Pivot-Post;* Dec., p. 9.
3698. *Basketball Styles for 1939;* Jan., p. 17.
3699. *National High School Basketball Review;* May, p. 13.
3700. *Progressive Action Pictures: Set, Foul and Pivot Shooting;* Nov., pp. 8, 10.
3701. *Progressive Action Pictures: Three Running Pivot Shots;* Dec., p. 38.
3702. *Progressive Action Pictures: Two-Man Screen-Plays;* Dec., pp. 9, 13.

Volume 9, 1939–40

3703. **Allen, F.C., Lapp, V.W., and Elbel, E.R.:** *Kansas Basketball Evaluation Study;* Jan., p. 44; Feb., p. 10.
3704. **Chandler, William:** *Marquette's Combination Offense;* Dec., p. 7.
3705. **Cox, Forrest:** *Colorado's Post and Screen Attack;* Nov., p. 7.
3706. **Elbel, E.R., Allen, F.C., and Lapp, V.W.:** *Kansas Basketball Evaluation Study;* Jan., p. 44; Feb., p. 10.
3707. **Ellsbury, C. Dale:** *Putting the Fun in Fundamentals;* Oct., p. 15.
3708. **Gullion, Blair:** *Building the Screen Attack;* Dec., p. 10; *Screen Plays;* Feb., p. 12.
3709. **Lapchick, Joe:** *St. John's Free-Style Offense;* Jan., p. 7.
3710. **Lapp, V.W., Allen, F.C., and Elbel, E.R.:** *Kansas Basketball Evaluation Study;* Jan., p. 44; Feb., p. 10.
3711. **Mitchell, Viola:** *Teach the Fundamentals First;* Dec., p. 34; *Individual and Team Defense;* Jan., p. 17; *A Team Attack for the Girls' Game;* Feb., p. 13.
3712. **Pagnucco, Grace:** *Advanced Two-Courts Basketball Plays;* Dec., p. 14.
3713. **Porter, H.V.:** *Basketball Rules Changes (1939-40);* Nov., p. 16; *Basketball Brain Teaser;* Feb., p. 16; *Basketball Rules Changes (1940-41);* May, p. 32.
3714. **Whitney, Franklin:** *The Closed Double-Pivot Offense;* Nov., p. 14.
3715. **Wood, William R.:** *Oh Captain, My Captain;* Jan., p. 27.
3716. *Clair Bee's Basketball Drills;* Oct., p. 14.
3717. *Colorado Basketball Notes;* Oct., p. 34.
3718. *Pivot Post Screen;* Nov., p. 12.
3719. *Progressive Action Pictures: A Defensive Stalemate;* Nov., p. 39.
3720. *Running Dummy Play;* Dec., p. 4.
3721. *State High School Basketball Tournaments;* May, p. 24.

Volume 10, 1940–41

3722. **Berger, Herbert:** *An Attack With a Double-Pivot-Post Motif;* Dec., p. 8.
3723. **Christenson, Irv:** *Basketball in Junior High;* Feb., p. 34.
3724. **Dell, Robert G.:** *Ups and Downs of Defensive Rebounding;* Nov., p. 8.
3725. **Iba, Henry P.:** *Oklahoma's Triple-Threat Offense;* Dec., p. 5.
3726. **Noble, Virgil J.:** *Shooting Drills;* Nov., p. 7.
3727. **Porter, H.V.:** *New Basketball Backboard;* Oct., p. 38; *Basketball Rules Changes (1940–41);* Nov., p. 22; *Basketball Brain Teasers;* Dec., p. 10; *Evolution of the Break;* Jan., p. 28; *Basketball Questionnaire;* Mar., p. 44; *Basketball Rules Changes (1941–42);* May, p. 36.
3728. **Robertson, A.J.:** *Bradley Tech's Three-Way Offense;* Jan., p. 7.
3729. **Ross, Roland F.:** *The Basketball Coaches Game Card;* Feb., p. 14.
3730. **Thomas, E.A.:** *How Strenuous Is Basketball?;* Mar., p. 26.
3731. **Turner, Ralph R.:** *A Four-Point Attack on a Set Zone;* Dec., p. 6.
3732. *Brief Suggestions for the Defense;* Dec., p. 12.
3733. *From Coaching School Notebooks (Keogan, Raese);* Nov., p. 14.
3734. *National High School Basketball Roundup;* May, p. 40.
3735. *Notre Dame Offense (Pictures);* Nov., p. 10.
3736. *Shots, Pivots and Passes (Pictures);* Feb., p. 20.

Volume 11, 1941–42

3737. **Baker, Floyd:** *You Can Beat the Zone by Jamming It;* Dec., p. 28.
3738. **Dahlberg, Al and Shaw, Harold:** *The Way of a Winner;* Apr., p. 42.
3739. **Fisher, Bruce:** *A Simplified Attack From a 2-1-2 Setup;* Dec., p. 16.

3740. **Gullion, Blair:** *Organization for Teaching Basketball;* Nov., p. 22.
3741. **Kennard, Ada:** *Girl's Basketball Groups Instruction;* Dec., p. 11.
3742. **Liebowitz, Charles:** *Two-Man Plays for Every Situation;* Nov., p. 18.
3743. **Morehouse, L.E. and Sterrett, J.E.:** *Basketball Exercises and Diet;* Nov., p. 26.
3744. **Noble, Virgil:** *An All Purpose Keyed Offense;* Dec., p. 8.
3745. **O'Dell, Griffith:** *Screen Escapes in the Backcourt;* Dec., p. 7.
3746. **Porter, H.V.:** *Basketball Brain Teasers;* Oct., p. 24; *Basketball Rules Changes (1941–42);* Nov., p. 32; *Fanning the Backboard;* Jan., p. 34; *Basketball Rules Changes (1942–43);* Apr., p. 44.
3747. **Presthus, Vance:** *A Fast Break Setup;* Dec., p. 38.
3748. **Quigley, James:** *Solving Your Big-Man Problem;* Nov., p. 40.
3749. **Ross, Roland:** *Basketball Skill Tests;* Oct., p. 20.
3750. **Shaw, Harold and Dahlbert, Al:** *The Way of a Winner;* Apr., p. 42.
3751. **Skiff, Nolan:** *A Scorer's Lot Is Not a Happy One;* Dec., p. 34.
3752. **Sterrett, J.E. and Morehouse, L.E.:** *Basketball Exercises and Diet;* Nov., p. 26.
3753. **Swenson, Ted:** *Aid to Referees;* Apr., p. 41.
3754. *From Coaching School Notebooks (John Lawther);* Nov., p. 13.
3755. *Short Shots and Passes;* Jan., p. 14.
3756. *State High School Basketball Tournaments;* May, p. 10.

Volume 12, 1942–43

3757. **Bee, Clair:** *Passing and Shooting Catalog;* Nov., p. 7; *Teaching Individual Defense;* Dec., p. 7.
3758. **Culp, Perry:** *Basketball Ability Tests;* Dec., p. 11.
3759. **Liebowitz, Charles:** *Five-Man Screen-Roll Continuity;* Nov., p. 14.
3760. **Mathews, Jack:** *The One-Man Officiating System;* Nov., p. 18.
3761. **Noble, Virgil:** *All-Year-Round Shooting Games;* Dec., p. 16.
3762. **Porter, H.V.:** *Basketball Rules Changes for 1943–44;* Apr., p. 19.
3763. *State High School Basketball Tournaments;* May, p. 16.

Volume 13, 1943–44

3764. **Abramoski, Edward:** *A Plan for Overcrowded Basketball Class;* Mar., p. 29.
3765. **Baker, Floyd:** *Center Play From the Floor Up;* Nov., p. 9.
3766. **Crawford, Wayne:** *Straight Shooting Pays;* Oct., p. 36.
3767. **Dickinson, Russell:** *Basketball Player at Work;* Dec., p. 25.
3768. **Kauffman, Morris:** *Whistle Blowing Made Easy;* Nov., p. 20.
3769. **Porter, H.V.:** *Basketball Rules (43–44);* Nov., p. 18; *Basketball Rules Changes (44–45);* May, p. 24.
3770. **Shaw, Harold:** *Open Your Season With a Jamboree;* Nov., p. 30.
3771. **Tobey, Dave:** *The "Bucket" Man as a Screener;* Dec., p. 7.
3772. **Weekley, Harold:** *Three-Man Half-Court Basketball;* Nov., p. 30.
3773. *Call 'Em as You See 'Em;* Dec., p. 13.
3774. *From the Coaching School Notebooks (Everett Shelton);* Nov., p. 7.
3775. *Screen and Switch-Dribble;* Dec., p. 30.
3776. *State High School Basketball Tournaments (1944);* May, p. 18.

Volume 14, 1944–45

3777. **Baker, Floyd:** *All Court Pressing Defense;* Nov., p. 12.
3778. **Dean, Everett:** *Elements of Team Offense;* Dec., p. 16.

3779. **Hall, Joel:** *Six Way Attack on a Zone Defense*; Feb., p. 7.
3780. **Juergensmeyer, Charles:** *State Basketball Regulations*; Sept., p. 24.
3781. **Lebowitz, Gordon:** *Quiz Your Basketball Varsity*; Oct., p. 32; *Master Plan for Basketball Practice*; Nov., p. 22; Dec., p. 18.
3782. **Malchavitz, Nat:** *Return to the 2-1-2 Zone*; Dec., p. 10.
3783. **Porter, H.V.:** *Rules Changes (1944–45)*; Nov., p. 26; *Rules Changes (1945–46)*; Apr., p. 30.
3784. **Rupp, Adolph:** *Winning Plays*; Dec., p. 7.
3785. **Spahn, Moe:** *Freezing the Ball—A Neglected Art*; Feb., p. 12.
3786. *State High School Basketball Tournaments, 1945*; May, p. 14.

Volume 15, 1945–46

3787. **Abramoski, Edward:** *Single Dribble Basketball*; Feb., p. 30.
3788. **Boell, Edward:** *Basketball Brain Busters*; Nov., p. 34.
3789. **Bunker, Herbert:** *(Air-Ating) Basketball*; Dec., p. 34.
3790. **Christenson, Richard:** *Center Open Offense*; Nov., p. 11; Dec., p. 14.
3791. **Copeland, T.D.:** *A Mass Teaching Plan for Basketball*; Feb., p. 28.
3792. **Crum, J. Birney:** *The Finals*; Feb., p. 7.
3793. **Dean, Everett:** *Stanford's Weave*; Nov., p. 13.
3794. **Kellar, Harry:** *Beating the Force*; Nov., p. 16.
3795. **Mack, Nat:** *Three Men on the Rebound*; Dec., p. 20.
3796. **Porter, H.V.:** *Official Signals*; Dec., p. 13; *Rules Changes (1946–47)*; Apr., p. 38.
3797. **Rupp, Adolph:** *Individual Defense*; Nov., p. 9.
3798. **Smith, Huron:** *Recess Basketball*; Nov., p. 54.
3799. *Pivot Play*; Dec., p. 7.
3800. *State Basketball Finals (National Report)*; May, p. 10.

Volume 16, 1946–47

3801. **Abramoski, Ed and Robb, R.T.:** *One-Hand vs. Two-Hand Shot*; Dec., p. 47.
3802. **Cook, Max:** *A Seven-Step Motivation Program*; Dec., p. 7.
3803. **Corb, I. Stanley:** *First Things*; Oct., p. 28; *When the Play Is the Thing*; Dec., p. 14.
3804. **Dean, Everett:** *Get Ready for Basketball*; Oct., p. 14.
3805. **Dudley, W.A.:** *Coaching School Report on Ray Meyer and Harold Olsen*; Nov., p. 20.
3806. **Ellis, Loren E.:** *"T" Attack*; Nov., p. 10.
3807. **Fisher, Bruce M.:** *A Simplified Offense*; Dec., p. 22.
3808. **Hall, J.W.:** *Five-Man Drills*; Dec., p. 24; *The Shift in the Zone*; Feb., p. 16.
3809. **Hanson, Ray:** *Coaching School Report on Officials Clinic*; Nov., p. 26.
3810. **Hellman, Walter H.:** *Coaching School Report on Blair Gullion*; Nov., p. 28.
3811. **Kellar, Harry:** *Outslicking the 2-1-2*; Nov., p. 7.
3812. **Lebowitz, Gordon:** *Defensive Drills*; Nov., p. 14.
3813. **Lustig, Arthur:** *Better Basketball Officiating*; Nov., p. 38.
3814. **Porter, H.V.:** *Rules Changes (1946–47)*; Nov., p. 35.
3815. **Thayer, J.A.:** *Play the Main Game First*; Dec., p. 34.
3816. *Bob Kurland on the Pivot*; Dec., p. 12.
3817. *Free Throwing*; Nov., p. 9.
3818. *1947 State Finals (National Round-up of High School Champions)*; May, p. 5.
3819. *One-Hand Shot (Kurland Shooting)*; Dec., p. 15.

Volume 17, 1947–48

3820. **Atkins, Gordon M.:** *Kentucky's Offense;* Nov., p. 7; *Coaching School Report on Peterson, Carnevale, Julian and Boyle;* Dec., p. 11.
3821. **Beck, Les:** *The Official in Action;* Nov., p. 54.
3822. **Durbin, Brice:** *The Gambling Menace;* Dec., p. 28.
3823. **Esposito, Michael:** *The Fast Break;* Dec., p. 7.
3824. **Knox, Robert D.:** *Basketball Ability Tests;* Nov., p. 45.
3825. **Lappenbusch, Chuck:** *Straight-Line Defense;* Dec., p. 26.
3826. **Lustig, Arthur:** *Make It Official;* Dec., p. 16.
3827. **Porter, H.V.:** *Basketball Rules Changes (1947–48);* Nov., p. 32; *Basketball Rules Changes (1948–49);* Apr., p. 42.
3828. **Shaw, Ross J.:** *Practice Drills;* Dec., p. 20.
3829. **Smith, A.N.:** *Educate Your Crowds;* Nov., p. 28.
3830. **Thomas, W.F.:** *Dominate the Zone;* Nov., p. 20.
3831. **Ward, Paul W.:** *Free-Throw Drill;* Feb., p. 26.
3832. *Flip and Go;* Dec., p. 10.
3833. *In the Bucket;* Nov., p. 12.
3834. *National Round-up of State High School Champions;* May, p. 7.
3835. *Scorers Manual;* Dec., p. 47.
3836. *Time-out With a Winning Coach;* Dec., p. 36.

Volume 18, 1948–49

3837. **Bee, Clair:** *Bench Strategy;* Nov., p. 8.
3838. **Burgoyne, Bus:** *Tip-Off Revival;* Nov., p. 8; *Free-Lane Attack;* Dec., p. 14.
3839. **Case, Everett N.:** *North Carolina State's Change of Pace Attack;* Dec., p. 7.
3840. **Clagg, Sam E.:** *The Basketball Crowd "Menace";* Apr., p. 40.
3841. **Gray, Jack:** *Texas' Custom-Fit Offense;* Dec., p. 12.
3842. **Hasser, George V.:** *Passing Thoughts;* Nov., p. 12.
3843. **Hobson, Howard:** *Material and System;* Nov., p. 10; *Yale's Fast Break;* Dec., p. 10.
3844. **Jones, E.D.:** *Building a Winning Attack;* Dec., p. 25.
3845. **Lappenbusch, Chuck:** *More on Straight Lane Defense;* Nov., p. 14.
3846. **Morris, Marty and Smith, Huron J.:** *Foul Shooting Drill;* Feb., p. 32.
3847. **Rarick, G.L. and Staton, W.M.:** *Free Throwing: Which Style?;* Feb., p. 48.
3848. **Rupp, Adolph:** *Kentucky's Pivot Post;* Nov., p. 7.
3849. **Scropos, Ted:** *Basketball Scouting;* Dec., p. 54.
3850. **Smith, Huron J. and Morris, Marty:** *Foul Shooting Drill;* Feb., p. 32.
3851. **Staton, W.M. and Rarick, G.L.:** *Free Throwing: Which Style?;* Feb., p. 48.
3852. **Sullivan, Kenneth G.:** *Basketball Officiating Survey;* Dec., p. 18.
3853. **Trythall, Don:** *Basketball Rules Quiz;* Dec., p. 38.

Volume 19, 1949–50

3854. **Carnevale, Ben:** *Navy's Fast Break;* Dec., p. 10.
3855. **Griffin, J.H.:** *Basketball Tip Sheets;* Nov., p. 28.
3856. **Hall, J.W.:** *Fast Break Drills;* Dec., p. 30.
3857. **Hickey, Eddie:** *St. Louis Defensive Control Pattern;* Nov., p. 8.
3858. **Horowitz, Leon D.:** *Get That Tap;* Dec., p. 23.
3859. **Iba, Hank:** *Oklahoma A. & M.'s Man to Man Defense;* Dec., p. 7.

3860. **Kaufman, Morris:** *Officiating Viewpoints;* Mar., p. 24.
3861. **Lebowitz, Gordon:** *City Slicker Basketball;* Nov., p. 18.
3862. **Lehsten, Nelson G.:** *Basketball Aptitude Tests;* Oct., p. 62.
3863. **Newell, Pete:** *Frisco Continuity Pattern;* Dec., p. 12.
3864. **Poten, George:** *Jump Ball Plays;* Oct., p. 22.
3865. **Wells, Cliff:** *Tulane's Double Pivot;* Nov., p. 7.
3866. **Wooden, John R.:** *U.C.L.A.'s Attack: Fast Break Set;* Nov., p. 12.
3867. *McGuire Passing;* Dec., p. 8.
3868. *Mikan Shooting;* Nov., p. 10.
3869. *Pivot Shot by Mikan;* Dec., p. 12.
3870. *Rules Changes for 1950-51;* May, p. 32.

Volume 20, 1950–51

3871. **Anderson, Forddy:** *Bradley Offense;* Dec., p. 10.
3872. **Burgoyne, Leon:** *Out-of-Bounds Plays;* Dec., p. 14.
3873. **Corb, I. Stanley:** *Getting an Offense Started;* Nov., p. 28.
3874. **Dye, Tippy:** *Ohio State's 1949–50 Set Attack;* Nov., p. 7.
3875. **Henderson, George L.:** *Stop the Fast Break!;* Feb., p. 26.
3876. **Hill, Elam R.:** *Passing Fancies;* Dec., p. 13.
3877. **Kaufman, Morris D.:** *"Mister Detective" of Basketball;* Dec., p. 24.
3878. **McCarthy, Thomas E. and Riggs, John D.:** *Third Man Theme in Hoop Officiating;* Nov., p. 14.
3879. **Penn, Edward C.:** *Zone Defense;* Nov., p. 38.
3880. **Ramsay, Jack:** *Foul Shooting;* Dec., p. 8.
3881. **Riggs, John D. and McCarthy, Thomas E.:** *Third Man Theme in Hoop Officiating;* Nov., p. 14.
3882. **Rupp, Adolph:** *Kentucky's Style of Pivot Play;* Nov., p. 8.
3883. **Wells, Cliff:** *Tulane's 3-Out 2-In;* Dec., p. 7.
3884. **Wooden, John R.:** *UCLA's Practice Schedule;* Nov., p. 12.
3885. *All American Jump Shooting;* Nov., p. 10.

Volume 21, 1951–52

3886. **Azary, John:** *Playing the Pivot;* Dec., p. 8.
3887. **Baker, Roy T.:** *A Compact, Flexible, Shifting Zone Defense;* Nov., p. 16.
3888. **Bee, Clair:** *Attacking the Press;* Oct., p. 11; *Attacking the Zone;* Nov., p. 10.
3889. **Burgoyne, Leon T.:** *Incentivized Foul Shooting;* Oct., p. 18.
3890. **Dallmer, Richard:** *Function of Statistics in Basketball Coaching;* Nov., p. 32.
3891. **Davis, Chick:** *Shifting Defensive Patterns;* Dec., p. 18.
3892. **Drake, Bruce:** *Oklahoma's Drake Shuffle;* Oct., p. 12; *Drake Shuffle vs. Special Defenses;* Nov., p. 12.
3893. **Flipper, J.S.:** *The 3-Man Zone;* Nov., p. 7.
3894. **Henderson, George L.:** *A "Haphazard" Press;* Oct., p. 24; *A Mid-Season Attack;* Nov., p. 28.
3895. **Hill, Elam R.:** *4-Man Weaving, 1-Man Posting;* Dec., p. 14.
3896. **Hobson, Howard:** *Competitive Defensive Drills;* Dec., p. 12.
3897. **Iba, Hank:** *Fundamental and Game-Situation Drills;* Nov., p. 9.
3898. **Kauffman, Morris D.:** *Consistency in Officiating;* Oct., p. 28.
3899. **McDowell, David D.:** *Basketball Coaching by Films;* Sept., p. 48.
3900. **McWilliams, Jay:** *Sliding Man-to-Man Defense;* Oct., p. 7.
3901. **Ramsay, Jack:** *Jump Shooting;* Nov., p. 14.

3902. **Rupp, Adolph:** *Kentucky's Fast Break*; Dec., p. 7.
3903. **Wood, Robin C.:** *A Unique All-Inclusive Net-Score Evaluation System*; Dec., p. 24.
3904. *Defense After a Shot (Picture Sequence)*; Dec., p. 13.
3905. *Give and Go (Picture Sequence)*; Nov., p. 8.
3906. *1952–53 Basketball Rules Changes*; May, p. 16.
3907. *Shooting From the Pivot (John Azary)*; Dec., p. 10.

Volume 22, 1952–53

3908. **Anderson, Forrest:** *Individual Offensive Stunts*; Dec., p. 8.
3909. **Bee, Clair:** *Weapons Against the Big Pivot*; Oct., p. 8.
3910. **Chambers, D.E.:** *Testing for Basketball Ability*; Oct., p. 36.
3911. **Combes, Harry:** *The Captain's Role*; Dec., p. 30.
3912. **Fleetwood, S.C.:** *Strategic Dribbling*; Nov., p. 20.
3913. **Gargan, J.E.:** *Ideal Junior High Varsity Basketball*; Nov., p. 36.
3914. **Henderson, George L.:** *Synchro-Shifts for the 1-3-1*; Nov., p. 10.
3915. **Hill, Elam R.:** *Basketball Coaches Survey*; Oct., p. 18.
3916. **Porter, H.V.:** *Basketball, 1952–53*; Nov., p. 38.
3917. **Riemeke, Cal:** *A Controlled 2-3 Offense*; Nov., p. 7.
3918. **Rossini, Lou:** *Individual Defense*; Nov., p. 8; *Sloughing Team Defense*; Dec., p. 5.
3919. *Feeding the Pivot (Demonstrated by Dick Dickey)*; Oct., p. 9.

Volume 23, 1953–54

3920. **Bee, Clair:** *Freezing the Ball*; Nov., p. 9.
3921. **Craig, Richard:** *Swap 1 Point for 2*; Dec., p. 7.
3922. **Gleason, Pat:** *28 Play Problems*; Nov., p. 10.
3923. **Greer, Hugh and Ward, Stan:** *Controlling the Defensive Board*; Oct., p. 22.
3924. **Henderson, George L.:** *The Whiz Kid's Inside Screen Attack*; Oct., p. 14.
3925. **Hickey, Eddie:** *St. Louis' Pre-Game Warm-Up Drill*; Oct., p. 10.
3926. **Lindeburg, Franklin A.:** *Animated Shooting Drills*; Dec., p. 14.
3927. **McGuire, Frank:** *North Carolina's Weave, Pivot and Post*; Dec., p. 10.
3928. **McWilliams, Jay:** *A 4-Man Weave*; Oct., p. 7; *Controlled Fast Break*; Nov., p. 16.
3929. **Porter, H.V.:** *1954 Rules*; Nov., p. 18.
3930. **Ramsay, Jack:** *Mix Your Defenses*; Dec., p. 20.
3931. **Rawlinson, Kenneth:** *Training and Conditioning for Basketball*; Oct., p. 30.
3932. **Stevenson, Chuck:** *Gauging Individual Performance*; Oct., p. 34.
3933. **Thompson, Donald B.:** *Simplified Scouting*; Nov., p. 24.
3934. **Watts, Stan:** *BYU's Combination Set-Free Lance Attack*; Nov., p. 7.
3935. *Cousy Shooting and Stunting*; Dec., p. 8–9, 12–13.
3936. *Rules Changes for 1954–55*; Apr., p. 55.
3937. *Stunts Off the Pivot*; Nov., p. 8.

Volume 24, 1954–55

3938. **Bach, Johnny:** *Fordham's Corner Clearout Series*; Dec., p. 7.
3939. **Byrne, John A.:** *Screen-Trap Offense*; Dec., p. 18.
3940. **Christenson, Irv:** *Basketball Tourney Management*; Oct., p. 40.
3941. **Cooper, S.A.:** *A Method of Recording Basketball Errors*; Oct., p. 16.

3942. **Gross, Elmer A.**: *Penn State's Full Court Press*; Oct., p. 14; *The 2-Out 3-In and 3-Out 2-In Set Offenses*; Nov., p. 20; *Penn State's Sliding Zone Defense*; Dec., p. 10.
3943. **Kruse, William L.**: *Kentucky's Scouting System*; Dec., p. 20.
3944. **Penn, Ed:** *Versatile Zone Defense*; Oct., p. 26.
3945. **Ramsay, Jack:** *Attacking the Various Zones*; Nov., p. 12.
3946. **Riemeke, Cal:** *Attacking the Collapsing Defense*; Oct., p. 10.
3947. **Sand, Bobby:** *5 Moving Pivots*; Oct., p. 8; *Give and Go*; Nov., p. 7.
3948. **Wood, Edward L.:** *The First 5 Days of Basketball Practice*; Sept., p. 50.
3949. *A Lesson in Man-to-Man Defense*; Nov., p. 30.
3950. *Arizin Shooting: Jump-Set-Hook (Picture Sequence)*; Dec., p. 12.
3951. *Basketball Rules Changes 1955–56*; May, p. 45.
3952. *Dayton's Criss-Cross Play (Picture Sequence)*; Dec., p. 30.
3953. *4 Pivot Shots by "Easy Ed" MacCauley (Picture Sequence)*; Oct., p. 12.

Volume 25, 1955–56

3954. **Henderson, George L.**: *The Trap Press*; Oct., p. 38.
3955. **Hickey, Eddie:** *St. Louis' Controlled 3-Lane Fast-Break*; Dec., p. 10.
3956. **Maravich, Press:** *7-Man Circle Option Drills*; Oct., p. 70.
3957. **Maravich, Press and Steel, James C.**: *Basketball Scouting Complete*; Nov., p. 22.
3958. **Masin, Herman L.**: *Defensing the Backboards*; Dec., p. 16.
3959. **McGinnis, Gordon:** *Screening for Basketball Attitude*; Nov., p. 44.
3960. **O'Haire, Ed:** *A Fluid 3-2 Pattern With Fixed Corner Men*; Oct., p. 26.
3961. **Picariello, S.J.**: *Defensive Dividends*; Oct., p. 72.
3962. **Pravda, Charles Liebowitz:** *Multi-Operation Drills*; Oct., p. 7; *Offensive Perpetuities Against All Zones*; Dec., p. 7.
3963. **Ramsay, Jack:** *A 3-2 Pattern Against the Man to Man*; Nov., p. 10.
3964. **Rupp, Adolph:** *"My 7 Cardinal Defensive Principles"*; Nov., p. 9.
3965. **Sand, Bobby:** *A Hybrid Defense Combining a Press and a 3-2 Zone*; Nov., p. 28.
3966. **Tarrant, Richard J.**: *Fast-Break Fundamentals*; Oct., p. 40.
3967. **Vanatta, Bob:** *Bradley's Box Weave*; Nov., p. 7.
3968. **Wooden, John R.:** *U.C.L.A.'s Coaching Pattern*; Dec., p. 12.
3969. **Woolpert, Phil:** *San Francisco's Balanced Offense*; Oct., p. 14.
3970. *Conlin Jumper (Action Pictures)*; Oct., p. 6.
3971. *Cousy Passing (Picture Sequence)*; Nov., p. 8.
3972. *Faking Off the Pivot (Picture Sequence)*; Dec., p. 12.
3973. *Key Lock: Lane of the Future*; Oct., p. 32.
3974. *Levitt Style of Foul Shooting*; Nov., p. 18.
3975. *1956 All American High School Basketball Squad*; May, p. 50.
3976. *10 Basketball Hints*; Dec., p. 41.

Volume 26, 1956–57

3977. **Bollinger, Dick:** *A 1-3-1 Revolving Offense Against All Defenses*; Oct., p. 66.
3978. **Boutrager, Ralph L.**: *A Good Sportsmanship Plan*; Nov., p. 16.
3979. **Comb, I. Stanley:** *Offerings to the Guards*; Sept., p. 40.
3980. **Dallmar, Howard:** *Stanford's 3-2 Post-Screen Attack*; Nov., p. 7.
3981. **Dell, Robert G.**: *Speed Up the Offense*; Oct., p. 28.
3982. **Diamond, Irwin P.**: *A Flexible "Switch" Offense*; Nov., p. 36.
3983. **Gruska, Jerry:** *The Half-and-Half Defense*; Oct., p. 40.

3984. **Hayes, E.C. (Dock):** *SMU's Post Series*; Oct., p. 17.
3985. **Hickey, Eddie:** *St. Louis' 2-3 Set Attack*; Nov., p. 10.
3986. **Masin, Herman L.:** *Foul Shooting Styles and Practice*; Dec., p. 12.
3987. **McGuire, Frank:** *Organization for Game Day*; Oct., p. 13.
3988. **Meyer, Ray:** *DePaul's Weave and Pivot Attack*; Nov., p. 8.
3989. **Picarello, S.J.:** *A Pre-Season Daily Dozen for Basketball*; Oct., p. 24.
3990. **Pinholster, Garland F.:** *A Fall Training Program for High School Basketball*; Nov., p. 30.
3991. **Ramsay, Jack:** *Developing the 3-Lane Controlled Fast Break*; Oct., p. 7.
3992. **Sand, Bobby:** *Feeding the Pivot Man*; Dec., p. 8.
3993. **Schaus, Fred:** *Time-Motion Study of Basketball Practice*; Dec., p. 7.
3994. **Toomasian, John:** *A Multiple Defense Featuring a Diamond and 1 Zone*; Nov., p. 18.
3995. **Wolfe, Herman:** *Figure-Eight Into a Pivot*; Dec., p. 10.
3996. **Woolpert, Phil:** *San Francisco's 3/4 Court Press*; Nov., p. 12.
3997. *1957 All American High School Basketball Squad*; May, p. 50.
3998. *Shaking Off a Tight Guard (Picture Sequence)*; Nov., p. 8.
3999. *That Extra Basket (Winning Plays)*; Oct., p. 10.
4000. *Uncovering the Pivot Man (Picture Sequence)*; Dec., p. 8.
4001. *Working off the Pivot (Picture Sequence)*; Oct., p. 12.

Volume 27, 1957–58

4002. **Carnesecca, Lou:** *Charting the Defensive Areas*; Nov., p. 50.
4003. **Curran, Joe:** *Canisius' Four-Man Close-Weave Attack*; Oct., p. 7.
4004. **Fears, Ernest and Lee, Robert:** *More Scoring in the Front Court*; Oct., p. 52.
4005. **Gleason, Pat:** *Multiple Team Defense*; Dec., p. 10.
4006. **Jarrett, Bill:** *A 1-3-1 Zone Attack*; Nov., p. 36.
4007. **Latham, George:** *Develop Your Own Coaching Philosophy*; Oct., p. 56; *A Screening-Continuity Against the Man-to-Man Defense*; Nov., p. 10.
4008. **Lee, Robert and Fears, Ernest:** *More Scoring in the Front Court*; Oct., p. 52.
4009. **McGuire, Frank:** *Defensing the Big Man Underneath*; Oct., p. 11.
4010. **Meyer, Ray:** *Developing the Big Boy*; Nov., p. 12.
4011. **Morris, Stanley:** *Attacking the 2-1-2 Zone With a Reverse Circle*; Oct., p. 30.
4012. **Munoz, Hector:** *Vibora's Post-Screen and Weave Pattern*; Oct., p. 14.
4013. **Ramsay, Jack:** *A Ball-Control Freeze*; Dec., p. 8.
4014. **Sand, Bobby:** *Outside Ball Scoring Plays*; Nov., p. 7.
4015. **Schaus, Fred:** *West Virginia's Free-Lance Offense*; Oct., p. 8.
4016. **Schayes, Dolph:** *Shooting Touch*; Nov., p. 8.
4017. **Wilkes, Glenn N.:** *Fast Break Theory and Drills*; Oct., p. 18.
4018. *Drives by Chet Forte (Picture Sequence)*; Oct., p. 12.
4019. *The Lakers' Pick-Off and Inside Roll (Picture Sequence)*; Oct., p. 9.
4020. *Two-Man Screen Plays (Picture Sequence)*; Dec., p. 12.

Volume 28, 1958–59

4021. **Bach, Johnny:** *Situation-Play Practice*; Dec., p. 10.
4022. **Bottom, Raymond:** *Basketball Coaching "Gimmicks"*; Nov., p. 36.
4023. **Carnesecca, Lou:** *15 Essentials of Game Strategy*; Nov., p. 14.
4024. **Durbin, Brice B.:** *Basic Points in Beating a Press*; Oct., p. 7.
4025. **Esposito, Michael:** *Defensing the Fast Break*; Oct., p. 14.
4026. **Grunska, Jerry:** *Four Principles of Effective Rebounding*; Oct., p. 30.

4027. **Hickey, Eddie:** *Stance and Footwork in Individual Defense*; Dec., p. 8.
4028. **McCafferty, Jim:** *Xavier's Moving Offense Against the Zone Defense*; Nov., p. 12.
4029. **McGuire, Frank:** *Individual Stunts*; Oct., p. 8.
4030. **Myers, Melvin:** *Basketball Coaching in Virginia*; Dec., p. 28.
4031. **Munoz, Dr. Hector:** *Coaching the 3-Lane Break and Variations*; Oct., p. 57.
4032. **Pickett, George:** *Screening the 2-1-2 Zone From a 1-3-1 Attack*; Nov., p. 7.
4033. **Sand, Bobby:** *Intensive Coaching Through Ten-Man Half-Court Drills*; Nov., p. 21.
4034. **Schayes, Dolph:** *Playing the Corner*; Nov., p. 8.
4035. **Sullivan, Don:** *Attacking Stacked Defenses*; Oct., p. 12.
4036. **Swegan, Don:** *10 Basic Basketball Coaching Points*; Oct., p. 20.
4037. **Ward, Charles R.:** *Study of Zone Defense*; Nov., p. 46.
4038. *Give-and-Go (Sequence Photos)*; Nov., p. 20.
4039. *1959 All-American H. S. Basketball Squad*; May, p. 48.

Volume 29, 1959–60

4040. **Barner, Chester:** *Keep Your System Simple*; Oct., p. 20.
4041. **Carnesecca, Lou:** *Zone Defense and Attack*; Nov., p. 14.
4042. **Davis, Bob:** *Ten Commandments for Tournament Play*; Nov., p. 18.
4043. **Dobbs, Wayne:** *Principles of Good Defense*; Oct., p. 50.
4044. **Fox, Lee:** *Buddy System in Teaching Foul Shooting*; Nov., p. 22.
4045. **Greenblatt, Jerry:** *Meaningful Pre-Game Warm-Ups*; Dec., p. 26.
4046. **Grenert, Al:** *Short Pass and Pivot Attack Against the Full-Court Press*; Dec., p. 10.
4047. **Griffin, J.H.:** *Keeping the Awkward Big Man in the Scoring Area*; Oct., p. 14.
4048. **Grigoriev, Victor and Spendoryan, Stepan:** *Basketball in Russia*; Nov., p. 36.
4049. **Hickey, Eddie:** *Teaching Principles for Individual and Team Defense*; Oct., p. 32.
4050. **Jacobs, George (Doc):** *Beating the Zone With a 1-3-1 Give-and-Go Attack*; Oct., p. 12.
4051. **Maravich, Press:** *Special-Situation Stunts (Part 1)*; Oct., p. 8; *Special-Situation Stunts (Part 2)*; Nov., p. 10.
4052. **Peck, Robert R.:** *The Best Out-of-Bounds Play in Basketball*; Oct., p. 7.
4053. **Sand, Bobby:** *Special Rotation Freeze Patterns*; Nov., p. 28.
4054. **Sterling, Robert M.:** *Make Your Practice Sessions Realistic*; Oct., p. 42.
4055. **Swegan, Don:** *Building Your Team Defense*; Oct., p. 46.
4056. **Tarrant, Richard:** *2-2-1 Moving Pattern Against Match-Up Zones*; Oct., p. 18.
4057. **Tener, Moe:** *Reverse Box Offense*; Nov., p. 7.
4058. **Toomasian, John:** *Defensing the Opposing Star*; Nov., p. 8.
4059. **Wolfe, Herman:** *Commerce's Around-the-Clock Pattern*; Dec., p. 12.
4060. *1960 All-American High School Basketball Squad*; May, p. 48.
4061. *Stunting Off the Pivot (Demonstrated by Joe Quigg)*; Dec., p. 8.

Volume 30, 1960–61

4062. **Baker, Paul M.:** *Mechanics of Shooting*; Dec., p. 8.
4063. **Burnham, Stan:** *Develop Your Rebounders With Weight Training*; Dec., p. 16.
4064. **Eaves, Joel:** *2nd Option in the Auburn Shuffle*; Oct., p. 10.
4065. **Gilliam, Joe H.:** *Overshifting Against the Zone*; Nov., p. 20.
4066. **Greenblatt, Dick:** *An "Angles" Pattern That Keys on the Defense*; Nov., p. 19.
4067. **Griffin, Tom:** *1-3-1 Versus All Defenses*; Oct., p. 76.

4068. **Grunska, Jerry:** *Defensing the Jump Shot;* Oct., p. 13.
4069. **LaGrand, Louis E.:** *Full-Court Zone Press;* Dec., p. 7.
4070. **Meadows, Paul E.:** *Hit the Zone With Movement;* Oct., p. 16.
4071. **Mulligan, Bill:** *1-2-2 Zone With a Chase;* Oct., p. 32.
4072. **Munoz, Hector:** *Meeting Changing Defenses With an Alternating Offense;* Dec.,
p. 20.
4073. **Rossini, Lou:** *One-on-One Defense;* Nov., p. 10.
4074. **Sand, Bobby:** *Moving Without the Ball;* Oct., p. 7.
4075. **Sonstroem, R.J.:** *Box-and-1 Running Zone;* Nov., p. 16.
4076. **Taylor, Fred:** *Ohio State's Patterned Front-Court Movements;* Nov., p. 7.
4077. **Tener, Moe:** *Double Post Versus the Man-to-Man;* Oct., p. 20.
4078. **Winter, Fred (Tex):** *Kansas State's Triangular Sideline Series;* Dec., p. 10.
4079. *Cliff Hagan's Moves From the Pivot (Photo Sequences);* Dec., p. 12.
4080. *Four Driving Moves by Bob Pettit (Photo Sequence);* Nov., p. 8.
4081. *Influencing the Backcourt Attacker (Symposium of 15 Famous College Coaches);*
Nov., p. 31.
4082. *1961 All-American High School Basketball Squad;* May, p. 52.

Volume 31, 1961–62

4083. **Albeck, Stan:** *Check That Defense!;* Dec., p. 26.
4084. **Bach, John W.:** *Integrating the Clear-Out With a Sideline Series;* Nov., p. 7.
4085. **Baker, Paul M.:** *Refining the Individual Offensive Techniques;* Dec., p. 12.
4086. **Bass, Bob:** *Charting the Man-to-Man Defense;* Oct., p. 14.
4087. **Boyer, Carl E.:** *Evolution of Zone Attack;* Dec., p. 38.
4088. **Coley, Ray C.:** *Weak-Side Post Pattern;* Oct., p. 8.
4089. **Dobbs, Wayne:** *Flexing Zone Defense;* Nov., p. 24.
4090. **Edmonds, Ed:** *A Seven-Pass Drill;* Oct., p. 38.
4091. **Eicher, Chester J.:** *A Moving 1-3-1 Versus Any Zone;* Nov., p. 14.
4092. **Friend, John:** *Rebounding ABC's;* Nov., p. 28.
4093. **Griffin, Tom:** *Simplified Offense for Beginning Coaches;* Nov., p. 40.
4094. **Hanlon, Thomas J.:** *1-2-2 Zone Attack;* Oct., p. 13.
4095. **Hunter, Ken:** *The Four Basic Defensive Moves;* Dec., p. 8.
4096. **Kloppenburg, Bob:** *Multiple Pressure Defenses;* Nov., p. 32.
4097. **LaGrand, Louis E.:** *A Complete Team Repertoire;* Oct., p. 22.
4098. **Maravich, Press:** *Organizing the Fast Break;* Nov., p. 12.
4099. **Peck, Robert R.:** *A Tailor-Made Offensive Continuity;* Dec., p. 10.
4100. **Schayes, Dolph:** *The Syracuse Nats' Famous "B" Series;* Dec., p. 7.
4101. **Smith, Chuck:** *Mix Your Defenses;* Oct., p. 42.
4102. **Smith, Pete:** *Interpreting the Trends in Basketball;* Oct., p. 48.
4103. **Swan, Jerry:** *Protect Your Lead With a Controlled Attack;* Dec., p. 24.
4104. **Travis, Bill:** *Pick That Zone!;* Oct., p. 11.
4105. **Wolfe, Herman:** *A Five-Man Move That Has Everything;* Oct., p. 7.
4106. *1962 All-American High School Basketball Squad;* May, p. 60.

Volume 32, 1962–63

4107. **Coley, Ray C.:** *Reverse Action From the Tandem Post;* Oct., p. 11.
4108. **Delaney, Donald G.:** *"Go Opposite" Zone Attack;* Nov., p. 40.
4109. **De Noon, Harold A.:** *The "Go-Between," a Simple Zone Offense;* Nov., p. 10.
4110. **Eason, John E.:** *Diversified Basketball Program for the Junior High School;* Nov.,
p. 22.

4111. **Haithcock, Maynard:** *Beating the Full-Court Zone Press;* Nov., p. 58.
4112. **Harkins, Harry:** *Zone Press;* Oct., p. 7; *Zoning by the Rules;* Nov., p. 28; *1-3-1 All-Purpose Attack;* Dec., p. 34.
4113. **Hastings, Glenn (Skip):** *Off-Season Check-List for the Junior High Basketball Player;* June, p. 40.
4114. **LaGrand, Louis E.:** *The Seven Lively Arts of One-on-One;* Nov., p. 14.
4115. **Leviton, Dan:** *Four Moves From the High Post;* Oct., p. 14.
4116. **Lewis, F. Dwain:** *Two-Footer Outside Play;* Oct., p. 8.
4117. **Lewis, Fred:** *Syracuse's Unique 1-4 Set;* Oct., p. 12.
4118. **Munoz, Hector:** *Fast Break and Zone Press;* Oct., p. 60.
4119. **Murrey, Bob:** *Survey of Working Conditions of High School Basketball Coaches;* Dec., p. 18.
4120. **Peck, Robert:** *Win the Close Ones;* Oct., p. 48.
4121. **Phillips, Pete:** *Spread-Stall Offense;* Nov., p. 48.
4122. **Ramsay, Jack:** *St. Joseph's 3-1-1 Half-Court Zone Press;* Dec., p. 7.
4123. **Rubin, Roy:** *1-2-2 Zone Press;* Oct., p. 32.
4124. **Samaras, Bob:** *Pivot Moves Complete;* Dec., p. 10.
4125. **Sand, Bobby:** *Attacking a Sloughing Defense;* Oct., p. 20.
4126. **Sells, Jim:** *Second Guard Through;* Nov., p. 7.
4127. **Silverberg, Stanley:** *Team Organization and Discipline;* Nov., p. 44.
4128. **Strohmeyer, Edward:** *15 Basic Defensive Drills;* Oct., p. 24.
4129. **Verderame, Sal (Red):** *Selecting Your Basketball Officials;* June, p. 24.
4130. **Wilkes, Glenn:** *Shuffling the Zone;* Nov., p. 9.
4131. *Back-Door Double Screen (Photos);* Nov., p. 58.
4132. *Horizontal Give and Go (Photos);* Nov., p. 8.
4133. *Inside Screen, Blur Screen (Photos);* Nov., p. 12.
4134. *1963 All-American High School Basketball Squad;* May, p. 60.

Volume 33, 1963–64

4135. **Carter, Bill:** *Recipe for Good Defense;* Jan., p. 42.
4136. **Coley, Ray C.:** *Odd and Even Offense With Reverse Action;* Oct., p. 11.
4137. **Fox, Phil and Usilaner, Dutch:** *Ball-Handling Specifics;* Oct., p. 42.
4138. **Fried, David H.:** *City-Slicker Defensive Drills;* Sept., p. 110.
4139. **Griffin, Tom:** *1-3-1 Shuffle;* Nov., p. 7.
4140. **Hatrak, Bob and Landa, Howie:** *Five-Man Continuity Stressing Isolation;* Oct., p. 20.
4141. **Harkins, Harry (Mike):** *Get-Away on the Controlled Break;* Oct., p. 14.
4142. **Hogeland, Zeke:** *Instant Offense: Attacking by the Numbers;* Nov., p. 22.
4143. **Jenkins, Paul E.:** *A Lonesome Guard Tight 1-4 Offense;* Oct., p. 12.
4144. **Kloppenburg, Bob:** *Individual Defense: Stance, Position, Movement;* Dec., p. 10.
4145. **LaGrand, Louis E.:** *Defensing the Four Common Attacking Moves;* Oct., p. 38.
4146. **Landa, Howie and Hatrak, Bob:** *Five-Man Continuity Stressing Isolation;* Oct., p. 20.
4147. **LeBlanc, Rene:** *Baseline Double Post;* Oct., p. 7.
4148. **McManus, John:** *Defensing the Blind Pick;* Oct., p. 8.
4149. **Merrill, Robert V.C.:** *Ohio Wesleyan's Freeze Attack;* Nov., p. 18.
4150. **Munoz, Hector:** *Installing the 2-2-1 Zone Press;* Oct., p. 60; *Beating the Zone Press;* Nov., p. 32.
4151. **Nida, Al:** *Concealed Switching Man-to-Man Defense;* Nov., p. 12.
4152. **Poulin, Art:** *Shuffle, Cut and Deal;* Dec., p. 7.
4153. **Rubin, Roy:** *A Switch in Time;* Dec., p. 9.
4154. **Samaras, Bob:** *Blitz Basketball System;* Nov., p. 10.

4155. **Usilaner, Dutch and Fox, Phil:** *Ball-Handling Specifics;* Oct., p. 42.
4156. **Van Gundy, William:** *Multi-Purpose 2-2-1 Delay Pattern;* Oct., p. 68.
4157. **Wilder, Robert:** *Mechanics of the Jump Shot;* Dec., p. 26.
4158. *Buddying-Up on Free-Lance Plays (Photos);* Nov., p. 8.
4159. *Checking the Give-and-Go (Photos);* Oct., p. 18.
4160. *1964 All-American High School Basketball Squad;* May, p. 76.

Volume 34, 1964–65

4161. **Baillie, Brian:** *Northwestern's Control Attack;* Nov., p. 20.
4162. **Baker, Paul M.:** *Revolving Continuity Offense;* Nov., p. 8.
4163. **Buxenbaum, Harris and Sells, Jim:** *Attacking the Multiple Zone;* Oct., p. 18.
4164. **Dalay, Charles J.:** *A Simplified Match-Up Defense;* Oct., p. 10.
4165. **Davis, Bob:** *Georgetown's Guard Offense;* Oct., p. 12.
4166. **Dawkins, John R.:** *Triple-Post Attack;* Oct., p. 7.
4167. **Ekker, Ron:** *Overplay, the Secret of Pressing Defense;* Oct., p. 14.
4168. **Grady, Rex:** *Double-Team Trapping;* Dec., p. 8.
4169. **Harkins, Mike:** *1-3-1 Semi-Stall;* Nov., p. 7.
4170. **Henry, Kent:** *Simplified 1-4 Attack;* Dec., p. 7.
4171. **Kilpatrick, Lloyd:** *Keep the Pressure On;* Oct., p. 38.
4172. **LaGrand, Louis E.:** *Three-Man Stall Offense;* Dec., p. 22.
4173. **Lockhart, Paul D.:** *Beating the Full-Court Zone Press With a 1-2-1-1;* Nov., p. 24.
4174. **Maynor, Cortez:** *1-2-1-1 Pressure Defense;* Nov., p. 48.
4175. **McGreevy, Mike:** *Free-FOUR-All Attack;* Nov., p. 12.
4176. **Munoz, Hector:** *Four Horsemen Out-of-Bounds Series;* Nov., p. 36.
4177. **Ramsay, Jack:** *St. Joseph's Multiple Man-to-Man Offense;* Nov., p. 10.
4178. **Sells, Jim and Buxenbaum, Harris:** *Attacking the Multiple Zone;* Oct., p. 18.
4179. **Silverberg, Stan:** *Fast-Break Situations;* Oct., p. 46.
4180. **Sullivan, William J.:** *Defensing the Man Without the Ball;* Dec., p. 28.
4181. **Vanderame, Sal (Red):** *Five Bread-and-Butter Plays;* Oct., p. 8.
4182. **Walters, Bucky:** *Defending the Low Post;* Nov., p. 14; *Six Steps to One-on-One Proficiency;* Dec., p. 12.
4183. **Wilder, Robert E.:** *Attacking the Zone With a Short Center;* Dec., p. 10.
4184. **Wilkie, Dennis:** *An Aggressive Fast-Break Defense;* Oct., p. 22.
4185. **Wolfe, Herman:** *Picking the Team;* Oct., p. 30.
4186. *1965 All-American High School Basketball Squad;* May, p. 62.

Volume 35, 1965–66

4187. **Bogonzi, John A.:** *Multi-Screening the Switching Man-to-Man;* Oct., p. 24; *A Seven-Set Rotating Defense;* Nov., p. 50.
4188. **Brown, James K.:** *Basketball "Scoring";* Nov., p. 45.
4189. **Burger, David L.:** *Penetrating the Full-Court Press;* Oct., p. 36.
4190. **Caine, John:** *Sell Your Defense!;* Oct., p. 50.
4191. **Canfield, Verne:** *Sell Your Basketball Program;* Nov., p. 58.
4192. **Clark, Dane E.:** *A Simple but Varied Shuffle Offense;* Nov., p. 42.
4193. **Covert, Mark:** *Double Low Attack vs. a Man-to-Man;* Oct., p. 28.
4194. **Enge, Charles:** *Defensive Change-Ups;* Nov., p. 18.
4195. **Harkins, Mike:** *1-2-2 Screening Offense;* Oct., p. 6; *The High-Low Shuffle;* Nov., p. 39.
4196. **Jack, Stan:** *Six Fast Options off a Double Post;* Nov., p. 7.

4197. **Jacobs, George (Doc):** *The Basketball Coach's Finest Half Hour;* Oct., p. 46.
4198. **Kloppenburg, Bob:** *Individual Defensive Post Play;* Oct., p. 48.
4199. **LaGrand, Louis E.:** *Jump-Ball Attack;* Nov., p. 32.
4200. **McKay, Joe:** *Mobile Rotating Attack vs. 1-3-1 and 1-2-2 Zones;* Oct., p. 44.
4201. **Mitchell, Warren:** *Combatting the Lateral Screen and the Tag and Body Contact;* Nov., p. 12.
4202. **Munoz, Hector:** *Vibora's Post-Screen and Weave;* Oct., p. 32.
4203. **Nissalke, Tom:** *New Thoughts on the Fast Break;* Dec., p. 24.
4204. **Quenette, Bill:** *Yo-Yo Zone Defense;* Nov., p. 24.
4205. **Ramsay, Jack:** *Ramsay on Defense: Part 1, The Pressing, Switching Man-to-Man;* Oct., p. 8; *Part 2, The Double-Team and Adjustments;* Nov., p. 8; *Part 3, The Zone Press;* Dec., p. 7.
4206. **Rickson, Ken:** *Rules of Action Set Offense;* Oct., p. 60.
4207. **Sauer, David W.:** *Surprise 3-2 Zone Press;* Dec., p. 26.
4208. **Waugh, Jim:** *Free-Throwing Under Pressure;* Oct., p. 42.
4209. **Williams, Carroll L.:** *Shuffling and Weaving;* Dec., p. 22.
4210. *Maneuvering From the Pivot;* Dec., p. 10.
4211. *1966 All-American High School Basketball Squad;* May, p. 60.

Volume 36, 1966–67

4212. **Anderson, Eugene W.:** *Eight Guiding Attacking Principles;* Nov., p. 8; *Defensing the Basic Seven;* Dec., p. 7.
4213. **Ankenbrand, Ralph J.:** *All-Purpose Shuffling;* Nov., p. 22.
4214. **Arnold, Frank H.:** *The 1-2-2 vs. Multiple Full-Court Presses;* Oct., p. 36.
4215. **Baudo, Charles J.:** *The Mid-Court Mix;* Nov., p. 16.
4216. **Borowetz, Walter:** *Dual Purpose Offense;* Dec., p. 38.
4217. **Bowman, Bill:** *A Loose 1-2-1-1 Full-Court Offense;* Oct., p. 18.
4218. **Cano, Albert M.:** *Attacking the Full-Court Zone Press;* Oct., p. 7.
4219. **Cook, J.R.:** *What Makes a Top College Basketball Coach?;* Mar., p. 17.
4220. **Costello, Chuck:** *Organizing the Jump Ball;* Oct., p. 60.
4221. **Craven, Len:** *A Penetrating Out-of-Bounds Play;* Dec., p. 16.
4222. **Earle, Jimmy:** *Match-Up Zone Defense;* Nov., p. 7.
4223. **Eskridge, Bill:** *That Half-Hour Before Practice;* Sept., p. 18; *High-Low Lopsided Offense;* Nov., p. 28.
4224. **Fershtman, Gil:** *Game-Situation Practice Drills;* Oct., p. 24.
4225. **Fisher, Willard:** *Beware the All-Out, All-Court "Mad Dog"!;* Nov., p. 12.
4226. **Griffin, Tom:** *A 3-in-1 Offense;* Nov., p. 24.
4227. **Handler, Fred D.:** *Continuity From a 2-1-2 High Post;* Oct., p. 52.
4228. **Harvey, John H.:** *Statistical Trends in Basketball;* Oct., p. 22.
4229. **Heathcote, Jud:** *2-2-1 High-Low Post;* Nov., p. 10; *Adjusting the High-Low Post;* Dec., p. 20.
4230. **Inglis, Dave:** *Double Low Post;* Dec., p. 7.
4231. **Kohl, William F.:** *Out-of-Bounds Plays;* Nov., p. 32.
4232. **Lewis, F. Dwain:** *Forward Play vs. Pressure;* Oct., p. 10.
4233. **Munoz, Hector:** *Full-Court, Full-Speed Attack: Part 1;* Nov., p. 18; *Part 2;* Dec., p. 24.
4234. **Nettles, Barry:** *The Power of the Press;* Oct., p. 13.
4235. **Peck, Robert R.:** *An Eclectic 1-2-1-1 Zone Press;* Oct., p. 8.
4236. **Rubin, Roy:** *Posting the Full-Court Zone Press;* Oct., p. 8.
4237. **Sand, Bobby:** *2-Up, 3-Under Total Offense;* Sept., p. 58.
4238. **Wiliams, Carroll L.:** *The "Candlestick" Auxiliary;* Dec., p. 8.
4239. **Woods, Edward L.:** *Zone and Ball Press Attack;* Oct., p. 28.

4240. **Zunic, Matt:** *A Simple High-Post Controlled Game;* Oct., p. 40.
4241. *Ambidexterity on the Pitch-Out (Photo Sequence);* Oct., p. 12.
4242. *1967 All-American High School Basketball Squad;* May, p. 44.

Volume 37, 1967–68

4243. **Albaugh, Glen:** *A High Post Continuity;* Oct., p. 54.
4244. **Alexander, Bill:** *A New Style of Basketball Conditioning;* Oct., p. 30.
4245. **Bien, Harvey J.:** *Pre-Game Basketball Ceremony;* Sept., p. 88.
4246. **Bolton, William D.:** *Developing the High Post Man;* Dec., p. 10.
4247. **Borowetz, Walter:** *Half-Court Zone Press Attack;* Dec., p. 35.
4248. **Carnesecca, Lou:** *Give and Go Behind;* Nov., p. 7.
4249. **Carrera, Michael A.:** *"Open the Gate" vs. Offensive Pressure;* Dec., p. 8.
4250. **Coniam, Jack:** *Score After the Second Pass!;* Nov., p. 42.
4251. **Crogan, Eli:** *All-Purpose Zone Attack;* Oct., p. 12.
4252. **Daly, Chuck:** *The One-Guard All-Purpose Offense;* Dec., p. 7.
4253. **Davis, Tom:** *Why Not a Defensive Coach in Basketball?;* Oct., p. 70.
4254. **Earle, Jimmy:** *"Basic Eight" Defensive System;* Nov., p. 37.
4255. **Eldred, Vince:** *After the Shot;* Oct., p. 18; *Golden Man-to-Man Offensive Rules;* Dec., p. 48.
4256. **Eskridge, Bill:** *Shuffle From 2-2-1 High-Low Lopsided Offense;* Oct., p. 10; *"Confidence" Plays From the High-Low Attack;* Dec., p. 44.
4257. **Gibson, Bill:** *The Shell Defensive Disguise;* Nov., p. 22.
4258. **Griffin, Tom:** *Control Continuity for the Small Team;* Nov., p. 20.
4259. **Harkins, Mike:** *Pressure Zoning With a Monster Man;* Nov., p. 17.
4260. **Jackson, Wilford:** *Multi-Presses off the Free Throw;* Dec., p. 30.
4261. **Jenkins, Paul:** *"Convertible" Out-of-Bounds Plays;* Oct., p. 7; *Jamming the Lay-Up Area;* Dec., p. 42.
4262. **LaGrand, Louis E.:** *Beating the Half-Court Zone Press;* Nov., p. 60.
4263. **Linder, Jack:** *Continuity From a 2-1-2 High Post;* Nov., p. 50.
4264. **Maratta, Roy:** *Controlling the Tap;* Nov., p. 48.
4265. **McKay, Joe:** *Ten Principles of Good Defense;* Oct., p. 40.
4266. **Pelcher, Jim:** *A Guard-Oriented Triple Post;* Nov., p. 30.
4267. **Phelps, Richard F.:** *Zone Press Drills;* Nov., p. 34.
4268. **Schultz, Jack E.:** *Reaction and Adjustment Drills;* Oct., p. 22.
4269. **Slough, Bob:** *The Sideline Fast Break;* Oct., p. 64.
4270. **Steffen, Ray:** *Kalamazoo's 1-2-1 Double Screen;* Oct., p. 26.
4271. **Stier, William F.:** *Stalling From a V;* Nov., p. 14.
4272. **Szymanski, Frank:** *A Clinical Analysis of the Jump Shot;* Oct., p. 8.
4273. **Thompson, Hugh:** *The Slot Offense;* Dec., p. 20.
4274. **Victor, Gene:** *"The Passing Game" Continuity;* Dec., p. 26.
4275. **Wyllie, Lawrence A.:** *Attacking the Box-and-One;* Oct., p. 36.
4276. *Basketball Rules Changes, 1967–68;* Nov., p. 47.
4277. *1968 All-American High School Basketball Team;* May, p. 66.
4278. *Telephonic Foul Shooting Contests;* Oct., p. 86.

Volume 38, 1968–69

4279. **Abramczyk, John:** *Look at the Statistics;* Nov., p. 64.
4280. **Albaugh, Glen and Graw, Herb:** *Continuous Action Fast-Break Drill;* Nov., p. 38.
4281. **Bagonzi, John A.:** *Continuity Zone Offense;* Nov., p. 34.
4282. **Barnabo, Don:** *A Twin-Optioned Press-Breaker;* Dec., p. 12.

4283. **Broaca, Peter:** *Reverse-Action Attack vs. the Man-to-Man*; Dec., p. 7.
4284. **Danforth, Roy:** *A Little-Man 3-2 Set*; Oct., p. 12.
4285. **Dooley, Jay:** *Fast Breaking After a Free Throw*; Dec., p. 36.
4286. **Englestead, Ray G.:** *Beat the Zone With "Musical Chairs"*; Nov., p. 46.
4287. **Gaffey, Bill:** *"Luck" = Preparation + Opportunity*; Nov., p. 50.
4288. **Graw, Herb and Albaugh, Glen:** *Continuous Action Fast-Break Drill*; Nov., p. 38.
4289. **Gray, Jerry:** *Three-Quarter Court Match-Up Pressure Defense*; Nov., p. 7.
4290. **Hankinson, Mel:** *The Complete Offensive Ball-Players*; Nov., p. 30.
4291. **Harkins, Mike:** *Overloaded 1-3-1 Continuity*; Oct., p. 54; *Monster Man Zone*; Nov., p. 12; *A Matching Zone Press*; Dec., p. 32.
4292. **Hulce, Larry:** *Guard Through and Forward Through Series*; Oct., p. 66.
4293. **Jones, Norm:** *Attacking the 1-2-2 Full-Court Zone Press*; Nov., p. 8.
4294. **Kemp, Phil:** *Attack With Continuous Movement*; Nov., p. 52.
4295. **Kloppenburg, Bob:** *Downcourt Guard Play in Man-to-Man Pressure Defense*; Dec., p. 44.
4296. **Kresse, John:** *How About a Four-Lane Fast Break!*; Dec., p. 40.
4297. **MacPhee, Len:** *Mechanical Principles of the Rocker Step*; Oct., p. 10.
4298. **Maddelena, Earl J.:** *Side-Saddle Offense*; Nov., p. 18.
4299. **Mulzoff, Frank:** *The Controlled 3-2 Free-Lane Attack*; Dec., p. 18.
4300. **Munoz, Hector:** *The Tornado Zone Offense*; Oct., p. 22.
4301. **Pinholster, Garland:** *Planning the Basketball Scouting Report*; Oct., p. 32.
4302. **Ross, Don:** *Versatile Conditioning Drills*; Nov., p. 42.
4303. **Stier, Wiliam F.:** *Revolving 1-2-2 Zone Defense*; Nov., p. 20.
4304. **Sweeting, Roger L.:** *A 2-2-1 Spread Against Pressure!*; Dec., p. 24.
4305. **Walker, Wilmer D.:** *Coaching the "Little Things"*; Oct., p. 42.
4306. **Watkins, David L.:** *Dickinson's "22" Series*; Oct., p. 18.
4307. **Williams, Carroll L.:** *1-3-1 Zone Attack*; Nov., p. 60.
4308. **Witthuhn, Bill:** *Motivation for Winning Teams*; Oct., p. 56.
4309. *Beating the Zone From the High Post*; Oct., p. 7.
4310. *Elements of Good Defense*; Nov., p. 10.
4311. *Jump-Shooting Moves in the Air Under Strong Pressure*; Oct., p. 12.
4312. *1969 All-American High School Basketball Team*; May, p. 56.
4313. *Two-Man Backcourt Plays*; Nov., p. 9.

Volume 39, 1969–70

4314. **Allen, Sonny:** *Simplified Fast Break*; Dec., p. 16.
4315. **Braun, Lee:** *Organization for That First Half Hour*; Oct., p. 70.
4316. **Broaca, Peter:** *The Double Stack Multi-Purpose Attack*; Nov., p. 46.
4317. **Earle, Jim:** *Organization for Offensive Planning*; Oct., p. 34.
4318. **Eberly, Stephen:** *Changing Offenses in Mid-Season*; Dec., p. 30.
4319. **Ellis, John:** *The Player Notebook*; Oct., p. 84.
4320. **Freund, Al:** *Beat the Zone With Movement*; Dec., p. 42.
4321. **Gideon, Donald L.:** *Locate the Shot and Control the Boards!*; Oct., p. 18.
4322. **Gonser, Jerry:** *1-2-1-1 Midcourt Zone Press*; Oct., p. 56.
4323. **Henson, Louis R.:** *New Mexico State's Multiple Series*; Oct., p. 14.
4324. **Mathiesen, Peter:** *A Splitting, Screening 2-3*; Nov., p. 16.
4325. **Musselman, Bill:** *Ashland's Matchup Zone Defense*; Nov., p. 12; *Stunting out of the Matchup Zone Press*; Dec., p. 14.
4326. **Newbold, Larry:** *Low-Post Offense*; Oct., p. 9.
4327. **Osborn, Bob:** *Multiple Offense From a Tandem Post*; Dec., p. 22.
4328. **Phillips, Goodrich K.:** *Umbrella Pressure Zone*; Nov., p. 9.

4329. **Ramsay, Jack:** *One-on-One Basketball*; Dec., p. 10.
4330. **Standlin, Fred:** *Shoot and Rebound Zone Offense*; Dec., p. 20.
4331. **Schakel, Doug:** *Auxiliary 1-4 vs. the 1-3-1 Zone*; Nov., p. 23.
4332. **Sledzik, Herm:** *3-2 Continuity Offense*; Nov., p. 10.
4333. **Stanley, Robert E.:** *3-2 Circle Offense*; Nov., p. 40.
4334. **Tattersall, Robert C.:** *Combining the Swing and Go and Backdoor Trap*; Nov., p. 24.
4335. **Underwood, Don:** *Rule-Defined Match-Up Zone Defense*; Oct., p. 22.
4336. **Williams, Carroll L.:** *Shuffle for the Big Men*; Oct., p. 50.
4337. **Wilson, Larry L.:** *Pressure Checks for the Shuffle*; Nov., p. 30.
4338. **Wince, Greg:** *The Corner Trap*; Dec., p. 9.
4339. *1970 All-American High School Basketball Team*; May, p. 62.

Volume 40, 1970–71

4340. **Alzina, Jack:** *A 1-2-1-1 Attack vs. All Types of Presses*; Nov., p. 32; *Attacking the Flexed Zone*; Dec., p. 24.
4341. **Bach, Johnny:** *Stopping the Fast Break*; Oct., p. 7.
4342. **Baker, Paul M.:** *Fast Break: Defense*; Dec., p. 11.
4343. **Carson, Glenn:** *Fast Break: Attack*; Dec., p. 10.
4344. **Coveleski, Don:** *Zoning With Man-to-Man Pressure*; Oct., p. 32.
4345. **Davenport, Dean:** *Basketball Pride-Builders*; Dec., p. 40.
4346. **Dudley, Jim:** *Pick and Roll*; Dec., p. 9.
4347. **Eberly, Stephen:** *Crash Course for the Inexperienced Big Man*; Nov., p. 8.
4348. **Ford, Jack S.:** *"The Fundamental Five"*; Nov., p. 40.
4349. **Gonzalez, Bill G.:** *A 2-3 Zone Buster*; Oct., p. 38.
4350. **Harnum, Don:** *Organization Against Full-Court Pressure*; Nov., p. 52.
4351. **Hogeland, Zeke:** *A "Reading" Zone Offense With Two Low Threats*; Nov., p. 14.
4352. **Kessler, Marv:** *A "Stall" Emergency Offense*; Nov., p. 22.
4353. **Klein, George:** *Multi-Purpose 1-2-1-1 Press*; Oct., p. 22.
4354. **Kresse, John:** *Scouting ABC's*; Oct., p. 35.
4355. **Jones, Jerry:** *Go Right at the 1-2-2 Zone!*; Nov., p. 7.
4356. **McAndrews, Tony:** *1-3-1 Quick-Cut Offense*; Oct., p. 54.
4357. **McGrath, Joseph P.:** *A High-Percentage End-Line Out-of-Bounds Play*; Oct., p. 70.
4358. **Nastase, Robert J.:** *"Starring" the Defense*; Oct., p. 58.
4359. **Sager, Thomas W.:** *In Season Weight Training for High School Basketball*; Oct., p. 42.
4360. **Scoble, Bill:** *Offside Defensive Help*; Dec., p. 12.
4361. **Stier, Bill:** *Double-Tandem Attack*; Oct., p. 8.
4362. **Ulmer, Pete:** *Cross-Over Step for the Big Man*; Nov., p. 26.
4363. **Updike, Buddy:** *Stopping the Isolated Dribbler From a Full-Court Press*; Nov., p. 30.
4364. **Wilson, Larry:** *Out-of-Bounds Plays for the Small Team*; Nov., p. 38.
4365. *Free-Lancing off a Shuffle*; Oct., p. 26.
4366. *1971 All-American High School Basketball Team*; May, p. 58.
4367. *Posting, Screening, Rolling (Photo Sequence)*; Nov., p. 10.

Volume 41, 1971–72

4368. **Bach, Johnny:** *Defensing the Low Post and the Lane Screen*; Oct., p. 14.
4369. **Bangerter, Blauer L. and Lilly, Rex:** *To Bank . . . or Not to Bank*; Nov., p. 35.

4370. **Bennett, Tom:** *Dribble Series off the 1-4;* Nov., p. 12.
4371. **Bond, Dale:** *Coaching the Special Situation;* Nov., p. 48.
4372. **Darnall, David D.:** *Power I Offense;* Oct., p. 40.
4373. **Dutcher, Jim:** *Patterned 2-1-2 for Two Sharp-Shooting Post Men;* Nov., p. 10.
4374. **Edelman, Sonny:** *Special 28-Foot Zone Defense;* Oct., p. 16.
4375. **Ellis, Cliff:** *1-2-1-1 and 2-1-2 Zone Presses;* Nov., p. 44.
4376. **Gordon, Duane F:** *Slow-Down Circle Continuity;* Dec., p. 28.
4377. **Halperin, Gary:** *Exploiting the Free-throw Set-Up;* Nov., p. 24.
4378. **Hermann, Dick:** *Double Stack Press Breaker;* Oct., p. 27.
4379. **Kaminer, Jack:** *3-1-1 Full Court Zone Press;* Oct., p. 50.
4380. **Kerns, James F.:** *A Dictating Funnel Defense;* Oct., p. 38.
4381. **Lilly, Rex and Bangerter, Blauer L.:** *To Bank . . . or Not to Bank;* Nov., p. 35.
4382. **MacCauley, "Easy Ed":** *Anatomy of the Jump Shot;* Oct., p. 8; *Going One-on-One;* Nov., p. 14; *Moves off the Dribble;* Dec., p. 14.
4383. **Mahoney, William J.:** *Last-Second Game Winner;* Oct., p. 73.
4384. **Miller, Ken:** *Double-Play Attack;* Nov., p. 40.
4385. **Morrison, Gary:** *Pressure-Simulated Free-Throw Practice;* Feb., p. 52.
4386. **Munoz, Hector:** *The Set 3-2 in the Full-Court Full-Speed Offense;* Nov., p. 28.
4387. **Paye, Burrall:** *Front Foot to Pivot Foot Stance;* Nov., p. 7; *Defensing the Inside;* Dec., p. 10.
4388. **Petro, Ron:** *Rebounding the Missed Foul Shot;* Dec., p. 34.
4389. **Queener, Duane:** *Man-to-Man Defensive Charting;* Dec., p. 16.
4390. **Riemcke, Cal:** *1-2-2 Extended Zone Attack;* Oct., p. 7.
4391. **Sakamoto, Oscar:** *1-2-2 Zone Press-Breaker;* Nov., p. 72.
4392. **Sand, Bobby:** *"Defense!";* Oct., p. 44.
4393. **Schoenherr, Steven:** *Power Options for Everyone;* Dec., p. 43.
4394. **Stier, Wiliam F.:** *Triple-Post Attack;* Nov., p. 20.
4395. **Taylor, Terry:** *1-2-2 Half-Court Trapping Defense;* Dec., p. 21.
4396. **Walters, Bill:** *Attacking the Zone With a Double High Post;* Oct., p. 22.
4397. *1972 All-American High School Basketball Team;* May, p. 48.

Volume 42, 1972–73

4398. **Allen, Sonny:** *Old Dominion's Last-Second Offense;* Oct., p. 36.
4399. **Bach, Johnny:** *Defensive Rebounding With a Purpose;* Oct., p. 14.
4400. **Baker, Paul:** *Master Plan for Basketball Practice;* Nov., p. 55.
4401. **Baschnagel, Norbert A.:** *2-3 Continuity Zone Attack With a Slide Series;* Oct., p. 40.
4402. **Collins, Darrell:** *Motivating the Basketball Player;* Oct., p. 50.
4403. **Dunaway, Larry:** *Shoot With the Inside Shoulder!;* Dec., p. 12.
4404. **Eldred, Vince:** *On Guard(s);* Nov., p. 50; *Basketball Coaching Guidelines;* Jan., p. 46.
4405. **Ellis, Cliff:** *A 1-2-1-1 Man-to-Man Press-Breaker;* Sept., p. 134.
4406. **Evans, Stan:** *Score From Out-of-Bounds;* Nov., p. 28.
4407. **Farrington, Robert:** *Multiple Offensive Sets;* Nov., p. 30.
4408. **Ferner, J. Alan:** *In Behalf of the 1-2-2 Stack;* Dec., p. 24.
4409. **Freund, Al:** *Eastern Michigan's Auxiliary 1-3-1 vs. the Man-to-Man;* Oct., p. 18.
4410. **Graw, Herb and Van Gundy, William:** *Beat the Zone From Inside;* Oct., p. 128.
4411. **Hall, Jim:** *Building a Disciplined Offense;* Dec., p. 34.
4412. **Hanada, Roger:** *Out-of-Bounds Plays With a Continuity;* Dec., p. 20.
4413. **Harnum, Don:** *Five-Option Open Offense;* Dec., p. 9.
4414. **Kahora, Jim:** *Accent the Offensive Rebound;* Dec., p. 10.

4415. **Kaminer, Jack:** *Step-by-Step Lead-Up Drills for Pressure Defense*; Nov., p. 14.
4416. **Kautzner, Ronald:** *"The Smasher" Full-Court Zone Press Breaker*; Dec., p. 30.
4417. **Kazanjian, Bob:** *Promoting P.R. and Team Unity*; Nov., p. 9.
4418. **Krause, Dr. J.V. and Meggelin, Gary:** *The Free Throw: A Precise Technique and Teaching Methodology*; Dec., p. 14.
4419. **Lawhead, Richard:** *1-3-1 Trap Defense*; Nov., p. 40.
4420. **Lien, Richard D.:** *X-Pattern Offense*; Oct., p. 7; *Organized Transition From Offense to Defense*; Dec., p. 29.
4421. **Lyons, Paul E.:** *Attacking the Full-Court Press From a 1-1-3*; Nov., p. 16.
4422. **Mahoney, William J.:** *Influencing the Referee*; Oct., p. 71.
4423. **Mathiesen, Pete:** *Pre-Season Camp for Basketball*; Nov., p. 60.
4424. **Meggelin, Gary and Krause, Dr. J.V.:** *The Free Throw: A Precise Technique and Teaching Methodology*; Dec., p. 14.
4425. **Murrell, James O.:** *Selecting a Summer Basketball Camp*; May, p. 78.
4426. **Odishoo, Daniel J.:** *For They Who Also Serve*; Sept., p. 138.
4427. **Paye, Burrall:** *Defensing Individual Movement*; Oct., p. 8; *Stunting Off the Man-to-Man Defense*; Nov., p. 10.
4428. **Stier, William F.:** *1-4 Baseline Attack*; Nov., p. 22.
4429. **Sweet, Virgil:** *Getting Your Players on the Rebound*; Sept., p. 128.
4430. **Van Gundy, William and Graw, Herb:** *Beat the Zone From Inside*; Oct., p. 20.
4431. **Wasem, Jim:** *Beating the Full-Court Zone Press by the Rules*; Nov., p. 44.
4432. **Willeford, Burt:** *"Clear-Out and Carry On"*; Oct., p. 28.

Volume 43, 1973–74

4433. **Abelsett, Bob:** *Rotating Invert-and-2 Matchup Defense*; Nov., p. 82.
4434. **Bach, John:** *Penn State's Freedom "Passing Game"*; Nov., p. 12.
4435. **Boyer, Steve and Randall, Chuck:** *Beating Every Kind of Press*; Nov., p. 28.
4436. **Breves, Ray:** *The Tryout Offense*; Nov., p. 37.
4437. **Carabajal, Frank:** *Simple Power Zone Attack*; Oct., p. 7.
4438. **Carroll, Mike J.:** *Building a Jayvee Basketball Program*; Dec., p. 56.
4439. **Chapman, Thomas R.:** *2-3 Rotating Match-Up Zone*; Oct., p. 28.
4440. **D'Amico, Rudy:** *Out-of-Bounds Continuities From the Side*; Oct., p. 88.
4441. **Dillon, Dick:** *The Total Match-Up Zone: Try It, Your Opponents Will Hate It!*; Dec., p. 18.
4442. **Dunaway, Larry:** *Sharpen Your Fast Break!*; Dec., p. 7.
4443. **Fails, Harry:** *Defensing the Out-of-Bounds Play*; Nov., p. 32.
4444. **Fisher, Steve:** *Double-Tandem All-Zone Offense*; Oct., p. 36.
4445. **Foss, Bill:** *Anticipating, All Purpose 2-1-2 Zone Attack*; Oct., p. 66.
4446. **Gotsill, Tom:** *A Philosophy and Offense for the Lower-Level Coach*; Nov., p. 7.
4447. **Hanna, George A.:** *Audible Out-of-Bounds Plays*; Dec., p. 24.
4448. **Hill, Betty L.:** *Kaycee at the Net*; Dec., p. 62.
4449. **Jones, Dwight:** *Long Beach State's High-Post Power Attack*; Oct., p. 12.
4450. **Lyons, Paul E.:** *Players' Progress Reports: Encouraging Self-Improvement During the Off-Season*; Nov., p. 40.
4451. **Miller, William:** *The Pressure Defense With Everything*; Dec., p. 32.
4452. **Randall, Chuck and Boyer, Steve:** *Beating Every Kind of Press*; Nov., p. 28.
4453. **Rinaldi, Tony:** *Man-to-Man Overload*; Oct., p. 78.
4454. **Roh, Les and Roundy, Elmo:** *Basketball Recruiting: What Influences the Prospects Most in Making Their Decisions?*; Dec., p. 44.
4455. **Roundy, Elmo and Roh, Les:** *Basketball Recruiting: What Influences the Prospects Most in Making Their Decisions?*; Dec., p. 44.
4456. **Ruesch, Robert G.:** *High-Post Attack*; Nov., p. 54.

4457. **Schofield, Jay:** *Screen-and-Weave Offense;* Dec., p. 42.
4458. **Stier, Wiliam F.:** *Working the Low Post in the 1-3-1;* Dec., p. 8.
4459. **Williams, Carroll L.:** *"Braking" the Fast Break;* Oct., p. 40.
4460. **Wissell, Dr. Harold R.:** *Fordham's 1-2-1-1 Match-Up Press: No. 1. Basic Principles;* Oct., p. 8; *No. 2. How It Works;* Nov., p. 8.
4461. *1974 All-American High School Basketball Team;* May, p. 68.

Volume 44, 1974–75

4462. **Alwine, Daryle:** *Simplified Cincinnati-Style Double Low Post and Variation;* Sept., p. 38.
4463. **Baumgartner, Dick:** *The Alignment of the Shooting Arm;* Oct., p. 18.
4464. **Berg, Roald O. and Proctor, Mark:** *Beating the Trappers;* Dec., p. 11.
4465. **Bussard, Dennis:** *Game Tempo and the Inside-Outside Offense;* Dec., p. 48.
4466. **Cotton, Richard:** *The Thinking Man's Offense;* Sept., p. 36.
4467. **Dunaway, Larry:** *The Art of Substituting;* Oct., p. 74.
4468. **Dutcher, Jim:** *The Michigan Fast Break;* Dec., p. 12.
4469. **Evans, Frank A.:** *Simple Two-Play 1-3-1 High-Low Series;* Nov., p. 32.
4470. **Fisk, Robert:** *Stall Set Off a Double Pick;* Dec., p. 52.
4471. **Fockler, Neil:** *"The Foul Five";* Dec., p. 6.
4472. **Fox, Robert A.:** *The Combination Press;* Nov., p. 64.
4473. **Froelich, Clyde W.:** *Beating the Box-and-One;* Nov., p. 15.
4474. **Gimblin, Ken and Taylor, John:** *John Wooden's Practice Philosophy;* Oct., p. 13.
4475. **Grebb, Budd:** *Trojan Multi-Drill;* Oct., p. 42.
4476. **Guerrera, Peter:** *A Meaningful Grade School Basketball Program ;* Sept., p. 107.
4477. **Hall, Ed L.:** *Rebounding on Both Ends of the Floor;* Nov., p. 16.
4478. **Ihnot, Thomas M.:** *Exploiting the "Lack of Sufficient Action";* Mar., p. 22.
4479. **Kaminer, Jack:** *Attacking the Various Full-Court Zone Presses;* Nov., p. 42.
4480. **Lyons, Paul:** *Harvard's #5 Offense;* Oct., p. 56.
4481. **Maravich, Press:** *Three Man Triangular "Bingo": Lead-Up Basketball at Its Best;* Oct., p. 14.
4482. **Mills, Sam:** *Beat the Match-Up With Movement;* Nov., p. 28.
4483. **Pancoast, Robert J.:** *Out-of-Bounds Plays for Everyone;* Nov., p. 46.
4484. **Post, Keith:** *Drawing the Charge;* Dec., p. 22.
4485. **Pratt, Michael J.:** *Out-of-Bounds Play vs. the Zone;* Oct., p. 32.
4486. **Proctor, Mark and Berg, Roald O.:** *Beating the Trappers;* Dec., p. 11.
4487. **Taylor, John and Gimblin, Ken:** *John Wooden's Practice Philosophy;* Oct., p. 13.
4488. **Wiener, David:** *Basic Zone Concepts;* Oct., p. 28.
4489. **Williams, Richard:** *The Streaker Break After an Opposing Basket;* Nov., p. 18.
4490. *1975 All-American High School Basketball Squad;* May, p. 80.

Volume 45, 1975–76

4491. **Alwine, Daryle:** *A Basketball Program for Elementary/Junior High Schools;* Sept., p. 51.
4492. **Baumgartner, Dick:** *Thrust, Release and Follow-Through in the Jump Shot;* Oct., p. 24.
4493. **Cavalcante, Cal:** *Blitz Press;* Nov., p. 46.
4494. **Conn, James H. and Krause, Jerry:** *Transition Offense vs. Half-Court Trapping Defenses;* Oct., p. 36.

4495. **Crawford, Larry:** *Getting That Clutch Two-Pointer;* Oct., p. 17.
4496. **David, Steve:** *Sideline Out-of-Bounds Plays;* Dec., p. 28.
4497. **Evans, Frank A.:** *Triple Threat Sideline Series;* Nov., p. 59.
4498. **Fockler, Neil:** *Pressing Off the Free Throw;* Oct., p. 62.
4499. **Froehlich, Clyde W.:** *Two-Guard Tandem Post vs. the Diamond-and-One;* Nov., p. 52.
4500. **Goetz, Lou:** *Push Them Baseline!;* Dec., p. 48.
4501. **Harter, Dick:** *Oregon's Fast Break;* Dec., p. 20.
4502. **Hoch, David A.:** *How About a Man Coaching a Girls' Basketball Team?;* Nov., p. 32.
4503. **Jack, Stan:** *Beat the Press—Simply;* Oct., p. 38.
4504. **Kitchens, Rich:** *"Revolver" Zone Offense;* Oct., p. 68.
4505. **Korobov, Glen:** *Stetson's Controlled "Motion Offense";* Dec., p. 40.
4506. **Krause, Jerry and Conn, James H.:** *Transition Offense vs. Half-Court Trapping Defenses;* Oct., p. 36.
4507. **Land, Harry L.:** *Double Stack to 1-3-1 Continuity;* Jan., p. 70.
4508. **LaRicca, Robert:** *Triple-Stack Press Breaker;* Oct., p. 40.
4509. **Lawhead, Rick:** *2-2-1 Full-Court Zone Press;* Jan., p. 62.
4510. **Lyons, Paul:** *Harvard's Run and Read Defense;* Jan., p. 94.
4511. **O'Neal, Louise:** *Pressure Defense Drills for Girls;* Oct., p. 32.
4512. **Schmidt, James:** *The 100 Tiger Defense;* Jan., p. 32.
4513. **Sheridan, Bill:** *Beating the Wide 1-3-1 Zone With a 1-4;* Oct., p. 49.
4514. **Smith, Dean:** *North Carolina's Pressure-Type Defense;* Sept., p. 22; *North Carolina's "T" Game, Part 1;* Nov., p. 17; *Part 2;* Dec., p. 15.
4515. **Somogyi, John:** *Gap Offense vs. Full-Court Pressure;* Nov., p. 30.
4516. **Swepston, Greg:** *"Mop" The Zone Defense;* Dec., p. 32.
4517. **Virtue, Frank:** *Blitz Offense;* Dec., p. 24.
4518. **Webster, Fran:** *Pittsburgh's Amoeba Defense;* Oct., p. 18.
4519. *1976 All-American High School Basketball Team;* May–June, p. 74.

Volume 46, 1976–77

4520. **Abelsett, Bob:** *Insurance Plays for "The Passing Game";* Mar., p. 33.
4521. **Aberdeen, Stu and Mears, Ray:** *Tennessee's Cinco-Man Quick Break;* Oct., p. 26; *Tennessee Quicksand Defense;* Nov., p. 17.
4522. **Archibald, Tony:** *Full-Court Man-to-Man Pressure: Part 1;* Dec., p. 28; *Part 2;* Jan., p. 82.
4523. **Clark, Gene A.:** *"Slide-Middle-Basket" Pressing Defense;* Jan., p. 94.
4524. **Conn, James H.:** *A Quick Fundamental—Review Drills;* Jan., p. 74.
4525. **Crawford, Charles L.:** *Five Keys to Defensive Rebounding;* Oct., p. 42.
4526. **Crawford, Larry N.:** *1-4 Baseline Offense vs. Odd-Front Zones;* Dec., p. 15.
4527. **Fershtman, Gil:** *Fast Break: The Pressure Defense;* Nov., p. 32.
4528. **Ford, Duane:** *Developing and Communicating a Defensive Philosophy in Basketball;* May, p. 66.
4529. **Frederick, Lee:** *The High-Percentage Stab Shot;* Oct., p. 31.
4530. **Gotsill, Tom:** *The Case for Half-Court Pressure;* Feb., p. 40.
4531. **Gray, Dick, Riese, Gordon, and Pennington, Hugh:** *Post Moves Low and High;* Dec., p. 16.
4532. **Hill, Andy:** *Team Contribution Index;* Jan., p. 96.
4533. **Korobov, Glen:** *"Motion Offense" vs. the Zone;* Aug., p. 68.
4534. **Layton, Terry:** *You Must Read the Defense;* Sept., p. 17.
4535. **Mathiesen, Pete:** *Progressive Drills for Team Defense;* Jan., p. 90.

4536. **Mears, Ray and Aberdeen, Stu:** *Tennessee's Cinco-Man Quick Break*; Oct., p. 26; *Tennessee Quicksand Defense*; Nov., p. 17.
4537. **Moro, John:** *Game Winners With 10, 5, 3, or 1 Second to Play!*; Jan., p. 56.
4538. **Patterson, Karlos:** *The "Passing Game," High School Style*; Dec., p. 64.
4539. **Pennington, Hugh, Riese, Gordon, and Gray, Dick:** *Post Moves Low and High*; Dec., p. 16.
4540. **Riese, Gordon, Gray, Dick, and Pennington, Hugh:** *Post Moves Low and High*; Dec., p. 16.
4541. **Rinaldi, Tony:** *Fast-Break Down the Sideline*; Dec., p. 42.
4542. **Samaras, Robert T.:** *New Dimensions in Basketball Stats*; Oct., p. 12.
4543. **Schakel, Doug:** *Baseline Shuffle Offense*; Dec., p. 22.
4544. **Schmidt, James:** *Angle-Stacked Triangle Stall*; Oct., p. 62.
4545. **Webster, Fran:** *Amoeba Area Zone Defense With Match-Up and Man-to-Man Principles: Part 1*; Oct., p. 32; *Part 2*; Nov., p. 24.
4546. *Corner Moves by Walter Davis*; Oct., p. 28.
4547. *1977 Adidas All-American High School Basketball Team*; May, p. 80.

Volume 47, 1977–78

4548. **Baumgartner, Dick:** *The Wrist Cock in Jump Shooting*; Nov., p. 28.
4549. **Blatt, Michele:** *"P.E.P." Up Your Basketball Program*; Oct., p. 53.
4550. **Brown, Bill:** *Defense From the Basket Out, Part 1*; Oct., p. 62; *Part 2*; Nov., p. 80.
4551. **Busone, Jerry:** *You Can Beat the Zone Press!*; Dec., p. 63.
4552. **Cottrell, Steve:** *Mini-Pressing After a Foul Shot*; Aug., p. 94.
4553. **Dougher, James D.:** *Holy Cross's Control Offense*; Oct., p. 24.
4554. **Fengler, Hank:** *Patterned Phase of the One-Guard Offense*; Nov., p. 38.
4555. **Fertig, Jack:** *Man-to-Man Structured Motion Offense*; Oct., p. 46.
4556. **Gilbert, Dale A.:** *Quick Transitions Can Make the Difference*; Dec., p. 34.
4557. **Gomulinski, Paul J.:** *Basic Six Agility Drills for the Green Big Man*; Dec., p. 80.
4558. **Gratz, Ron:** *Big-Play Strategy*; Oct., p. 97.
4559. **Jackson, Jack:** *Delaying . . . and Scoring!*; Nov., p. 34.
4560. **Jenkins, Red:** *Win the Big Ones From the Foul Line*; Dec., p. 42.
4561. **Jenkins, Red and Wootten, Morgan:** *Late-Game-Situation Winners: Woodson's #8 Play: DeMatha's Ladder*; Oct., p. 70.
4562. **Kershner, Ed:** *Multi-Purpose Flash Offense*; Oct., p. 23.
4563. **Loftus, John:** *Complementary Plays for the "Motion Game"*; Nov., p. 36.
4564. **Lyons, Paul:** *Full-Court Zone Press*; Sept., p. 84.
4565. **Masters, George D.:** *"22" Pressure-Defense*; Feb., p. 92.
4566. **McCrea, Dotty:** *The 3-2 Matchup Zone*; Sept., p. 62.
4567. **Murphy, James:** *Get the High Percentage Shot With a Box Offense*; Nov., p. 21.
4568. **Nagle, Jack:** *Shallow Guard Zone Attack*; Dec., p. 22.
4569. **Pelliccioni, Louis:** *Press off a Missed Foul*; Oct., p. 7.
4570. **Phillips, Bucky:** *Junior High Press Breakers*; Sept., p. 34.
4571. **Piscopo, Joe:** *"T" Match-Up Defense*; Nov., p. 22.
4572. **Robinson, Jim:** *Beating the 2-3 Zone*; Nov., p. 42.
4573. **Rojcewisz, Sue:** *Defensing the Post*; Oct., p. 56.
4574. **Schacht, Charles A.:** *"Mousetrap" Full-Court Pressure Defense*; Dec., p. 90.
4575. **Schakel, Doug:** *Basketball . . . From March to November*; Dec., p. 12.
4576. **Schakel, Doug:** *Fund Raising for Basketball*; Feb., p. 103.
4577. **Schoyler, Paul:** *Defensive Corner Drill*; Nov., p. 73.
4578. **Simpson, Alice:** *Only Road to "Greatness" in Basketball*; May/June, p. 83.
4579. **Staak, Bob:** *All-Purpose Rotation Zone Offense*; Jan., p. 108

4580. **Underwood, Don:** *7-12 Stack Continuity;* Oct., p. 76.
4581. **Williams, Carroll L.:** *Out-Of-Bounds Series From a Shuffle;* Oct., p. 40.
4582. **Wootten, Morgan and Jenkins, Red:** *Late-Game-Situation Winners: Woodson's #8 Play: DeMatha's Ladder;* Oct., p. 70.
4583. *Big-Man Drills in the University of Tennessee Program;* Nov., p. 26.
4584. *Inside Moves for the Big Guard or Forward;* Dec., p. 26.
4585. *1978 Adidas All-American High School Girls Basketball Team;* May, p. 112.
4586. *1978 Adidas All-American High School Basketball Team;* May, p. 110.

Volume 48, 1978–79

4587. **Aponte, Angelo and Munoz, Hector:** *The Concealed Moving Screen: An Un-switchable Play;* Jan., p. 66.
4588. **Beecroft, John R.:** *Interchangeable "Spread" Delay Offense;* Oct., p. 91.
4589. **Byers, John R., III:** *Try the One-Hand Chest Pass!;* Oct., p. 30.
4590. **Comstock, Marc:** *Pressure Defense Without Fouling;* Nov., p. 74.
4591. **Cotton, Gene:** *Power-Stack Offense;* Dec., p. 64.
4592. **Foster, Bill [of Clemson]:** *Clemson's "Passing Game";* Nov., p. 28.
4593. **Foster, Bill [of Duke]:** *Free Throw Shooting the Duke Way;* Oct., p. 20.
4594. **Gappy, Bill:** *Michigan Tech's 2-3 Match-Up Zone;* Dec., p. 28.
4595. **Gundy, Bill Van:** *Variety in Offensive Initiation;* Oct., p. 34.
4596. **Haklin, Joe:** *Beat the Stall With a 10-Point Plan;* Nov., p. 6.
4597. **Hartwig, James:** *Camouflaging Your Zone Defense;* Nov., p. 78.
4598. **Kloppenburg, Bob:** *Progressive "On the Ball" Defense;* Oct., p. 22; *Progressive "On the Ball" Drills;* Nov., p. 2; *Progressive "Off the Ball" Defense;* Dec., p. 18.
4599. **Kornhauser, Sam:** *Triangle-and-2 With a Mousetrap;* Sept., p. 23.
4600. **Kresse, John:** *50 Tips on Beating Pressure;* Dec., p. 42.
4601. **Layton, Terry:** *A New "Angle" on Rebounding;* Oct., p. 26.
4602. **Lopez, Bill:** *Full-Court Zone Press-Breaker;* Dec., p. 32.
4603. **Masters, George D.:** *Make Press Time Lay Up Time;* Aug., p. 60.
4604. **Miller, David:** *Complete Inbounds System;* Sept., p. 92.
4605. **Mims, Ray:** *Press "Buster";* Nov., p. 21.
4606. **Munoz, Hector and Aponte, Angelo:** *The Concealed Moving Screen: An Un-switchable Play;* Jan., p. 66.
4607. **Noice, Bob:** *Defensive Game Drill;* Sept., p. 34.
4608. **Ostby, Marnold:** *Start Your Shooters One-Handed!;* Dec., p. 17.
4609. **Pelliccioni, Louis:** *Scramble Drills for "Neglected" Situations;* Oct., p. 88.
4610. **Potter, Dr. Glenn R.:** *Beat Pressure With a Six-Area "Passing Game";* Aug., p. 80.
4611. **Ridley, Cornelius and Travis, Frank:** *"Streaking" for the Sidelines;* Dec., p. 48.
4612. **Snyder, Jack:** *Drill With a Purpose;* Nov., p. 10.
4613. **Stier, William F.:** *Inside Motion Continuity Offense;* Dec., p. 22.
4614. **Swartz, Steven:** *The 1-2-2 Ball-Control Offense;* Nov., p. 34.
4615. **Travis, Frank and Ridley, Cornelius:** *"Streaking" for the Sidelines;* Dec., p. 48.
4616. **Van Gundy, Bill:** *Variety in Offensive Initiation;* Oct., p. 34.
4617. **Webster, Fran:** *Sound Off on the Officiating: Part 1;* Sept., p. 138; *Part 2;* Oct., p. 80.
4618. **Wilk, John F.:** *Tempo Control: The Best Way to Beat a Better Team;* Oct., p. 86.
4619. *1979 Adidas All-American High School Basketball Team (Boys);* May, pp. 6, 54.
4620. *1979 Adidas All-American High School Basketball Team (Girls);* May, p. 72.

Volume 49, 1979–80

4621. **Borkowicz, Ron:** *The 2-1-2 Circle Continuity*; Aug., p. 62.
4622. **Brown, Bruce:** *Self-Substitution System for Basketball*; Oct., p. 70.
4623. **Capano, Vincent L.:** *Rotation System of Pressure Defense*; Nov., p. 63.
4624. **Davison, Bill:** *Teaching That All-Important Sense of Where You Are*; Dec., p. 30.
4625. **DeVenzio, Dave:** *Motivating Your Bench Warmers*; Jan., p. 78.
4626. **Edwards, Mark:** *Washington State's Double-Low Post*; Oct., p. 21; *Situation Moves From the Low Post*; Nov., p. 21.
4627. **Findura, Thomas:** *Freedom and Safety of the Press*; Dec., p. 19.
4628. **Gibson, Mel:** *Double-Stack Tease Offense*; Oct., p. 36.
4629. **Hankinson, Mel:** *Defensing the Four-Corner Game*; Nov., p. 38.
4630. **Hartwig, James:** *Last-Minute Strategy When the Game Is on the Line*; Oct., p. 50.
4631. **Huckle, Bruce:** *Continuous, Unpredictable "Motion Offense"*; Apr., p. 58.
4632. **Hutchens, Ron:** *Simple Press Offense*; Apr., p. 49.
4633. **Kennedy, Barry:** *Developing the High School Basketball Feeder System*; Jan., p. 82.
4634. **Kobel, Butch and Miller, David:** *Beat Motion Offense With a "23X" Zone*; Nov., p. 42.
4635. **Mili, Vinnie:** *Developing a Winning Defensive Attitude*; Dec., p. 36.
4636. **Miller, David and Kobel, Butch:** *Beat Motion Offense With a "23X" Zone*; Nov., p. 42.
4637. **Miller, Jim:** *Extend Your Pressure by Double-Teaming the Inbounder*; Nov., p. 36.
4638. **Munoz, Dr. Hector:** *Getting the High-Percentage Shot vs. the Zone*; Dec., p. 28.
4639. **Murphy, Dianne:** *Eastern Kentucky's 1-4 Stack Offense*; Feb., p. 66.
4640. **Piscopo, Joe:** *An Out-of-Bounds Play for All Occasions*; Mar., p. 37.
4641. **Potter, Dr. Glenn R.:** *Zone Defense by the Rules*; Sept., p. 34.
4642. **Stier, William H.:** *1-3-1 High-Post Continuity*; Nov., p. 33.
4643. **Summers, Al:** *A Junior High 1-3-1 Zone Defense*; Oct., p. 26.
4644. **Tarkanian, Jerry and Warren, William:** *Sideline-Influence Pressure Defense*; Oct., p. 28.
4645. **Toomasian, John:** *The Pre-Practice 100*; Dec., p. 70.
4646. **Warren, William and Tarkanian, Jerry:** *Sideline-Influence Pressure Defense*; Oct., p. 28.
4647. **Weinstein, Paul:** *Fast-Breaking Off a Converted Free Throw*; Nov., p. 54.
4648. **Wendelkin, Maureen and John:** *Single Stack Series, Stressing the Inside Game*; Sept., p. 76; *Special-Situation Defense, the Winning Edge*; Oct., p. 64; *Montclair State's 2-3 Zone Defense*; Nov., p. 66.
4649. *1980 Adidas All-American High School Basketball Team*; May, p. 30.
4650. *Situation Moves From the Low Post*; Dec., p. 26.

Volume 50, 1980–81

4651. **Ammirnate, Gene:** *Building Blocks for Practice Organization*; Oct., p. 38.
4652. **Andrews, Arthur:** *Diamond and One Star-Stopped Press*; Sept., p. 72.
4653. **Balliet, Glenn L.:** *Rebounding From Pressure Defense*; Oct., p. 70.
4654. **Boosalis, John and Margaritis, John:** *1-1-3 Man-Zone Half-Court Trap Defense*; Nov., p. 50.
4655. **Dobbins, Terry:** *Seeding and Building the Girls Basketball Program*; Oct., p. 58.
4656. **Doperalski, Vic:** *Beat the Zone With a 1-2-2 Rotation Offense*; Oct., p. 32.
4657. **Dunavant, Mike:** *"Box" In That Full-Court Man-to-Man Pressure!*; Oct., p. 31.
4658. **Framer, Larry and O'Connor, Kevin:** *UCLA High-Post Offense*; Oct., p. 21.
4659. **Hainje, Robert:** *"Float" Your Way Through the Press*; Nov., p. 42.

4660. **Handler, Fred D. and Satalin, Jim:** *St. Bonaventure's Patterned Inside Game;* Nov., p. 32.
4661. **Hart, Dave, Jr.:** *Promoting and Funding the High School Basketball Program;* Sept., p. 25.
4662. **Malone, Brendan:** *Syracuse's Big-Man Moves in Low;* Oct., p. 26; *Syracuse's Dozen and One Big-Man Drills;* Nov., p. 21.
4663. **Margaritis, John and Boosalis, John:** *1-1-3 Man-Zone Half-Court Trap Defense;* Nov., p. 50.
4664. **Masters, George D.:** *Time-Out! The Forgotten Equalizer;* Nov., p. 58.
4665. **McCrea, Dotty:** *Stanford's 1-2-1-1 Denial, All Out Full-Court Press;* Sept., p. 52.
4666. **Morros, Jim:** *Fairfield's "2-Game" (Getting the Ball Inside);* Dec., p. 32.
4667. **O'Connor, Kevin and Farmer, Larry:** *UCLA High-Post Offense;* Oct., p. 21.
4668. **Ostby, Marnold:** *Jump Ball Rotations;* Dec., p. 48.
4669. **Phipps, Jerry:** *Defense vs. the Four-Corner Offense;* Jan., p. 80.
4670. **Pike, John:** *Crossover Dribble Illustrated;* Dec., p. 24.
4671. **Rataiczak, Thomas E.:** *"Stats" Amore!;* Nov., p. 72.
4672. **Reid, Larry:** *A "Go" Offense From Optional Sets;* Dec., p. 28.
4673. **Samaras, Robert T.:** *The Automatic 20-Second Man Offense;* Oct., p. 72.
4674. **Satalin, Jim and Handler, Fred D.:** *St. Bonaventure's Patterned Inside Game;* Nov., p. 32.
4675. **Schoepfer, Martin:** *Gap and Rotate Zone Offense;* Oct., p. 42.
4676. **Shogon, Debra A.:** *And Now for the One-Hand Chest Pass;* Oct., p. 52.
4677. **Summers, Al:** *A Trapping, Rotating 2-2-1 Press;* Dec., p. 22.
4678. **Warren, William:** *Nine Principles of Zone Offensive Strategy;* Dec., p. 64.
4679. *1981 Adidas All-American High School Boys Basketball Team;* May, p. 30.
4680. *1981 Adidas All-American High School Girls Basketball Team;* May, p. 34.
4681. *UCLA Duck and Backdoor Moves;* Nov., p. 24.

Volume 51, 1981–82

4682. **Ammirante, Gene:** *Ten Proven Drills for the Young Post Player;* Dec., p. 42.
4683. **Brann, David and Pearcy, Terry:** *Exploiting the Free-Throw Rebounding Rule Change;* Feb., p. 52.
4684. **Brown, Charles A.:** *2-1-2 Overload vs. the Zone Defense;* Nov., p. 64.
4685. **Davis, Tom:** *Boston College's Continuity vs. the Zone;* Nov., p. 21; *Boston College's Full-Court Denial Defense;* Dec., p. 22.
4686. **Duke, Dr. Derwood and Pim, Dr. Ralph:** *Field-Goal Shooting;* Dec., p. 58.
4687. **Fiske, William A.:** *The "45" Man Offense;* Oct., p. 60.
4688. **Ford, Duane:** *Sticking the Axe Into Some Sacred Basketball Axioms;* Nov., p. 32.
4689. **Lambert, Randy:** *Attacking the One-Guard Front-Zone Defense;* Dec., p. 32.
4690. **Miller, Ralph and Van Eman, Lanny:** *Oregon State's 1-4 Half-Court Offense;* Oct., p. 21.
4691. **Pearcy, Terry and Brann, David:** *Exploiting the Free-Throw Rebounding Rule Change;* Feb., p. 52.
4692. **Pelcher, Stan:** *Team Free-Throw Shooting Regimen;* Sept., p. 30.
4693. **Pike, John:** *Drilling the Crossover Dribble;* Oct., p. 18.
4694. **Shambarger, Jake:** *Shuffling to a High Post Offense;* Sept., p. 88.
4695. **Spinelli, Joseph A.:** *Think" Press Break!;* Dec., p. 21.
4696. **Van Gundy, Bill:** *What To Do About the Triangle and 2;* Nov., p. 30.
4697. **Watson, Edwin R.:** *Try the Full-Court Parallel Zone Press;* Oct., p. 26.
4698. **Zigler, Ted:** *Skip" The Zones!;* Nov., p. 56.
4699. *1982 Adidas All-American Girls High School Basketball Team;* May/June, p. 42.
4700. *1982 Adidas All-American High School Basketball Team;* May/June, p. 30.

Volume 52, 1982–83

4701. **Johns, Ellen:** *The Foul-Shot Situation: Key to Switching Defense*; Jan., p. 66.
4702. **Orshoski, Paul:** *A Top Pressure Free Throw Shooting Drill*; Feb., p. 16.
4703. **Simmons, Ted:** *Nine Game Objectives for the High School Team*; Jan., p. 55.
4704. **Stier, Dr. William F.:** *Recruiting on the Small College Level*; May/June, p. 49.
4705. **Wolfsohn, Edward T.:** *Don't Fold Against the Press (Sure)*; Mar., p. 32.
4706. *All-American Girls High School Basketball Team*; May/June, p. 49.
4707. *All-American High School Team*; May/June, p. 42.

Volume 53, 1983–84

4708. **Beach, Richard C. and Simpson, Warren K.:** *Pinpointing the Common Elements in Our Successful Women's Basketball Programs*; Sept., p. 42.
4709. **Bedingfield, Donald:** *Going Into the Whole Against the Zone*; Nov., p. 62.
4710. **Brown, Dale D.:** *Box and Chaser Continuity Offense*; Nov., p. 34.
4711. **Brown, Dale D.:** *Freak Defense Does Everything*; Dec., p. 26.
4712. **Comstock, Marc L.:** *25 Components of a Successful Basketball Drill*; Oct., p. 60.
4713. **Creutzberger, Peter:** *"Look to Score" Delay Offense*; Oct., p. 24.
4714. **Davis, Tom:** *The Stanford Bounce Pass: Key to Zone Penetration*; Nov., p. 30.
4715. **Fiske, William:** *Box-and-One Combination Zone Offense*; Oct., p. 45.
4716. **Hearn, Jeffery N.:** *5-Player 1-2-2 Press Breaker*; Nov., p. 66.
4717. **Hudson, Steve:** *OBU's 1-2-2 Half Court Zone Trap*; Aug., p. 40.
4718. **Keller, Butch:** *Winning Words on the Court*; Nov., p. 22.
4719. **King, Don:** *Training Your Big Men With an Inside Power Station*; Dec., p. 38.
4720. **Maravich, Press:** *80 Checkpoints for the Player and Coach*; Nov., p. 29.
4721. **McDougall, Kelly:** *Flex Continuity, Offense of the '80s*; Dec., p. 22.
4722. **Pike, John:** *Quick Score Inbounding Series*; Oct., p. 30.
4723. **Sanderford, Paul:** *Getting the Tip 90% of the Time*; Oct., p. 58.
4724. **Schrier, Jeff:** *1-3-1 Quick Scramble Trap*; Nov., p. 32.
4725. **Starsinic, Bill:** *5-Play Inbound Package*; Dec., p. 46.
4726. **Walker, Lee:** *Power and Finesse at the "Windows"*; Oct., p. 26.
4727. **Webb, Dr. Wyatt M.:** *Going the Full Route Against All-Court Pressure*; Oct., p. 38.
4728. **Whitney, Craig L.:** *Alternating Your Defense*; Nov., p. 46.
4729. **Zigler, Ted:** *"Volunteer" One-on-One Drills*; Feb., p. 70.
4730. Interview: *Bill Bradley Out of the Corner and Into the White House*; Oct., p. 32.
4731. Interview: *Bill Foster: Man to Man Against Stress*; Feb., p. 38.
4732. *1984 All-American Girls High School Team*; May/June, p. 80.
4733. *1984 All-American High School Team*; May/June, p. 74.
4734. *Shoe Survey: What's New in Athletic Shoes*; May/June, p. 57.

Volume 54, 1984–85

4735. **Brandt, John:** *Jumping for Joy—and Power, Agility, and Stamina*; Jan., p. 60.
4736. **Cameron, D. J.:** *Score From the Sideline*; Dec., p. 44.
4737. **Cox, Tom:** *Stack Rover Inbound Series vs. a Rover Defense*; Nov., p. 22.
4738. **Darnell, Dave:** *Eureka's Fast Break Down the Side*; Oct., p. 24.
4739. **Drake, Leonard:** *Beating the 4-Corner Game*; Nov., p. 20.
4740. **Edinges, Dave:** *Simple Screening Continuity off the Passing Game*; Dec., p. 38.
4741. **Evans, Frank:** *How to Win on the Road*; Oct., p. 36.
4742. **Fox, Dr. Robert A.:** *A Stack Stall for Outsized Teams*; Feb., p. 34.

4743. **Jarrett, Richard:** *Color Coded System for Changing Defenses on Run;* Sept., p. 46.
4744. **Kitchens, Rich:** *Progressive Man-to-Man Defensive Help Drills;* Oct., p. 56.
4745. **Nolan, Michael:** *A 2-3 Zone That Keeps It Simple;* Oct., p. 32.
4746. **Oliver, Peter:** *High-Tech and the Modern Athletic Shoe;* May/June, p. 52.
4747. **Reilly, Tom:** *The Expanded Pick and Roll;* Nov., p. 26.
4748. **Reisman, Lonn:** *Southeastern's Reverse-Lob Half Court Press Offense;* Oct., p. 72.
4749. **Robinson, Robert:** *Cornering the Four Corners;* Sept., p. 46.
4750. **Southworth, Mike:** *Big Guard Oriented Offense;* Sept., p. 32.
4751. **Taylor, Dick:** *10 Basic Principles in Beating a Help Type Man;* Dec., p. 20.
4752. **Wellenreiter, Doug:** *Simplified Passing Game;* Oct., p. 41.
4753. **Winston, Lloyd K.:** *Variations on the Basic 2-3 Zone Theme;* Dec., p. 24.
4754. **Wolfe, Thomas W.:** *Computerized Stats;* Dec., p. 18.
4755. Interview: *The Power and the Glory—The Coach's Art (Jack Ramsay);* Sept., p. 38.
4756. *1985 All-American High School Team (Boys);* May/June, p. 46.
4757. *1985 All-American High School Team (Girls);* May/June, p. 72.

Volume 55, 1985–86

4758. **Andrist, Ed:** *Pressuring the Four-Corner Offense;* Nov., p. 38.
4759. **Baker, Dee:** *The "Seven" Last-Second Special;* Dec., p. 9.
4760. **Capra, Carl:** *Triangle-and-Two "Heart Defense";* Nov., p. 26.
4761. **Cluztens, Wim:** *A Good, Simple Two Man Fast Break Drill;* Nov., p. 40.
4762. **de Vandrecourt, Billy R.:** *Try the 1-1-3 Halfcourt Tandem Zone;* Nov., p. 18.
4763. **Fox, Dr. Robert A.:** *Ark Concepts for Determining Your Best Starting Team;* Dec., p. 28.
4764. **Gilbert, Dale A:** *"Designate" Your Fast Break;* Dec., p. 34.
4765. **Hoch, David A.:** *Make Up Your Own Combo Defense;* Oct., p. 16.
4766. **LaRose, Michael:** *Three Psychological Keys to Success in Coaching;* May/June, p. 78.
4767. **May, Joseph A.:** *A Defensive Package vs. the Fast Break;* Jan., p. 28.
4768. **Nagle, Jack:** *Triangle and Two Delay Pattern Game;* Dec., p. 26.
4769. **Parsley, Chip:** *"Deuce" the 1-3-1 Zone;* Dec., p. 18.
4770. **Philips, Bob:** *Basketball's Legend (John Wooden) Revisited: Part 1;* Nov., p. 43.
4771. **Philips, Bob:** *Basketball's Legend (John Wooden) Revisited: Part 2;* Dec., p. 42.
4772. **Philips, Bob:** *Checking for the Right Shoe;* May/June, p. 50.
4773. **Powell, C.W. (Butch):** *"Flex"-ibility in Your Offense;* Dec., p. 32.
4774. **Pike, John:** *Block-Out Technique off the Defensive Board;* Feb., p. 40.
4775. **Sheehy, Harry:** *A 1-2-1-1 Full-Court Pressure Breaker;* Oct., p. 52.
4776. **Taylor, Dick:** *Assigned Lane Transition Game;* Oct., p. 46.
4777. **Travis, Russell:** *Team Leadership, a Guardsend;* Oct., p. 44.
4778. **Underwood, Don:** *Fastbreak: The Offset Plan;* Nov., p. 34.
4779. **Walkes, Fred:** *Take P.R.I.D.E. in Your Free Throwing: It Will Win for You;* Oct., p. 18.
4780. *1986 All-American (Boys);* May/June, p. 80.
4781. *1986 All-American (Girls);* May/June, p. 84.

Volume 56, 1986–87

4782. **Andrist, Eddie A.:** *Fundamental Drills, the Short, Intense Way;* Nov., p. 18.
4783. **Bassett, Matt:** *A Power Series vs. the Zone Defense;* Oct., p. 34.

4784. **Boone, Jim:** *Aggressively Attacking From the Transition Game;* Dec., p. 66.
4785. **Duncan, Anna May B. and Menapace, Larry:** *A 1-3-1 Half-Court Zone Trap;* Dec., p. 70.
4786. **Ellsworth, Keith:** *A Double-Front Pure 2-1-2 That Plays Like a One-Front Zone;* Sept., p. 76.
4787. **Frank, Richard S.:** *A Zone Offense for the Middle School;* Oct., p. 31.
4788. **Hecker, Barry:** *Shooting for Practice (Pre-Practice Shooting Routine);* Aug., p. 44.
4789. **Hess, Chic:** *What the Blue-Chip Players Think of Their Recruitment;* Nov., p. 30.
4790. **Howard, Robert K.:** *Quick-In Baseline to Baseline Fast Break Offense;* Oct., p. 18.
4791. **Kellner, Stan:** *The Cybernetic Way to Superior Free Throwing;* Sept., p. 50.
4792. **Kimble, John:** *Free-Throw Situation Drill;* Jan., p. 119.
4793. **Lambert, Ward:** *Do You Have Your Best Five Players on the Floor?;* Dec., p. 88.
4794. **McKown, Mark:** *A Simple but Multifaceted 1-3-1 Attacking Defense;* Nov., p. 24.
4795. **Menapace, Larry and Duncan, Anna May B.:** *A 1-3-1 Half-Court Zone Trap;* Dec., p. 70.
4796. **Muse, Bill:** *Out of Bounds;* Nov., p. 54.
4797. **Nolan, Michael P.:** *When the Clock Stops;* Nov., p. 38.
4798. **Parkinson, Craig:** *Closing Off the New 3-Point Shot;* Sept., p. 30.
4799. **Paschal, Art:** *Fast-Breaking Into the Flex;* Mar., p. 19.
4800. **Sabatino, Jeff:** *Beat the Defense With the Pure Passing Game;* Nov., p. 20.
4801. **Sallade, Randy:** *Testing Your Young Basketball Players' Knowledge of the Game;* Dec., p. 84.
4802. **Santos, Robert D.:** *Cornerstones of the Basketball Coaching Structure;* Nov., p. 64.
4803. **Taylor, Dick:** *Options and Strategy on the Free Throw (Defense);* Nov., p. 34.
4804. **Wenning, Bill:** *Simple 1-3-1 Zone Press;* Feb., p. 38.
4805. **Wilson, Russ:** *Three "Constants" of Multiple Defense;* Oct., p. 28.
4806. **Zinn, David:** *Zone Offense by the Rules;* Oct., p. 66.
4807. Interview: *Dale Brown: Tiger, Tiger Burning Bright;* Sept., p. 40.
4808. Interview: *Denny Crum: One Large Crum of Comfort;* Nov., p. 42.
4809. *1987 All-American High School Basketball Team (Boys);* May/June, p. 1.
4810. *1987 All-American High School Basketball Team (Girls);* May/June, p. 44.

Volume 57, 1987–88

4811. **Alofs, Jack:** *Trap the Ball, Steal the Ball, Fast Break With the 1-3-1 Zone Trap!;* Oct., p. 30.
4812. **Burson, Jim:** *Offensive Recovery: How to React to the Ball;* Feb., p. 14.
4813. **Carlson, Tom and Termeer, Steve:** *Make Way for the Three-Point Shot;* Oct., p. 26.
4814. **Cavallini, M. Felicia:** *Guidelines for Aerobics Basketball Conditioning;* Aug., p. 50.
4815. **Cluztens, Wim:** *Simple Stack for Two Good Shooting Forwards;* Dec., p. 30.
4816. **Davis, Tom:** *Iowa's Zone Offense;* Nov., p. 22.
4817. **Fields, Marvin R.:** *Breaking After the Made Free Throw;* Oct., p. 76.
4818. **Fitzgerald, Gene and Stern, Will:** *Try the "14" Zone Breaker;* Dec., p. 78.
4819. **Hanrahan, Mike and Renkens, Jack:** *The Secondary Break in the Transition Game;* Nov., p. 34.
4820. **Hoch, David:** *High Post Options for Your Zone Offense;* Oct., p. 24.
4821. **Hoppenstedt, Bob:** *The 1-3-1 Match-Up Zone, Zone Defense at Its Best!;* Dec., p. 86.
4822. **McKown, Mark:** *Why You Should Use Set Plays—Lots of Them!;* Oct., p. 70.

4823. **Mikes, Jay:** *A Computer Breakdown of Percentage Basketball—Part I*; Nov., p. 52; *Part II*; Dec., p. 94; *Part III*; Jan., p. 82.

4824. **Mollberg, Kent:** *Coaching That Crucial Timeout*; Mar., p. 56.

4825. **Nall, Thomas D.:** *A Simple #2 Offense*; Sept., p. 22.

4826. **Nolan, Michael and Sharrow, Michael:** *A 4-Step Progressive Shooting Drill*; Jan., p. 75.

4827. **Ostro, Harry:** *Sin Number One: Pulling a Team Off the Floor*; May/June, p. 4.

4828. **Pearcy, Terry:** *Try the 15-Man Scrimmage*; Sept., p. 56.

4829. **Rehak, Miroslav:** *Czech Out This Out-of-Bounds Sideline Series*; Nov., p. 30.

4830. **Reidburn, Bill:** *Pick 'n' Roll for the Junior High Team*; Jan., p. 116.

4831. **Renkens, Jack and Hanrahan, Mike:** *The Secondary Break in the Transition Game*; Nov., p. 34.

4832. **Samaras, Bob:** *Basketball 1987, a Ten-Man Game*; Nov., p. 38.

4833. **Schrier, Jeff:** *Double-Stack Your Offensive Troubles Away*; Oct., p. 73.

4834. **Sharrow, Michael and Nolan, Michael:** *A 4-Step Progressive Shooting Drill*; Jan., p. 75.

4835. **Spinelli, Joe:** *What To Look for in a Swingman*; Nov., p. 78.

4836. **Stern, Will and Fitzgerald, Gene:** *Try the "14" Zone Breaker*; Dec., p. 78.

4837. **Sullivan, James:** *"Passing Game"—The Ultimate Free-Lance Offense*; Sept., p. 38.

4838. **Termeer, Steve and Carlson, Tom:** *Make Way for the Three-Point Shot*; Oct., p. 26.

4839. Interview: *A Chat With a Legend—Hank Iba*; Apr., p. 52.

4840. *1988 All-American High School Basketball Team (Boys)*; May/June, p. 1.

4841. *1988 All-American High School Basketball Team (Girls)*; May/June, p. 114.

Chapter 3

Visual Resources

Chapter 3 presents a compilation of organizations that distribute basketball-related visual resources. NOTE: Contact each organization for a current listing of basketball-related materials.

4842. AAHPERD (American Alliance for Health, Physical Education, Recreation and Dance) Educational Media Sources 1201 16th Street, N.W. Washington, DC 20036

4843. ACC Video History P.O. Box 22032 Greensboro, NC 27420-2032 919-967-9890

4844. Alford-Wright Productions, Inc. P.O. Box 9721 Fort Wayne, IN 46899-0721 1-800-552-4837 (in Indiana) 1-800-348-0951 (outside Indiana)

4845. Athletic Supply of Dallas, Inc. 10812 Alder Circle Dallas, TX 75238

4846. BFA Division of Phoenix Films 468 Park Avenue South New York, NY 10016 1-800-221-1274

4847. Bob Knight Basketball Aids, Inc. 1113 South High Street Bloomington, IN 47401 812-334-3422

4848. Cambridge Physical Education and Health One Players Club Drive, Dept. PE2 Charleston, WV 25311 1-800-468-4227

4849. Champions on Film and Video 745 State Circle P.O. Box 1941 Ann Arbor, MI 48106

4850. Colorado State Pressure Defensive System c/o Fred Litzenberger Basketball Offices Colorado State University Fort Collins, CO 80523 303-491-6232

4851. Competitive Edge 16006 Waterloo Road Cleveland, OH 44110

4852. Converse 55 Fordham Road Wilmington, MA 01887

4853. Coronet Films 108 Wilmot Road Deerfield, IL 60015

4854. Drill for Skill—"The Miller Way" 1077 North Brodhead Road Aliquippa, PA 15001

4855. Embassy Home Entertainment 1901 Avenue of the Stars Los Angeles, CA 90067

4856. ESPN Home Video Youth Coaching Library P.O. Box 3390, Dept. YC Wallingford, CT 06494

4857. The Film Library 616 South Westmoreland Avenue Los Angeles, CA 90005

4858. *Final Four— The Movie*
P.O. Box 3395
Champaign, IL 61821
1-800-292-NCAA

4859. Karol Video
Division of Karol Media
22 Riverview Drive
Wayne, NJ 07470

4860. Lord and King Associates
Box 68
Winfield, IL 60190
312-231-0102

4861. MacGregor Sports Education
Library
2236B Blue Mound Road
Waukesha, WI 53186
1-800-633-2823

4862. The Master Teacher
Leadership Lane
P.O. Box 1207
Manhattan, KS 66502
913-539-0555

4863. Modern Talking Picture Services, Inc.
5000 Park Street North
St. Petersburg, FL 33709

4864. National Association of Inter-
collegiate Athletics (NAIA)
Film Library
University of Wisconsin—
La Crosse
1705 State Street
La Crosse, WI 54601

4865. National Instructional Sports
Videos (A Division of MF
Athletic)
P.O. Box 8188
Cranston, RI 02920
1-800-556-7464

4866. NCAA Library of Films
P.O. Box 15602
Kansas City, MO 64106
816-471-7800

4867. New Star Video
260 South Beverly Drive
Suite 200
Beverly Hills, CA 90212-3813
1-800-453-7600
213-205-0666 (in California)
FAX 213-205-0511

4868. Odyssey Distribution Systems,
Inc.
123 NW 2nd Avenue
Portland, OR 97209

4869. The Official NBA Catalog
Dept. QZ-3063
Building #73
Hanover, PA 17333
1-800-972-1000

4870. Pitino Video
P.O. Box 34
Queens, NY 11357

4871. Pro Keds Lessons From
Lehmann
P.O. Box 157
Riverside, NJ 08075

4872. Publishers Central Bureau
Dept. 235
One Champion Avenue
Avenel, NJ 07001-2301

4873. Quality Coaching
P.O. Box 11051
Burbank, CA 91510-1051
1-800-541-5489 (outside
California)
818-842-6800 (in California)

4874. Scotch Home Video
Dept. B 525
11300 Rupp Drive
Burnsville, MN 55337
1-800-328-5727, ext. 21 (outside
Minnesota)
1-800-742-5685 (in Minnesota)

4875. Sports Books
7073 Brookfield Plaza
Springfield, VA 22150
703-451-1884

4876. Sports Films and Talents, Inc.
12755 State Highway 55
Minneapolis, MN 55441

4877. Sports-R-Us
Box 5852
Denver, CO 80217
1-800-525-9030 (outside
Colorado)
1-800-428-1118 (in Colorado)

4878. Sunkist Growers, Inc.
Media Library
14130 Riverside Drive
Sherman Oaks, CA 91423

4879. Tossback, Inc.
Box 64
Dorrance, KS 67634

4880. University Film Center
Boston University
Boston, MA 02215

4881. University Film Center
Central Washington University
Ellensburg, WA 98926

4882. University Film Center
Idaho State University
Pocatello, ID 83209

4883. University Film Center
Indiana State University
Terre Haute, IN 47809

4884. University Film Center
Portland State University
Portland, OR 97207

4885. University Film Center
Southern Illinois University
Carbondale, IL 62901

4886. University Film Center
1325 South Oak
Champaign, IL 61820

4887. University Film Center
University of Arizona
Tucson, AZ 85720

4888. University Film Center
University of Colorado
Boulder, CO 80309

4889. University Film Center
University of Texas
Austin, TX 78713-7399

4890. University Film Center
University of Wisconsin
Madison, WI 53711

4891. University Film Center
Washington State University
Pullman, WA 99164-1610

4892. Video Tech
RMI Media Productions
19346 Third Avenue, N.W.
Seattle, WA 98177

■ Chapter 4

Pamphlets, Yearbooks, and Commercial Publications

Chapter 4 lists all current pamphlets, yearbooks, and commercial publications specializing in basketball-related materials. Contact each organization directly for additional information.

4893. *The Athletic Directory*
Scholastic Resources Unlimited (SRU)
20622 Ottawa Road
Apple Valley, CA 92307

4894. *Basketball Coaches Digest*
c/o Seal O San
P.O. Box 710
Huntington, IN 46750

4895. *Basketball Times*
P.O. Box 833
Rochester, MI 48063

4896. *Beacon Falls Coaches Digest*
c/o Beacon Falls Rubber Footwear
Beacon Falls, CT 06403

4897. *Blue Ribbon College Basketball Yearbook*
1 Christopher Lane
Buckhannon, WV 26201

4898. *Converse Inside Coaching*
Converse, Inc.
One Fordham Road
North Reading, MA 01864

4899. *Converse Yearbook*
One Fordham Road
North Reading, MA 01864

4900. *Dick Vitale Basketball Yearbook*
c/o Preview Publishing
P.O. Box 19200
Seattle, WA 98119

4901. *HOOP!-NBA Today*
P.O. Box HOOP
Lowell, MA 01852

4902. *Let's Teach Basketball News*
P.O. Box 1481
St. Cloud, MN 56301

4903. *Pro Keds Coaches Digest*
c/o The Keds Corporation
675 Massachusetts Avenue
Cambridge, MA 02403

4904. *Sporting News College Basketball Yearbook*
c/o The Sporting News
1212 Lindbergh Boulevard
St. Louis, MO 63132

4905. *Street & Smith's Basketball Yearbook*
c/o Street & Smith's Sports Group
304 East 45 Street
New York, NY 10017

4906. *Today's Coach*
c/o MacGregor Sports Education
2236B Blue Mound Road
Waukesha, WI 53186

Unpublished Materials

Chapter 5 is a compilation of all unpublished basketball-related research materials, especially theses and dissertations. Entries are arranged with the author's name appearing first, followed by material title, university granting degree, degree program, and date of degree. To obtain a copy of one of these research studies, contact a librarian at a college or public library near you.

4907. **Abernathy, Kyle G.** *An Analysis of the Coaching Techniques Used in High School Basketball.* University of Wyoming, Master's, 1951.

4908. **Ahart, Frederick C.** *The Effect of Score Differential on Basketball Free Throw Shooting.* Ithaca College, Master's, 1973.

4909. **Al-Sarraj, Foad Ibrahim.** *History of Basketball in the United States and Its Implication Upon Basketball in Iraq.* Colorado State University, Master's, 1976.

4910. **Alaspa, Hugo Winfield.** *A Basketball Ability Test for High School and College Male Students.* University of New Mexico, Master's, 1949.

4911. **Albaugh, Glen Reuben.** *A Comparative Study of the Ability of Basketball Coaches to Assess the Personality Traits and Profiles of Their Players.* University of Utah, Doctorate, 1970.

4912. **Albeck, Charles Stanley.** *Comparative Evaluation of the Two Hand Underhand Free Throw to the One Hand Push Free Throw.* Michigan State University, Master's, 1961.

4913. **Albert, Russell Dean.** *Physical Effects of Competitive Basketball on Pleasant Plains Junior High School Students.* Illinois State Normal University, Master's, 1958.

4914. **Aldrich, A. Everett, Jr.** *The Effect of Weight Training on Vertical Jumping Ability of Springfield College Freshman Basketball Players.* Springfield College, Master's, 1958.

4915. **Alexander, Mary Virginia.** *What Parents Think About Interscholastic Basketball for High School Girls.* University of Alabama, Master's, 1940.

4916. **Alexander, William Little, Jr.** *Biographies of Leading Living Coaches of Basketball, Baseball, and Track in the United States.* University of Texas at Austin, Master's, 1951.

4917. **Alfes, Marilyn.** *The Effect of Circuit Training on Physical Fitness and Basketball Skills in Selected High School Girls.* Montclair State College, Master's, 1973.

4918. **Alheim, William.** *An Experimental Investigation of the Predictive Ability of a Selected Battery of Basketball Tests and a Method of Measuring Improvement of Basketball Playing Skills.* Appalachian State University, Master's, 1958.

4919. **Allen, Edward Pike.** *A Survey of Certain Factors Associated With Free Throwing Ability Under Game Conditions.* Boston University, Master's, 1949.

4920. **Allen, Frank E.** *The Relationship of Strength and Fatigue to Accuracy in Shooting Free Throws in Basketball.* University of Iowa, Master's, 1954.

4921. **Allen, R.L.** *The Effect of Fatigue on the Accuracy of the One Hand and the Underhand Free Throw.* Brigham Young University, Master's, 1965.

4922. **Alley, James William.** *An Analytical Study of Team Play in Basketball.* University of Cincinnati, Master's, 1945.

4923. **Allison, Maria Teresa.** *A Structural Analysis of Navajo Basketball.* University of Illinois, Doctorate, 1980.

4924. **Al-Saiedi, Abdullatif.** *A Comparative Study of Sports in Kuwait Society Before and After the Discovery of Oil.* University of Toledo, Master's, 1983.

4925. **Alten, Steven Robert.** *The Effects of Mental Practice and Visualization on Basketball Free-Throw Shooting Among Junior Varsity Intercollegiate Basketball Players.* University of Delaware, Master's, 1984.

4926. **Altergott, James A.** *An Analytical Survey of State Championship Basketball Teams in Colorado During the Last Five Years as Related to Selected Variables.* Adams State College, Master's, 1970.

4927. **Alverson, G.D.** *The Effectiveness of the Match-up Zone Defense in Basketball.* Brigham Young University, Master's, 1986.

4928. **Ammermdm, Alan.** *Comparative Effects of Two Practice Foul Shooting Techniques at Junior High Level.* Montclair State College, Master's, 1972.

4929. **Amsler, Connie Marie.** *A Survey of Selected Factors in the Organization of Practice Sessions for Women's Intercollegiate Basketball Teams in Southern California.* California State University, Long Beach, Master's, 1972.

4930. **Anderson, Ann C. Paluck.** *The Relationship Between Personal Performance Expectations and Actual Competitive Performance of High School Basketball Players.* Central Washington University, Master's, 1979.

4931. **Anderson, Eugene W.** *A Coordinated Program of Basketball Instruction for Grades Five to Eight.* Fort Hays State College, Master's, 1959.

4932. **Anderson, Kenneth A.** *The Effect of Weighted Ankle Spats on the Jumping Performance, Agility, and Endurance of High School Basketball Players.* University of Wisconsin, Master's, 1961.

4933. **Anderson, Richard.** *The Effect of Weight Training on the Vertical Jump.* University of Tennessee, Master's, 1966.

4934. **Anderson, Wade L.** *A Study of Selected Personality Characteristics of Collegiate Sports Participants.* Utah State University, Master's, 1964.

4935. **Andrew, John Albert.** *An Analysis of Home and Away Game Performance of Atlantic Coast Conference Basketball Teams.* University of North Carolina, Master's, 1984.

4936. **Andrews, Linda Kathleen.** *The History of Boys' Basketball at Oakland High School from 1958–1979.* Eastern Illinois University, Master's, 1980.

4937. **Andrews, Mary F.** *Emotional Response to Participation in Basketball and Swimming by College Women.* University of Maryland, Master's, 1970.

4938. **Annadale, Arthur David.** *Creative Thinking Abilities in High School Basketball Players.* University of Arizona, Master's, 1968.

4939. **Anspaugh, David James.** *Leader Characteristics of Basketball Players as Perceived by Team Members and as Measured by Selected Evaluative Instruments.* Indiana University, Master's, 1971.

4940. **Antrim, Mary Margaret.** *Construction and Validation of a Basketball Skill Test.* Texas Tech University, Master's, 1972.

4941. **Appel, V. E.** *A Study of Basketball Shots Made by Junior and Senior High School Girls from the Free Throw Line During Practice.* University of Southern California, Master's, 1935.

4942. **Applin, Albert G.** *In Search of a Model: The Institutionalization of Basketball.* University of Massachusetts–Amherst, Master's, 1977.

4943. **Applin, Albert Gammon.** *From Muscular Christianity to the Market Place: The History of Men's and Boys' Basketball in the United States (1891–1957).* University of Massachusetts, Master's, 1982.

4944. **Archer, Nancy.** *A Model Goal Setting Program for Individual and Team Basketball Performances.* Winthrop College, Master's, 1987.

4945. **Argotsinger, Jack D.** *A Study of Field Goal Attempts in Girls' Basketball.* University of Iowa, Master's, 1959.

4946. **Arietta, Ralph J.** *Defensive Positioning for Rebounding Free Throws.* Springfield College, Master's, 1967.

4947. **Arnett, Philip M.** *A Study of Ratings of High School Basketball Officials.* University of Kansas, Master's, 1959.

4948. **Arnold, Frank Harold.** *A Comparative Study of Free-Lance, Set-Pattern, and a Combination of Set-Pattern and Free-Lance Styles of Offensive Play in High School Basketball.* Brigham Young University, Master's, 1960.

4949. **Arnold, Guy Edward.** *Team Cohesiveness, Personality and Final League Standings of High School Varsity Basketball Teams.* Ithaca College, Master's, 1972.

4950. **Arrighi, Margarite Ann.** *A Study of the Effects of Competitive Basketball on the Motor Efficiency of College Women as Measured by a Selected Battery of Tests.* University of Maryland, Master's, 1962.

4951. **Arwood, Victor B.** *The History of Varsity Basketball at the University of Tennessee.* University of Tennessee, Master's, 1968.

4952. **Ashley, Donald Walker.** *The Origin and Development of Basketball.* Southwest Missouri State Teachers College, Master's, 1941.

4953. **Askins, Roy Leland, Jr.** *Acting as Social Work: An Interpretive Approach to the Constitutive Traits of Basketball Officials.* University of Tennessee, Doctorate, 1976.

4954. **Asmussen, Kelly Jay.** *The Relationship of Sex-Selected Factors to Winning in Basketball.* Colorado State University, Master's, 1976.

4955. **Atnips, Mary C.** *Conditioning Programs for Girls in Basketball.* North Texas State University, Master's, 1960.

4956. **Augustine, Jack.** *The Relationship of Galvanic Skin Response to Game Performance in College Basketball.* University of Rhode Island, Master's, 1972.

4957. **Aus, Melford L.** *The Effect of Weight Training and Isometric Contractions on the Vertical Jump and Leg Strength of Basketball Players.* University of North Dakota, Master's, 1964.

4958. **Austin, Ellis W.** *Effect of Fatigue on Free Throw Shooting Accuracy of High School Basketball Players.* Northern Illinois University, Master's, 1966.

4959. **Bachman, Ronald Lee.** *An Analytical Study of the Characteristics of Intramural Basketball Officials at the University of Nebraska.* University of Nebraska, Doctorate, 1980.

4960. **Backstrom, Kurt Alan.** *Personalities of Seventh and Eighth Grade Basketball Players as Affected by Participation and Coach's Personality.* University of Kentucky, Master's, 1974.

4961. **Badger, Edward William.** *A Study of the Accuracy of the Set Shot and the Jump Shot.* University of Iowa, Master's, 1954.

4962. **Bailey, Jay G.** *A Comparative Analysis of the Results Obtained From Selected Tests and the Ability to Participate in Basketball.* Louisiana State University, Master's, 1945.

4963. **Bailin, Stuart.** *The Effect of Formal, Informal, and Lack of Warm-Up Upon the Accuracy of the Basketball Free Throw.* University of Massachusetts, Master's, 1964.

4964. **Baker, Fred.** *The Effect of Various Warm-Up Methods on Basketball Shooting Accuracy.* Western Maryland College, Master's, 1973.

4965. **Baker, Harlan, II.** *The Development and Implications of a Unified System for Securing Team and Individual Statistical Data in Basketball at San Benito High School.* Texas A&I University, Master's, 1950.

4966. **Baker, John T.** *A Film Study of Selected Basketball Conditioning Drills.* California State University, Master's, 1965.

4967. **Ballinger, Robert Dale.** *A Study of Basketball Field Goal Shooting Deviations for Selected Male College Students at Montana State University.* University of Montana, Master's, 1962.

4968. **Baltzer, Thomas Allen.** *The Effect of the Winning-Losing Record of Selected Basketball Teams on Team Cohesion.* Brigham Young University, Master's, 1977.

4969. **Barbini, Annette Marie.** *A Comparative Study of Junior High School Girls and Their Achievements in Using Selected Basketball Drills.* East Stroudsburg State College, Master's, 1967.

4970. **Barclay, G.D.** *The Relationship Between Efficient Vision and Certain Sensory Motor Skills.* New York University, Doctorate, 1938.

4971. **Barker, Gene Allen.** *The Relationship Between Total Leisure Behavior of Persons Within Selected Oklahoma Communities and the Success of High School Football and Basketball Programs in Their Communities.* Oklahoma State University, Doctorate, 1974.

4972. **Barker, John Tiffany.** *A Mechanical Analysis of the Two-Hand Set Shot in Basketball.* Springfield College, Master's, 1955.

4973. **Barker, Rex.** *A Comparison of Sportsmanship Attitudes of Basketball Fans at Emotional and Non-Emotional Games.* Kansas State University, Master's, 1971.

4974. **Barkey, Ralph Ralston.** *A Comparison of the One Minute Step Test and the Three Minute Step Test as Reflected by Circulatory Changes Occurring During a Period of Athletic Training.* University of California, Santa Barbara, Master's, 1963.

4975. **Barnes, Jack F.** *A Study of High School Basketball Tournament and League Play in Washington State.* Washington State University, Master's, 1962.

4976. **Barrette, Gary T.** *The Effect of Blindfold Practice on Basketball Free Throw Accuracy.* Penn State University, Master's, 1969.

4977. **Barrows, George F.** *A Manual on the Educational Problems of High School Basketball Coaches.* Colorado State University, Master's, 1941.

4978. **Barry, Patricia Elaine.** *Use of the Video Tape Recorder in Teaching the Free Throw and Lay-up Shots in Basketball to College Women.* Florida State University, Master's, 1969.

4979. **Bartel, Roy Allen.** *Testing Basketball Ability of Senior High School Boys.* Kansas University, Master's, 1949.

4980. **Bash, M. Ronald.** *A Study of the Effect of Varsity College Basketball Participation on the Self-Concept of Players on Selected Teams.* Boston University, Doctorate, 1972.

4981. **Bassy, Emilio.** *A Comparison of the Orange Net and the White Net in Basketball Free Throw.* Springfield College, Master's, 1955.

4982. **Baugh, Evan A.** *A Historical Sketch and an Evaluation of the Utah State Agricultural Coaching School and Its Results in Terms of the Judgment of Coaches Who Participated in 1948.* Utah State University, Master's, 1948.

4983. **Beard, Michael.** *Mental Imagery in Free-Throw Shooting.* Northwest Missouri State University, Master's, 1988.

4984. **Beasley, M.** *A Discussion of the Problems in Basketball for Girls.* George Peabody College for Teachers, Master's, Date unknown.

4985. **Beattie, Mendeil E.** *A Compilation and Analysis of Various Devices Used in Coaching Basketball.* University of Cincinnati, Master's, 1952.

4986. **Bechtold, Warren Willard.** *Standards for Speed Passing and Dribble Shooting Basketball Tests for Huckingham Junior High Boys.* Springfield College, Master's, 1958.

4987. **Beck, Douglas J.** *The Difference Between High Top and Low Cut Basketball Shoes in Defensive Footwork.* Brigham Young University, Master's, 1964.

4988. **Becker, Marc Barnett.** *An Investigation Into the Cognitive and Personality Dimensions of Basketball Athletes.* United States International University, Doctorate, 1981.

4989. **Becknell, Ray Stuart.** *A Study of New England College Basketball Officials Decisions in the 1950–51 Season.* Springfield College, Master's, 1951.

4990. **Beeson, William Henry.** *A Study of Basketball in Louisiana High Schools.* Louisiana State University, Master's, 1936.

4991. **Beetz, Robert R.** *A Comparative Study of the Overhand and Underhand Methods of Free Throws.* Springfield College, Master's, 1949.

4992. **Beitzel, Michael Lynn.** *An Analysis of the Techniques Employed by College Basketball Coaches to Identify Athletes.* Ohio State University, Doctorate, 1981.

4993. **Belko, Stephen.** *History, Organization and Problems of Interscholastic Basketball in Idaho.* University of Idaho, Master's, 1947.

4994. **Bell, Mary.** *The Construction and Standardization of Knowledge Tests in Basketball for College Women.* Smith College, Master's, 1951.

4995. **Bell, Mary Monroe.** *Measurement of Selected Outcomes of Participation in Girls' High School Interscholastic Basketball.* University of Iowa, Doctorate, 1955.

4996. **Bell, Steve.** *Averages of the SAT and Class Rank of Ballplayers in Connecticut.* University of Connecticut, Master's, 1972.

4997. **Bell, William G.** *Principles of Zone Offense in Basketball.* Northern Illinois University, Master's, 1963.

4998. **Bellairs, Wesley.** *Western Illinois University Basketball Handbook.* Western Illinois University, Master's, 1986.

4999. **Ben Scoter, Judith L.** *Effects of a Strength Training Program on Basketball Playing Ability of College Women.* Temple University, Master's, 1972.

5000. **Bennett, Colleen L.** *The Relative Contributions of Modern Dance, Folk Dance, Basketball, and Swimming to Selected and General Motor Abilities of College Women.* Indiana University, Doctorate, 1956.

5001. **Bennice, Donn Alan.** *A Survey of Evaluation Procedures for Basketball Coaching in Ohio's High Schools.* Ohio State University, Doctorate, 1979.

5002. **Berg, Howard.** *The Effect of Fatigue on Performance in the Foul Shot for College Varsity Players.* Lehman College, Master's, 1971.

5003. **Berger, David Dean.** *The Effect of Systematic Weight Training on Leg Power of Varsity High School Basketball Players.* Mankato State College, Master's, 1961.

5004. **Bergstrom, Arthur J.** *A Study of Basketball Courts in an Attempt to Discover the Optimum Size for High School Games.* University of Iowa, Master's, 1935.

5005. **Bernard, Barbara R.** *Establishment of Norms for Skill Test of Basketball Ball Handling Ability for Junior High School Girls.* Kansas State Teachers College, Master's, 1966.

5006. **Bertholf, David L.** *A New Test to Predict Basketball Ability.* University of Kansas, Master's, 1968.

5007. **Bertinetti, Dominie, Jr.** *Equalizing Intramural Basketball Competition for Junior High School Boys.* Illinois State Normal University, Master's, 1960.

5008. **Bettencourt, R.M.** *The Relationship Between Selected Fundamental Skills and Team Success in Intramural Junior College Basketball.* Springfield College, Master's, 1970.

5009. **Bettes, Lawrence E.** *The Status of Coaches of Boys' Interscholastic Basktball in Class A High School in Texas.* North Texas State University, Master's, 1964.

5010. **Bevell, Roland E.** *Administrative Practices Related to Safety in the Football and Basketball Programs in Oregon High Schools.* Utah State University, Master's, 1970.

5011. **Bevington, Raymond H.** *A Study of the Indiana High School Basketball Tournaments.* Indiana State Teachers College, Master's, 1949.

5012. **Bicknell, Ray S.** *A Study of New England College Basketball Officials' Decisions in the 1950–51 Season.* Springfield College, Master's, 1951.

5013. **Bieber, Merle.** *A Study to Compare the Reaction Times of Simmons Junior High Ninth Grade Basketball Players and Non-Basketball Players.* Northern State College, Master's, 1969.

5014. **Biewen, Eugene R.** *Effectiveness of the Minnesota State High School League Alcohol Rule Among the Basketball Players of District VI.* Mankato State University, Master's, 1969.

5015. **Bigham, Eldon M.** *A Study of Selected Factors That Contribute to the Home-Court Advantage in Illinois High School Basketball Games.* Southern Illinois University, Undergraduate, 1969.

5016. **Bigsbee, J.H.** *An Analysis of the Springfield College Strength Test as a Means of Equalizing Intramural Teams in Basketball.* New York University, Master's, 1941.

5017. **Bill, Alban Joseph.** *The Effect of an Off-Season Skill Development Program on High School Basketball Players.* University of Wisconsin–La Crosse, Master's, 1975.

5018. **Bingner, Charles.** *A Study of Rating Scales for Boys' Interscholastic High School Basketball Officials in the United States.* University of Wisconsin, Master's, 1959.

5019. **Bird, Anne Marie.** *A Comparative Study of Certain Personality Characteristics of College Women Participating in Basketball and Modern Dance.* University of Maryland, Master's, 1965.

5020. **Blackborn, Frank Delana.** *The Correlation of Shoulder Strength to Basketball Field Goal Shooting Performance.* Kansas State Teachers College, Master's, 1968.

5021. **Blake, Raymond.** *Distance Traversed by Basketball Players in Different Types of Defenses.* University of Iowa, Master's, 1939.

5022. **Blanton, Lynn Suzanne.** *Instructional Super 8MM Film—Basic Offensive Basketball Patterns for Women.* California State University, Master's, 1974.

5023. **Blazer, Joelle J.** *A Comparison of Grade Point Averages in the Required and Elective Courses of Senior Varsity Basketball Lettermen in Class C Oklahoma Panhandle High Schools.* Emporia Kansas State College, Master's, 1973.

5024. **Blish, Russell R.** *An Investigation of Basketball Fouls and Violations, Delay in Player Substitutions, and the Time Lost Due to Player Violations.* University of Wisconsin, Master's, 1960.

5025. **Block, Cherri Marie.** *A Comparison of the Pre-Season Self-Concepts of Winning and Losing Female Basketball Coaches.* Western Illinois University, Doctorate, 1984.

5026. **Blurton, Richard Ray.** *Effects of Group Behavior Therapy Imagery on Basketball Performance.* University of Southern California, Doctorate, 1968.

5027. **Bobb, Moeberta.** *Survey of Injuries in Women's Intercollegiate Basketball.* Winthrop College, Master's, 1974.

5028. **Boetel, Norma.** *Basketball: August 1975–August 1976.* University of North Carolina at Greensboro, Doctorate, 1975.

5029. **Bode, Sandra Ann.** *Telemetered Cardiac Response and Energy Expenditures of Two Women Engaging in Intercollegiate Basketball.* South Dakota State University, Master's, 1972.

5030. **Boes, Charles A.** *Factors Which Influenced Freshmen Basketball Grants-in-Aiders in the Selection of Different Types of Colleges.* Bowling Green State University, Master's, 1973.

5031. **Boetell, Norma M.** *A Factorial Approach in the Development of a Basketball Rating Scale to Evaluate Players in a Game Situation.* University of North Carolina at Greensboro, Doctorate, 1981.

5032. **Boggio, Henry R.** *The Effect of Experience and Floor Position Upon Basketball Officiating Performance.* Penn State University, Master's, 1962.

5033. **Boldin, Charles Theo.** *A Study of the Validity of Brace's Basketball Achievement Tests as a Measure of Real Playing Ability of Individual Players of District 35B University of Texas Interscholastic League for the 1950 Season.* North Texas State University, Master's, 1950.

5034. **Boller, Leo Paul.** *The Effect of the Free Throw on the Outcome of Basketball Games.* Western Michigan University, Master's, 1958.

5035. **Bolstorff, Frank.** *The Effects of Postseason Shooting Practice on Basket Shooting Ability.* University of Minnesota, Master's, 1966.

5036. **Bomar, William McKinley, Jr.** *Abstract of a Study in Relationship of Individual Ability in Certain Fundamental Shots in Basketball During Practice Sessions.* University of Georgia, Master's, 1951.

5037. **Bonczyk, Edmund Anthony.** *Basketball Rule Changes: Opinions of Illinois High School Basketball Coaches.* Illinois State Normal University, Master's, 1960.

5038. **Bond, Charles Levi.** *Pre-Season Practice of Football and Basketball in the State Associated High Schools of the United States and Canada.* Northern Illinois University, Master's, 1963.

5039. **Bonner, Donald.** *A Comparative Study of the Ability of High School Basketball Players to Perform Basic Skills at Three Stages of the Season: Pre-Season, In-Season and Post-Season.* North Carolina Central University, Master's, 1963.

5040. **Booth, Harry.** *The Effects of Interscholastic Basketball on Levels of Self-Esteem of 5th and 6th Grade Athletes.* Westchester State College, Undergraduate, 1981.

5041. **Borke, Lon B.** *A Study of Whether or Not the Men's Basketball Coaches of South Dakota Are in Favor of the No-Foul-Out Rule, a Three-Point Line and a Shot Clock.* Northeastern State University, Master's, 1986.

5042. **Bosch, Raymond A.** *The Effect of Leg Strength Training Upon the Execution of the Vertical Jump.* University of California, Santa Barbara, Master's, 1966.

5043. **Boutin, Kenneth James.** *Relationship of Anxiety Level and Performance in NAIA Intercollegiate Basketball Games.* Oregon State University, Doctorate, 1983.

5044. **Bova, Philip M.** *The Development of a Basketball Officials Training Program.* Ashland College, Master's, 1983.

5045. **Bowden, Ronnie D.** *The Effects on the Mood State of Intramural Basketball Officials.* University of Wyoming, Master's, 1983.

5046. **Boyer, Lisa Ann.** *A Kinematic Analysis of Successful and Unsuccessful Jump Shots Performed by Female Shooters.* University of North Carolina at Greensboro, Master's, 1986.

5047. **Bradley, Carroll.** *A Study of the Organization of Pre-Season Basketball Practice Among Kentucky High Schools.* Springfield College, Master's, 1953.

5048. **Bradley, William Earl.** *Effects of Practice With a Rubber Basketball on Shooting Accuracy.* University of Mississippi, Master's, 1971.

5049. **Braithwaite, Wilbur T.** *A Statistical Analysis of Officiating Calls in 342 College Basketball Games Played in the Fourth NCAA District During 1950–51.* University of Michigan, Master's, 1951.

5050. **Brassie, Paul Stanley.** *Effectiveness of Intermittent and Consecutive Methods of Practicing Free Throws.* University of Iowa, Master's, 1965.

5051. **Bray, Clifford C.** *The Relationship of Basketball Coaching Success to Educational Background, Athletic Experience, Coaching Experience, Skill Level and Game Knowledge.* Kent State University, Master's, 1983.

5052. **Bredice, Frederick A.** *Effects of Skill Performance on Game Outcome in Basketball.* Springfield College, Master's, 1965.

5053. **Breding, Virgil D.** *A Comparison of Intrinsic and Extrinsic Motivation Used to Improve Free Throw Shooting Accuracy of High School Boys.* University of North Dakota, Master's, 1968.

5054. **Brees, Clifford D.** *The Effects of Trampoline Upon the Jumping Performance, Agility, Running Speed and Endurance of High School Basketball Players.* University of Wisconsin, Master's, 1961.

5055. **Brennan, James Francis.** *A Study of the Relative Effectiveness of Four Basketball Shooting Methods Commonly Used and Taught at the Eleventh Grade Level.* Boston University, Master's, 1950.

5056. **Brennan, Stephen James.** *Intrinsic Motivation of Intercollegiate Male and Female Athletes in Team and Individual Sport Groups.* University of Nebraska at Lincoln, Master's, 1986.

5057. **Brennan, Stephen James.** *Perceptions and Expectations of NCAA Division I Basketball Referees Regarding Game Coaching Behavior.* Peak Performance Consultants, 14728 Shirley Street, Omaha, NE 68144. National study conducted by independent consulting company, 1987.

5058. **Brent.** *A Comparison of Turnovers by the Dallas City Junior High School and Senior High School.* Western Illinois University, Master's, 1977.

5059. **Brett, Patricia.** *An Assessment of Variations in the Skilled Performance of Female Intercollegiate Basketball Players as a Function of the Competitive Circumstances.* University of Wisconsin–Madison, Master's, 1978.

5060. **Bridges, Dennis Lynn.** *The History of Basketball at Illinois Wesleyan University.* Illinois State University, Master's, 1965.

5061. **Brinkerhoff, Dennis R. and Friedow, Monty D.** *Visual Enhancement of Pacific University's Women's Basketball Team.* Pacific University, Doctorate, 1983.

5062. **Broadfoot, Clarence Peter.** *An Investigation to Support the Forming of a New Basketball Classification in the Kansas State High School Activities Association.* University of Kansas, Master's, 1952.

5063. **Brockinton, William Joseph.** *Effects of Upper Body Endurance Weight Training on Power Output Capability.* University of Kentucky, Master's, 1983.

5064. **Bromley, Zoe.** *An Experiment in Concentrated Versus Distributed Learning in Basketball Achievement for Ninth Grade Girls.* UCLA, Master's, 1941.

5065. **Brooks, Dana Demarco.** *A Comparison of Recruitment Networks of Selected AAA High School Basketball Programs Within the State of West Virginia.* West Virginia University, Doctorate, 1979.

5066. **Brooks, Mark A.** *The Relationship of Selected Variables to Successful Basketball Performance in High School Boys Varsity Basketball Players.* Northeast Missouri State University, Master's, 1986.

5067. **Brown, Betty J.** *Correlation of Scores Made in a Basketball Test With Experts' Ratings of Basketball Playing Ability of Junior High School Girls.* Penn State University, Master's, 1962.

5068. **Brown, James Keith.** *A Survey of Fouls Committed and Free Throws Converted and Attempted by Basketball Teams that Participated in Both Class A Sectional and State Basketball Tournaments in South Dakota in 1958.* University of South Dakota, Master's, 1960.

5069. **Brown, Michael E.** *The Effect of Plyometric Training on the Vertical Jump of High School Boys Basketball Players.* Northeast Missouri State University, Master's, 1984.

5070. **Browne, Thomas James.** *History and Philosophy of Basketball.* Springfield College, Master's, 1898.

5071. **Broxton, Cleo Cook.** *A Proposed Program for Teaching Basketball to High School Girls.* Southwest Texas State University, Master's, 1957.

5072. **Bruce, R.M.** *An Annotated and Indexed Bibliography of Basketball Publications.* Springfield College, Master's, 1946.

5073. **Brumbak, Ralph.** *A Guide for Teaching Basketball in the Secondary School.* Kansas State Teachers College, Master's, 1963.

5074. **Brunnemer, James Leroy.** *Characteristics and Attributes of Highly Successful Intercollegiate Football and Basketball Coaches.* Indiana University, Doctorate, 1980.

5075. **Bryant, James E.** *Percentage Rebounding of Selected Varsity High School Basketball Teams Under Game Conditions in Illinois.* Northern Illinois University, Master's, 1965.

5076. **Bryant, James Edward.** *Four Descriptive Case Study Analyses of the Basketball Jump Shot and the Effect of Fatigue in the Jump Shot.* University of Missouri, Doctorate, 1969.

5077. **Buck, Marilyn Margaret.** *Performance Motives of Girl Basketball Players in Iowa High Schools.* University of Utah, Master's, 1978.

5078. **Buckles, Tina Marie.** *The Effects of Visuo-Motor Behavior Rehearsal on Competitive Performance.* University of Oregon, Master's, 1987.

5079. **Bucklew, Mark Williams.** *An Instructional Tape of the Defensive Fundamentals of Basketball.* Sonoma State University, Master's, 1978.

5080. **Buecheler, Charles M.** *The Effect of Using Lighter and Smaller Balls on the Learning of Selected Basketball Skills by Fifth Grade Boys and Girls.* West Chester University, Master's, 1977.

5081. **Buehler, Clyde W.** *A Survey of Basketball Offenses Used in Class A High Schools in the Northwest District of Iowa as Specified by the Iowa High School Athletic Association.* University of South Dakota, Master's, 1953.

5082. **Bulat, Carl J.** *The Effects of Motivational Techniques on the Win-Loss Record of High School Boys' Basketball Teams.* Western Illinois University, Master's, 1987.

5083. **Burger, William R.** *The Comparative Effects of Three Levels of Noise on Free Throw Shooting in Basketball.* Pennsylvania State University, Master's, 1969.

5084. **Burk, Otis Elbert.** *Procedures in Basketball.* West Texas State University, Master's, 1933.

5085. **Burke, Edmond Joseph, Jr.** *A Comparison of the Effects of Two Conditioning Methods Designed to Increase Circulorespiratory Endurance in Candidates for a College Basketball Team.* East Carolina University, Master's, 1969.

5086. **Burkhammer, Billy L.** *A Comparison of a Written Psychological Anxiety Test With the Number of Turnovers in a Basketball Pressure Situation.* Lamar University, Master's, 1973.

5087. **Burkhart, Ralph Clayton.** *An Analysis of the Most Influential Factors in the Development of Interscholastic Basketball in the Cumberland Valley Conference.* College of William and Mary, Master's, 1950.

5088. **Burkness, Julien.** *An Experimental Standardization of a Modified Basketball for Junior High School Boys.* University of Iowa, Master's, 1939.

5089. **Burley, Morse R.** *A Survey and Analysis of Basketball Zone Defenses Employed by a Selected Group of Western High School Coaches.* University of Wyoming, Master's, 1952.

5090. **Burnett, Tannye.** *The Motion Picture as a Visual Aid in the Training of Officials for Women's Basketball.* University of North Carolina, Master's, 1951.

5091. **Burnham, Stanley.** *A Study of the Effects of Weight Training Combined With Drills Upon the Rebounding Performance of Basketball Players.* University of Texas, Master's, 1961.

5092. **Burr, Wendell Pomeroy.** *The Development of a Classification Test of Basketball Ability.* Springfield College, Master's, 1950.

5093. **Burson, James Fredrick.** *The Development of a Systematic Procedure for Basketball Video/Film Analysis and Utilization.* Ohio State University, Doctorate, 1974.

5094. **Bush, Paul C.** *An Analytical Survey and Collection of Basketball Drills.* California State University at Humboldt, Master's, 1968.

5095. **Byrd, Richard F.** *The Effects of Competitive Practice of Foul Shooting on Accuracy in Games.* University of Tennessee at Knoxville, Master's, 1977.

5096. **Cabalka, Leo J.** *An Analysis of Offensive Rebounding in Basketball.* University of Iowa, Master's, 1948.

5097. **Cada, Dean A.** *A Survey of Summer Basketball Programs in Class AA High Schools of Illinois.* Western Illinois University, Master's, 1976.

5098. **Cafer, Glenn Ezra.** *Study of the Basic Tactical, Education and Motor Skill Methods in the Teaching of Adolescent Basketball.* Northeast Missouri State University, Master's, 1956.

5099. **Cain, Gary Kay.** *A Comparison of Certain Administrative Practices and Conditions With the Sportsmanship Ratings for Interscholastic Basketball Contests in Selected Missouri Schools.* University of Missouri, Master's, 1967.

5100. **Caldwell, Evangeline.** *California Psychological Inventory Scores of Women Varsity Basketball Members of Varying Performance and Different Academic Levels.* Xavier University, Master's, 1979.

5101. **Calihan, Robert J.** *Proposal for the Formation of a New Catholic Intercollegiate Basketball Conference.* Wayne State University, Master's, 1961.

5102. **Callaway, Deborah Johnson.** *A Comparison of Leadership Styles of Successful and Unsuccessful Collegiate Women Basketball Coaches.* Virginia Polytechnic Institute and State University, Master's, 1982.

5103. **Calvert, Marvin E.** *An Analysis of Errors in Ball Control Leading to the Loss of Possession of the Ball in Basketball.* University of Iowa, Master's, 1949.

5104. **Campbell, Judith May.** *Selected Factors and Practices in the Competitive Basketball Programs for High School Girls in Indiana 1975–1976.* Indiana University, Doctorate, 1978.

5105. **Caney, James Hendrix.** *History of Intercollegiate Basketball at the University of Georgia.* University of Georgia, Master's, 1969.

5106. **Cardey, Charlotte.** *Six Learning Activity Packages in Beginning Basketball for Junior High School Girls.* California State University, Sacramento, Master's, 1972.

5107. **Carlson, Donald W.** *A Study of the Cardiovascular Condition of Selected College Basketball Players.* Southwest Missouri State University, Master's, 1968.

5108. **Carlstrom, Leonard A.** *An Analysis of Home and Visiting Team Fouling in Basketball with Regards to Officials.* University of Oregon, Master's, 1972.

5109. **Carroll, Wanda.** *An Analysis of the Value of Interscholastic Basketball for Girls.* Arkansas State University, Master's, 1960.

5110. **Carter, George Franklin.** *A Comparison of Selected Instructional Methods in Teaching Basketball Skills.* University of Utah, Doctorate, 1971.

5111. **Caruthers, Joey.** *Proposed Rule Changes in College Basketball.* Old Dominion, Master's, 1980.

5112. **Carver, Edgar Charles.** *Basketball Skills as Related to Manual Dexterity.* University of Kansas, Master's, 1954.

5113. **Case, E.N.** *An Analysis of the Effects of Various Factors in the Accuracy of Shooting Free Throws in Basketball.* University of Southern California, Master's, 1934.

5114. **Case, Robert Wayne.** *An Examination of the Leadership Behaviors of Selected Successful Basketball Coaches at Four Competitive Levels.* Ohio State University, Doctorate, 1980.

5115. **Casey, Claudine Estelle.** *The Construction of a Sound-Slide on the Techniques of Officiating Girls' and Women's Basketball.* University of Colorado, Master's, 1956.

5116. **Cassidy, Peter L.** *Varied Target Size and Basketball Shooting Accuracy.* California State University, Northridge, Master's, 1969.

5117. **Castrovillo, Gene.** *The Effect of Dominant Eye and Non-Dominant Eye Vision on Basketball Foul Shooting Accuracy.* Alfred University, Master's, 1975.

5118. **Chaloupecky, Robert F.** *A Comparison of Basketball Shooting Skill at a 10-Foot and 11-Foot Basket.* Illinois State University, Master's, 1967.

5119. **Chamberlain, Oris D.** *A Comparative Study of the One and One Free-Throw Rule in Basketball at the University of Wyoming.* University of Wyoming, Master's, 1954.

5120. **Chambers, Donald E.** *An Experiment to Determine the Reliability of an Ability Test as a Basis for Selecting Basketball Candidates for Varsity and Reserve Squads.* Indiana State Teachers College, Master's, 1952.

5121. **Chan, Roy Chin Ming.** *The Effects of Single and Combined Psyching Up Strategies on Basketball Free-Throws and Leg Strength.* North Texas State University, Master's, 1982.

5122. **Chandler, William S.** *Basketball: A Scientific Study of Free-Throw Performance.* University of Wisconsin, Master's, 1952.

5123. **Chappell, Robert H.** *The Development of a Basketball Battery for Middle School Male Students.* Western Kentucky University, Master's, 1971.

5124. **Cherry, Aubrey L.** *An Evaluation of Two Selected Basketball Skills Tests in the Light of Recent Changes in the Style of Play.* University of Texas at El Paso, Master's, 1969.

5125. **Chestnut, Clark E.** *A Survey of Basketball Team Records in Relation to Strength Index and Scholastic Ability.* University of Kentucky, Master's, 1941.

5126. **Childress, James Thomas.** *A Factor and Discriminant Analysis to Identify and Determine the Effectiveness of Selected Physical Variables in Predicting a Successful Basketball Performer.* Northwestern State University of Louisiana, Doctorate, 1972.

5127. **Chomeau, Bernal T.** *A Study of the Relationship of Basketball Passing to Team Performance.* University of Wisconsin, Master's, 1956.

5128. **Christensen, Lot B.** *The Value of Skill Tests in Selecting a Basketball Squad.* Utah State University, Master's, 1960.

5129. **Christian, Hallie Mae (Shupe).** *An Experimental Study in the Acquisition of Skills in Girls' Basketball at Princeton High School, Princeton, West Virginia.* West Virginia University, Master's, 1946.

5130. **Christopulos, John T.** *Examination of Conditions Involved in a Proposed Basketball Rule Change.* University of Utah, Master's, 1967.

5131. **Cione, Jean Shirley.** *The Effect of a Modified Basketball Size on the Performance of Selected Basketball Skills by Senior High School Girls and College Women.* University of Illinois, Master's, 1962.

5132. **Clark, Donald Franklin.** *An Analysis of the Advantage of the Home Court in Southwest Conference Basketball Competition.* University of Texas, Master's, 1959.

5133. **Clark, Eugene.** *Film: The FTU Break Execution and Patterns.* University of Central Florida, Degree program unknown, 1972.

5134. **Clark, Eugene A.** *Fast Break Basketball.* Florida Institute of Technology, Master's, 1970.

5135. **Clark, Jay T.** *The Effect of Varying Height on Power Generated During Rebound Jumping.* University of Northern Iowa, Master's, 1986.

5136. **Clark, Joseph J.** *The Role of the College Assistant Basketball Coach.* Western Illinois University, Master's, 1985.

5137. **Clark, M.F.** *Some of the Physiological Effects of a Girls Rules Basketball Game With Special Emphasis on Time.* New York University, Master's, 1932.

5138. **Clark, Michael James.** *A Study of Major Problems Confronting Interscholastic Basketball Coaches.* University of Central Florida, Master's, 1979.

5139. **Clark, William James.** *Development Validation of a Basketball Potential Skill Test.* Ohio State University, Doctorate, 1973.

5140. **Clauson, Donald Bruce.** *The Analysis of Body Positions in the Game of Basketball.* George Peabody College, Master's, 1931.

5141. **Clay, Reda Faye.** *Effects of Massed and Distributed Practice on Basketball Shooting of Free Throws.* Texas Tech University, Master's, 1968.

5142. **Clayton, Kelvin C.** *Analysis of Methods Used in Selecting High School Basketball Team Members as Related to Coaching Success.* Brigham Young University, Master's, 1969.

5143. **Clifton, Robert L.** *Effect of Weight Training Upon Accuracy in Shooting Field Goals in Basketball.* University of Iowa, Master's, 1955.

5144. **Cloyd, Edward Lamar, Jr.** *A Study of Girls Interscholastic Basketball in North Carolina.* University of North Carolina, Master's, 1951.

5145. **Cocula, John.** *Comparative Effectiveness of Two Methods of Instructions on Basketball Skills of Eighth Grade Boys.* Montclair State College, Master's, 1968.

5146. **Codispoti, James C.** *Effects of Mental and Physical Practice With and Without a Basketball on Accuracy as Measured by Basketball Foul Shooting.* University of Maryland, Master's, 1965.

5147. **Coffman, Gary Glenn.** *Personality as Compared to Performance of Basketball Players.* University of Mississippi, Doctorate, 1974.

5148. **Cohen, Dorothy Ann.** *An Epidemiological Study of Women's High School Basketball Injuries.* University of Illinois, Doctorate, 1977.

5149. **Colbert, Charles.** *Descriptive Study of Early Life Factors Contributing to the Development of Professional Baseball, Basketball, and Football Players.* University of Georgia, Doctorate, 1972.

5150. **Colclough, Scott Haines.** *A Survey of North Carolina High School Basketball Coaches' Attitudes Toward Officials.* Middle Tennessee State University, Doctorate, 1986.

5151. **Coldwell, Donald A.** *Improving the Field Goal Shooting Percentage of the Ridgedale Girls' Varsity Basketball Team.* Ashland College, Master's, 1981.

5152. **Cole, George.** *Testing for Basketball Ability in Elementary School Children.* Northern Illinois University, Master's, 1960.

5153. **Cole, Jack.** *The Effects of Weight Training on Basketball Shooting Accuracy.* Ashland College, Master's, 1984.

5154. **Colebank, Albert Deahl.** *A History of Intercollegiate Basketball in the United States With Special Reference to West Virginia University.* West Virginia University, Master's, 1939.

5155. **Colla, Marilyn M.** *Investigation of Aggression and Assertiveness of High School Female Varsity Basketball Players.* Mankato State University, Master's, 1982.

5156. **Collins, Catherine Mae.** *A Comparison of Selected Personality Traits Between Female Varsity Basketball Players in Catholic and Public Coeducational High Schools in Northern New Jersey.* East Stroudsburg State College, Master's, 1973.

5157. **Collins, Greg.** *Drills for a High School Basketball Program.* Ashland College, Master's, 1983.

5158. **Colvin, V., Glassow, R., and Schwartz, M.** *Studies on Testing Basketball Skills.* University of Wisconsin, Master's, 1937.

5159. **Connolly, Steven Renton.** *A Statistical Analysis of Basketball's Home Court Advantage—Theory at California State University, Chico.* California State University, Chico, Master's, 1981.

5160. **Connor, Doran L.** *The Use of the Exer-Genie Machine to Improve Flexibility and Strength for Basketball Players.* Utah State University, Master's, 1966.

5161. **Conoley, Merton Gilbert.** *The Expenditures for Basketball in Selected AA High Schools of Texas.* University of Texas, Master's, 1954.

5162. **Cook, Timothy Brian.** *A Handbook of Basketball Plays and Techniques Beneficial to High School and College Coaches.* University of Dayton, Master's, 1987.

5163. **Cooper, Katherine Jean.** *Comparison of Changes in Foot and Ankle Strength of College Women in Basketball and Modern Dance.* University of Illinois, Master's, 1957.

5164. **Cooper, Stewart A.** *A Study of Basketball Errors as a Determining Factor in the Outcome of the Game.* University of Iowa, Master's, 1951.

5165. **Copeland, Barry Wilson.** *A National Survey of Basketball Recruiting Procedures From Selected Successful National Collegiate Athletic Association Division I, II, and III Schools.* Northwestern State University of Louisiana, Doctorate, 1982.

5166. **Coppedge, Norman Gerald.** *The Effects of Strength on the Accuracy of Basketball Shooting.* Texas Tech University, Master's, 1967.

5167. **Corizzi, Harold Samuel.** *Comparative Effects of Isometric and Isotonic Exercises on Vertical Jumping Ability of Basketball Players at Ramapo High School, New Jersey, Spring 1969.* Montclair State College, Master's, 1969.

5168. **Coslet, Francis Rae.** *An Analysis and Classification of Structural Elements in a Selected Basketball Offense.* Chico State College, Master's, 1971.

5169. **Cotter, Linda Louise.** *Group Cohesiveness and Team Success Among Women's Intercollegiate Basketball Teams.* Indiana University, Doctorate, 1978.

5170. **Coughlin, Mary Ann.** *The Effects of Goal Setting on Basketball Foul Shooting Performance.* Springfield College, Master's, 1984.

5171. **Coulfield, Roberta.** *Effect of Pre-game Warm-up on Free Throw Accuracy in Basketball for Freshmen and Sophomore Women.* Montclair State College, Master's, 1967.

5172. **Coutts, Robert L.** *A Rating System for Evaluating Florida High School Basketball Officials.* Florida State University, Master's, 1954.

5173. **Coward, Isham Aquilla.** *A Case Study of Basketball Ability of High School Boys.* University of Texas, Master's, 1954.

5174. **Cox, Vernon W.** *A Study of the Comparison of Basketball Skill Tests With the Coach's Judgment of Varsity Basketball Candidates.* Springfield College, Master's, 1949.

5175. **Cracraft, Joe David.** *A Basketball Bibliography of Books, Selected Periodical Articles, Unpublished Theses and Dissertations, and Films Produced from July 1, 1957, through June 30, 1968, Including Annotations and Comments on Selected Materials.* California State University, Sacramento, Master's, 1971.

5176. **Crafts, Virginia R.** *Common Elements of Movement in a Selected Groups of Sports and Suggestions for Utilizing These Common Elements in the Teaching of Sports.* Columbia University, Doctorate, 1964.

5177. **Crain, Owen Burnell.** *The Effect of Training With the Dynabalometer on Jump Shooting Ability.* Southwest Missouri State University, Master's, 1967.

5178. **Cram, E. C.** *A Study of the Knowledge of Rules and Nomenclature of Football, Basketball, Volleyball, and Tennis as Demonstrated by Junior High Boys of Des Moines, Iowa.* University of Iowa, Master's, 1939.

5179. **Crawford, Micky D.** *Manual for Prospective Athletic Trainers.* University of Toledo, Degree program unknown, 1977.

5180. **Crawley, Richard Francis.** *Basketball Coaching for Beginners.* Springfield College, Master's, 1936.

5181. **Cress, Carolyn Louise.** *A Study to Compare the Effect of Single Instruction Periods With That of Double Instruction Periods in the Learning of Basketball Skills for Girls.* Springfield College, Master's, 1955.

5182. **Cromer, Dennis.** *A Study to Determine the Effects Shots Attempted and Shooting Percentage Have on Winning and Losing.* Western Illinois University, Master's, 1978.

5183. **Crooke, Sharon L.** *Personality Traits of Successful High School Male and Female Basketball Coaches.* Bowling Green State University, Master's, 1974.

5184. **Cross, T.J.** *A Comparison of the Whole Method, the Parts Method, and a Minor Games Method of Teaching Basketball to Ninth Grade Boys.* University of Iowa, Master's, 1934.

5185. **Crum, Cecilia A.** *A Comparative Study of Personality Traits of Women Intercollegiate and Women Intramural Basketball Players.* University of Minnesota, Master's, 1925.

5186. **Culver, Elizabeth Jean.** *The Effect of a Ten Minute Period of Body Conditioning Exercises on Certain Elements of Physical Fitness and Basketball Skill of High School Girls.* University of Washington, Master's, 1958.

5187. **Cunningham, Gary Allen.** *Forearm Strength and Distance Shooting in Basketball.* UCLA, Master's, 1965.

5188. **Cunningham, Phyllis.** *Measuring Basketball Playing Ability of High School Girls.* University of Iowa, Doctorate, 1964.

5189. **Curtin, Robert Saunders.** *A Study of Self-Perception, Personality Traits, and Player Perceptions of Selected Male High School Basketball Coaches.* Boston University, Doctorate, 1977.

5190. **Curtis, Milton Bishop.** *A Comparison of Certain Physical Abilities with Basketball Skill Among Girls in a Small High School.* University of Texas, Master's, 1952.

5191. **Cutter, Elizabeth D.** *A Study of College Women's Attitudes Toward Different Types of Competition in Basketball.* University of Iowa, Master's, 1951.

5192. **Czarnowski, Edward Joseph.** *A Study of Pre-Game Emotions of High School Basketball Players.* Boston University, Master's, 1950.

5193. **Dahl, Donald.** *The Relationship of Jump Shooting Ability in Basketball to Selected Measurement Traits.* South Dakota State University, Master's, 1972.

5194. **Dahlgren, Leroy Leonard.** *An Analytical Survey of Basketball Turnovers in the AA Tournament of Washington State, 1963, as They Related to Winning and Losing Games.* University of Washington, Master's, 1967.

5195. **Dalker, Beatrice Elton.** *The Status of Varsity Basketball Competition for Girls in the Public Junior Colleges.* University of Alabama, Master's, 1942.

5196. **Damon, E. Lyle.** *An Experimental Investigation on the Predictive Ability of a Basketball Readiness Test.* University of Nevada, Reno, Master's, 1966.

5197. **Darracott, Charles Risdon.** *Expectancies and Attributions as Mediators of Coaching Behavior in Youth League Basketball.* Wake Forest University, Master's, 1980.

5198. **Daugherty, Bailey Eugene.** *The Effect of a Power Jumping Exercise With Moderately Heavy Resistance Weights on the Jumping Ability of High School Basketball Players.* University of Texas, Master's, 1959.

5199. **Daugherty, Fred William.** *A Proposed Coaches' Basketball Manual for a Monett, Missouri, Senior High School.* Kansas State College of Pittsburg, Master's, 1957.

5200. **Davidson, George A.** *Factors Which Contribute to Success in Winning Basketball Games.* University of Kansas, Master's, 1966.

5201. **Davidson, Joel H.** *Opinions and Attitudes of Girls Toward Interschool Basketball in Selected High Schools of Metropolitan Winnipeg.* University of North Dakota, Master's, 1970.

5202. **Davies, William Thomas.** *Motivation in Intramural Basketball Skills.* Springfield College, Master's, 1933.

5203. **Davis, Benjamin H., III.** *A Study of the Time Involved in the Basketball Throw-In.* Springfield College, Master's, 1967.

5204. **Davis, Carl Aaron.** *An Experiment in Measuring Ability and Progress in Basketball Skills.* Springfield College, Master's, 1932.

5205. **Davis, Cathy Jean.** *A Comparison of Three Women's Basketball Circulorespiratory Endurance Groups at Utah State University to Determine Which Has the Most Significant Effect on Oxygen Uptake.* Utah State University, Master's, 1972.

5206. **Davis, Ivan Dariel.** *Individual Basketball Effectiveness as Related to Personality Variables and Its Use in Basketball Coaching.* Utah State University, Master's, 1966.

5207. **Davis, Walter G.** *A Comparative Analysis of Basketball Coaching Methods, Techniques, and Schedule Procedures for Girls in Georgia High Schools, Abstract 40.* Middle Tennessee State University, Master's, 1962.

5208. **Davis, William Eugene.** *A Study to Determine the Best Floor Locations for Obtaining Rebounds of Basketball Jump Shots From Selected Areas.* University of North Carolina, Master's, 1973.

5209. **Davison, Richard N.** *A Study of Reaction Time, Choice Movement Reaction Time, Movement Time, Choice Movement Time and Strength Among Various Basketball Ability Groups.* Montclair State College, Master's, 1976.

5210. **Deary, Michael.** *A Correlation Study to Predict Success in Basketball: Basketball Officiating.* Springfield College, Master's, 1982.

5211. **Debate, Wayne Charles.** *The Effect of the Personal Foul and the Free Throw on the Outcome of High School Basketball Games.* San Diego State College, Master's, 1965.

5212. **Dedoshka, Donna.** *A Basketball Coaching Manual for the Physical Conditioning of Women Without the Use of Heavy Resistive Equipment.* University of California, San Diego, Master's, 1982.

5213. **DeFrank, Sheila L.** *The Effects of Training and Detraining on Body Composition and Physiological Parameters of Collegiate Basketball Players.* University of Massachusetts–Amherst, Master's, 1984.

5214. **Dehnert, Annette Ella.** *A Comparison of the Effects of Two Methods of Instruction Upon Free Throw Shooting Ability.* University of Wisconsin, Master's, 1962.

5215. **DeKalb, Susan Elaine.** *Expectancies, Casual Attributions, and Anxiety in Collegiate Women Basketball Players.* Pennsylvania State University, Master's, 1981.

5216. **DeMichael, John Anthony.** *The History of Basketball at Stongington High School.* Eastern Illinois University, Master's, 1962.

5217. **Dempsey, Bruce Clark.** *A Survey of Policies Regarding Interscholastic Basketball in Junior High Schools in Illinois.* Northern Illinois University, Master's, 1965.

5218. **Denby, Preston Allen.** *Basketball Participation and the Self Concept.* Springfield College, Doctorate, 1977.

5219. **Des Jardins, Dennis.** *A Study of Physiological Parameters Before and After a Season of Wheelchair Basketball Competition.* University of Rhode Island, Master's, 1981.

5220. **Dessureault, Jacques.** *Reaction, Movement, and Competition Times of Basketball Players at Grade Nine Level.* University of Oregon, Master's, 1970.

5221. **Deterding, Don.** *The History of Basketball of the Effingham High School.* Eastern Illinois University, Master's, 1965.

5222. **Deutach, Helgo Meta.** *The Effect of Two Selected Distributions of Practice on the Acquisition of Skill in Basketball.* University of Illinois, Master's, 1960.

5223. **Deutch, Robin.** *History of Northeastern University Basketball: From Foster to Calhoun.* Northeastern University, Undergraduate research report, 1983.

5224. **DeWaard, Linda Susan.** *Validation of a Conceptual Model Characterizing Gender Based Stereotypes in Ballet and Basketball.* West Virginia University, Master's, 1981.

5225. **Dewar, John Duncan.** *The Life and Professional Contributions of James Naismith.* Florida State University, Doctorate, 1965.

5226. **DeWitt, Norval.** *Effects of the Iowa Weight Training and the Army Dozen on the Jumping Ability of Basketball Players.* Drake University, Master's, 1963.

5227. **Diana, Edward Anthony.** *Personality Traits of National Basketball Officials.* Ithaca College, Master's, 1972.

5228. **Dickson, Joseph Fletcher.** *The Relationship of Depth Perception to Goal Shooting in Basketball.* University of Iowa, Doctorate, 1953.

5229. **Dickson, Leland H.** *A Comparative and Experimental Study of Three Basic Methods of Basketball Free Throws.* Texas A&I University, Master's, 1950.

5230. **Dickyson, Charles.** *A Basketball Handbook for the Beginning Basketball Coach.* Northwest Missouri State University, Master's, 1978.

5231. **DePersio, Edward R.** *The Evaluation of Basketball Rules From 1936–1954.* Springfield College, Master's, 1954.

5232. **Diehl, Pamela Sue.** *Effects of a Season of Training and Competition on Selected Physiological Parameters in Female College Basketball Players.* Ohio State University, Doctorate, 1974.

5233. **Dillingham, Vicki Lynn.** *Effect of an "Instructional Conceptualization" Video Tape Replay on Maximum Strength and Maximum Power Output in College-Age Females.* University of Kentucky, Master's, 1982.

5234. **Dittebradt, Catherine Harker.** *Objective Method of Measuring the Development of Skill in the Basketball Free Throw.* Washington State University, Master's, 1935.

5235. **Doan, Edna K.** *A Study of the Effectiveness of Video Tape as a Supplement to Traditional Methods in a Women's Basketball Class.* Pacific University, Master's, 1971.

5236. **Dodson, Nathan Taylor.** *A Study of the Effects of Basketball Upon the Physical Condition of the Players.* University of North Carolina, Master's, 1948.

5237. **Doherty, Michael Thomas.** *An Analysis of the Relationship Between Selected Autobiographical Data and the Personality Traits of High School Basketball Players.* Oregon State University, Doctorate, 1975.

5238. **Donkhorst, Jane.** *Cohesion in Girls' Basketball Teams in the Davis School District.* University of Utah, Master's, 1973.

5239. **Dooley, John B.** *A Comparison of Basket Shooting Proficiency When Shots Are Aimed at the Backboard and at the Basket.* Northern Illinois University, Master's, 1963.

5240. **Dorinson, Joseph.** *Sports and Social Mobility: A Look at Connie Hawkins and Jack Molinass.* Long Island University, Master's, 1978.

5241. **Dorsey, Pamela Florence.** *The Relationship to Visual Perceptual Speed to Basketball Play Ability of High School Females.* Illinois State University, Master's, 1985.

5242. **Douglas, Robert A.** *A Study to Determine Time Loss After Violations in Basketball.* Springfield College, Master's, 1958.

5243. **Downing, Margaret.** *Women's Basketball: A Historical Review of Selected Organizations Which Influenced Its Ascension Toward Advanced Competition in the United States.* Texas Woman's University, Doctorate, 1973.

5244. **Draper, Mary Vanessa.** *Goal Orientation as a Function of Sport Team Cohesion.* University of Oregon, Master's, 1987.

5245. **Dray, D.A.** *The Effect of Various Factors Upon Heart Rates of Girls Engaged in Playing Competitive Basketball.* Mills College, Master's, 1936.

5246. **Drury, Leon A., III.** *An Evaluation of an In-Season Isometric Strength Training Program for Basketball.* Springfield College, Master's, 1967.

5247. **Drysdale, Sharon J.** *A Cinematographic and Comparative Analysis of the Basketball Jump Shot.* University of Iowa, Doctorate, 1972.

5248. **DuCharme, Pierre L.** *A Survey of the Home Court Advantage in Basketball as Found in North Dakota and South Dakota High School During 1969–1970.* Northern State College, Master's, 1970.

5249. **Dudduth, Solon Bluch.** *A Summary of Essentials From Selected Bibliographies on Teaching Basketball.* Vanderbilt University–Peabody College, Master's, 1934.

5250. **Dudek, David M.** *Factors for Selection of Junior College Basketball Players.* Ithaca College, Master's, 1975.

5251. **Dudley, Jimmie E.** *The Effect of the One Point Field Goal on the Outcome of Selected College Basketball Games.* Eastern Illinois University, Master's, 1967.

5252. **Duff, Barbara Arlene.** *The Relative Effectiveness of Physical Practice and a Combination of Mental and Physical Practice in Improving the Underhand Free Throw as Used in Basketball.* University of Colorado, Master's, 1963.

5253. **Dufford, Carl L.** *The Development of a High School Aggressive Pressure Defensive Basketball Program.* Ashland College, Master's, 1981.

5254. **Duffy, Bernard Eugene.** *The Effect of Prescribed Weight Training on a Selected Group of Varsity Basketball Players.* South Dakota State University, Master's, 1956.

5255. **DuFrane, Stanley J.** *The Relationship of Ball Possession, Foul Location and Bonus Free Throwing on Varsity Basketball Team Performance.* University of Wisconsin, Master's, 1956.

5256. **Duka, Michael.** *Effectiveness of a Rim-Reducer on Foul Shooting Accuracy.* West Chester State College, Master's, 1971.

5257. **Duncan, Weldon.** *A Study of the Junior High Basketball Program of the Class AA Schools in Texas.* Sam Houston State College, Master's, 1955.

5258. **Dunger, C.** *Teaching Aids for Girls' Basketball.* University of Iowa, Master's, 1945.

5259. **Dunn, Linda Marie.** *A Comparative Analysis of Girls' High School Basketball Rules from Thirteen Southern States.* University of Tennessee, Master's, 1970.

5260. **Durentini, Carol L.** *The Relationship of a Purported Measure of Kinesthesis to the Learning of a Simple Motor Skill, the Basketball Free Throw, Projected With and Without Vision.* University of Massachusetts, Master's, 1967.

5261. **Dutot, Norman Emile.** *A Comparison of Anxiety Levels of College and High School Female Basketball Players and Father's Basketball Background.* Central Missouri State University, Master's, 1987.

5262. **East, Ruby J.** *The Effect of Coaching Upon the Acquisition of Skill in the Basketball Free Throw.* University of Wisconsin, Master's, 1927.

5263. **Easturn, Warrine.** *A Survey of the ''B'' League Basketball Competition for Girls in Lane County, Oregon.* University of Oregon, Master's, 1938.

5264. **Ebel, Harold K.** *A Study of the Accuracy of One-Handed and Two-Handed Set Shots in Basketball.* University of Iowa, Master's, 1951.

5265. **Echert, Richard L.** *The Apparent Effect of Interscholastic Competition in Basketball on Scholastic Achievement of Boys in DeKalb County, Illinois, High Schools.* Northern Illinois University, Master's, 1955.

5266. **Ecklund, John Albin.** *A Comparison of the Effect of Variation in Task Difficulty in the Transfer of Basketball Shooting Accuracy Among College, Senior High, and Junior High Females.* University of Minnesota, Doctorate, 1975.

5267. **Edgren, Harry.** *An Experiment in the Testing of Ability and Program in Basketball.* George Williams College, Master's, 1931.

5268. **Edmonstron, Craig Alan.** *Professionalization of Attitude Toward Play of Intramural Basketball Participants.* University of Kansas, Master's, 1978.

5269. **Edwards, John Hardy, Jr.** *A Cinematographical Study of Field Goal Shooting Characteristics as Indicated by Successful College Basketball Teams.* University of Maryland, Master's, 1958.

5270. **Egge, James.** *The Probability of a Basketball Rebounding in a Specific Area After a Missed Shot Is Taken From a Certain Area.* South Dakota State University, Master's, 1974.

5271. **Eggebrecht, C.A.** *Effect of Basketball on Weight and Heart Rate.* Springfield College, Master's, 1920.

5272. **Ehrenfried, Michael J.** *The History of Basketball at Bowling Green State University.* Bowling Green State University, Master's, 1975.

5273. **Eickhorst, Willard A.** *Comparative Study of Three Free Throw Shooting Techniques.* University of Wisconsin, Master's, 1967.

5274. **Eidsness, John.** *The Effects of a Collegiate Basketball Season on Selected Fitness Measurements.* South Dakota State University, Master's, 1971.

5275. **Elbert, Patty.** *The Relationship of Selected Measurable Traits to Success in Basketball.* Indiana University, Doctorate, 1953.

5276. **Elders, Olive Boone.** *A Handbook for Basketball Coaches of Hall High School.* Indiana University, Doctorate, 1972.

5277. **Eliowitz, Samuel.** *Testing to Determine Basketball Ability of Large Groups.* Wayne State University, Master's, 1964.

5278. **Ellenburg, Joe K.** *The Predictive Value of Selected Physical Variables in Determining Competitive Performance in High School Basketball.* University of Alabama, Doctorate, 1970.

5279. **Elorza, Jesus.** *Venezuela Sport Law and Its Influence on the Formation or Development of Human Resources in Physical Education and Sports.* University of Toledo, Master's, 1981.

5280. **Elston, Donald W.** *A Biography of Forest C. "Phog" Allen.* University of Kansas, Master's, 1967.

5281. **Emerson, Phyllis Ann.** *Basketball of the Woman Physical Education Teacher and Coach.* Springfield College, Master's, 1961.

5282. **Emil, Bernard.** *The Development of Techniques of Officiating Men's Basketball With Special Reference to the Eastern College Athletic Conference.* Queens College, Master's, 1971.

5283. **Engelland, Cheryl Rene.** *A Comparison of Reaction Times of Women Varsity Basketball Players and Women Non-Varsity Athletes at Fort Hays Kansas State College.* Fort Hays Kansas State College, Master's, 1974.

5284. **Englese-Dellaserva, Frances.** *A Comparison Between Accumulated Playing Time and Academic Performance Among Female High School Basketball Players.* University of California, San Diego, Master's, 1985.

5285. **Enty, Frank Edward.** *The Analysis and Implication of the Status of Interscholastic Competitive Athletics in Selected States.* North Carolina Central University, Master's, 1955.

5286. **Erans, Bernice M.** *The Size of the Ball as One Factor Influencing Skill in Basketball.* Washington State University, Master's, 1957.

5287. **Erdman, Robert.** *The Relationship of the Success in Making Free Throws in Game Competition With the Time They Were Attempted in Practice.* University of Minnesota, Master's, 1959.

5288. **Erickson, Ralph Winthrop.** *Balance as a Means of Measuring Body Control in Relation to the Teaching of Basketball Skills to Children in Elementary Grades.* Springfield College, Master's, 1935.

5289. **Erikson, Anders E.** *An Experimental Visual Training Method for a Selected Shooting Skill in Basketball.* Central Washington University, Master's, 1975.

5290. **Esboldt, Gary.** *The Effects of Participation in Competitive Basketball on Weight-Loss and Selected Measures of Basketball Related Skills.* South Dakota State University, Master's, 1979.

5291. **Espe, Brian.** *A Study of the Relationship of Selected Game Factors to Success in High School Basketball.* Mankato State University, Master's, 1978.

5292. **Estes, James William.** *A Preliminary Investigation of Some Effects of Activation on the Performance of College Basketball Players.* George Peabody College for Teachers, Master's, 1978.

5293. **Esworthy, Raymond Wayne.** *Types of Muscular Coordination in Basket Throwing.* University of Illinois, Master's, 1930.

5294. **Evanoas, David.** *A Brief Basketball Screening Test to Classify Boys Into Homogeneous Groups for Instructional Purposes.* Oregon State University, Master's, 1952.

5295. **Evans, Floyd Collins.** *A History of Varsity Basketball at Texas Tech College.* Texas Tech University, Master's, 1965.

5296. **Evans, Frank A.** *The History of Basketball in the Interstate Intercollegiate Athletic Conference 1950–70.* Eastern Illinois University, Master's, 1970.

5297. **Evans, Linda Marie.** *The Relationship Between Self-Concept and Team Cohesiveness of Basketball and Swimming Teams.* Washington State University, Master's, 1980.

5298. **Evans, Virginia Lou.** *The Formative Years of Women's College Basketball in Five Selected Colleges.* University of Maryland, Master's, 1971.

5299. **Evenhouse, John Allen.** *An Analysis of Game Statistics in Basketball.* George Williams College, Master's, 1979.

5300. **Evjen, Gary C.** *Effects of a Six Week Depth Jumping Program on Vertical Jumping Ability of Male College Basketball Players.* University of North Dakota, Master's, 1979.

5301. **Excell, Evan K.** *An Investigation Into the Home Court Advantage of Utah Class B High School Basketball.* University of Utah, Master's, 1967.

5302. **Fahey, Brian William.** *Basketball: A Phenomenological Perspective of Livedbody Experience.* University of Washington, Master's, 1971.

5303. **Farley, William.** *The Effects of Instruction and Use of a Mechanical Device Based Upon a Scientific Principle as Applied to Basketball Shooting.* University of Northern Colorado, Doctorate, 1967.

5304. **Farmer, Daniel Scott.** *Changes in Blood Pressure Incidental to Training and Activity in Football and Basketball.* University of California, Master's, 1934.

5305. **Farmer, James E.** *Variables Affecting Performance Levels of Basketball Officials.* University of Southern California, Master's, 1981.

5306. **Feasel, John Wesley.** *A Handbook of Drills to Teach the Fundamentals of High School Basketball.* University of Dayton, Master's, 1986.

5307. **Felder, Sidney F.** *Weight Training for Varsity Basketball Players in Selected Northern Illinois Schools.* Northern Illinois University, Master's, 1963.

5308. **Feldmann, John A.** *The Apparent Advantages for the Home Team in Basketball.* Northern Illinois University, Master's, 1963.

5309. **Fellows, Frank C.** *A Comparison of the Visual Performance of Nine College Varsity Basketball Players With Visual Test Norms.* University of Maryland, Master's, 1957.

5310. **Femrite, Arnold S.** *Relationship of the Personality of Selected Basketball Coaches to Their Coaching Success.* Mankato State University, Master's, 1967.

5311. **Ferazzi, Gabriel Ernest.** *A Study of Shooting Methods Employed by Basketball Players in the Professional Basketball Association of America.* Boston University, Master's, 1949.

5312. **Ferguson, John A.** *The Effects of Rebounding on the Outcome of High School Basketball Games.* San Diego State College, Master's, 1970.

5313. **Ferrigno, Edward N.** *A Study of Basketball Skills Tests Conducted in Selected High Schools.* Springfield College, Master's, 1955.

5314. **Finanger, Kenton E.** *The Relationship of Rebounding, Free Throw Shooting, and Field Location to High School Basketball Team Performance.* University of Wisconsin, Master's, 1957.

5315. **Fisbeck, Weldon.** *Prediction of Basketball Ability in High School Girls.* University of Texas, Master's, 1961.

5316. **Fishback, Herbert O.** *A Study of Factors Used to Recruit Basketball Players in the Atlantic Coast Conference and the Pacific Ten Conference.* Washington State University, Master's, 1986.

5317. **Fisher, Edward Samuel.** *A Comparison of the Conventional and Zones Systems of Basketball Scoring.* University of Washington, Master's, 1961.

5318. **Fisher, Roger L.** *The Effect of Backboard and Rim Alterations on Basketball Shooting Accuracy.* Illinois State University, Master's, 1968.

5319. **Fisk, Timothy.** *Development of Basketball Shooting Accuracy as Affected by Varying Goal Sizes.* South Dakota State University, Master's, 1967.

5320. **Flack, H.M.** *Basketball Systems Evaluated and Adapted for High School Coaching.* George Peabody College for Teachers, Master's, 1935.

5321. **Flack, Howard Watson.** *Selected Basketball Systems Evaluated and Adapted for High School Coaching.* George Peabody College, Master's, 1935.

5322. **Flanagan, Jerome J.** *Different Sized Balls Involved in 8th Grade Boys' Basketball Skills.* Mankato State College, Master's, 1973.

5323. **Flatt, Jerry Edward.** *A Study of the Professional Preparation of Football, Basketball, Baseball, and Track Coaches of the Tennessee Secondary Schools.* Middle Tennessee State University, Dissertation abstract, 1975.

5324. **Fleming, Edmund John.** *A Simplified Revolving Basketball Offense.* University of Texas, Master's, 1954.

5325. **Flickner, Robert E.** *A Study of the Characteristics of Play in Intercollegiate Basketball With the 30-Second Time Limit Rule in Effect.* University of Kansas, Master's, 1974.

5326. **Fliss, Cindy Jane.** *Accuracy of College Women Shooting Set Shots as Affected by Selected Training Programs.* South Dakota State University, Master's, 1974.

5327. **Fong, Dexter.** *A Socio-Historical Study of the California Nisei Athletic Union "AA" North-South Basketball Championship Games for Men From 1934 to 1971.* California State University, Master's, 1973.

5328. **Fontis, Dave.** *History of Basketball at San Diego State University.* San Diego State University, Master's, 1975.

5329. **Ford, Don Ray.** *A Comparison of Massed and Distributed Practice on Free Throw Practices.* Texas Tech University, Master's, 1972.

5330. **Forker, Barbara Ellen.** *The Effects of a Season of Basketball Practice on Male College Freshmen as Indicated by Selected Tests of Fatigue.* University of Michigan, Doctorate, 1957.

5331. **Forsyth, Harry.** *The Effects of a Basketball Training Program on Cardiovascular Condition as Shown by the Cameron Heartometer.* South Dakota State University, Master's, 1956.

5332. **Foster, Evie Gooch.** *Personality Traits of Highly Skilled Basketball and Softball Women Athletes.* Indiana University, Doctorate, 1971.

5333. **Fowler, Dianne Elaine.** *The Effect of Cohesion, Participation Motivation, and Satisfaction on Performance in Women's Intercollegiate Basketball.* University of Arizona, Undergraduate, 1982.

5334. **Fox, Barbara Jean.** *Cinematographic Analysis of the Point of Release in the Basketball Jump Shot.* Northeast Missouri State University, Master's, 1986.

5335. **Fox, Rene Marie.** *Smaller and Lighter Ball Influences: NorPac Women Basketball Players' Perspectives.* Washington State University, Master's, 1985.

5336. **Fox, Richard Anthony.** *Basketball Syllabus for High Schools.* University of Idaho, Master's, 1935.

5337. **Fox, Sidney.** *A Comparison of the Whole Method vs. the Part-Whole Method of Teaching Basketball to 6th Grade Boys.* Wayne State University, Master's, 1969.

5338. **Fraase, Jennifer.** *An Investigation of Drug and Alcohol Use by North Dakota High School Class "B" Girls' Varsity Basketball Players: A Research Paper.* North Dakota State University, Master's, 1986.

5339. **Frank, Omer K.** *A Comparison of the Social and Emotional Adjustment of Basketball Players and Wrestlers.* Central Missouri State University, Master's, 1968.

5340. **Fraser, Art.** *A Comparison of the Effect of Two Weight Training Programs on the Vertical Jump of Freshmen Basketball Players.* University of Minnesota, Master's, 1962.

5341. **Fraser, R.A.** *A Study of the Frequency and Court Placement in Women's Basketball as Related to the Problem of Officiating Women's Basketball Games.* New York University, Master's, 1942.

5342. **Fratzke, Melvin Reuben.** *Discriminant Analysis of Intramural Basketball Officials.* Indiana University, Doctorate, 1973.

5343. **Frazer, R., Mauer, M., and Nautz, A.** *Testing the Ability of Basketball Forwards Objectively.* University of Wisconsin, Master's, 1930.

5344. **Freeborn, Richard D.** *The Professional Preparation of High School Male Head Coaches in the State of Ohio.* University of Toledo, Master's, 1974.

5345. **Freeman, Charles G.** *The Effects of Post Season Weight Training on the Vertical Jumping Ability of Male High School Players.* Northwestern State University of Louisiana, Master's, 1961.

5346. **Friedrichs, Warren David.** *The Influence of Leader Behaviors, Coach Attributes, and Institutional Variables on Performance and Satisfaction of Collegiate Basketball Teams.* University of Oregon, Doctorate, 1984.

5347. **Friery, Robert Joseph.** *Evolution of the Rules of Basketball.* Springfield College, Master's, 1936.

5348. **Frigard, Wilho.** *Effect of the Elimination of the Center Jump on the Game of Basketball.* University of Massachusetts, Master's, 1938.

5349. **Frye, Barbara.** *The Influence of Visual Feedback on Accuracy of the Underhand Toss in Foul Shooting in Basketball for High School Girls.* East Tennessee State University, Master's, 1972.

5350. **Frye, Gregory.** *A Comparison of Attitudes—Christian and Basketball Coaches—Toward Basketball Incidents.* Western Illinois University, Master's, 1976.

5351. **Fuller, Chester.** *A Survey of Football and Basketball Officials in the High Schools of Salt River Valley.* Northern Arizona University, Master's, 1941.

5352. **Fulton, Clifton Dale.** *Progressive Changes in Heartometer Pulse Wave Tracings During a Season of Basketball.* University of Illinois, Master's, 1951.

5353. **Fulton, Robert D.** *Relationship Between Achieving Tendency and Sport Motivation of College Basketball Players.* University of North Carolina at Greensboro, Master's, 1984.

5354. **Funk, Durward Rose.** *An Analysis of Two Methods of Teaching Girls' Basketball.* West Virginia University, Master's, 1941.

5355. **Galbreath, Carl Sylvio.** *A Study of the Intramural Sports and Programs in Negro Colleges and Universities in North Carolina.* North Carolina Central University, Master's, 1957.

5356. **Gallagher, Arlea.** *Relationship Between Fundamental Skill Performance Level and Subjective Rankings of Basketball Game Play Ability of Selected Female High School Basketball Players.* Montclair State College, Master's, 1972.

5357. **Gallagher, Donna.** *The Relationship of Agility to Performance in Women's Intercollegiate Basketball.* Springfield College, Master's, 1969.

5358. **Gallatin, Harry J.** *A Study of the Relation of Field Goals Attempted and Field Goals Made to Winning or Losing in Basketball.* University of Iowa, Master's, 1954.

5359. **Ganey, James H.** *History of Intercollegiate Basketball at the University of Georgia.* University of Georgia, Master's, 1969.

5360. **Gant, Katherine Anne.** *The Relationship Between Anxiety and Performance in a Women's Intercollegiate Basketball Team in the Course of a Regular Season.* University of North Carolina at Chapel Hill, Master's, 1982.

5361. **Garchow, Kenneth E.** *The Relationship Between Tachistoscopic Performance and Athletic Training.* Pacific University, Doctorate, 1984.

5362. **Gardiner, William C.** *A Study of the Most Apparent Weaknesses of High School Basketball Players Entering College.* University of Maryland, Master's, 1952.

5363. **Gardner, C. Michael.** *The Effect of Raising the Height of the Basketball Goal From a Height of Ten Feet to Heights of Eleven and Twelve Feet on Shooting Accuracy in the Game of Basketball.* Brigham Young University, Master's, 1966.

5364. **Garretson, Rodney R.** *An Analysis of Selected Basketball Skills Used by Coaches of the Institutions of Higher Learning of the Pacific Northwest, 1962.* University of Washington, Master's, 1962.

5365. **Garrett, Kevin.** *The Effects of an Off-Season Weight Training Program on the Strength of Male Basketball Players.* Slippery Rock University, Master's, 1984.

5366. **Garvin, Lorraine and O'Reilly, Ann.** *Effect of Mental and Physical Practice Combined With Massed and Distributed Practice in the Learning of the Foul Shot by Players of Three Levels of Skills.* Herbert H. Lehman College, Master's, 1971.

5367. **Gaultiere, William.** *A Study of the Effect of the Figure Eight Ankle Wrap Bandage on Performance in Selected Basketball Skills.* Ohio University, Master's, 1961.

5368. **Gaunt, Sharon Jeannette.** *A Cinematographic and Comparative Analysis of the Basketball Jump Shot as Performed by Male and Female Shooters.* Eastern Kentucky University, Independent, 1976.

5369. **Gaunt, Sharon Jeannette.** *Factory Structure of Basketball Playing Ability.* Indiana University, Doctorate, 1979.

5370. **Gebhardt, F. Don.** *A Study of the Use of McCloy Classification Index I in Classifying Boys of the Eighth and Ninth Grades for Participation in Interscholastic Basketball.* University of Michigan, Master's, 1935.

5371. **Gee, Ada J.** *Physiological Characteristics of the Female Basketball Player: A Review.* Ball State University, Master's, 1986.

5372. **Gelina, Anthony L.** *Relationship Between Selected Warm-up Experiences to Performance of the Jump Shot in Basketball.* University of Wisconsin, Master's, 1973.

5373. **George, Phillip Morgan.** *A Continuity Tandem Post Basketball Offense.* University of Texas, Master's, 1954.

5374. **Gephart, Gene Charles.** *The Relative Effect of Blindfold, Sighted, and No Practice on Free Throw Accuracy.* University of Illinois, Master's, 1954.

5375. **Gertler, Richard W.** *Factors Affecting Student Attendance at 1983–1984 Men's Football and Basketball Games at Western Illinois University.* Western Illinois University, Doctorate, 1985.

5376. **Geurin, William L.** *A Study to Determine the Effects of Extraneous Visual Cues on the Accuracy of Shooting a Basketball.* Eastern Illinois University, Master's, 1966.

5377. **Giambrone, Charles Paul.** *The Influence of Situation Criticality and Game Criticality on Basketball Free Throw Shooting.* University of Illinois, Master's, 1973.

5378. **Gibbens, Denzel R.** *A Basketball Skill Test.* University of Kansas, Master's, 1947.

5379. **Gibson, Herbert Wayne.** *The Effects of Two Training Methods on Vertical Jumping Ability of Intermediate Basketball Players.* East Carolina University, Master's, 1970.

5380. **Gideon, Donald L.** *A Basketball Study to Determine the Relation of Shots Taken From Certain Areas and Their Probability of Rebounding to Another Specified Area.* Western Illinois University, Master's, 1968.

5381. **Gienger, Dennis W.** *The Effect of Ankle Weights on the Jumping Performance of a Selected Group of Basketball Players.* University of North Dakota, Master's, 1968.

5382. **Gilbert, Marc-Andre.** *An Organizational Approach to the Study of Productivity, Efficiency and Satisfaction of AAA High School Basketball Teams Based on Fielder's Contingency Model and Taylor and Bowers' Survey of Organization Conditions.* University of Oregon, Doctorate, 1977.

5383. **Gilbert, Raymond.** *A Study of Selected Variables in Predicting Basketball Players.* Springfield College, Master's, 1968.

5384. **Gillespie, William John.** *An Experiment to Determine Incomplete Shots for Basketball Shooting.* San Diego State College, Master's, 1965.

5385. **Gillett, Ronald Earle.** *Intrinsic Factors That Relate to High School Basketball Success in Idaho.* Brigham Young University, Master's, 1971.

5386. **Gilman, Joseph Richard, Jr.** *Basketball Skills as Related to Manual Dexterity.* University of Kansas, Master's, 1954.

5387. **Gingerich, Roman.** *A Study of the Control of the Basketball From the Offensive and Defensive Backboard.* University of Iowa, Master's, 1946.

5388. **Giorgis, Ann Marie.** *Attribution and Goal Expectancy With Two Different Methods of Task Structure Presentation in a Basketball Shooting Unit.* Bowling Green State University, Master's, 1986.

5389. **Girouard, J.E.** *The Effect of Practice Position on Accuracy in Goal Shooting in Basketball.* Springfield College, Master's, 1967.

5390. **Givone, Robert.** *The Personality of Basketball Players From Rural and Urban Areas as Measured by the Cattell Sixteen Personality Factor Questionnaire.* University of Massachusetts, Master's, 1969.

5391. **Glas, Richard.** *Effects of Foot Positioning Upon Reaction Movement Time of Defensive Basketball Players.* Western Illinois University, Master's, 1971.

5392. **Glaz, Doris.** *Alternations of Hematological Indices of Intercollegiate Female Basketball Players.* Bowling Green State University, Master's, 1978.

5393. **Glick, Lester R.** *An Attempt to Devise a Simple Method of Measuring Potential Basketball Intelligence.* University of Iowa, Master's, 1941.

5394. **Glore, James LeRoy.** *Survey of Injuries Sustained by the St. Louis McKinley High School Football and Basketball Teams in the 1956–57 Seasons.* New Mexico State University, Master's, 1957.

5395. **Glowatzke, Dianne K.** *A Comparative Study of the Incidence of Injury in Female and Male Basketball Players.* St. Cloud State University, Master's, 1977.

5396. **Goldsmith.** *The History of the National Junior College Athletic Association National Basketball Tournament.* Kansas State Teachers College, Master's, 1962.

5397. **Goldstein, Barbara Zona.** *The Relationship Between Threat and Cohesiveness on the Process and Outcome of Basketball Games.* University of California, Los Angeles, Doctorate, 1981.

5398. **Goldstein, Norman.** *Techniques Utilized to Determine Basketball Ability for Selecting High School Sophomore Players.* University of Washington, Master's, 1967.

5399. **Goodard, Russell E.** *A Plan for Athletic Officiating in the High Schools of Arizona.* Northern Arizona University, Master's, 1945.

5400. **Goodson, Michael.** *The Influence of Failure at Basketball Tryouts Upon Self-Esteem of Ninth Grade Boys.* University of Rhode Island, Master's, 1974.

5401. **Gordon, Patricia Ann.** *Prediction of Basketball Playing Ability of College Women by Selected Tests.* University of Arkansas, Doctorate, 1978.

5402. **Gorman, Robert H.** *Comparison of Response Times of Intercollegiate Basketball Players and Non-Players.* University of Oregon, Master's, 1958.

5403. **Gorton, Beatrice Ann.** *Selected Kinetic and Kinematic Factors Involved in the Basketball Jump Shot.* Indiana University, Doctorate, 1979.

5404. **Gourdouze, Frank Rex.** *An Analysis of the Indiana High School Athletic Association Tourneys Home Court Winners' Percentages From 1936–1949 Inclusive.* Indiana State Teachers College, Master's, 1950.

5405. **Grace, Gary.** *An Analysis of How College Basketball Coaches Spend Their Time.* University of Nebraska at Lincoln, Master's, 1988.

5406. **Graham, Eddie.** *A Study in Foul Shooting.* Southwest Texas State University, Master's, 1959.

5407. **Grant, Martin Trygstad.** *A Comparison of Personalities of Lake Conference Basketball Players for the Year 1970–71.* Bemidji State University, Master's, 1973.

5408. **Grantham, Joseph Miles.** *An Investigation of the Priority, Accomplishment and Distortion of Objectives of Intercollegiate Basketball Programs in N.A.I.A. Schools.* University of Missouri at Kansas City, Doctorate, 1975.

5409. **Grassini, Doris Ann.** *Methods of Pre-Season Basketball Conditioning for Female Varsity Players in Selected Secondary Schools in New Jersey.* Montclair State College, Master's, 1973.

5410. **Grastorf, Jane E.** *Nonverbal Behaviors of Collegiate Female Volleyball and Basketball Coaches as Recalled by Athletes and Coaches.* University of North Carolina at Greensboro, Doctorate, 1980.

5411. **Graves, Francis Anne.** *Effect of Coaching and Motion Picture Study on the Attitudes of Elementary and Junior High School Basketball Players.* Texas Tech University, Master's, 1969.

5412. **Graves, Marilyn Lou.** *Stress in College Women Basketball Players and Coping Techniques of Coaches.* University of Arkansas, Doctorate, 1981.

5413. **Gray, Gary Robert.** *The Relationship Between Elements of Team Cohesiveness and Team Success at Various Levels of Basketball Competition.* University of Kentucky, Master's, 1975.

5414. **Gray, Gene Edwin.** *The Effect of Selected Game Factors and Team Height Upon the Outcome of Interscholastic Basketball Games.* Northern Illinois University, Master's, 1966.

5415. **Green, George H.** *The Defensive Tactics of North Carolina Basketball Coaches.* North Carolina Central University, Master's, 1963.

5416. **Green, Marjorie L.** *Effects of Competitive Basketball Experiences of Girls in the Gainesville State Training School.* North Texas State University, Master's, 1969.

5417. **Green, William J.** *The Effect of Two Types of Training on Accuracy of Basketball Free Throw Shooting.* East Tennessee State University, Master's, 1971.

5418. **Greene, Herald T.** *The Point Cost of Errors in Basketball Made by the Team in Possession of the Ball.* University of Iowa, Master's, 1954.

5419. **Greenfield, Stanley.** *A Comparison of the Relationship Between Anxiety and Free Throw Shooting Ability of College and High School Varsity Basketball Players.* Kearney State College, Master's, 1972.

5420. **Greenlee, Virginia.** *The Development of Strength as One Component of Skill in Basketball for Ninth Grade Girls.* Washington State University, Master's, 1957.

5421. **Greer, Alfred Edgar.** *A Study of the Validity of the Brace Basketball Achievement Tests for Girls as a Measure of Real Playing Ability of Individual Players of District 30B University of Texas Interscholastic League for the 1954 Season.* North Texas State University, Master's, 1954.

5422. **Gregg, Michael Miller.** *A Study of Basketball Coaching Ethics in Selected Northern California High Schools.* California State University, Chico, Master's, 1972.

5423. **Gregory, Gerald.** *Ability Basketball Manual for Youth-Serving Agencies.* George Williams College, Master's, 1963.

5424. **Gregory, Hallie E.** *A Survey of Free Throw Practice Methods Employed by Coaches in the State of Minnesota.* Moorhead State College, Master's, 1965.

5425. **Grenier, Jacques.** *The Effectiveness of the Jump Shot in Relation to Angles and Distances.* University of Oregon, Master's, 1970.

5426. **Gribben, Tom L.** *High School Basketball Coaching Method in the San Juan Basin.* Adams State College of Colorado, Master's, 1958.

5427. **Griffin, Norma Sue.** *A Comparison of the Heart Rates of Female College Participants in Field Hockey and Basketball.* University of Oregon, Doctorate, 1967.

5428. **Grishman, Robert D.** *The Effect of Mental Practice on Competitive Free Throw Performance of Intercollegiate Basketball Players.* Western Washington University, Master's, 1985.

5429. **Gross, Elmer Alfred.** *The History of Basketball at the Pennsylvania State College.* Pennsylvania State University, Master's, 1947.

5430. **Grossman, Raymond Allen.** *A Study of Tests of Inherent Ability and Acquired Skills as Indices of Basketball Ability.* George Williams College, Master's, 1949.

5431. **Gruber, Samuel C.** *Development of a Pressure Basketball Program.* Western Maryland College, Master's, 1970.

5432. **Grubbs, Paula J.** *Reliability of the AAHPER Basketball Skills Test for Ninth and Tenth Grade Girls and the Establishment of Local Norms.* Pennsylvania State University, Master's, 1967.

5433. **Gruentzel, Paul J.** *The Relation Between High School Basketball Players' Ability to Shoot Free Throws in Practice Versus Game Conditions.* University of Wisconsin, Master's, 1954.

5434. **Gruetter, Dan Emerson.** *Relationship of Leadership Styles of Selected Division I Athletic Directors With Winning Percentages in Football and Basketball.* University of Utah, Doctorate, 1979.

5435. **Gudknecht, Janice E.** *An Assessment of Athletic Scholarship Opportunities for Female Basketball Athletes in Region VI for One (1976–77) School Year.* Kearney State College, Master's, 1977.

5436. **Guerin, William L.** *A Study to Determine the Effects of Extraneous Visual Cues on the Accuracy of Shooting a Basketball.* Eastern Illinois University, Master's, 1966.

5437. **Gunther, David.** *Turnovers in Winning and Losing Basketball Games.* Wayne State University, Master's, 1967.

5438. **Gunther, John Stephen.** *Player Dissidence as Related to Sentient Attitudes.* University of the Pacific, Master's, 1972.

5439. **Gustafson, Carl Marvin.** *A Survey of Basketball Programs in AA Texas High Schools.* University of Texas, Master's, 1959.

5440. **Gustafson, Merle W.** *A Comparison of Basketball Shooting Percentages at Home and Away.* University of North Dakota, Master's, 1965.

5441. **Guthrie, Julia A.** *A Study of Girls' Basketball in Kentucky High Schools.* University of Kentucky, Master's, 1932.

5442. **Haines, Danell Jean.** *Women Coaching Boys Interscholastic Sports in the State of Ohio: The Demographics and Situational Differences That Exist Between Boys and Girls Interscholastic Sports.* Ohio State University, Master's, 1986.

5443. **Haldeman, Neil Dean.** *A Cinematographical Analysis of the Standing High Jump as Related to the Basketball Jump Ball Situation.* Penn State University, Master's, 1958.

5444. **Hall, Barbara Anne.** *The Establishment of Norms and Standards in Badminton, Basketball, Speedball, and Volleyball for High School Girls in the State of North Carolina.* University of North Carolina, Master's, 1953.

5445. **Hall, Garth V.** *Factors Influencing Student Athletes to Enroll in Utah Colleges.* Utah State University, Master's, 1972.

5446. **Hall, M.H.** *A Study of the Factors of Tension and Fatigue Affecting Free Throwing Ability in Basketball.* New York University, Master's, 1935.

5447. **Halley, Kenneth R.** *An Approach to Improve Basketball Officiating in North Dakota.* University of North Dakota, Master's, 1962.

5448. **Halverson, Donald E.** *Validation of the AAHPER Basketball Skills Test for Male Physical Education Majors at University of North Dakota.* University of North Dakota, Master's, 1968.

5449. **Hamieleski, Henry Louis.** *A Cinematographic Analysis of the Hook Pass.* Springfield College, Master's, 1956.

5450. **Hamilton, George R.** *A Comparative Analysis of the Long Baseball Pass Versus the Long Hook Pass in Basketball.* Springfield College, Master's, 1963.

5451. **Hamilton, Jim Tudder.** *A Basketball Skill Test for Classifying Candidates for College Freshmen Basketball Teams.* University of North Carolina, Master's, 1949.

5452. **Hamilton, Penelope A.** *A Mechanical Analysis and Comparison of Two Jump Shots Performed by a Female Basketball Player.* University of Massachusetts, Master's, 1970.

5453. **Hammersmith, Veronica A.** *An Evaluation of Cardiac Activity in Young Women as Spectators and Participants in Competitive Basketball.* University of Kansas, Master's, 1969.

5454. **Hammig, Jack G.** *A Historical Sketch of Doctor James Naismith.* University of Kansas, Masters, 1962.

5455. **Hampton, Gerald Elmer.** *The Effects of Manipulating Two Types of Feedback, Knowledge of Performance and Knowledge of Results, in Learning a Complex Motor Skill.* Columbia University, Doctorate, 1970.

5456. **Hamton, Charles M.** *A Study of the Relation Between the Psychological Principles of Learning and Coaching in Basketball Team.* San Diego State College, Master's, 1953.

5457. **Handel, Randy Michael.** *Comparison Between the Family Background Traits of ''Blue Chip'' and Average High School Basketball Players.* Colorado State University, Master's, 1980.

5458. **Hanson, Terance M.** *A History of Intercollegiate Basketball at St. Benedict's From Its Installation in 1919–1969.* Southwest Missouri State College, Master's, 1970.

5459. **Hanson, William C.** *An Investigation of the Variables Relating to Basketball Coaching Success.* Kansas State College of Pittsburg, Master's, 1970.

5460. **Harmon, Harlan LeRoy.** *The Relationship Between Size and the Ability to Shoot and Handle a Basketball.* University of Kansas, Master's, 1952.

5461. **Harpster, Virginia C.** *A Comparison of Three Basketball Skills for College Women.* Pennsylvania State University, Master's, 1967.

5462. **Harris, Betty June Smith.** *Initial Status of Basketball for Girls Under the University Interscholastic League.* University of Texas at Austin, Master's, 1951.

5463. **Harrison, Edward Roy.** *A Test to Measure Basketball Ability for Boys.* University of Florida, Master's, 1969.

5464. **Harshbarger, Ivan Leroy.** *The Effects of Height and Weight in Predicting Success in Basketball.* University of Oregon, Master's, 1969.

5465. **Hart, David E.** *How Physical Education Helps Build Character; and Methods of Achieving a Game Situation in Foul Shot Practice.* Utah State University, Master's, 1967.

5466. **Hart, Elizabeth Kaye.** *The Effect of Competitive and Non-Competitive Situations Upon the Accuracy of Basketball Shooting for College Women Majoring in Physical Education.* Utah State University, Master's, 1969.

5467. **Hartman, David.** *Leadership Behavior of Head Basketball Coaches of Boys' Teams in Minnesota AA Schools.* Mankato State University, Master's, 1977.

5468. **Hartwell, Bobby J.** *A Brief History of Pontiac Central's Golden Era of Basketball: 1967–73.* Wayne State University, Master's, 1976.

5469. **Harwick, John.** *Factors That Influence College Basketball Game Coverage.* West Virginia University, Master's, 1981.

5470. **Hastad, Douglas Noel.** *Authoritarianism and Its Relationship to Success in Coaching High School Football and Basketball.* Washington State University, Master's, 1972.

5471. **Hastings, Mary J.** *The Effects of Hypnosis on the Free Throw Shooting Performance of Highly Susceptible Subjects.* Sonoma State University, Master's, 1980.

5472. **Hasty, Marie D.** *Minnesota Basketball Coaches Survey.* Bemidji State University, Master's, 1978.

5473. **Hatlem, Roger B.** *The Development of a Standardized Form for Scouting in Basketball.* Springfield College, Master's, 1956.

5474. **Hause, Gerald William.** *A Comparison of the Progressive-Part Method and the Whole Method in Teaching Basketball Shooting Skills to High School Boys.* University of Alabama, Master's, 1944.

5475. **Hawkin, John K.** *Factors Which Affect the Administration of Interscholastic Basketball Games in Ohio.* Bowling Green State University, Master's, 1957.

5476. **Hay, Philip.** *The Effects of Weight Training Upon the Accuracy of Basketball Jump Shooting.* Indiana University at Bloomington, Doctorate, 1972.

5477. **Haycock, Marvyn B.** *A History of Intercollegiate Basketball at the University of Illinois.* University of Illinois, Master's, 1958.

5478. **Hays, John W.** *A Comparison of Supplementary Training Programs in Basketball Activity Classes at Tennessee Technological University.* Tennessee Technological University, Master's, 1967.

5479. **Haywood, Kathleen M.** *Children's Basketball Performance With Regulation and Junior-Sized Basketballs.* University of Missouri at St. Louis, Doctorate, 1978.

5480. **Hazel, Marion W., III.** *Relationship of Response Time to Success in Selected Basketball Skills.* West Chester State College, Master's, 1970.

5481. **Hazen, Robert L.** *A Statistical Analysis of Rebounds After Missed Free Throws Under Normal and Controlled Conditions.* Springfield College, Master's, 1949.

5482. **Healey, William A.** *An Investigation of the Relationship of Playing Ability and Knowledge of the Rules in Boys' Basketball.* University of Iowa, Master's, 1938.

5483. **Hearne, Michael Douglas.** *Types of Defenses in Basketball.* Louisiana Tech University, Master's, 1970.

5484. **Heathcote, George ("Jud").** *A Chronological Review of Washington State High School Basketball Tournaments Held at the University of Washington From 1923 Through 1960.* University of Washington, Master's, 1961.

5485. **Hebel, Susan Lee.** *Selected Physical Training Effects of Female Basketball Players.* California State University, Long Beach, Master's, 1977.

5486. **Heck, Klaus.** *A Study of Attribution Theory and Achievement, Related to Coaches, Teachers and Administrators. (A Study of British Columbia Basketball Players).* Western Washington University, Master's, 1986.

5487. **Heitz, Gilman.** *The Effectiveness of Three Methods of Instruction in One-Hand Foul Shooting.* Indiana University, Doctorate, 1956.

5488. **Helixon, Dennis J.** *The Relationship of Player Performance to Basketball Team Play.* Northern Illinois University, Master's, 1967.

5489. **Helling, Teri.** *Effects of Isotonic Training, Isokinetic Training and Jumping Practice on the Vertical Jump Performance of College Age Women.* South Dakota State University, Master's, 1980.

5490. **Helms, Carol Sue.** *A Study of the Personality Traits of Selected 1979–1980 AIAW Division I Basketball Coaches.* Stephen F. Austin State University, Master's, 1980.

5491. **Henderson, Dana Roc Thomas.** *Group Cohesion as Related to the Success of Basketball Teams.* University of California, San Diego, Master's, 1981.

5492. **Hendricks, Elbridge Troy.** *The Organization and Administrative Operation of Physical Education Service Programs in Land-Grant Colleges and Universities.* University of Missouri, Doctorate, 1951.

5493. **Henman, Jane Lynn.** *The Interpersonal Relationship of the Montana State University Women's Varsity Basketball Team.* Montana State University, Master's, 1981.

5494. **Henry, George Martin.** *The Shooting Accuracy of Third Grade Students' Practice Shooting at Goals Less Than 10 Feet High.* Indiana University, Doctorate, 1974.

5495. **Henry, Spencer L.** *The Rebound Characteristics of Shots Attempted by Left-Handed and Right-Handed Shooters.* West Chester State College, Master's, 1970.

5496. **Hensarling, Anne.** *Comparison of the Use of a Large Basketball and Small Basketball by College Women.* Central Missouri State University, Master's, 1986.

5497. **Henschen, Keith Page.** *The Effects of a Small Basket Upon Basketball Shooting Accuracy with the Non-Dominant Hand.* Indiana University, Doctorate, 1971.

5498. **Hesalroad, L.** *Comparison of the Response of the Heart of College Women to Swimming and Basketball.* University of Iowa, Master's, 1939.

5499. **Hess, Charles J.** *The Relationship Between the AAHPER Basketball Skill Test and Judges' Ratings of Basketball Players' Ability.* East Stroudsburg State College, Master's, 1972.

5500. **Hetzel, Michael W.** *Assessment of Aerobic and Anaerobic Energy Cost of College Basketball Players.* University of Wisconsin, Master's, 1972.

5501. **Hey, John Philip.** *The Effects of Weight Training Upon the Accuracy of Basketball Jump Shooting.* Indiana University, Doctorate, 1972.

5502. **Hickerson, Doyle B.** *Development of Achievement Standards in Boys' Basketball at Baer Junior High School, Austin, Texas.* University of Texas at Austin, Master's, 1956.

5503. **Hidinger, George W.** *A Comparative Study and Analysis of High School Basketball Tournaments.* University of Iowa, Master's, 1947.

5504. **Higgins, Charles Roger.** *An Analysis of Selected Mechanical Factors That Contribute to Vertical Jumping Height of Four Basketball Players.* University of North Carolina at Greensboro, Doctorate, 1972.

5505. **Higgins, Joseph Ronald.** *The Effect of Basketball Playing Time on Explosive Power.* Utah State University, Master's, 1962.

5506. **Hile, Mary Elizabeth.** *Leadership Behavior of Male and Female Coaches of Women's Intercollegiate Basketball Teams.* California State University, Long Beach, Master's, 1985.

5507. **Hill, Daniel N.** *The Effect of Ankle Taping on a Basketball Player's Running Speed.* California State University, Fresno, Master's, 1969.

5508. **Hill, Donna Faye Becking.** *Improvement in the Motor Fitness of High School Girls Developed Through Participation in an Instructional Unit in Basketball and Volleyball.* University of Oregon, Master's, 1958.

5509. **Hill, Elam Richard.** *An Analysis and Comparison of the Practices and Procedures Used by High School Basketball Coaches of Central California and the Percentages of Games Won During the 1951–52 Season.* California State University, Fresno, Master's, 1952.

5510. **Hill, Leo J.** *Determining Basketball Ability Through the Use of Basketball Skills Tests.* Washington State University, Master's, 1956.

5511. **Hilmer, Robert.** *The Relative Effects of Selected Stress Conditions on Free Shooting Conditions.* Mankato State University, Master's, 1976.

5512. **Hines, Douglas J.** *The Effects of Direct Practice, Calisthenics, Sprint Training, and Weight Training on Performance in Selected Basketball Skills Tests.* Indiana University, Doctorate, 1968.

5513. **Hinton, Evelyn Alberta.** *The Correlation of Rogers's Test of Physical Capacity and the Cubberley and Cozens Measurement of Achievement in Basketball.* University of Washington, Master's, 1938.

5514. **Hisey, Carol Nan.** *Comparison of Selected Physical Performance and Emotional Characteristics of Two Groups of Former High School Athletes in Girls' Basketball.* University of North Carolina, Master's, 1953.

5515. **Hitner, John Waren.** *The Learning Curve in Basketball Technique Among High School Boys.* Temple University, Master's, 1926.

5516. **Hobson, Howard Andrew.** *A Study of Basket Shooting in College Basketball Games—Basketball Scouting.* Columbia University, Doctorate, 1949.

5517. **Hoch, Kenneth R.** *Effects on the "Big Four" Isometric Exercises on Accuracy in Foul Shooting Under the Fatigue Factor.* West Chester State College, Master's, 1975.

5518. **Hodges, Carolyn Virginia.** *Comparison of Responses of Basketball Coaches and Players to Situation-Response Survey.* University of North Carolina at Greensboro, Doctorate, 1982.

5519. **Hodges, Dennis.** *Relationships Between the Value of Humboldt State College Basketball Players to Their Team and Certain Physical and Mental Traits.* Humboldt State University, Master's, 1967.

5520. **Hoehn, Jorja Eileen.** *The Knox Basketball Test as a Predictive Measure of Overall Basketball Ability in Female High School Basketball Players.* University of Oregon, Master's, 1981.

5521. **Hofer, Herbert.** *Cinematographic Analysis of Ball Trajectory During Free Throw Shooting.* South Dakota State University, Master's, 1978.

5522. **Hoffman, Charles.** *The Relationship of Selected Objective Factors to Team Success in Basketball.* University of Minnesota, Master's, 1961.

5523. **Hohman, Howard Rolf.** *The Effect of Pre-Activity and Muscular Warmup on Motor Performance as Indicated by Basketball Shooting Ability.* University of Maryland, Master's, 1959.

5524. **Hole, Martin Norman.** *Sport Spectatorship and Social Integration: A Study of Basketball at the University of Illinois.* University of Illinois, Master's, 1970.

5525. **Holland, Gary Leon.** *A Study of Winning at Home and on the Road in Selected Collegiate Basketball Conferences and in Selected Major Independents in the United States.* Arkansas State University, Master's, 1965.

5526. **Holland, John Christopher.** *Heart Rates of Indiana High School Basketball Officials, as Measured by Electro-Cardiographic Radio Telemetry.* Indiana University, Master's, 1971.

5527. **Holland, Kenneth Alphonse.** *The Predictive Value of Selected Variables in Determining the Ability to Play Basketball in Small High Schools.* University of Arkansas, Doctorate, 1963.

5528. **Holland, Robert H.** *Comparative Analysis of Basketball Coaching Methods for Boys in Georgia High Schools.* University of Georgia, Master's, 1955.

5529. **Holley, Jack D.** *The Effect of Weight Training Upon the Vertical Jump of Secondary School Basketball Players.* Stephen F. Austin State University, Master's, 1961.

5530. **Holman, Pettiford.** *A Study of Interscholastic Athletic Programs in Selected Secondary Schools of Northeastern North Carolina.* North Carolina Central University, Master's, 1959.

5531. **Holmquist, David Gordon.** *Comparisons Between Self and Player Perceptions of Empathic Understanding, Unconditionability of Regard, and Level of Regard of High School Basketball Coaches.* University of Southern California, Doctorate, 1983.

5532. **Holmquist, David Gordon.** *Differences Between Actual, Perceived and Ideal Personality Traits of NAIA Basketball and Baseball Coaches.* California State University, Fullerton, Master's, 1976.

5533. **Holoweskik, Alfred Richard.** *Individual and Team Concepts of the Man to Man Denial Defense in Basketball.* Southern Connecticut State College, Master's, 1975.

5534. **Holt, Richard H.** *Fan Hostility in Relation to the Observation of Men's and Women's College Basketball Games at Western Illinois University.* Western Illinois University, Master's, 1976.

5535. **Holt, Sandra Sueanna.** *Predictive Validity of the Basketball Distance Throw Test as a Measure of Potential Tennis Playing Ability on College Women.* Drake University, Master's, 1969.

5536. **Hooks, David Taylor.** *Team and Individual Motivation in Collegiate Basketball: Perspectives of Successful Coaches.* University of North Carolina at Greensboro, Master's, 1985.

5537. **Hoover, Betty.** *Effects of an Undersized Basketball on Shooting and Ball Handling.* West Chester State College, Master's, 1970.

5538. **Hoover, Francis L.** *A History of the National Association of Intercollegiate Athletics.* Indiana University, Doctorate, 1976.

5539. **Hopewell, Theodore Russell.** *Investigation of the Suitable Height of the Basketball Goal for 11 and 12 Year Old Boys.* Western Maryland College, Master's, 1970.

5540. **Hopkins, David Ray.** *A Factor Analysis of Selected Basketball Skill Tests.* Indiana University, Doctorate, 1976.

5541. **Horst, Robert W.** *An Analysis of Two Selected Distributions of Practice on the Accuracy of Free Throw Shooting of Male High School Players.* Southern Illinois University, Master's, 1979.

5542. **Horstmann, Carla D.** *The Relationship Between Self-Concept and Average Playing Time Per Game of Intercollegiate Female Basketball Players.* University of North Carolina at Chapel Hill, Master's, 1983.

5543. **Hosinski, John Philip.** *An Investigation of the Use of Computer Assisted Instruction in Teaching the Shuffle Offense in Basketball.* Florida State University, Doctorate, 1965.

5544. **Hoss, Robert Joseph.** *The Effects of Grip Strength Improvement on the Accuracy of Jump Shot Shooting.* San Diego State College, Master's, 1971.

5545. **Hostenstein, Charles S.** *Effect of Seventeen Inch Rims on the Improvement of the Basketball Shooter During Practice.* West Chester State College, Master's, 1971.

5546. **Houlton, Fred R.** *An Investigation of Desireable Practices of Coaching High School Basketball.* Western Illinois University, Master's, 1956.

5547. **Hovis, Jeffrey.** *Effect of Dark Glasses on Dribbling a Basketball.* West Chester State, Master's College, 1969.

5548. **Howard, Edward T.** *Effects of Different Lengths of Practice Periods on Learning of Gross Motor Basketball Skills Among Ninth Grade Boys.* Glassboro State College, Master's, 1972.

5549. **Howard, Glen Willard.** *A Measurement of the Achievement in Motor Skills of College Men in the Game Situation of Basketball.* Columbia University, Doctorate, 1938.

5550. **Howard, William George.** *Machiavellianism and Performance Among Male High School Basketball Players.* University of Oregon, Master's, 1982.

5551. **Howell, William.** *The Influence of Ankle Weights on Jumping Height of High School Basketball Players.* Drake University, Master's, 1967.

5552. **Hubbard, W.V.** *Achievement Tests in Basketball for Use in Teacher Training Institutions.* Stanford University, Master's, 1937.

5553. **Huber, Christopher.** *The Relationship Between Vertical Jump, Leg Strength and Shooting Accuracy.* Humboldt State University, Master's, 1979.

5554. **Hudson, Allan J. and Padrnos, Patrick E.** *Development of a Vision Screening Program for Athletic Teams.* Pacific University, College of Optometry, Doctorate, 1981.

5555. **Huff, Horace G.** *Suggested Method of Organizing and Administering an Interscholastic Basketball Program for Boys and Class A High Schools in the State of Georgia.* University of Georgia, Master's, 1954.

5556. **Huffman, Billy Rex.** *Presentation and Evaluation of Techniques Used in Teaching the Men's Required Physical Education Basketball Classes at the University of Texas.* University of Texas, Master's, 1955.

5557. **Hughes, James E.** *An Investigation of the Effects of Ankle Weights on the Vertical Jumping Ability of Basketball Players.* East Tennessee State University, Master's, 1968.

5558. **Hughes, James Marshall.** *A Personnel Study of Members of Undefeated Basketball Teams of John Tarleton Agricultural College from 1934 through 1938.* North Texas State University, Master's, 1946.

5559. **Hughes, Lawrence James.** *Comparison of the Validities of Six Selected Basketball Ability Tests.* Pennsylvania State University, Master's, 1957.

5560. **Hughes, Robert Collings.** *A Study of the Offensive Patterns Used Against the Pennsylvania State College Varsity Basketball Team's Zone Defense for Twelve Games of the 1951–52 Season.* Pennsylvania State University, Master's, 1952.

5561. **Humphrey, Fred N.** *An Analysis of Factors in Ball Control as Related to the Ball Possession of the Winning and Losing Teams in Basketball.* University of Iowa, Master's, 1953.

5562. **Hunter, Bob.** *The Effects of Two Isokinetic Training Programs on the Vertical Jump Performance of Male Varsity College Basketball Players.* Western Illinois University, Master's, 1976.

5563. **Hunter, Martha Jean.** *An Analysis of the Skills and Techniques Used in an Official and Experimental Game of Women's Basketball.* Smith College, Master's, 1971.

5564. **Hurt, Marcia L.** *Development of Skills for the Female Baketball Player.* George Williams College, Master's, 1979.

5565. **Husbands, Arlie Jay.** *A Survey of the Coaching Turnover and Coaching Drop-Outs of Class A High Schools in Utah.* Utah State University, Master's, 1965.

5566. **Huston, Donald A.** *The Effect of Weight Vests on the Jumping Performance, Ability and Endurance of College Basketball Players (Bellingham), 1967.* Western Washington State College, Master's, 1967.

5567. **Hutchinson, Jill.** *The Effects of Situational Stress on Women Basketball Players.* Illinois State University, Master's, 1969.

5568. **Hutchinson, Jill.** *Measurement of Attitudes Toward the Conduct of Intercollegiate Basketball for Women.* University of North Carolina at Greensboro, Master's, 1976.

5569. **Igbagnugo, Veronica.** *The Effect of Task Difficulty on Transfer of Accuracy Training (Basketball).* Smith College, Master's, 1972.

5570. **Inciong, Phillip Alexander.** *Leadership Styles and Team Success.* University of Utah, Doctorate, 1974.

5571. **Indiana State Teachers College.** *Souvenir Program: Annual Terre Haute Jaycee Midwest Collegiate Basketball Tourney.* Indiana State Teachers College, Master's, 1955.

5572. **Inglis, Gordon Walter.** *Discriminatory Factors That Identify Successful Basketball Performers.* Washington State University, Master's, 1980.

5573. **Ingram, Dorothy C.** *A Study of Existing Practices in the Programs of Girls' Physical Education in Junior High School in Texas.* East Texas State University, Master's, 1958.

5574. **Ingram, Mary C.** *A Comparative Study of the Completions and Attempts on the First Shot of the One-and-One and Two Shot Awards in Three Female Intercollegiate Basketball Tournaments.* St. Cloud State University, Master's, 1978.

5575. **Insana, Craig.** *The Duties, Salary Structure, and Qualification of Scouts of the Basketball Teams in the National Basketball Association.* Western Illinois University, Doctorate, 1981.

5576. **Irome, Gail Robert.** *Direction of Foul Shots in Basketball Rebound.* Pennsylvania State University, Master's, 1963.

5577. **Irwin, Stephen E.** *Approach Angle of the Basketball to the Basket Using Different Levels of Male Players.* George Williams College, Master's, 1977.

5578. **Jable, John T.** *The Relative Effects of Training with Basketballs of Varying Weights Upon Free Throw Shooting Accuracy.* Pennsylvania State University, Master's, 1965.

5579. **Jackson, George Paul.** *The Status of Basketball Coaching in Selected Elementary Schools of King County, Washington.* University of Washington, Master's, 1963.

5580. **Jacobs, Jean Gills.** *A Study of High School Girls' Interscholastic Basketball in Tennessee.* George Peabody College, Doctorate, 1956.

5581. **Jacobs, Virgil Morris.** *A History of Basketball at Eastern Illinois University.* Eastern Illinois University, Master's, 1959.

5582. **Jacobsen, Donald.** *The Effects of a Basketball Season on Leg Strength and Explosive Power as Shown on a Select Group of Players at South Dakota State University.* South Dakota State University, Master's, 1962.

5583. **Jacobsen, Farrel.** *Surface Temperature, Body Temperature, and Heart Rate as Affected by Immersing the Feet of Conditioned Basketball Players in a Cold Water Bath.* South Dakota State University, Master's, 1968.

5584. **Jacoby, Harry Joseph.** *Showing Correlations Between Basketball Ability and Certain Psychophysical Traits.* University of Idaho, Master's, 1940.

5585. **Jamarik, Sherry L.** *A Personality Profile of Women Basketball Officials in Virignia.* Madison College, Master's, 1973.

5586. **James, Ted.** *A Guide to Teaching the Major Sports in the Classroom.* Northern Arizona University, Master's, 1955.

5587. **Januszuvski, Frank A.** *A Study to Determine the Duration of Ball Control in Basketball.* Springfield College, Master's, 1955.

5588. **Jenkinson, Roger Louis.** *The Geography of Indiana Interscholastic and Intercollegiate Basketball.* Oklahoma State University, Doctorate, 1974.

5589. **Jennings, Jack L.** *A Summary of Individual Basketball Fundamentals.* Central Washington University, Master's, 1953.

5590. **Jennings, Larry.** *An Analysis of Floor Shooting Percentages in High School Basketball.* California State University, Sacramento, Master's, 1966.

5591. **Jensen, Judith Lee.** *The Development of Standards for Women's Athletics and Their Influence on Basketball Competition in the State of New York.* Ohio State University, Doctorate, 1972.

5592. **Jensen, Robert Harry.** *The Influence of Instant Replay of a Video Taped Recording of Performance on the Development of Selected Basketball Skill.* Chico State College, Master's, 1971.

5593. **Jenson, D.L.** *The Effectiveness of the Knox and the Wolfe Basketball Ability Tests and Their Various Sub-Tests in Selected Junior High School Basketball Players.* Brigham Young University, Master's, 1969.

5594. **Jessen, LaVern M.** *The Effect of Competitive and Non-Competitive Free Throw Shooting Practice on Free Throw Shooting Accuracy.* University of North Dakota, Master's, 1962.

5595. **Jester, Michael R.** *Evaluation of the Jester Basketball Test of Predicting Basketball Ability.* Ball State University, Master's, 1970.

5596. **Jirsak, Jan.** *Self-Image, Achievement, Motivation and Fear of Success Among Female Basketball Coaches in Colleges and Universities in the State of Nebraska.* Kearney State College, Master's, 1977.

5597. **Johns, Ellen J.** *The Development of a Statistics Sheet to Aid a Coach in the Selection of Female Basketball Scholarship Athletes.* Eastern Kentucky University, Master's, 1976.

5598. **Johnsen, William Sharr.** *A Study of All-State Basketball Players in Utah.* University of Utah, Master's, 1956.

5599. **Johnson, Gay Jeanine.** *Comparison of Personality Traits Between Highly Skilled Female Basketball, Softball, and Volleyball Performers at the High School Level.* California State University, Long Beach, Master's, 1980.

5600. **Johnson, Howard L.** *A Study of the Free Throw in Basketball.* University of Wisconsin, Master's, 1934.

5601. **Johnson, Joann Marlene.** *The Relationship Between Skill as Measured by a Combination of Selected Basketball Tests and Judges' Ratings of Basketball Playing Ability.* University of Colorado, Master's, 1958.

5602. **Johnson, L. William.** *Objective Basketball Tests for High School Boys.* University of Iowa, Master's, 1934.

5603. **Johnson, Leslie Willis.** *Determination of the Status of Football and Basketball Officiating in the Secondary Schools of the State of Washington.* University of Washington, Master's, 1933.

5604. **Johnson, Robert Bruce.** *An Experiment With a Small Goal Device Designed to Improve Free Throw Shooting Accuracy.* California State University, Chico, Master's, 1981.

5605. **Johnson, Rodney William.** *Statistical Analysis of Pass Evaluation in Basketball.* George William College, Master's, 1977.

5606. **Johnson, Scott J.** *Attributes Perceived as Essential for Hiring Football and Men's Basketball Coaches at NCAA Division IA Schools by University Officials.* Oregon State University, Doctorate, 1986.

5607. **Johnson, Susan Jean.** *Recruitment Factors Identified by Female Basketball Players and Head Coaches of Women's Basketball Teams on the Small College Level.* Washington State University, Master's, 1987.

5608. **Jones, Bronson.** *The Effects of Distributed Practice on the Learning of a Basketball Skill.* Western Maryland College, Master's, 1970.

5609. **Jones, Dan A.** *A Survey of the Existing Artifical Lighting Facilities of Certain High School Basketball Courts in Oregon as Compared With Recommended Minimum Standards.* University of Oregon, Master's, 1951.

5610. **Jones, Edith.** *A Study of Knowledge and Playing Ability in Basketball for High School Girls.* University of Iowa, Master's, 1941.

5611. **Jones, Patricia Long.** *A Survey of Southeastern Conference Women's Basketball Coaches and Ohio Valley Conference Women's Basketball Coaches on the Overall Effects of Pre-Season Weight Training.* Middle Tennessee State University, Doctorate, 1979.

5612. **Jones, Ruth Jean.** *The Effects of Contingency Management on Competitive Game Practice and Selected Managerial Behaviors at Girls Basketball Camp.* Ohio State University, Doctorate, 1979.

5613. **Jones, Thomas J.** *The Relationship Between the Position of the Shot and the Flight of the Rebound of a Basketball in a Game.* University of the Pacific, Master's, 1972.

5614. **Jones, William M.** *The History of Offensive Basketball.* Washington State University, Master's, 1951.

5615. **Jonston, Jeanne L.** *The Revision of a Basketball Knowledge Test for College Women, and the Construction of Equivalent Forms of This Test.* Smith College, Master's, 1951.

5616. **Joynes, Garland Phillips.** *A Study of the Environmental and Psychological Factors Affecting the Abilities of a Basketball Official.* University of Tennessee, Master's, 1965.

5617. **Kaberna, Karen Mae.** *The Effect of a Progressive Weight Training Program for College Women on Selected Basketball Skills.* South Dakota State University, Master's, 1968.

5618. **Kamieneski, Carla Dupuis.** *The Effectiveness of an Instructional Unit in the Analysis and Correction of Selected Basketball Skills.* Brigham Young University, Doctorate, 1980.

5619. **Kampe, Greg C.** *The Sports Physician's Defense: A Survey of Legal Literature.* University of Toledo, Master's, 1984.

5620. **Kanten, Steven C.** *Hypnosis and Freethrow Shooting Performance.* University of Utah, Master's, 1982.

5621. **Kasson, Peter L.** *An Analysis of College Basketball Officiating.* University of Wisconsin, Master's, 1960.

5622. **Katsiaficas, Charles G.** *A Mechanical Analysis of the One-Hand Set Shot.* Springfield College, Master's, 1957.

5623. **Kellogg, Willard C.** *A History of Lightweight and Junior Basketball in the Chicago Area.* George Williams College, Master's, 1972.

5624. **Kelly, Clair Cornelius.** *An Experiment in Measuring Accuracy and Reaction Time in Basketball Officiating.* Springfield College, Master's, 1933.

5625. **Kelly, Daniel Joseph.** *Basketball for Coaches, Players and Officials.* Springfield College, Master's, 1923.

5626. **Kelly, Patricia E.** *The Professional Status of Boys' and Girls' Interscholastic Basketball Coaches in the State of Illinois.* Western Illinois University, Master's, 1980.

5627. **Kennedy, Robert M.** *The Effects of Basketball Competition on Emotional Behavior of Boys in Junior High School.* Northern Illinois University, Master's, 1967.

5628. **Kennett, Ronald Dean.** *A Survey of Methods of Play in Basketball.* Arkansas State University, Master's, 1960.

5629. **Keplinger, Sandra M.** *Values That Women Expect to Realize Through Participation on Intercollegiate Basketball Teams.* University of Wisconsin, Master's, 1973.

5630. **Kerans, Lori Ann.** *The Relationship of Leadership and Personality to Success in Coaching Collegiate Women's Basketball.* Illinois State University, Master's, 1986.

5631. **Kimball, E.R.** *A Comparative Study of the Whole and Part Methods of Teaching Basketball Fundamentals.* University of Southern California, Master's, 1935.

5632. **Kindig, Louise Elizabeth.** *The Production of a Film to Aid in the Instruction of Basketball Officiating for Women.* University of North Carolina, Master's, 1953.

5633. **Kindle, Hellon Gean.** *A Test for the General Knowledge of Sports.* East Texas State University, Master's, 1956.

5634. **King, Donald C.** *A Comparative Study of Errors Committed in Junior and Senior High School Basketball.* University of Iowa, Master's, 1956.

5635. **King, Robert F.** *A History of Girls' Basketball in the State of Arkansas.* State College of Arkansas, Master's, 1962.

5636. **King, Robert Jackson.** *A One-Item Offensive Basketball Skills Test for High School Boys.* Chico State College, Master's, 1971.

5637. **Kingsmore, John Mack.** *The Effect of a Professional Wrestling and Professional Basketball Contest Upon the Aggressive Tendencies of Male Spectators.* University of Maryland, Doctorate, 1968.

5638. **Kint, Bruce E.** *A Comparison of the Effectiveness of Light Weight and Regulation Practice Balls on Basketball Free Throw Shooting Accuracy for Selected Chico State College Males.* Chico State College, Master's, 1968.

5639. **Kiomourtzoglou, Efthimis.** *The Effects of Massing vs. Distributing Practice Within Practice Sessions on the Acquisition of Basketball Skills.* University of North Carolina at Chapel Hill, Master's, 1983.

5640. **Kirchner, Jon Wayne.** *The Relationship of State-Trait Anxiety Levels and Basketball Free-Throw Shooting Proficiency Among Selected High School Male Basketball Players.* Northeast Missouri State University, Master's, 1981.

5641. **Kirkpatrick, Robert Perry.** *A Study of the Errors and Violations Committed by College and High School Basketball Teams.* Boston University, Master's, 1948.

5642. **Kitchen, Gregory J.** *Effects of Conditioning on Various Physiological Responses in Basketball Players.* Utah State University, Master's, 1978.

5643. **Kite, Joseph C.** *The Effects of Variations in Target Size and Two Methods of Practice on the Development of Accuracy in Motor Skills.* Louisiana State University, Doctorate, 1964.

5644. **Kizer, David L.** *Attitudes and Basketball Skill: The Effects of Calisthenics and Pre-Activity Warm-Up Upon Basketball Skill and Attitudes Toward Physical Education.* California State University, Fresno, Master's, 1964.

5645. **Klassen, Richard.** *The Effects of Two Distributions of Practice and Rest on the Performance of the Basketball Free Throw.* University of Minnesota, Master's, 1964.

5646. **Kleinfelter, Eileen Rose.** *The Perceptions of Female High School Varsity Basketball Players.* University of Oregon, Master's, 1985.

5647. **Klink, Allen A.** *A Study of Ball Handling Proficiency Comparing Large and Small Basketballs.* University of Wisconsin, Master's, 1964.

5648. **Klipp, Kenneth P.** *The Effects of Sight and Sound Inhibitors on the Dribbling Ability of Basketball Players.* Eastern Illinois University, Master's, 1972.

5649. **Klitzing, Melvin Ray.** *The Effect of Foot Position on Accuracy in Shooting Free Throws.* University of Illinois, Master's, 1951.

5650. **Klock, Gail Patricia.** *The Background Experiences and Current Status of Women Intercollegiate Basketball Coaches in the State of North Carolina.* University of North Carolina, Master's, 1974.

5651. **Klovdahl, D.** *A Comparison of Intelligences and Motivation with Basketball Ability.* Central Washington State College, Master's, 1973.

5652. **Kmucha, Orlena W.** *The Significance of Free Throws on Game Success Among High School Girls' Varsity Teams.* Southern Illinois University, Master's, 1980.

5653. **Knapp, Vicki.** *The Relationship of Attentional Style and Anxiety Levels to Team Success in Selected Female High School Varsity Basketball Players.* Northeast Missouri State University, Master's, 1986.

5654. **Knight, Thomas.** *The Athletic Equipment of the High School Teams of Arizona and Its Relationship to Injuries and Winning Percentages.* Northern Arizona University, Master's, 1941.

5655. **Knoh, R.D.** *An Experiment to Determine the Relationship Between Performance in Skill Tests and Success in Playing Basketball.* University of Oregon, Master's, 1937.

5656. **Knowlton, Glenn E.** *Comparison of Two Treatment Components of an Anxiety Management Program to Improve the Free Throw Performance on a Women's Collegiate Basketball Team.* Mankato State University, Master's, 1987.

5657. **Knox, R.** *Prediction of Basketball Ability in Eight Class B High Schools.* University of Oregon, Master's, 1938.

5658. **Knox, Willie Samuel.** *A Test of Basketball Ability for Boys of Junior High School Level.* University of Kansas, Master's, 1947.

5659. **Knudson, Thomas Allan.** *The Evolution of Men's Amateur Basketball Rules and the Effect Upon the Game.* Springfield College, Doctorate, 1972.

5660. **Knudtson, Paul O.** *A Study of the Effect of Weight Training and Jumping Exercises on the Jumping Ability of Girl Basketball Players.* University of Iowa, Master's, 1957.

5661. **Knuttgen, Howard C.** *The Evaluation of Potential Athletes by Coaches of Intercollegiate Soccer, Basketball and Lacrosse.* Pennsylvania State University, Master's, 1953.

5662. **Koch, Warren Edward.** *The Calorie Cost of Playing Basketball.* University of Illinois, Master's, 1965.

5663. **Koehler, Gretchen Margaret E.** *Perception of Motivational Agents: Selected Male and Female Intercollegiate Basketball Players.* Brigham Young University, Doctorate, 1978.

5664. **Koehler, Linda Sue.** *Social Structure and Interaction in Girls' Basketball: A Contribution to Socialization and Sport.* University of Illinois, Doctorate, 1982.

5665. **Koenig, Francis Becher.** *Comparative Analysis of Selected Personal and Social Background Characteristics of High School Girls at Three Levels of Participation in Basketball.* Michigan State University, Doctorate, 1969.

5666. **Kolf, Robert M.** *Theory and Practice of Defense in Basketball.* University of Wisconsin, Doctorate, 1931.

5667. **Kolodziejezyk, Lula Bella.** *Attitudes Toward Competitive Girls' Basketball in Texas Schools.* Southwest Texas State University, Master's, 1958.

5668. **Kolonay, Barbara Jean.** *Personality Profiles of Winning and Losing Basketball Teams.* Tulane University, Doctorate, 1979.

5669. **Koon, Loren Dean.** *An Analysis of the Effects of Weight Training on Selected Measures of Girth, Strength, Power, Agility of Basketball Skills in College Men.* University of North Dakota, Master's, 1951.

5670. **Kootnekoff, John Lee.** *A Study of the Academic Preparations, Teaching Responsibilities, Athletic Experiences and Duties of Basketball Coaches in Selected Secondary Schools in Canada, 1965–66.* University of Washington, Master's, 1968.

5671. **Kostenbauder, Karen.** *The Relationship Between Explosive Strength of the Extensor Muscles of the Arms and Accuracy Shooting in Basketball.* West Chester State College, Master's, 1971.

5672. **Kouri, Ronald L.** *The Comparison of Using the Backboard Versus the Basket Rim as a Point of Aim in Basketball Shooting.* South Dakota State University, Master's, 1970.

5673. **Kowalkowski, Eugenie L.** *The Proper Arc as a Device to Improve Free Throw Shooting.* University of Wisconsin, Master's, 1974.

5674. **Kowalski, Pearl Hunsberger.** *A Comparison of the Caloric Expenditure for Women's Five and Six Player Basketball.* Temple University, Doctorate, 1971.

5675. **Kragness, Ronald D.** *The Effects of Depth Perception Training Upon Basketball Shooting Ability.* Moorhead State College, Master's, 1971.

5676. **Krahenbuhl, Gary S.** *The Comparison of Home and Away Shooting Percentages in Basketball.* Northern Illinois University, Master's, 1966.

5677. **Kramer, Duane Paul.** *The Professional Status of Boys' Basketball Coaches in Iowa Class AA High Schools, 1968.* Drake University, Master's, 1969.

5678. **Kranking, James D.** *A History of the Zone Defense in Men's Intercollegiate Basketball 1891–1950.* University of Maryland, Master's, 1954.

5679. **Kregel, Marinus John.** *The Part Method Versus the Whole Method in Teaching Basketball Free Throw Shooting.* Indiana University at Bloomington, Doctorate, 1959.

5680. **Kregel, Marinus John.** *A Study of the Effectiveness of the One Hand and the Two Hand Underhand Free Throw Shot in Basketball.* University of Colorado, Master's, 1952.

5681. **Krem, Alexander.** *A Study in Basketball Shooting.* George Williams College, Master's, 1940.

5682. **Krentz, Terrill Jane.** *Effects of a Weight Training Program on Skilled Basketball Skills: A Study of Females Aged 12 to 14.* George Williams College, Master's, 1984.

5683. **Kretzechmar, Judith Carol.** *Skill Testing and Player Selection in Women's Basketball.* University of Nebraska, Master's, 1966.

5684. **Kruse, Bill R.** *The Effect of No Practice on the Free Throw Shooting Accuracy Among Skilled Basketball Players at the U. of North Dakota.* University of North Dakota, Master's, 1934.

5685. **Kruse-Yoder, Carol.** *Psychological Comparisons of College and High School Female Basketball Players.* Arizona State University, Master's, 1981.

5686. **Kubachka, Joseph.** *A Compilation of Basketball Drills.* Springfield College, Master's, 1951.

5687. **Kupersanin, Michael.** *Intercollegiate Athletics at Duquesne University in Historical Perspective.* University of Pittsburgh, Master's, 1980.

5688. **Kurth, Bertram M.** *A Survey of Iowa High School Boys' Basketball Shooting Percentages from Various Distances.* University of Iowa, Master's, 1948.

5689. **Kurth, Stephen J.** *The Acquisition of Shooting Skill in Basketball, Using Balls of Different Weight.* Washington State University, Master's, 1966.

5690. **Kurtt, John F.** *A Comparison of the Accuracy of the Jump Shot, the One-Hand Set Shot, and the Two-Hand Set Shot.* University of Iowa, Master's, 1958.

5691. **Kutnink, P.** *An Experimental Comparison of the Effect of Praise and Reproof Upon Group Performance Basketball.* Kansas State Teachers College, Master's, 1935.

5692. **Kuwada, Gordon Yutaka.** *A Manual for Players and Coaches of Wheelchair Basketball.* University of Illinois, Master's, 1959.

5693. **Labanowich, Stanley.** *Wheelchair Basketball: A History of the National Association and an Analysis of the Structure and Organization of Teams.* University of Illinois, Doctorate, 1975.

5694. **LaBaw, Nye Lee.** *Effect of Basketball Conditioning on the Brachial Pulse Wave.* University of Illinois, Master's, 1951.

5695. **LaBella, Joseph E.** *The Development of a Fundamental Defensive System for All Levels of Competition in the Basketball Program at Cleveland Central Catholic High School.* Ashland College, Master's, 1981.

5696. **Lamb, Don W.** *A Survey and Analysis of Opinions Relating to Televised Basketball Games in the Wichita, Kansas, Area.* Kansas State Teachers College, Master's, 1962.

5697. **Lamph, James A.** *The Effect of Two Different Basket Heights on Rebound Area.* Brigham Young University, Doctorate, 1976.

5698. **Lande, Leon Alvin.** *A Study of the Trends of Basketball Offenses and Defenses in North Dakota High Schools.* University of North Dakota, Master's, 1950.

5699. **Landry, David D.** *Relationship Between Technical Execution and Success in the Standing Jump Shot.* Montclair State College, Master's, 1977.

5700. **Lane, Vern.** *An Analytical Study of Basketball Shooting in 20 Intercollegiate Basketball Games for Men in Selected Colleges in the Southwest Region of the United States 1948-49.* North Texas State University, Master's, 1948.

5701. **Langdon, John J.** *A Historical Development of Girls' Basketball.* University of Wyoming, Master's, 1953.

5702. **Langlois, Susan E.** *The Effects of Mental and Physical Practice on Basketball Foul Shooting Accuracy.* Springfield College, Master's, 1980.

5703. **Langston, William Francis.** *The Professional Preparation of Head Coaches in Central Illinois.* Illinois State University, Master's, 1978.

5704. **Lappenbusch, Charles Frank.** *Basketball, Straight Line Defense.* Western Washington State College, Master's, 1953.

5705. **Larson, Edgar Ole.** *Emotional Responses of College Basketball Players.* University of Oregon, Doctorate, 1966.

5706. **Larson, James Allen.** *The High School Head Basketball Coach: Perceptions of Real Behavior and Expectations of Ideal Behavior.* University of California, Los Angeles, Doctorate, 1973.

5707. **Lash, D.W.** *A Statistical Study of College Basketball Measured in Terms of Basket Shooting.* New York University, Master's, 1931.

5708. **Lawler, William J.** *The Validity of Certain Basketball Skills Tests for Rating High School Basketball Players.* Springfield College, Master's, 1949.

5709. **Lawrence, David.** *A Study of the 1971-72 Big 8 Conference Varsity Basketball Players' Opinions Concerning Their Work Load While Pursuing a College Degree.* Kansas State University, Master's, 1972.

5710. **Lawrence, H.B.** *A Handbook for Women's Basketball.* George Washington University, Master's, 1938.

5711. **Layton, Terry.** *The Effect of a Basketball Training Glove on Shooting Accuracy.* Mankato State College, Master's, 1971.

5712. **Leach, George.** *Analysis of Variations in Pulse Rates of Basketball Players Throughout the Training Season.* University of Texas at Austin, Master's, 1939.

5713. **Leary, John Edward.** *Personality, Physiological and Demographic Traits of Collegiate and Professional Basketball Officials.* Ithaca College, Master's, 1971.

5714. **Leddy, Matthew Hamilton.** *Personality Differences Between Successful and Unsuccessful Male Community College Basketball Players.* San Jose State University, Master's, 1986.

5715. **Lee, Joseph Lynn.** *Developing a Program for Reduction of Athletic Injuries in Small High Schools, Through a Study of Hydro-Therapy and Sonic Therapy.* Northern Arizona University, Master's, 1959.

5716. **Lee, M. Gene.** *A Study of the Formal Education of Selected University of Utah Football and Basketball Athletes Receiving Full Grants-in-Aid.* University of Utah, Doctorate, 1969.

5717. **Lee, Norvell T.** *Offensive Trends in North Carolina 4A High School Basketball.* North Carolina Central University, Master's, 1977.

5718. **Lee, Robert M.** *The Effects of Three Forms of Observing a Basketball Game on Subsequent Aggression.* University of the Pacific, Master's, 1971.

5719. **Lehr, Carolyn Ann.** *The Relationship Between Self-Concept, Skill-Related Behavior and Team Status of Women Basketball Players.* University of New Mexico, Doctorate, 1972.

5720. **Leilich, Avis F.** *The Primary Components of Selected Basketball Tests for College Women.* Indiana University, Doctorate, 1953.

5721. **Leishman, Courtney Maughan.** *Three Styles of Defensive Play Used in High School Basketball.* Brigham Young University, Master's, 1962.

5722. **Lemberger, Kathleen F.** *The Performance of Female Basketball Point Guards and Accuracy of Response to Open Play Identification.* University of Wisconsin–La Crosse, Master's, 1982.

5723. **LeMoine, Mitchell Brooks.** *The Effect of Strength Improvement on Basketball Shooting Accuracy Among High School Girls.* Texas Tech University, Master's, 1968.

5724. **Lenahan, Rita Janice.** *A Study of the Contribution of Selected Fundamental Factors to Success in Women's University Intramural Basketball.* University of Tennessee, Master's, 1970.

5725. **Lenguadoro, James R.** *Relationship Between the Time Taken to Execute Free Throws and Success in Free Throw Shooting in Basketball.* University of Iowa, Master's, 1961.

5726. **Leo, C. David.** *A Comparison of the Heart Rates and Work-Load Levels of Selected Male Freshmen Basketball Players at Utah State University During Actual Game Competition.* Utah State University, Master's, 1973.

5727. **Leo, Toni R.** *Visuo-Motor Behavior Rehearsal, Physical Practice and Performance of Selected Basketball Skill Tests by Senior High Girls.* University of North Carolina at Greensboro, Master's, 1984.

5728. **Leone, Gerald.** *The Effect of a Season of Variety Basketball on the Cardiovascular System for High School Boys.* West Chester State College, Undergraduate research report, 1982.

5729. **Lewis, Donald G.** *An Approach to the Problem of Time Allotted for Basketball Practice in the Small Kansas High School.* Kansas State College of Pittsburg, Master's, 1958.

5730. **Lewis, Frederick B., Jr.** *A Comparison of Three Methods of Conditioning Upon Strength, Speed, Endurance and Selected Basketball Skills.* New York University, Doctorate, 1967.

5731. **Lewis, Raymond Lee.** *The Effect of Self-Concept and Various Conceptual and Physical Practice Methods Upon the Performance of a Selected Basketball Motor Skill.* North Texas State University, Doctorate, 1971.

5732. **Lidstone, James Edward.** *The Relationships of Selected Psycho-Social Variables Associated With Achievement to the Performance of Male and Female Intercollegiate Basketball Players.* University of North Carolina at Greensboro, Doctorate, 1982.

5733. **Lilly, Rex A.** *A Study to Determine the Most Effective Method of Shooting Basketball Short Shots: Banking Versus Straight In.* Brigham Young University, Master's, 1970.

5734. **Limke, Dennis J.** *A Study of Zone Offense Techniques Used by Class A High School Basketball Coaches in North Dakota.* University of North Dakota, Master's, 1968.

5735. **Lipp, Brady.** *Factors Influencing Recruitment: North Central Conference Basketball.* North Dakota State University, Master's, 1985.

5736. **Little, Mildred Jess.** *Use of Achievement Standards in Physical Skills as a Means of Motivating and Classifying Girls for Interschool Basketball.* University of Texas, Master's, 1955.

5737. **Loader, Eric C.** *Field-Dependent/Field-Independent Characteristics of Male and Female Basketball Players.* University of Utah, Master's, 1981.

5738. **Long, Edwin.** *A Study of Team Defenses in College Basketball.* Arizona State University, Master's, 1950.

5739. **Longley, J.H.** *A Personnel Study of the Basketball Coaches of the Class A Senior High School of Ohio.* University of Michigan, Master's, 1938.

5740. **Loose, W. A. Robert, Jr.** *A Study to Determine the Validity of the Knox Basketball Test.* Washington State University, Master's, 1961.

5741. **Lorenz, Gene.** *A Study of the Home Court Advantage at Northern State College, 1981–82 Through 1984–85.* Northeastern State University, Master's, 1986.

5742. **Lorton, Frank.** *A Study of the Relation of Fouls Committed and Free Throws Made to Winning in Basketball.* University of Iowa, Master's, 1940.

5743. **Lorton-Gregerson, Sharon K.** *A Comparative Study of the Success of Girls' and Boys' Basketball Teams in the Central Gopher Conference.* St. Cloud State University, Master's, 1977.

5744. **Lorts, Buck Allen.** *A Descriptive Analytical Case Study of the Verbal Behavior of Basketball Coaches.* University of Montana, Master's, 1973.

5745. **Louis, Benjamin Eugene.** *The Effect of a Six Month Period of Training Competition and Detraining on the Estimated Percent Body Fat of College Basketball Players.* University of Illinois, Master's, 1971.

5746. **Loughton, Spencer Jackson.** *The Effect of a Basketball Season Upon Cardiovascular Condition of Selected Athletes.* Utah State University, Master's, 1972.

5747. **Louri, Ronald L.** *The Comparison of Using the Backboard Versus the Basket Rim as a Point of Aim in Basketball Shooting.* South Dakota State University, Master's, 1970.

5748. **Lowry, Carla.** *A Comparative Study of the Effects Two Sets of Dissimilar Basketball Rules Have on General Motor Ability.* Texas Woman's University, Master's, 1963.

5749. **Lowry, F.W.** *An Educational Analysis of Basketball.* Ohio State University, Master's, 1940.

5750. **Loy, James R.** *The Duties of the Division I College Assistant Basketball Coach.* Western Illinois University, Master's, 1986.

5751. **Luckenbach, Guenther Edward.** *Present Status and Suggested Modifications of Junior High School Football and Basketball.* Southwest Texas State University, Master's, 1950.

5752. **Luitjens, Larry.** *Leg Strength and Vertical Jump of Basketball Players as Affected by Two Selected Exercise Programs Conducted Throughout the Competitive Season.* South Dakota State University, Master's, 1969.

5753. **Lukas, D. Wayne.** *The Effect of the Weighted Training Shoe on the Jumping Performance, Agility, Running Speed, and Endurance of College Basketball Players.* University of Wisconsin, Master's, 1960.

5754. **Luke, Steve John.** *Hostility Levels of Male Basketball and Hockey Spectators.* Mankato State University, Master's, 1978.

5755. **Lukens, Fred A.** *Dave Gunther: A Study of a Successful Coach and the Application of the Contingency Model of Leadership.* University of North Dakota, Master's, 1977.

5756. **Lundeen, David E.** *Effects of Training for Basketball Free-Throw Shooting by Means of Mental Practice.* St. Cloud State University, Master's, 1978.

5757. **Lundin, Arthur A.** *A Study of Basketball Shooting Based on High School Tournament Play and Opinions of Coaches.* Pacific University, Master's, 1956.

5758. **Luoma, Robert O.** *Elementary School Basketball.* Western Montana College, Master's, 1967.

5759. **Lutes, Warren C.** *A Study to Determine the Best Locations for Obtaining Rebounds.* Springfield College, Master's, 1961.

5760. **Luther, Wesley M.** *A Study of the Physical Characteristics of Preparatory Background and Coaching Methods of State High School Basketball Champions.* University of North Carolina, Master's, 1965.

5761. **Luymes, LuVerne L.** *An Evaluation of Methods in Basketball Scouting.* University of Iowa, Master's, 1950.

5762. **Maaske, Paul M.** *The Effect of the Practice of Shooting at Small Baskets on the Accuracy of Shooting in Basketball.* University of Arkansas, Master's, 1972.

5763. **MacDonald, Ron.** *Syracuse Basketball 1900–1975.* Syracuse University, Master's, 1976.

5764. **Mack, Arthur E.** *The Relationship of Selected Traits to Basketball Success.* University of Massachusetts, Master's, 1964.

5765. **Madsen, Mac O.** *A Study of the Effects of Adding a Medium Distance Shooting Test to the Knox Basketball Ability Test.* Brigham Young University, Master's, 1961.

5766. **Magini, Evelyn Louise.** *A Comparison of Five- and Six-Player Basketball for Women.* University of Montana, Master's, 1971.

5767. **Malaise, John W., Jr.** *The Relationship Between Running Speed and Lateral Movement.* Texas Tech University, Master's, 1969.

5768. **Manahan, William L.** *Measurement of Individual Basketball Skill in College Men.* University of Iowa, Master's, 1935.

5769. **Mandel, Frank J.** *The Effects of the Use of Hand Weights on Selected Basketball Skills for Elementary School Boys.* Northern Illinois University, Master's, 1965.

5770. **Manfredik, Alfred.** *A Brief History of the Zone Defense in Men's Intercollegiate Basketball.* California State University, Sacramento, Master's, 1971.

5771. **Mangus, Brent Charles.** *Pilot Study Investigating the Absence of the Palmaris Langus Muscle in High School Basketball Players.* University of Oregon, Master's, 1978.

5772. **Marberry, James W.** *A Mechanical Analysis and Experimental Study of Technique in the Foul Throw in Basketball.* University of Iowa, Master's, 1949.

5773. **Marcus, Bill.** *A Survey Concerning the Administrative Attitudes of the Participating High Schools Toward the Tournament of Champions in Northern California, 1947–53.* Chico State College, Master's, 1954.

5774. **Maroney, Robert Eugene.** *The Status of Coaches of Boys' Interscholastic Basketball in Class A High Schools of Texas.* North Texas State University, Master's, 1961.

5775. **Marshall, D. Alfred.** *Effect of Varying the Rim Size on Basketball Foul Shooting.* Utah State University, Master's, 1964.

5776. **Martel, Thelma E.** *The Development of a Motion Picture for Use in Teaching Foul Shooting in Girls Basketball.* Boston University, Master's, 1950.

5777. **Marticke, Linda Kay.** *Racial Attitudes of Male Basketball Team Participants.* University of Montana, Master's, 1978.

5778. **Martin, Dean Steven.** *The Relationship of Field Goal and Free Throw Percentages to Winning in Basketball.* California State University, Chico, Master's, 1982.

5779. **Martin, James L.** *A Study to Determine the Frequency and Effectiveness of Field Goal and Free Throw Shooting in Relation to Portion of Game, Area of Court, and Varying Defenses.* Western Illinois University, Master's, 1969.

5780. **Martin, Jean C.** *A System for Rating the Performance of Interscholastic Basketball Players.* California State University, Los Angeles, Master's, 1961.

5781. **Martin, John W.** *Effects of Basketball Free Throw Shooting Accuracy During Game Situations.* Southern Illinois University, Master's, 1970.

5782. **Martin, Lawrence A.** *The Effects of Competition Upon the Aggressive Responses of Basketball Players and Wrestlers.* Springfield College, Doctorate, 1969.

5783. **Martin, Peggy Elizabeth.** *Attributes of Nationally Rated Intercollegiate Basketball Officials.* Indiana University, Doctorate, 1981.

5784. **Martin, R.F.** *Equilibrium as a Factor in Foul Shooting in Basketball.* Springfield College, Master's, 1935.

5785. **Martin, Richard G.** *A Comparative Study Between the Foot Reaction Time of Interscholastic Basketball Players and Male Physical Education Students.* University of Wisconsin, Master's, 1970.

5786. **Martin, Rose Lee.** *A Study to Determine the Status of Interscholastic Athletics for Women in Selected Secondary Schools in North Carolina.* North Carolina Central University, Master's, 1956.

5787. **Martin, William H.** *Index to the Basketball Case Book.* Springfield College, Master's, 1949.

5788. **Martinek, Thomas Jerry.** *A Study of High School Offensive Basketball Strategy.* George Williams College, Master's, 1971.

5789. **Marvin, Albert Jerrold.** *The Effect of Selected Fundamental Basketball Drills on Game Performance.* University of California, Los Angeles, Master's, 1968.

5790. **Masotti, Bruno.** *An Investigation of the Effects of Exercise (Basketball) on Blood Sugar Concentrations.* Michigan State University, Master's, 1960.

5791. **Massaro, Ray.** *A Survey to Determine Preferred Methods of Selected Basketball Officials in Essex and Union Counties, New Jersey.* Montclair State College, Master's, 1968.

5792. **Masteller, Jerry P.** *A Study of Basketball as an Interscholastic Game in Transition.* Bowling Green State University, Master's, 1961.

5793. **Mather, Marilyn J.** *The Relationship of Self-Concept and Group Perceived Self-Concept of Female High School Basketball Players.* Southern Connecticut State University, Master's, 1983.

5794. **Mathes, Lee K.** *A Study of the Net Gain in Points Resulting from Fouling in Basketball.* University of Iowa, Master's, 1940.

5795. **Mathesius, Peter J.** *The Relationship Between Predicted and Actual Maximum $\dot{V}O_2$ Determinations of Three Stress Tests Among Basketball Players.* Utah State University, Master's, 1981.

5796. **Mathews, Leslie E.** *A Battery of Basketball Skills Tests for High School Boys.* University of Oregon, Master's, 1963.

5797. **Matson, Andrew A.** *Small Group Dynamics and Their Application to Coaching Basketball.* Montana State University, Master's, 1968.

5798. **Mattes, Aaron Lloyd.** *A History of Intercollegiate Basketball at the University of Illinois, Urbana–Champaign, 1959–1971.* University of Illinois, Master's, 1972.

5799. **Mattiache, Michael R.** *Individual Instruction in the Physical Skills of Basketball, Volleyball, and Tennis Compared to a Traditional Program in Physical Education.* University of Kansas, Master's, 1976.

5800. **Maxsey, Mary Frances.** *A Comparison of Two Physiological Indices of Emotional Reactions of High School Girls to Competitive Basketball.* University of Maryland, Master's, 1953.

5801. **May, Carolyn Jeannette.** *A Comparison of Three Basketball Free Throw Practice Situations' Effects on Accuracy Performance and Evidence of Ball Trajectory Transfer.* University of Wisconsin, Master's, 1968.

5802. **Maybauer, Ruth A.** *Effect of High School Basketball on the Menstrual Health of College Freshmen.* University of Iowa, Master's, 1928.

5803. **Mays, Tracey L.** *An Analysis of Factors Influencing the Outcomes of Women's Basketball Seasons at the University of Alabama–Birmingham from 1978–1984.* University of Kansas, Master's, 1985.

5804. **McCarthy, Eugene F., Jr.** *A Comparison of the Personality Characteristics of Highly Successful, Moderately Successful, and Unsuccessful High School Basketball Coaches as Measured by the Cattell Sixteen Personality Factor Questionnaire.* University of Maryland, Master's, 1973.

5805. **McCarthy, Neil N.** *An Examination of the Results of One Method of Teaching Free Throw Shooting Form.* California State University, Sacramento, Master's, 1970.

5806. **McClements, Lawrence E.** *A Comparative Analysis of Methods of Attacking the Zone Defense.* Springfield College, Master's, 1956.

5807. **McClendon, McKee Jared.** *Interracial Contact on Collegiate Basketball Teams: A Test of Sherif's Theory of Superordinate Goals.* University of Kansas, Doctorate, 1972.

5808. **McConnell, Richard Lee.** *An Evaluation of the Present Method of Rating and Assigning Officials for the Washington State Basketball Tournaments.* Washington State University, Master's, 1971.

5809. **McCormick, Lawrence F.** *A Guide for Ninth Grade Basketball for the Sweet Home Central School.* State University of New York at Buffalo, Master's, 1968.

5810. **McCray, Mary E.** *A Documented Analysis of Rule Changes in Women's Basketball from 1935–1970.* Springfield College, Master's, 1971.

5811. **McDaniel, Gary L.** *A Twenty Year Review of Basketball Literature (1948–1968).* Southwest Missouri State University, Master's, 1969.

5812. **McDaniel, Thomas Carlyle.** *A Comparative Study in Basketball Free Throwing.* George Peabody College, Master's, 1938.

5813. **McDonald, Andrew Jesse.** *A Study of the Contributions Made by Men to the Development of the Game of Basketball.* Louisiana State University, Master's, 1944.

5814. **McDowell, Betsy and Schneeback, Jeri.** *An Investigation of Visual Skills in Athletics.* Pacific University, College of Optometry, Doctorate, 1982.

5815. **McDuffie, Richard Adrian.** *An Investigation of Performance Consistency of Intercollegiate and Interscholastic Basketball Officials.* University of North Carolina at Greensboro, Doctorate, 1980.

5816. **McGinnis, Michael Joseph.** *Personality Changes as a Result of a Selected Basketball Program for a College Freshman Basketball Team.* University of Florida, Master's, 1971.

5817. **McIlwain, James Dixon.** *A Study of Methods and Procedures of Basketball Scouting.* Arizona State University, Master's, 1952.

5818. **McIntosh, Donald V.** *The Effects of Fatigue on Basketball Shooting.* Brigham Young University, Master's, 1967.

5819. **McKelhen, Joe.** *A Survey for the Need for a Coach's Handbook Pertaining to the Individual Administration Duties of a Prospective Basketball Coach.* Western Montana College, Master's, 1969.

5820. **McKenna, Ralph J.** *A Study of Basketball Errors and Their Relationship to Winning and Losing Games in the Northeastern Wisconsin Conference During the 1958-1959 Season.* University of Wisconsin, Master's, 1959.

5821. **McKenzie, Flora.** *Basketball Clinic for High School Leaders.* University of Toledo, Master's, 1961.

5822. **McKissick, Scott.** *A Comparison of Hostility Levels of Male Intramural Basketball Participants at Western Illinois University.* Western Illinois University, Master's, 1984.

5823. **McLaughlin, Maureen.** *Relationship of Two Measures of Shooting Ability of Selected Girls Parochial High Schools Varsity Basketball Players.* Montclair State College, Master's, 1969.

5824. **McLean, Edward.** *The Relationship of Attentional Style and Anxiety Patterns to Performance Tendencies in Intercollegiate Basketball Competition.* University of Tennessee at Knoxville, Doctorate, 1984.

5825. **McLemore, Matthew Hunter.** *An Analysis of Interpersonal Group Structures and Personality Profiles of Team Members Representing Two Categories of Junior College Basketball Teams.* North Texas State University, Doctorate, 1967.

5826. **McNabb, Chester Derald.** *Opinions of Recognized Collegiate Basketball Coaches Pertaining to the Use of the Two-Handed and One-Handed Basketball Set Shot.* Arizona State University, Master's, 1949.

5827. **McNerney, James Benson.** *A Study of the Amount of Activity of High School Players in the Game of Basketball.* Kansas State Teachers College, Master's, 1961.

5828. **McNickleg, Reinold G.** *A Weight Training Questionnaire for Basketball Coaches.* Herbert H. Lehman College, Master's, 1978.

5829. **Meister, Richard W.** *The Relationship of Basketball Officiating to Basketball Team Performance.* University of Wisconsin, Master's, 1958.

5830. **Melograno, Vincent J.** *Effects of Teacher Personality, Teacher Choice of Educational Objectives, and Teaching Behavior on Student Achievement.* Temple University, Doctorate, 1971.

5831. **Menacof, Nick Eugene.** *A Proposed Simplified Basketball Scouting Report.* University of Tennessee, Master's, 1966.

5832. **Mende, David T.** *Five Individualized Instructional Programs in Beginning Basketball for Boys.* California State University, Sacramento, Master's, 1973.

5833. **Menser, Linda Jean.** *Forces Which Influence Women to Compete in Basketball.* California State University, Long Beach, Master's, 1974.

5834. **Merritt, Anthony Louis.** *A Study of the Effect of a Progressive Isometric Training Program on the Basketball Ability of Ninth Grade Boys.* University of Utah, Master's, 1966.

5835. **Merritt, Myrtle A.** *Achievement Tests in Basketball for College Women.* University of Iowa, Master's, 1951.

5836. **Messer, Buerdon Norris.** *Techniques of Basketball.* Springfield College, Master's, 1909.

5837. **Messerich, Sandra.** *A Cinematographic Study of the Basketball Dribble.* Texas Woman's University, Master's, 1973.

5838. **Messersmith, L.** *The Development and Application of a Measuring Technique for the Distance Traversed by Participants in Certain Athletic Events.* Indiana University, Doctorate, Date unknown.

5839. **Messner, Robert L.** *A Study to Determine the Difference in a Basketball Skill Utilizing Defense.* University of Wisconsin, Master's, 1972.

5840. **Mester, Vicki R.** *The Relationship Between Female Basketball Players' Vertical Jumping Ability to Basketball Ability Tests and Judges Rating.* West Chester State College, Master's, 1976.

5841. **Metcalf, Robert Leo.** *Transfer of Training Effect of Basketball Shooting Practice on Free Throw Shooting Accuracy.* Indiana University, Doctorate, 1971.

5842. **Metcalf, Shelby Robinson.** *Variables Affecting Crowd Behavior at Basketball Games in the Southwest Conference.* Texas A&M University, Doctorate, 1974.

5843. **Meyer, Donald Wayne.** *A Comparison of Perceptions of University Basketball Coaches.* University of Utah, Doctorate, 1972.

5844. **Meyer, Gerald B.** *The Effect of Weight Lifting and Isometric Contractions Exercises on the Height of the Vertical Jump.* University of North Dakota, Master's, 1965.

5845. **Meyer, Joseph E.** *The Effectiveness of Practice Shooting on a Smaller Rim on the Improvement of Basketball Free Throw Shooting.* George Williams College, Master's, 1975.

5846. **Meyernoff, John W.** *History of Basketball, Old Dominion University 1930–1974.* Old Dominion University, Master's, 1974.

5847. **Michaelson, Maren Elaine.** *Prediction of Efficient Player Combinations Among Members of the South Dakota State University Women's Basketball Squad.* South Dakota State University, Master's, 1976.

5848. **Miletich, Nick J.** *Skills Basic to Basketball Taught in Grades Four Through Nine in Communities of 10,000 or More in the State of Iowa.* University of Iowa, Master's, 1948.

5849. **Miller, David L.** *The Effectiveness of Selected Warm-Ups on the Vertical Jump Reach Performance of Seventeen Male Students.* Florida Institute of Technology, Master's, 1972.

5850. **Miller, Donald C.** *Techniques of Shooting Free Throws.* University of Wyoming, Master's, 1952.

5851. **Miller, Robert A.** *Tachistoscopic Training of High School Basketball Players.* California State University, Los Angeles, Master's, 1966.

5852. **Miller, Robert C.** *The Effect of the Size of Ball and Height of the Basket on the Learning of Selected Basketball Skills by Fifth Grade Boys.* Springfield College, Doctorate, 1971.

5853. **Miller, Steven E.** *A Behavioral Descriptive Study of the Communication Variables Utilized by Coach Larry Brown of the University of Kansas.* University of Kansas, Master's, 1985.

5854. **Millslagle, Duane Gordon.** *Visual Perception, Recognition Recall and Mode of Search Control in Basketball Involving Novice and Experienced Woman Basketball Players.* University of Tennessee at Knoxville, Doctorate, 1986.

5855. **Milne, Duane Conrad.** *The Effects of a Cold Hip Bath on Accuracy in Basketball Shooting.* Michigan State University, Master's, 1967.

5856. **Milne, Richard Kenneth.** *A Survey of Half-Time Procedures Used by High School and College Basketball Coaches.* University of Utah, Master's, 1966.

5857. **Milner, Edward Keith.** *Interaction of Personality With Activity, Participation, and Competition of Basketball Players at Different Educational Levels.* University of Wisconsin, Master's, 1967.

5858. **Milner, Orlin G.** *The Historical Development of Basketball at Kansas State College of Pittsburg, Kansas.* Kansas State College of Pittsburg, Master's, 1967.

5859. **Milner, Robert K.** *The Difference Between Converse Canvas and Adidas Leather Basketball Shoes as Shown by Various Performance Tests.* Brigham Young University, Master's, 1970.

5860. **Minahan, Fred B.** *An Experiment With a Restrictive Goal Device Designed to Improve Basketball Free Throw Shooting Accuracy.* University of Washington, Master's, 1963.

5861. **Mischler, Marion E.** *A Graded Lesson Plan in Basketball for Nationally Enrolled Leaders Clubs.* George Williams College, Master's, 1933.

5862. **Mitchell, A.V.** *A Scoring Table for College Women in the Fifty-Yard Dash, the Running Broad Jump, and the Basketball Throw for Distance.* University of Iowa, Master's, 1932.

5863. **Mitchell, Lisa Lyn.** *Coaching Gender Differences on the Leader Behavior Satisfaction of Female Intercollegiate Basketball Players.* University of Tennessee at Knoxville, Master's, 1986.

5864. **Mitchell, Samuel Edward.** *A Study of Basketball Organizational Materials and the Development of an Organizational Handbook for Beginning Basketball Coaches.* Central Washington State College, Master's, 1961.

5865. **Mitchelson, Edward Barry.** *The Evolution of Men's Basketball in Canada, 1892-1936.* University of Alberta, Master's, 1968.

5866. **Mittun, James A.** *An Analysis of the Effects of a Weight Training Program on Selected Measures of Power, Agility, and Basketball Skills in Adolescent Boys.* University of North Dakota, Master's, 1960.

5867. **Mixon, Donna O'Steen.** *A Study of Posture, Somatotype and Varsity Athletic Participation of College Men.* Auburn University, Master's, 1973.

5868. **Moawad, Robert Abraham.** *A Study of the Effects of Democratic Coaching Procedures Upon Members of a High School Basketball Squad.* Central Washington State College, Master's, 1967.

5869. **Mock, R.G.** *The Correlation of Games Won in Basketball with Offense, Defense, and a Combination of Offense and Defense.* New York University, Master's, 1932.

5870. **Moessmang, Virginia L.** *The Analysis of the Emotional Reaction of High School Girls Participating in Interscholastic and Intramural Basketball.* Boston University, Master's, 1950.

5871. **Moffitt, David Clair.** *A Measure of Basketball Skills for Fifth and Sixth Grade Boys.* Central Washington State College, Master's, 1970.

5872. **Moffitt, James Irvin.** *Male Basketball Players and Coaches' Perceptions of Factors Influencing Players' Choice of University.* North Texas State University, Doctorate, 1982.

5873. **Molgard, Robert Kent.** *Team Rules and Regulations Used by Football and Basketball Coaches in Utah High Schools.* Utah State University, Master's, 1973.

5874. **Monahan, W.L.** *The Measurement of Individual Basketball Skills in College Men.* University of Iowa, Master's, 1935.

5875. **Montgomery, Michael John.** *Personality Traits of Men and Women Basketball Players at the College Level.* Colorado State University, Master's, 1976.

5876. **Mooney, Shirlee Ann Beaudreau.** *A Comparative Analysis of Physiques and Performances of University of Kentucky Basketball Teams, 1948–1968.* University of Kentucky, Master's, 1970.

5877. **Moore, Jacqueline.** *An Investigation of a Criterion for Establishing the Validity of Tests of Performance in Team Sports.* Smith College, Master's, 1960.

5878. **Moore, Neile D.** *A Case Study of the Effects of Interscholastic Basketball on the Health of High School Girls.* Oklahoma State University, Master's, 1936.

5879. **Moore, Warren Everett and Rose, John Alton.** *A Study of the Correlation Between Reaction Time, Depth Perception, Visual Span of Apprehension and a Basketball Skills Test of High School Male Basketball Players.* Boston University, Master's, 1951.

5880. **Mordy, M.** *A Study of Officiation in Women's Basketball.* University of Iowa, Master's, 1942.

5881. **Moreman, Vernon H.** *A Study of the Development of the Jump Shot and the Two Hand Set Shot in Basketball.* Washington State University, Master's, 1959.

5882. **Morgan, Wayne B.** *A Comparison of the Effects of Three Warm-Up Techniques on Various Basketball Skills.* Ithaca College, Master's, 1972.

5883. **Morris, Charles McKay.** *The Construction of a Basketball Motor Ability Test for College Men Through Factor Analysis.* George Peabody College, Doctorate, 1966.

5884. **Morrison, Carolyn Jean.** *Methods of Teaching Girls Basketball.* West Virginia University, Master's, 1961.

5885. **Morrison, Stanley Mach.** *The Advantages and Disadvantages in Raising the Height of the Goal in Basketball from Ten Feet to Twelve Feet.* California State University, Sacramento, Master's, 1966.

5886. **Morrow, Ellen Ruth.** *Latitude of Sportsmanship Behavior Deemed Acceptable by Spectators of Basketball Games.* Texas Woman's University, Doctorate, 1981.

5887. **Mortimer, Elizabeth.** *Trajectory Studies in Relation to Specific Goals for Basketball Shooting.* University of Wisconsin, Master's, 1950.

5888. **Moseley, Kenneth.** *A Historical Study of Basketball in the North State Intercollegiate Athletic Conference.* Appalachian State University, Master's, 1958.

5889. **Moser, Dayton Donald.** *An Investigation of the Duties Performed by Head Coaches of Boys' Basketball and Football Teams Within the Secondary High School of Tennessee.* Middle Tennessee State University, Master's, 1979.

5890. **Moser, Helen A.** *A Preliminary Selection of Tests to Measure Essential Skills in Basketball for Women.* University of California, Berkeley, Master's, 1933.

5891. **Motta, John R.** *The Effect of Weight Training on Selected Gross Motor Skills Related to Basketball Playing Ability.* Utah State University, Master's, 1960.

5892. **Mottinger, Sue Glover.** *Salary Comparison of Female and Male Intercollegiate Basketball Coaches: An Equal Opportunity Study.* Texas Woman's University, Doctorate, 1981.

5893. **Mouw, Robert J.** *An Analysis of Objective Factors Associated with Interscholastic Basketball Team Success.* California State University, Long Beach, Master's, 1971.

5894. **Moyer, I.C.** *History of College Basketball.* Springfield College, Master's, 1911.

5895. **Moyer, Lou Jean.** *The Construction of Films Designed for Practice in Officiating Women's Basketball.* University of Iowa, Doctorate, 1968.

5896. **Muehlfield, Phil P.** *The High School Coach as a Helping Person.* University of Toledo, Master's, 1977.

5897. **Mueller, Paul Otto.** *The Effect of Christmas Vacation on Selected Intercollegiate Basketball Players.* University of Wisconsin, Master's, 1971.

5898. **Mularz, Thad J.** *A Semantic Differential Analysis of Attitudes Toward Certain Concepts Held by Male Basketball Officials.* University of New Mexico, Doctorate, 1973.

5899. **Mullan, A.** *The Study of Some Effects of Participation in Field Hockey and Basketball by Junior High School Girls.* New York University, Master's, Date unknown

5900. **Muller, Paul Andrew.** *A Study of Fouling in Basketball.* Springfield College, Master's, 1955.

5901. **Mullins, Peter M.** *An Experimental Study of the Value of Kinesthesis in Learning the Basketball Free Throw.* Washington State University, Master's, 1954.

5902. **Munroe, Richard Allen.** *The Effect of Systematic Weight Training on the Performance of Beginning Basketball Players.* University of Illinois, Master's, 1956.

5903. **Murphy, Charles S.** *Why Girls' Interscholastic Basketball is Unpopular in West Virginia Schools.* West Virginia University, Master's, 1938.

5904. **Murphy, Chester Walter.** *An Experiment in the Use of Strength, Ability and General Ability Tests as Indices of Basketball Ability.* George Williams College, Master's, 1941.

5905. **Murphy, Thomas J.** *The Effect of Mental Warm-Up on Jump Shooting Accuracy Among Selected Boys High School Basketball Players.* South Dakota State University, Master's, 1977.

5906. **Murphy, Thomas Michael.** *The Relationship Between the AAHPER Youth Fitness Test Scores and the Athletic Ability in Football, Basketball, and Paddleball.* Florida State University, Master's, 1971.

5907. **Murrey, Thomas Henning.** *Development of Basketball Skill Test Norms for Austin Peay State University College Freshmen and Sophomores.* Austin Peay State University, Master's, 1968.

5908. **Myron, Clifford W.** *Determining the Validity of Basketball Test Scores Compared With Game Performance.* Washington State University, Master's, 1963.

5909. **Nachtigal, Frank G.** *An Investigation of the Effects of a Season of Varsity Football or Basketball Participation Upon Hand Reaction Time of High School Athletes.* Kansas State Teachers College, Master's, 1968.

5910. **Nadeau, Andre Joseph.** *The Construction and Evaluation of Objective Tests for Football and Basketball Officials.* University of Iowa, Doctorate, 1966.

5911. **Napier, William James.** *The Effectiveness of Honor System Basketball in Teaching Individual Skills and Teamwork on the College Service Course Level.* University of Colorado, Master's, 1954.

5912. **Nardone, Leonard J.** *A Comparison in the Accuracy of the Jump Shot, Hook Shot, and Jump-Hook Shot at Various Distances from the Basket.* Springfield College, Master's, 1972.

5913. **Nayler, William Chastain.** *Effect of Wrist and Elbow Power on Jump Shot Accuracy.* University of Southern Mississippi, Doctorate, 1971.

5914. **Naylor, Richard Wayne.** *Three Methods of Practice Relative to Developing Free Throw Accuracy in Basketball.* Indiana University, Doctorate, 1973.

5915. **Neely, Janice Jean.** *The Construction and Evaluation of a Knowledge Examination for Women's Basketball Classes at the University of Washington.* University of Washington, Master's, 1952.

5916. **Nelson, George B.** *Efficiency in Field Goal Shooting in Basketball.* University of Wisconsin, Doctorate, 1934.

5917. **Nelson, Irwin L.** *An Analysis of Goal Shooting Accuracy in Basketball of High School Boys and Girls.* University of Iowa, Master's, 1947.

5918. **Nelson, Judith Ann.** *Effect of Modern Rhythmic Gymnastics, Physical Conditioning, Basketball, and Gymnastics on the Physical Fitness Status and Professed Self-Concept of University of Florida Freshmen Women.* University of Florida, Master's, 1973.

5919. **Neve, Kyle K.** *A System for the Evaluation of Basketball Officials.* Virginia Polytechnic Institute and State University, Master's, 1986.

5920. **Newlee, John Barney.** *Historical Analysis of Basketball.* San Diego State College, Master's, 1954.

5921. **Newlin, Charles Samuel.** *Suggested Standards for the Qualifications and Requirements of Kansas High School and Basketball Officials.* Kansas State Teachers College, Master's, 1964.

5922. **Newton, Reason George.** *A Study of Basketball Tournament Teams in Relation to Strength Index.* University of Kentucky, Master's, 1938.

5923. **Nick, David Harry.** *A Comparison of Ratings and Qualifications of Basketball Officials in the Catholic Youth Organization in Counties in Kansas.* University of Kansas, Master's, 1976.

5924. **Nicolai, Richard.** *A Workbook for Beginning Coaches of High School Basketball.* Chico State College, Master's, 1962.

5925. **Nielsen, Gerald Orsen.** *The Effect of Weight Training on Basketball Shooting Accuracy.* University of Utah, Master's, 1963.

5926. **Noakes, Sandra Dee.** *A Course for Teaching Girls and Women the Techniques of Officiating Basketball.* Brigham Young University, Master's, 1966.

5927. **Nogawa, Haruo.** *A Study of a Japanese-American Basketball League and the Assimilation of Its Members Into the Mainstream of United States Society.* Oregon State University, Doctorate, 1984.

5928. **Nordyke, T.** *Influence of Basketball in the Improvement of Kinesthetic Sense.* Springfield College, Master's, 1941.

5929. **Norenberg, Lynn A.** *Cardiorespiratory Fitness of Women Basketball Players Throughout the Course of a Competitive Season.* University of Kentucky, Master's, 1983.

5930. **Norris, Edward M.** *An Experiment in New Mechanics of Officiating in College Basketball.* University of Texas, Master's, 1952.

5931. **Nourse, Howard Francis.** *A Process for Determining the Influence of Television Advertising Promoting Game Attendance for a Specific Division I Women's Basketball Program Upon Individual Spectator Decisions to Attend a Home Contest at the Institution.* Ohio State University, Doctorate, 1986.

5932. **Novak, Michael F.** *The Effect of Massed Versus Distributed Practice on Free Throw Shooting Accuracy.* University of Wisconsin–La Crosse, Master's, 1980.

5933. **Nuccio, John Robert.** *National Collegiate Athletic Association Recruiting Regulations Under Rules Manual Article One–A Study of Needed Changes in Recruiting Practices: A Survey of American Basketball Coaches.* University of Southern California, Doctorate, 1981.

5934. **Null, Richard William.** *High School and College Sports Participation of Basketball Players From Five Midwest Intercollegiate Conferences, 1968–1969.* Drake University, Master's, 1969.

5935. **Nutgrass, Robert D.** *An Investigation of the Career Patterns of University Assistant Basketball Coaches.* Western Illinois University, Master's, 1982.

5936. **Nycum, Richard L.** *A Study of Young Men's Christian Association Organized Basketball Programs in Ohio, West Virginia, and Indiana.* Springfield College, Master's, 1950.

5937. **Oakes, Michael D.** *The Herman Wolfe Basketball Test as a Predictor of Basketball Ability, Spring 1970.* Montclair State College, Master's, 1970.

5938. **Odom, Bentley Robert.** *The Effect of an Eleven Foot Basket on Shooting Accuracy.* Mankato State College, Master's, 1973.

5939. **Odoms, Connie Marie Amsler.** *A Survey of Selected Factors in the Organization of Practice Sessions for Women's Intercollegiate Basketball Teams in Southern California.* California State University, Long Beach, Master's, 1972.

5940. **Olds, Lloyd W.** *Study of the Effects of Competitive Basketball Upon the Physical Fitness of High School Boys as Determined by McCurdy-Larson Organic Efficiency Tests.* University of Michigan, Doctorate, 1939.

5941. **Oliphant, Harvey A.** *A Study of Improvement in Shooting Baskets as Related to the Amount of Practice.* University of Iowa, Master's, 1939.

5942. **Oliveira, Edwin L.** *An Analysis of Five Selected Fundamentals of Offensive Basketball.* California State University, Humboldt, Master's, 1960.

5943. **Oliver, John Newton.** *A Comparative Study of Free Throw Techniques in a Selected Group of Ohio High Schools.* University of Wyoming, Master's, 1952.

5944. **Oliver, Pamela Sue.** *A Study of the Relative Value of Selected Factors Which Contribute to Winning in Girls Basketball.* University of Tennessee, Master's, 1966.

5945. **Olney, Cless LeRoy.** *Motor Ability as a Predictive Measure of Potential Basketball Ability.* Utah State University, Master's, 1953.

5946. **Olson, Anne Kruse.** *The Relationship of Selected Tests to Evaluations of Basketball Playing Ability.* Montana State University, Master's, 1980.

5947. **Olson, Ruth.** *The Effects of a Season of Training and Competition on Aerobic Capacity, Blood Lactate Levels, and Body Composition in Female Intercollegiate Basketball Players.* Bowling Green State University, Master's, 1982.

5948. **Opperman, Ernest F.** *A Study of Shoulder Strength in Relation to Basket Shooting.* Moorhead State College, Master's, 1966.

5949. **Ordyna, Richard Franklin.** *Seasonal Stress Level Development of Intercollegiate Basketball Players.* Brigham Young University, Doctorate, 1975.

5950. **Oreak, William T.** *The Effect of Weighted Inner-Soles on the Vertical Jump of High School Basketball Players.* Moorhead State College, Master's, 1966.

5951. **Orr, Leonard R.** *A Six Week Pre-Season Practice Plan.* Northwest Missouri State University, Master's, 1978.

5952. **Osborn, Michael Lee.** *A Comparison of Three Basketball Skill Tests.* Central Washington State College, Master's, 1969.

5953. **Osborne, D.E.** *Coaching Basketball in the Secondary School.* George Washington University, Master's, 1940.

5954. **Osborne, Vernon.** *A Basketball Charting System.* College of William and Mary, Master's, 1953.

5955. **Osborne, William Terry.** *The Relative Accuracy of Officiating Basketball From Different Positions.* New York University, Doctorate, 1941.

5956. **Ostrem, Roderick L.** *A Study of the Shooting Frequency of Selected High School Basketball Teams as Related to the Thirty Second Time Period.* University of Wisconsin–La Crosse, Master's, 1981.

5957. **Owen, Joseph P.** *The Effect of Practice with Weighted Basketballs on Shooting Accuracy of Fifth and Sixth Grade Boys.* Northern Illinois University, Master's, 1965.

5958. **Owens, Dennis P.** *A Study to Determine the Relationship Between the Physical Fitness of a Selected Group of Boys and Their Ability to Perform Certain Selected Basketball Skills.* Southern Connecticut State College, Master's, 1970.

5959. **Pace, Paula Kay.** *A Suggested Marketing Strategy for the Montana State University Women's Basketball Program.* Montana State University, Master's, 1982.

5960. **Page, Weston O.** *An Analysis of Fouls Committed in Thirty Intercollegiate Basketball Games and Their Effect on Successful Team Performance.* Boston University, Master's, 1948.

5961. **Paine, Thomas A.** *A Study of the Relationship of Arm and Wrist Strength and Basketball Shooting Accuracy.* University of Wisconsin–La Crosse, Degree program unknown, 1965.

5962. **Palmer, Anita M.** *The Effects of a Pre-Season Conditioning Program and a Season of Competition on Selected Physical Fitness Measures of Women's Intercollegiate Basketball Players.* University of Wisconsin–La Crosse, Master's, 1983.

5963. **Pampuch, Elroy J.** *Effect of Type of Foul, Foul Location, Six-Foul Rule and Rebounding After Missed Free Throws on Varsity Basketball Performance.* University of Wisconsin, Master's, 1958.

5964. **Pangman, John Russell.** *Weight Variance of Basketballs Related to Kinesthetic Sense in Free Throw Shooting.* Indiana University at Bloomington, Doctorate, 1982.

5965. **Paramore, Jim.** *A Survey of Selected Kansas High Schools Concerning the Optimum Number of Basketball Games to Be Played in a Season.* Kansas State Teachers College, Master's, 1963.

5966. **Parchman, Linda Lou.** *A Comparative Study of the Development of Leg Strength and Endurance of College Women in Basketball and Swimming.* University of Illinois, Master's, 1961.

5967. **Pariseau, John.** *The Relationship of Selected Statistical Data to Team Success in the Athletic Association of the Western University Basketball Conference, 1959–1962.* University of Washington, Master's, 1962.

5968. **Parker, Harold.** *An Evaluation of the Factors Contributing to a Sound Program of Conditioning for Basketball.* Kansas State College of Pittsburg, Master's, 1956.

5969. **Parker, Lauris Joan.** *Expectancies and Perceived Effort as Mediators of Coaching Behavior and Players' Self-Concept in Youth League Basketball.* Wake Forest University, Master's, 1980.

5970. **Parkhill, Richard Blair.** *An Experimental Study of Two Supplementary Basketball Conditioning Programs.* Ohio University, Master's, 1970.

5971. **Parr, Richard B., Wilmore, Jack H., et al.** *Professional Basketball Players: Athletic Profiles.* Unviersity of Arizona, Master's, 1978.

5972. **Pete W.S., Jr.** *Factors Affecting the Athletes' Choice of College: a Comparison of Basketball Coaches' and Athletes' Perceptions.* University of North Carolina, Master's, 1986.

5973. **Patty, Elbert K.** *The Relationship of Selected Measurable Traits to Success in Basketball.* Indiana University, Doctorate, 1953.

5974. **Pavlich, Mary.** *The Validation of a Battery of Basketball Tests in a Teaching Situation.* Smith College, Master's, 1949.

5975. **Payne, Marsha A.** *The Use of Selected Drills for a Girls' Varsity Basketball Team.* Western Maryland College, Master's, 1972.

5976. **Pearson, Carol Lee Couberly.** *Is Coeducational Physical Education a Hindrance to Girls and Boys Learning Basketball Skills?* California State University, Chico, Master's, 1979.

5977. **Pease, Dale Gordon.** *The Relationship of Selected Hand and Wrist Measurements to the Ability to Shoot in Basketball.* University of Colorado, Master's, 1965.

5978. **Pederson, Robert Duane.** *Effectiveness of the Problem Solving Method in Coaching Junior High School Basketball.* Central Washington University, Master's, 1970.

5979. **Pennypacker, Janis.** *The Relationship Between the Strength of the Extensor Muscles of the Elbow and the Flexor Muscles of the Wrist on the Ability of High School Girl Basketball Players to Execute the Jump Shot.* West Chester State College, Master's, 1976.

5980. **Perez, J. Gregory.** *Offensive Basketball Progressions for the Souers Junior High School Program.* Ashland College, Master's, 1984.

5981. **Perkerson, Gladys Loraine.** *A Correspondence in Coaching Basketball for Girls.* George Peabody College, Master's, 1927.

5982. **Perkins, Thomas Martin.** *The Relationship of Selected Biorhythms to Intercollegiate Offensive Basketball Performance.* University of Utah, Master's, 1978.

5983. **Persciano, J.F.** *A Comparative Study of Three-Division and Two-Division Girls Rules Basketball for Women.* New York University, Master's, 1938.

5984. **Pershouse, John Stanley.** *A Comparison of Certain Physical Abilities With Basketball Skill Among Junior High School Boys.* University of Texas, Master's, 1953.

5985. **Perszyk, John J. and Trejo, Bernie.** *Stereolocalization as It Relates to Athletic Performance.* Pacific University, College of Optometry, Doctorate, 1984.

5986. **Peterich, Russell Edward.** *Changes in Negative Attitudes of Selected Tenth Grade Boys Toward Basketball.* Chico State College, Master's, 1969.

5987. **Peters, Charles William.** *The Post-Forward Option Offensive Pattern for High School Basketball Teams.* Adams State College, Master's, 1958.

5988. **Peters, Gerald Vernon.** *The Reliability and Validity of Selected Shooting Tests in Basketball.* University of Michigan, Master's, 1964.

5989. **Peterson, Herbert D.** *A Study of Certain Objective Factors in High School Basketball and Their Relationship to Team Success.* Indiana University, Doctorate, 1953.

5990. **Peterson, James A.** *Success and Residential Affiliation as Determinants of the Group Cohesiveness of Intramural Basketball Teams.* University of Illinois, Master's, 1970.

5991. **Peterson, Joan.** *The Prediction of Basketball Performance Using Psychomotor, Cognitive and Anthropometric Measures.* Northeast Missouri State University, Master's, 1979.

5992. **Peterson, Karen Marie.** *The Effect of Mental Imaging and Relaxation on the Basketball Shooting Performance of Female College Players.* California State University, Long Beach, Master's, 1985.

5993. **Petit, Thomas Patrick.** *Effects of Modification of Ball Size and Basket Height Upon Performance of Selected Basketball Skills.* Illinois State University, Master's, 1970.

5994. **Petrich, Fred.** *Basketball Skill Tests for Junior High School Boys.* University of North Dakota, Master's, 1955.

5995. **Pfeifer, Vernon.** *Rebound Tendencies and Their Possible Effect on Basketball Strategy.* Northern State College, Master's, 1972.

5996. **Phelps, Thomas Lewis.** *The Effect of Dribbling Practice with Blinder Glasses on Basketball Dribbling Speed.* East Tennessee State University, Master's, 1973.

5997. **Pheneger, James W.** *A Basketball Manual Covering Grades Five Through Twelve for the Berea City School District.* Ashland College, Master's, 1981.

5998. **Phillips, Carl William.** *A Proposal for the Improvement of Basketball Officiating in Southeastern Ohio.* Ohio University, Master's, 1957.

5999. **Phillips, Carol Linda.** *The Effect of Crowd, Coaches, and Team Members on the Self-Confidence of Basketball Players.* University of Oregon, Master's, 1985.

6000. **Phillips, Penelope Ruth.** *A Comparison of Two Methods of Shooting the Lay-Up Shot in Basketball Among College Women.* University of Arizona, Master's, 1972.

6001. **Picard, John E. and Jankowski, Christian.** *Consumer's Choice in Protection Eyewear.* Pacific University, Doctorate, 1984.

6002. **Pickman, Evan T.** *A Contingency Approach to Successful Basketball Coaching for Men.* University of Utah, Doctorate, 1980.

6003. **Pierce, Paul Edward.** *The Construction of Scales for Predicting Ability to Play Interscholastic Basketball.* University of Houston, Doctorate, 1961.

6004. **Pierce, Raymond E.** *A Survey of Selected Methods of Coaching Boys' Interschool Basketball Teams in Class A Public High Schools in Washington State for the Year 1960–1961.* University of Washington, Master's, 1962.

6005. **Pilch, Andrew W.** *A Comparison of Two Methods of Practicing Basketball Shooting and Their Effect on Shooting Accuracy.* University of Wisconsin–La Crosse, Master's, 1971.

6006. **Pim, Ralph L.** *An Investigation of Selected Division I Basketball Conferences to Determine Statistical Variables That Lead to Winning or Losing Games.* Northwestern State University of Louisiana, Doctorate, 1981.

6007. **Pinkston, Gerry Camilla.** *Personality Traits of Coaches of Women's Intercollegiate Basketball.* Oklahoma State University, Doctorate, 1982.

6008. **Pintor, Jaime M. Cabrera.** *The Effect of a Season of Basketball on Body Composition and Selected Cardiorespiratory Parameters.* Florida State University, Doctorate, 1974.

6009. **Pipho, Armin P.** *Shot Position and Rebound Location for Missed Field Goals and Missed Free Throws.* University of Iowa, Master's, 1963.

6010. **Pitney, Ben E.** *Some Factors Affecting the Hiring and Dismissal of High School Basketball Coaches in Illinois.* New Mexico State University, Master's, 1962.

6011. **Pitol, Frank R.** *The History of Basketball in the Collinsville High School.* Eastern Illinois University, Master's, 1962.

6012. **Pitts, Dorothy Carla.** *Aggressive Tendencies of Men and Women Varsity Basketball Players at Indiana State University.* Indiana State University, Master's, 1974.

6013. **Plinke, John Frederick.** *The Development of Basketball Physical Skill Potential Test Batteries by Height Categories.* Indiana University, Doctorate, 1966.

6014. **Pohl, William G.** *Effects of a Junior Size Basketball on the Skill Level of Ninth Grade Girls.* St. Cloud State College, Master's, 1979.

6015. **Polland, Michael.** *Validation of the Cook Age Height Classification Index for Use in Basketball Team Selection for Boys 10–15 Years of Age.* Montclair State College, Master's, 1972.

6016. **Poon, Joe.** *A Cinematographical Analysis of the Arm Action in the Basketball Jump Shot.* Springfield College, Master's, 1965.

6017. **Poplin, Ann Shappard.** *The Relationship Between Sociometric Status and Basketball Ability of College Women.* Florida State University, Master's, 1965.

6018. **Popp, Rod.** *The Development of a Strength Training Program for Collegiate Basketball Players Based on a Survey Study of College Players With Prestigious Basketball Programs.* University of Wisconsin–La Crosse, Master's, 1981.

6019. **Poppe, Kenneth H.G.** *The Effect of Distance and Direction on the Relative Accuracy of One-Hand and Two-Hand Basketball Shooting.* University of Kansas, Master's, 1953.

6020. **Porretta, David Louis.** *Patella Tendon Reflex Time in Black as Compared to White Basketball Players.* Ithaca College, Master's, 1972.

6021. **Porter, Alva L.** *A Comparison of the Percentage of Conversion of One-Hand Basketball Shots to the Percentages of Conversion of Two-Hand Basketball Shots.* Pennsylvania State University, Master's, 1948.

6022. **Porter, Carol.** *A Comparative Study of Personality Traits of Girls High School Coaches in the State of Tennessee.* University of Tennessee, Master's, 1973.

6023. **Porter, David T.** *The Effects of the Heart Rates of Head and Assistant Basketball Coaches During Game Situations.* Brigham Young University, Master's, 1977.

6024. **Poteet, Jim.** *A Comparison of the Bank Jump Shot and Direct Jump Shot From Certain Angles on the Floor With Experienced Basketball Players.* California State University, Los Angeles, Master's, 1965.

6025. **Potter, Douglas E.** *Comparison of Judges' Ratings of Basketball Tipping Ability with Objective Measure Using McCall's Rebounding Machine.* University of Wisconsin, Master's, 1972.

6026. **Potter, Glenn R.** *An Analysis of Selected Variables in NCAA Division I Basketball During the Last Three Minutes of Play with Implications for a Thirty Second Time Limitation on Team Possession.* Brigham Young University, Doctorate, 1976.

6027. **Potts, Charles A.** *The Effects of Isometric Weight Training on the Basic Skills of the Basketball Players at Salpoint High School.* Northern Arizona University, Master's, 1964.

6028. **Powell, Richard B.** *Historical Development of the American Game of Basketball.* University of Cincinnati, Master's, 1947.

6029. **Prescott, Roger L.** *The Evolution of Basketball from 1891 to 1964.* Northeast Missouri State University, Master's, 1964.

6030. **Price, Franklin Sarcy.** *Criteria for Determining Success in Basketball.* University of Alabama, Doctorate, 1969.

6031. **Price, Joy Ann.** *The Prevalence of 47,XYY Males Among Collegiate Basketball Players.* Western Michigan University, Master's, 1976.

6032. **Pritchett, Rita J.** *Reliability and Validity of a Passing Skill Test in Women's Basketball.* Eastern Kentucky University, Master's, 1971.

6033. **Prochaska, William J.** *Iowa Basketball Camps.* Mankato State University, Master's, 1969.

6034. **Pruitt, Warren B.** *A Study of Coaching Techniques Employed by Coaches of the Interscholastic League Boys' Championship Class B Basketball Teams of Texas.* North Texas State University, Master's, 1967.

6035. **Pruner, Sherry W.** *The Effects of Three Methods of Practice on Improving the Performance of a Modified Free Throw on Sixth Grade Girls.* North Texas State University, Master's, 1971.

6036. **Quincy, Floyd W., Jr.** *The Effect of the Resilience of Basketballs on Game Strategy.* Kansas State Teachers College, Master's, 1965.

6037. **Rampey, Mark S.** *The Effects of Spectator Anti-Social Behavior on the Performance of College Basketball Players.* Southern Illinois University, Master's, 1978.

6038. **Rancourt, Diana M.** *The Effect of Goal-Setting Upon a Test of Physical Skill in Basketball.* Southern Illinois University, Master's, 1972.

6039. **Ranes, Raymond S.** *A Comparative Study of the Bounce Pass and Direct Pass in Basketball as Related to the Systems Used by Coaches in the Big Ten Conference.* University of Iowa, Master's, 1939.

6040. **Ranklin, John.** *An Investigation of the Effect of Increased Arm and Shoulder Strength on the Basketball Set Shooting Accuracy of Ninth Grade Boys.* California State University, Sacramento, Master's, 1971.

6041. **Ranniger, Duane Stephen.** *The Effect of Using Ankle Weights on the Vertical Jumping Ability, Leg Strength, and Agility of Male High School Basketball Players.* Washington State University, Master's, 1965.

6042. **Rapp, Earl W.** *The Administration of Basketball in Indiana High Schools.* University of Wisconsin, Doctorate, 1930.

6043. **Rappaport, Michael.** *The Frequency of Held Balls Called by Collegiate Basketball Officials During Player Control.* Springfield College, Master's, 1974.

6044. **Raspberry, Drucilla Ann.** *A Ranking Model for Two Women's Team Sports (Basketball and Hockey).* Virginia Polytechnic Institute and State University, Master's, 1986.

6045. **Ray, Carl L., Jr.** *Offensive Basketball Fundamentals for High School.* University of Wyoming, Master's, 1957.

6046. **Ray, Joseph J.** *The Spectator Control Problem at Basketball Games at Eastman High School.* North Carolina Central University, Master's, 1973.

6047. **Raymond, Lloyd E.** *Identification of the Important Characteristics of Potential College Basketball Players.* Mankato State University, Master's, 1969.

6048. **Read, H.W.** *Demonstration of Pedagogy in Basketball.* Western State Teachers College, Master's, 1936.

6049. **Rearick, Nancy Naylor.** *The Wood Brothers Basketball Team of Portsmouth, New Hampshire, 1900 to 1906.* Springfield College, Master's, 1974.

6050. **Redden, Hugh Felix.** *The Relative Accuracy of Basketball Shooting With One and Two Hands at Different Distances.* University of Illinois, Master's, 1950.

6051. **Reed, Dale Leonard.** *The Effects of Lengths of Drills Practice on the Performance of Certain Fundamental Skills Among College Varsity Basketball Players.* East Texas State University, Master's, 1977.

6052. **Reed, Frederick L.** *The Status of Interscholastic Basketball for Junior High School Age Boys in Sedgwick County During the Year 1963.* Kansas State Teachers College, Master's, 1964.

6053. **Reeves, William Charles.** *Weight Training for Basketball Players.* San Diego State College, Master's, 1961.

6054. **Reichenstein, William.** *Effect of an Upper Body Strength Training Program on Power Output as Measured During Bouts of Arm Cranking.* University of Kentucky, Master's, 1983.

6055. **Reid, Jack L.** *A Study of Basketball Field Goal Attempts in Certain High School Games to Determine the Relative Accuracy of Different Kinds of Shots from Various Areas and Distances from the Goal.* Brigham Young University, Master's, 1963.

6056. **Reilly, Joseph F.** *Fundamentals of Basketball, Emphasizing Individual Skills.* Southern Connecticut State College, Master's, 1969.

6057. **Reinhard, Bernadine Marie.** *A Comparison of Two Methods of Teaching High School Girls the Limited Dribble, Lay-Up Shot and Recovery of the Rebound in Basketball.* University of Colorado, Master's, 1957.

6058. **Renick, Jobyann.** *An Analysis of Women's Basketball Rules.* University of Southern California, Doctorate, 1972.

6059. **Renshaw, J.E.** *An Analysis of High School Girls Basketball in Terms of Frequency of Occurrence of Technical Elements of the Game.* Wellesley College, Master's, 1933.

6060. **Repass, Ivan.** *Effects of Additional Exercise Programs During a Basketball Practice Season on Vertical Jumping Performance and Shuttle Run.* Florida Institute of Technology, Master's, 1972.

6061. **Repass, Ivan.** *Student-Developed Materials for Units on the Human Body.* University of Central Florida, Master's, 1978.

6062. **Retherford, Claude.** *A Study of a Time, Sequence, and Scope Approach for the Operation of a High School Varsity Basketball Program.* California State University, Los Angeles, Master's, 1962.

6063. **Reynolds, H.A.** *A Manual of Lead-Up Games for Eight Popular Sports.* New York University, Master's, 1934.

6064. **Rhodes, Eugene Neal.** *A Study of the Effects of a Pre-Season Ankle Exercise Program on the Prevention of Ankle Injuries in Michigan State High School Basketball.* Michigan State University, Master's, 1956.

6065. **Richards, James and Portillo, Richard.** *Development of Two Tachistoscopic Slide Series for Sports Vision.* Pacific University, College of Optometry, Doctorate, 1984.

6066. **Richmond, Kay.** *Effects of Isometric Strength Training on Basketball Shooting Accuracy.* Texas Tech University, Master's, 1969.

6067. **Rickman, John V. and Splinter, Kenneth W.** *A Public Survey of Athletic Eyewear.* Pacific University, Doctorate, 1984.

6068. **Rider, Richard Hall.** *The Influence of Basketball Coaches on Their Players' Personalities.* University of Utah, Doctorate, 1973.

6069. **Rider, Richard Hall.** *Personality Traits of Basketball Coaches as Perceived by Coaches and Their Players.* University of Utah, Master's, 1971.

6070. **Rider, William H.** *Development of a Junior High Basketball Offense.* State University of New York at Buffalo, Degree program unknown, 1965.

6071. **Riehl, Anthony T.** *Factors in College Basketball Recruiting That Influence Prospective Student-Athletes in Their Selection of a College or University.* Indiana State University, Master's, 1975.

6072. **Rife, Mas L.** *Basketball In Its Early Years at the University of Kansas, 1898–1925.* University of Kansas, Master's, 1967.

6073. **Righter, C.E.** *A Preliminary Study of the Relation of Personality Traits to Success in Basketball.* Stanford University, Master's, 1936.

6074. **Rindt, Ralph H.** *Techniques of Teaching Full Court Pressure Defense in Basketball.* Kansas State Teachers College, Master's, 1967.

6075. **Riokin, Francine Vicky.** *Predicting Basketball Standings Using Dominance Hierarchies.* University of Illinois, Master's, 1982.

6076. **Ritchie, Gwendolyn H.** *A Comparison of the Problem-Solving Explanation/ Demonstration Method of Teaching Basketball.* University of Massachusetts–Amherst, Master's, 1966.

6077. **Roberson, Johnny Lee.** *A History of Intercollegiate Basketball at East Carolina University from 1931–1972.* East Carolina University, Master's, 1972.

6078. **Roberts, Dan W.** *Comparison of Various Levels of Ability and Practice Conditions When Shooting Basketball From Three Different Distances With and Without the Use of a Basketball.* Temple University, Master's, 1973.

6079. **Roberts, Jack E.** *Changes in Basketball.* Wayne State University, Master's, 1965.

6080. **Roberts, John A.** *A Comparison of the Effectiveness of Two Methods of Training Upon the Jumping Ability of Basketball Players.* University of Iowa, Master's, 1956.

6081. **Roberts, John W.** *The Effects of the Degree of Involvement Upon the Level of Aggression of Spectators Before and After a University Basketball Game.* University of Maryland, Master's, 1972.

6082. **Roberts, William.** *College Basketball Bribery Scandals, 1947–1951.* California State Polytechnic University, Pomona, Master's, 1979.

6083. **Rochelle, Margery Edith.** *An Evaluation of College and University Professional Courses in Basketball by Coaches of Girls Interscholastic Basketball Teams in the Public Secondary Schools of Texas.* Texas Woman's University, Master's, 1959.

6084. **Rockland, Edward.** *An Investigation of the United States Participation in Olympic Basketball, 1936–1968.* University of Massachusetts, Master's, 1970.

6085. **Rockstad, Donald L.** *A Study of Selected Performance Factors and Their Relationship to Team Success in College Basketball.* St. Cloud State University, Master's, 1978.

6086. **Rodenberger, Miriam Latta.** *A Study of the Reliability Among High School Girls of Three Tests of Fundamental Abilities in Basketball.* University of Missouri, Master's, 1941.

6087. **Rodgers, Randall Rene.** *A History of the Illinois State High School Basketball Tournament (1908–1971).* University of Illinois, Master's, 1971.

6088. **Rogan, Lesley.** *Effects of Stress Management Training on Anxiety and Basketball Shooting Accuracy.* Cleveland State University, Master's, 1982.

6089. **Rogers, Albert Paul.** *What Should Coaches Teach Freshman Basketball Players in High School?* Arizona State University, Master's, 1953.

6090. **Rogers, Robert L.** *A Study of the Effects of Non-Dominant Hand Practice on the Acquisition of Skill in Basketball Shooting.* Central Missouri State University, Master's, 1968.

6091. **Rolando, James H.** *A Survey of Adminstrative Attitudes Towards Boys High School Basketball in the State of North Dakota.* University of Wyoming, Master's, 1959.

6092. **Rolek, Gary Lee.** *Opportunities Afforded Participants to Develop Character Through the Basketball Program of the Roosevelt Church Athletic Association, Minneapolis, Minnesota.* George Williams College, Master's, 1961.

6093. **Ross, James Raye.** *The Effects of Weight Training Upon the Charge, Initial Speed of Running and Jumping Ability.* University of Texas, Master's, 1958.

6094. **Rouse, Eldon C.** *The Relationship of the Free Throw to the Outcome of High School Basketball Games.* Wayne State University, Master's, 1968.

6095. **Rowe, Leslie.** *Effects of Conditioning Upon the Learning of Basketball.* Colorado State University, Master's, Date unknown.

6096. **Ruffner, William R.** *The Relationship Between the Type of Pass and the Loss of the Ball in Seventy-two Selected Basketball Games.* Brigham Young University, Master's, Date unknown.

6097. **Ruley, Amy Joyce.** *The Effects of Isotonic and Isokinetic Training on the Vertical Jump.* University of Oregon, Master's, 1981.

6098. **Rundio, Stephen Joseph.** *Status as a Factor Affecting Decisions of Members of a Youth Basketball Team.* University of North Carolina at Greensboro, Doctorate, 1975.

6099. **Russell, John.** *The Status of Interscholastic Athletics in Eight Selected Union Schools in Bobeson County.* University of North Carolina, Master's, 1960.

6100. **Rutte, Joseph Wenzel.** *An Exploration of Ego Development in Late Adolescence: Case Studies of Male Collegiate Seminarians and Male Collegiate Basketball Athletes.* University of Oregon, Doctorate, 1977.

6101. **Saba, Donald Daniel.** *A Comparison of the Performance of Basketball Teams of High School Age Selected by Test Results and by the Judgment of the Coach.* Northern Illinois University, Master's, 1960.

6102. **Sabo, John Phillip.** *An Empirical Study of Types of Muscular Coordination in Throwing Baskets.* University of Illinois, Master's, 1934.

6103. **Sackbauer, Mary Elizabeth.** *Personality Characteristics of Intramural Basketball Officials.* Colorado State University, Master's, 1979.

6104. **Sage, Larry Allan.** *The Effect of a Target Rim on Basketball.* Eastern Washington University, Master's, 1985.

6105. **Salmons, Neveto.** *The Influence of Dance on the Ability to Jump in Basketball.* Eastern Illinois University, Master's, 1964.

6106. **Salmons, Robert Harold.** *A Study of the Development of the Rules and Playing Style in the Game of Amateur Basketball.* Columbia University, Doctorate, 1954.

6107. **Saltis, Lawrence Robert.** *A Study to Determine the Effects of Various Factors on Basketball Foul Shooting Accuracy During Game Competition.* University of Michigan, Master's, 1942.

6108. **Salvo, Paul A.** *A Study of Present Basketball Officiating Qualification Practices of Class A High Schools in Utah.* Utah State University, Master's, 1968.

6109. **Samara, Robert Theofilos.** *A Curriculum in Basketball Offense for Programs at High School and College Level.* Wayne State University, Doctorate, 1973.

6110. **Sancken, Judith K.** *An Investigation of Selected Factors Associated With the Basketball Jumpball.* Bowling Green State University, Master's, 1978.

6111. **Sanderson, Douglas R.** *A Statistical Analysis of the Authenticity of the Home Court Advantage Theory in Intercollegiate Basketball.* Chico State College, Master's, 1969.

6112. **Sanford, Lynn Edmund.** *A Correlation Between Space I.Q. and Space Performance in Basketball.* Central Washington State College, Master's, 1961.

6113. **Sappington, Vera Ellen.** *The Role of the Women's Basketball Official as Perceived by Selected Groups of Subjects.* University of Iowa, Doctorate, 1976.

6114. **Sarelakos, Charles P.** *A Study of the Effect of Lay-Up Accuracy Before and After Strenuous Exercise.* West Chester State College, Master's, Date unknown.

6115. **Sarubbi, Kenneth Francis.** *The Effectiveness of Two Methods of Practice and Three Different Size Rims on the Improvement of Basketball Shooting.* Indiana University, Doctorate, 1970.

6116. **Satern, Miriam N.** *The Effect of Two Basket Heights and Two Ball Sizes on the Mechanics of the One-handed Basketball Free Throw as Performed by 13-Year-Old Boys.* University of North Carolina at Greensboro, Doctorate, 1984.

6117. **Sauers, Richard J.** *An Analysis of Ball-Control Periods in the Twelve Home Games of the Pennsylvania State University Varsity Basketball Team During the 1954–1955 Season.* Pennsylvania State University, Master's, 1955.

6118. **Saunders, Delmagene V.** *Effects of Three Types of Audiences on the Performance of Basketball Free Throw Shooting.* Texas Tech University, Master's, 1971.

6119. **Saunders, Glenn Arthur.** *The Effect Upon Accuracy in Goal Shooting with Basketballs of Different Weights.* University of Kansas, Master's, 1957.

6120. **Saunders, Harold Leslie, II.** *A Cinematographic Study of the Relationship Between Speed of Movement and Available Force.* Texas A&M University, Doctorate, 1980.

6121. **Sawyer, Fred Michael.** *The Effect of Training Methods on Basketball Field Goal Shooting Accuracy and Ball Toss Distance.* Indiana University, Doctorate, 1970.

6122. **Scaduto, Leonard J.** *Apparent Emotional Effects of Basketball Competition on Eighth Grade Boys.* Northern Illinois University, Master's, 1958.

6123. **Scanlon, William M.** *A Study to Determine the Results of Focusing Attention on a Point of Reference in Basketball Field Goal Shooting.* University of Arkansas, Master's, 1972.

6124. **Scerra, Anthony W.** *TOTE Model in Comparison to Traditional Method of Teaching the Foul Shot.* Herbert H. Lehman College, Master's, 1971.

6125. **Schaefer, Otto J.** *Tensions and Anxieties: A Study of the Causes of Failure in Athletic Performance in Basketball.* St. Cloud State College, Master's, 1956.

6126. **Schagel, Kevin.** *An Analysis of Field Goal Percentages in Basketball From Designated Shooting Areas.* St. Cloud State University, Master's, 1982.

6127. **Scheller, Thomas J.** *The Use of Guidance and Counseling Techniques in Coaching.* University of Toledo, Master's, 1978.

6128. **Schellhase, David G., Jr.** *Determination of the Best Items Which Discriminate Between Winning and Losing in the Big Ten.* Purdue University, Master's, 1972.

6129. **Schlekeway, LaVern.** *The Effect of Weight Training on Explosive Power and Leg Strength During a Basketball Season.* South Dakota State University, Master's, 1965.

6130. **Schmiesing, Frederick.** *Personality Traits of Varsity High School Basketball Players.* Mankato State College, Master's, 1969.

6131. **Schmitt, Janet Clare.** *An Investigation of Two Tests Used as a Basis of Selection for Women's Intercollegiate Basketball and Volleyball Teams.* Ohio University, Master's, 1970.

6132. **Schneebeck, Jeri and McDowell, Betsy.** *An Investigation of Visual Skills in Athletics.* Pacific University, Doctorate, 1982.

6133. **Schneeberger, Robert W.** *Experimental Study to Determine the Effect of Practicing Free Throws at Small Baskets.* University of Wisconsin, Master's, 1968.

6134. **Schneider, John E.** *Improving the Basketball Jump Shooting at Brunswick High School.* Ashland College, Master's, 1981.

6135. **Schoolmester, Vernon L.** *A History of Intercollegiate Basketball at South Dakota State University.* South Dakota State University, Master's, 1969.

6136. **Schromm, Richard A.** *Survey of Basketball Scouting Procedures in 96 Selected Large Class Missouri High Schools.* Northeast Missouri State University, Master's, 1958.

6137. **Schriener, Lynn R.** *Comparative Effects of Two Training Programs on Fitness Components of Girls Participating in Interscholastic Basketball.* Northern Illinois University, Master's, 1977.

6138. **Schultz, Robert L.** *A Study of the Use of the Fast Break in Basketball.* University of Iowa, Master's, 1951.

6139. **Schwan, Kristen.** *The Academic Preparation of the 1983–1984 High School Basketball Coaches in Minnesota, North Dakota, and Oregon.* University of Oregon, Master's, 1983.

6140. **Schwomeyer, Herbert Frederic.** *A History of Indiana High School Basketball.* Indiana University at Bloomington, Doctorate, 1970.

6141. **Scobell, Elizabeth H.** *West Virginia State College Basketball 1960–61: A Compilation of Reprints of Newspaper Articles.* West Virginia State College, Special librarian project, 1986.

6142. **Scobie, William C.F.** *The Relationship of High School Basketball Teams' Defense to Success in the Seattle Metropolitan League.* University of Washington, Master's, 1966.

6143. **Scoggin, James Steven.** *The Influence of Aubrey Bonham on Basketball Players at Whittier College.* California State Polytechnic University, Pomona, Master's, 1979.

6144. **Scolnick, Anthony.** *An Electrogoniometric and Cinematographic Analysis of the Action of Expert Basketball Jump Shooters.* Springfield College, Doctorate, 1968.

6145. **Scopinich, June Townsend.** *The Effect of Detraining on Cardiorespiratory Endurance in Female High School Basketball Players.* Smith College, Master's, 1971.

6146. **Scott, Charles Howard.** *The Effect of a Pre-Season Conditioning Program on the Endurance of Selected Male Candidates for Interscholastic Basketball Teams, 1961–62.* University of Washington, Master's, 1962.

6147. **Scott, Harold Alfred.** *An Analysis of Fouls and Violations Occurring in 60 Nebraska High School Basketball Games.* University of Nebraska, Master's, 1950.

6148. **Sebold, H.H.** *The Dickinson System of Team Ranking.* Ohio State University, Master's, 1936.

6149. **Seibel, Debra A.** *Maintaining the Girls' Basketball Program.* Ashland College, Master's, 1984.

6150. **Selk, Larry B.** *A Comparison of Different Methods of Free Throwing Practice Among Selected High School Basketball Players in North Dakota and Minnesota With Respect to Accuracy in Games.* University of North Dakota, Master's, 1966.

6151. **Sell, Veryl L.** *Use of Fifteen-Inch Goals in Development of Shooting Accuracy in Basketball (High School).* University of Iowa, Master's, 1963.

6152. **Sellers, Dorothy Gray.** *A Teaching Handbook in Basketball for High School Girls.* Louisiana State University, Master's, 1937.

6153. **Seni, Patricia Ann.** *The Effects of Volleyball, Basketball and Hockey on the Development of Three Components of General Motor Skill.* Pennsylvania State University, Master's, 1962.

6154. **Serfustini, Leonard Thomas.** *The Theoretical Approaches to Learning as Revealed by the Association and Field Psychologists With Their Implications for the Coaching of Intercollegiate Basketball.* State University of New York at Buffalo, Doctorate, 1956.

6155. **Shaeffer, Lynn E.** *The Effect of the Universal Gym Training Program on the Vertical Jumping Ability of a High School Basketball Team.* West Chester State College, Undergraduate research report, 1981.

6156. **Shaner, Armand L.** *Materials for a Filmstrip and Manual on Individual Techniques of Defensive Man-to-Man Play for the Beginning Basketball Coach and Players.* Springfield College, Master's, 1959.

6157. **Shaw, Catherine Fraser.** *Measurement of Motor Skill: A Statistical Study of Basketball Testing.* Smith College, Master's, 1946.

6158. **Shaw, Willie George.** *The Effect of Two Methods of Practice on Basketball Free Throw Shooting.* University of Tennessee, Master's, 1968.

6159. **Sheppard, Roy Wayne.** *A Brief History of Varsity Basketball at Highlands High School From 1958 Through March 1971.* California State University, Sacramento, Master's, 1972.

6160. **Sheridan, Leslie Thomas.** *The Personal and Professional Backgrounds and Roles of General Managers of Professional Baseball, Basketball, and Football.* Pennsylvania State University, Master's, 1984.

6161. **Shiley, Catherine Jonne.** *A Knowledge Test in Basketball for Ninth Grade Girls.* University of Michigan, Master's, 1964.

6162. **Shockley, Sarah Lednum.** *The Effect of the Five Player Basketball Game on Women's Basketball at Western Maryland College.* Western Maryland College, Master's, 1970.

6163. **Shollenberger, Allan E.** *The Effectiveness of Foul Shooting Practice in Relationship to Rated Reaction Under Stress.* East Stroudsburg State College, Master's, 1969.

6164. **Shults, Cathie L.** *A Comparison of Aggression Levels in Men and Women Intercollegiate Basketball Players.* Mankato State University, Master's, 1980.

6165. **Siehl, James William.** *A Study of Possible Relationship Between Scholastic Attainment and Basketball Team Success in a Small Missouri High School.* Northeast Missouri State University, Master's, 1958.

6166. **Sigafoos, Dave.** *Effect of Ankle Wraps on Reducing Injury in Basketball.* Colorado State University, Master's, Date unknown.

6167. **Silverstein, Fay Edith.** *The Effect of Warm-up on the Basketball Throw for Distance.* San Diego State College, Master's, 1969.

6168. **Sim, Lionel.** *A Comparison of the Tactual and Kinesthetic Senses in Good and Poor Basketball Shooters.* Indiana University at Bloomington, Doctorate, 1973.

6169. **Simmons, James Robert.** *The Influence of Goal Height Upon Shooting Accuracy in Basketball.* Tennessee Technological University, Master's, 1968.

6170. **Simmons, Victoria.** *Measurement of Moral Maturity of Female Interscholastic Basketball Players Based on Kohlberg's Cognitive-Development Approach to Moral Judgement.* University of North Carolina at Greensboro, Master's, 1984.

6171. **Simpson, Dallas R.** *Attitudes of Varsity Athletes Toward Physical Activity.* Stephen F. Austin State University, Master's, 1970.

6172. **Simpson, Erwin H.** *A Study of the Effect of Jump Balls in Basketball on the Continuity of the Play, on Fouling, and on Stalling.* University of Iowa, Master's, 1941.

6173. **Sims, Alfred Dean.** *A Comparative Study of the One-Hand and Two-Hand Method of Shooting in Basketball.* Ohio University, Master's, 1952.

6174. **Sims, Willard.** *A History of Boys' Interscholastic Basketball at the Kirksville Senior High School, 1916–1955.* Northeast Missouri State University, Master's, 1955.

6175. **Singer, Robert Norman.** *Massed and Distributed Practice Effects on the Acquisition and Retention of a Novel Basketball Skill.* Ohio State University, Doctorate, 1964.

6176. **Singleton, Ronald W.** *The Effects of Practicing Free Throw Shooting on a Fifteen-Inch Basket as Compared to an Official Eighteen-Inch Basket.* Tennessee Technological University, Master's, 1973.

6177. **Sitter, Leon R.** *A Study of Interscholastic Competition in Basketball in the Elementary Schools of Southern Illinois.* Southern Illinois University, Master's, 1958.

6178. **Skagen, James C.** *Pre-Season Basketball Organization.* Central Washington University, Master's, 1961.

6179. **Slaughter, James.** *Personality Traits as Compared to Performance Areas of Basketball Players in the Southwest Preparatory Conference of the 1977-78 Season.* Southwest Texas State University, Master's, 1978.

6180. **Smith, Barbara A.** *Women's Basketball, 1891-1961.* University of North Carolina, Master's, 1971.

6181. **Smith, Betty.** *The Effect of Anxiety on Shooting Proficiency Among College Women Basketball Players.* South Dakota State University, Master's, 1978.

6182. **Smith, Beverly A.** *An Investigation of the Effectiveness of Two Conditioning Programs in Reducing the Number of Injuries in Women's Intercollegiate Basketball.* Chico State University, Master's, 1964.

6183. **Smith, Brent E.:** *The Relationship of Personality Traits to Ratings of Basketball Officials.* University of Utah, Master's, 1972.

6184. **Smith, Carole Frances.** *Effect of Anxiety Levels of Women Intercollegiate Basketball Players on Their Performance in a Laboratory Setting and a Game Situation.* Texas Woman's University, Doctorate, 1973.

6185. **Smith, Carroll Hayden.** *Analysis of Offensive and Defensive Efficiency to Winning High School Basketball Games.* University of Tennessee, Master's, 1972.

6186. **Smith, Daniel Elon.** *Evaluation of an Imagery Training Program With Intercollegiate Basketball Players.* University of Illinois, Doctorate, 1986.

6187. **Smith, Everest Paul.** *The Effects of a Progressive Weight Training Program on Competitive Basketball Rebounding and on the Tibial Tuberosity of Collegiate Basketball Players.* Michigan State University, Master's, 1963.

6188. **Smith, Flavius J.** *The Prediction of Basketball Ability Through an Analysis of Selected Measures of Structure and Strength.* George Peabody College for Teachers, Doctorate, 1962.

6189. **Smith, Gary.** *Factors Which Influence the Likelihood of Extra Practice on a Novel Basketball Skill.* Herbert H. Lehman College, Master's, 1975.

6190. **Smith, Harlan King.** *A Study of Football and Basketball Officials Associations Serving Interscholastic Athletics.* University of Texas at Austin, Master's, 1951.

6191. **Smith, Hubert H.** *Administration and Educational Values of a District Basketball Tournament.* Columbia University, Doctorate, 1926.

6192. **Smith, John.** *Effects of Team Participation on the Personality of High School Freshmen Basketball Players.* Montclair State College, Master's, 1972.

6193. **Smith, L.C.** *A Study of the Objectives in Archery and Basketball.* Stanford University, Master's, 1938.

6194. **Smith, Marily Elaine.** *Attributional Control Processes in the Player-Coach Interaction.* University of Oregon, Master's, 1984.

6195. **Smith, Ralph Welby.** *The Progressive Preseason, Competitive and Postseason Changes in Selected Physical Fitness Characteristics of Eleven Wheelchair Basketball Players.* University of Illinois, Master's, 1967.

6196. **Smith, Wilbur.** *A Research of Basketball Programs and Philosophies as a Guide for Inexperienced Teacher-Coaches.* Chico State College, Master's, 1970.

6197. **Smithson, Alton Gene.** *Comparative and Mechanical Analysis of the Jump Shot by Use of Cinematography.* Indiana State Teachers College, Master's, 1963.

6198. **Sneddon, Russell Clyde, Jr.** *The Teaching and Coaching Contribution of Vadal Peterson.* University of Utah, Master's, 1963.

6199. **Sneller, Robert M.** *A Study of Basketball Coaching Methods in the Areas of Squad Selection and Promotion of Team Unity.* Kansas State College of Pittsburg, Master's, 1957.

6200. **Snouffer, John Irving.** *Major Problems and Suggested Solutions in the Administrative Organization and Design of a Suburban Junior High School Boys' Basketball Program.* Ashland College, Master's, 1980.

6201. **Snowden, Frederick.** *Testing to Determine the Effect of Fatigue on Free Throw Shooting Accuracy of High School Varsity Basketball Players.* Wayne State University, Master's, 1965.

6202. **Snyder, John Jay.** *An Experiment Involving Proficiency in Performing Four Selected Physical Skills as a Basis for Predicting Basketball Playing Ability.* University of Washington, Master's, 1964.

6203. **Snyder, Karen.** *Vertical Jumping Ability in Female Basketball Players.* West Chester State College, Master's, 1969.

6204. **Snyder, Ray.** *The Effects of the Use of a Backboard Visual Aid on Basketball Shooting Accuracy.* Pennsylvania State University, Master's, 1967.

6205. **Somerville, Thomas Robert.** *A History of the National Association of Basketball Coaches of the United States.* Ohio State University, Doctorate, 1981.

6206. **Sonstoem, Robert J.** *An Investigation of the Offensive Aspects of Basketball.* Springfield College, Master's, 1957.

6207. **Sorg, L.E.** *Albuminuria in Basketball Men.* Springfield College, Master's, 1916.

6208. **Souder, Donald E., Jr.** *A Selection of Desirable Reference Materials on the Science or Art of Coaching Four Sports: Football, Basketball, Baseball, and Track.* Ohio University, Master's, 1949.

6209. **Spear, Frank Allen.** *Effect of Basketball on Scholarship in High School.* George Peabody College, Master's, 1933.

6210. **Spear, Karl E.** *The Effect of Distance and Angle on Basketball Goal Shooting Accuracy.* Kansas University, Master's, 1951.

6211. **Speck, Margaret Anne.** *The Effects of a Stress Management Program on the Anxiety Levels and Free Throw Shooting of Moderately Skilled Female Basketball Players.* University of California, San Diego, Master's, 1986.

6212. **Spencer, Henry.** *Rebound Characteristics of Shots Attempted by Left Handed and Right Handed Shooters.* West Chester State College, Master's, Date unknown.

6213. **Spencer, William L.** *A Comparison of Personality Traits Between Participants and Discontinued Participants in High School Basketball.* Marshall University, Master's, 1975.

6214. **Spicer, Patricia L.** *A Comparison of Self-Concept of Full Scholarship and Non-Scholarship Freshmen Women Intercollegiate Basketball Players.* Western Illinois University, Master's, 1982.

6215. **Spielman, Jeff.** *The Influence of Isotonic and Isokinetic (Leaper) Weight Training on Vertical Jumping Proficiency.* South Dakota State University, Master's, 1978.

6216. **Spika, Daniel J.** *Effect of Type of Foul, Foul Location, and Basketball Officiating on Varsity Team Performance.* University of Wisconsin, Master's, 1957.

6217. **Spink, Kevin Stirling.** *Attribution and Athletics.* University of Western Ontario, Master's, 1977.

6218. **Spinner, Ellen.** *The Personality Differences Between Field Hockey Players and Basketball Players.* Smith College, Master's, 1972.

6219. **Spitz, Donald Andrew.** *Developing a Man for Man Defense.* University of Texas at Austin, Master's, 1959.

6220. **Splinter, Kenneth W. and Rickman, John V.** *A Public Survey of Athletic Eyewear.* Pacific University, College of Optometry, Doctorate, 1984.

6221. **Spotts, Gloria Jean.** *The Construction of Tests for Measuring Girls' Ability to Dribble, Shoot, and Recover the Rebound of a Basketball.* University of Colorado, Master's, 1953.

6222. **Sprenger, Joanne Govier.** *A Study of the Changes Occurring in the Basketball Throw for Women Following a Weight Training Program.* University of North Dakota, Master's, 1966.

6223. **Squibb, Dennis Duane.** *Evaluation of Basketball Player Combinations by Use of the Offensive and Defensive Efficiency Rating System.* South Dakota State University, Master's, 1971.

6224. **Staheli, Wendell Kent.** *Effect of Varied Music Intensity on Basketball Foul Shooting.* Utah State University, Master's, 1963.

6225. **Stahle, Leo H.** *The Relationship of Playing Ability and Knowledge of the Rules and Play Situations in Boys' Basketball.* University of Iowa, Master's, 1948.

6226. **Stai, Harry A.** *The Effect of an In-Season Weight Training Program on Selected Basketball Skills.* University of Wisconsin, Master's, 1968.

6227. **Stallard, Mary Louise.** *Female Intercollegiate Basketball Players' Perception of Their Coaches.* University of Utah, Doctorate, 1974.

6228. **Stallcup, William Clyde.** *A Study of the Offensive System of Team Play in Basketball.* Louisiana State University, Master's, 1937.

6229. **Stallings, Martha Jeanne.** *The Development of an Instructional Motion Picture to Be Utilized as an Aid in Teaching Individuals to Officiate Basketball for Girls or Women.* Texas Woman's University, Master's, 1961.

6230. **Stannard, Dennis R.** *The Effects of a Holiday Lay-off Period Upon the La Crosse State University 1966 Freshman Basketball Team.* University of Wisconsin–La Crosse, Master's, 1967.

6231. **Stanton, Wesley Morgan.** *A Study of Certain Factors Associated With Individual and Team Performance in Collegiate Basketball.* Boston University, Master's, 1947.

6232. **Staples, Lionel.** *A Comparison of the Effects of Binocular Vision and Monocular Vision on Accuracy in Basketball Shooting.* Springfield College, Master's, 1971.

6233. **Stauffer, Gordon Carl.** *An Investigation of the Effects of Conditioning on the Ballistocardiogram of Varsity Basketball Players.* Michigan State University, Master's, 1955.

6234. **Stautz, Daniel Frederick.** *A History of Men's Basketball in the Seattle Area of the Pacific Northwest Association of the Amateur Athletic Union.* University of Washington, Master's, 1966.

6235. **Steigelman, Owen.** *An Investigation of the Relationship of Lateral Dominance to Selected Basketball Skills of Junior High School Girls.* Smith College, Master's, 1973.

6236. **Steward, Lawrence James.** *A Comparison of Three Basketball Skill Tests and Two Innate Capacity Tests.* Boston University, Master's, 1953.

6237. **Stewart, Larry.** *A Comparative Study Measuring the Psychological Make-up Among Groups of Basketball Players and Coaches.* Western Washington State College, Master's, 1971.

6238. **Stewart, Ralph Edward.** *Origin and Development of Intramural Sports for Men at the University of Missouri.* University of Missouri, Master's, 1964.

6239. **Stinar, Raymond Andrew.** *The Effects of Modified and Regulation Basketball Equipment on the Shooting Ability of Nine-to-Twelve-Year-Old Children.* University of Maryland, Doctorate, 1981.

6240. **Stine, C. Douglas and Arterburn, Michael R.** *Vision and Sports.* Pacific University, College of Optometry, Doctorate, 1981.

6241. **Stockdale, James E.** *The Relationship of Seven Elements in Basketball to Success in Winning.* University of Tennessee, Master's, 1955.

6242. **Stockton, Gerald Ethan.** *The Relationship of Four Time Schedules to the Development of Selected Basketball Skills.* University of Utah, Doctorate, 1970.

6243. **Stockton, James John.** *A Study of Home Court Advantages in College Basketball.* University of Arkansas, Master's, 1980.

6244. **Stockton, William Turner.** *The History of Basketball in the Mountain States Athletic Conference.* Eastern New Mexico University, Master's, 1958.

6245. **Stofko, Henry.** *The Effect of the Arch Builder on Accuracy While Shooting the Jump Shot.* West Chester State College, Master's, 1971.

6246. **Stone, Thomas E.** *The Effect of Mental Practice and Film Viewing on the Basketball Jump Shot.* Mankato State College, Master's, 1967.

6247. **Stoppels, Paul J.** *A Comparison of the Effectiveness of Non-Visual and Visual Methods of Practicing Free-Throw Shooting in Basketball.* University of Iowa, Master's, 1957.

6248. **Stork, Brenda A.** *A Comparison of the Changes in Physical Performance of Ball-Handling Skills of Girls in Basketball and Fitness Classes.* California State University, Sacramento, Master's, 1967.

6249. **Stotts, James E.** *Height as Related to the Success of Basketball Players.* University of Kansas, Master's, 1967.

6250. **Strain, David.** *Predicting Future High School Basketball Player Success as Measured by Estimated Varsity Game Point Production From Individual Sophomore Game Statistics.* South Dakota State University, Master's, 1969.

6251. **Strausberger, Janet B.** *Women's Basketball Rule Infringements in Seasonal and National Tournament Play.* University of North Carolina, Master's, 1972.

6252. **Strecker, Gerald D.** *The Effect of Major Varsity Athletic Participation on Academic Achievement at Fort Hays Kansas State College.* Fort Hays Kansas State College, Master's, 1964.

6253. **Strickland, Samuel P., Jr.** *A Survey of Thirty-Five Massachusetts High School Gymnasiums for Hazards in Basketball Under Playing Conditions.* Boston University, Master's, 1949.

6254. **Strike, Mary Sheila.** *Role Models and Females in Athletics: Selected Case Studies.* University of Oregon, Master's, 1984.

6255. **Stroede, Dennis J.** *The History and Development of Basketball Rule Changes in the United States From 1891 to 1954.* University of Wisconsin, Master's, 1953.

6256. **Strom, Jerry A.** *A Statistical Analysis of Home and Away Game Performance of Male College Basketball Teams—The Big Ten Conference, 1980–1981 Season.* Western Illinois University, Doctorate, 1981.

6257. **Strommen, Steven Terence.** *Offensive and Defensive Styles of Basketball in Minnesota's Lake Conference High Schools.* San Diego State University, Master's, 1970.

6258. **Stroup, Francis E.** *Relationship Between Measurements of the Field of Motion Perception and Basketball Ability in College Men.* University of Southern California, Doctorate, 1955.

6259. **Stuart, Helen B.** *A Study of Girls' Interscholastic Basketball in Arkansas.* University of North Carolina, Master's, 1950.

6260. **Stuart, Rubard A.** *The Relevance of Successful Coaching Psychology to Secondary Classroom Teaching.* Glassboro State College, Master's, 1980.

6261. **Stubbs, Helen Carol.** *An Exploratory Study in Girls' Basketball Relative to the Measurement of Ball Handling Ability.* University of Tennessee, Master's, 1968.

6262. **Stucker, Darryl Gene.** *A Survey of Techniques of Shooting Free Throws.* California State University, Long Beach, Master's, 1973.

6263. **Stutsman, J.D.** *A Study of Girls Basketball in Kansas.* Kansas State Teachers College, Master's, 1938.

6264. **Sudduth, Dolon.** *A Summary of Essentials from Selected Bibliographies on Teaching Basketball.* George Peabody College, Master's, 1933.

6265. **Sullivan, David M.** *The Development and Evaluation of a Weight Training Program to Improve Basic Skills in Basketball.* Western Maryland College, Master's, 1968.

6266. **Sullivan, Kenneth George.** *An Evaluation of the Administration of Basketball Officiating in the United States.* Springfield College, Master's, 1947.

6267. **Sunderlin, Jeffrey Clark.** *The Relationship of Biorhythms to Selected Aspects of Basketball Performance.* Illinois State University, Master's, 1977.

6268. **Suran, Cade.** *Current Trends in Basketball Coaching.* Fort Hays State College, Master's, 1950.

6269. **Swalgin, Kenneth Lee.** *A Computer Assisted Quantitative Analysis and Evaluation System of Individual Basketball Performance by Position of Play for Men's Division I College Basketball.* Ohio State University, Doctorate, 1987.

6270. **Swan, Kenneth N.** *The Cinematographic Analysis of High School Performers Shooting the Basketball One-Handed Jump Shot.* Northern Illinois University, Master's, 1964.

6271. **Swanberg, Phillip H.** *The Investigation of Basketball Coaching Techniques Utilized in Meeting Environmental and Personal Situations in Basketball Games in Selected High Schools in the State of Washington.* University of Washington, Master's, 1963.

6272. **Swander, Robert Dean.** *The Effects of Varied Distances and Basket Sizes on Basketball Shooting Ability.* Indiana University, Master's, 1969.

6273. **Swartz, Jack Hazen.** *The First Years of Varsity Basketball at Chico State College.* Chico State College, Master's, 1960.

6274. **Swartzendruber, Lowell.** *A Comparison of Physical and Mental-Physical Practice on the Performance of Basketball Shooting.* Pennsylvania State University, Master's, 1965.

6275. **Sweet, Dyer N.** *A Study to Determine the Factors That Affect the Accuracy of Shooting Set and Running Set Shots in Basketball.* University of Michigan, Master's, 1938.

6276. **Sweet, Van.** *The Value of Fundamentals and Fundamental Drills to the Coaching of Basketball.* University of the Pacific, Master's, 1948.

6277. **Switzer, John L.** *A History of Inter-Collegiate Basketball at Wayne State University.* Wayne State University, Master's, 1968.

6278. **Szymanski, Frank A.** *A Cinematographical Analysis of Professional Basketball Players.* University of Maryland, Master's, 1966.

6279. **Takacs, Robert F.** *A Comparison of the Effects of Two Methods of Practice on Basketball Free Throw Shooting.* Arkansas State University, Master's, 1965.

6280. **Tangen, Elnar.** *Methods of Teaching Reasoning Skills in Basketball.* University of Wisconsin, Master's, 1935.

6281. **Tao, Donald Te-Yeuh.** *An Analysis of Offensive and Defensive Team Play of Basketball in the United States.* University of Iowa, Master's, 1950.

6282. **Taylor, Carl Leslie.** *A Study of Statistics for Eight Returning Basketball Lettermen at Austin Peay State University.* Austin Peay State University, Master's, 1969.

6283. **Taylor, David Warren.** *Differences Between Female and Male Basketball Players as Regards Causal Attributions of Successes and Failures in 1985 Carolina Intercollegiate Athletic Conference.* Winthrop College, Master's, 1985.

6284. **Taylor, John R.** *Specific Factors Which Contribute to Interscholastic Football and Basketball Success in Selected Ohio and Michigan Cities.* Bowling Green State University, Master's, 1956.

6285. **Taylor, John W.** *The Objectives in Intercollegiate Basketball.* Brigham Young University, Master's, 1967.

6286. **Taylor, Richard W.** *Aggressive Responses of High and Low Skilled Basketball Competitors of Two Age Levels.* Springfield College, Doctorate, 1974.

6287. **Taylor, W.J.** *The Relation Between Kinesthetic Judgment and Success in Basketball.* Pennsylvania State College, Master's, 1933.

6288. **Terribile, Rosemary.** *A Basketball Skills Test for College Women.* Pennsylvania State University, Master's, 1971.

6289. **Test, Mary Jean.** *The Basketball Skill Test for Guarding, Dribbling and Shooting.* San Diego State College, Master's, 1969.

6290. **Thanassoulas, George P.** *Dr. James Naismith, 1861–1939, Inventor of Basketball.* Wake Forest University, Master's, 1972.

6291. **Thatcher, John Robert.** *An Analysis of Three Selected Protective Techniques for the Knee.* East Stroudsburg State College, Master's, 1972.

6292. **Thayer, Gerald.** *A Ten Year Analysis of Scoring and Team Success of St. Cloud Varsity Basketball.* St. Cloud State College, Master's, 1963.

6293. **Theige, Howard M.** *The Effects of Basketball Participation on Sportsmanship Attitudes of Selected Seventh-Grade Boys.* Moorhead State College, Master's, 1966.

6294. **Thomas, Earnestine.** *Teaching for Ambidexterity Versus Unilaterality in the Development of Fundamental Basketball Skills in Fifth Grade Athletics.* Texas Woman's University, Master's, 1970.

6295. **Thomas, Jerry D.** *An Experimental Study of the Effectiveness of Instructional Television as a Supplement to Conventional Instruction in the Teaching of Free Throw Shooting.* University of Wisconsin–La Crosse, Master's, 1968.

6296. **Thomas, Laverne R.** *The Bases of the Distribution of the District B Basketball Tournaments of South Dakota for 1948 and 1949.* University of South Dakota, Master's, 1949.

6297. **Thomassen, Wesley Hal.** *The Life and Service of Elnar Nielsen.* University of Utah, Master's, 1958.

6298. **Thompson, Carol Ann.** *The Development of Girls' Interscholastic Basketball in Ohio, 1940–1976.* Ohio State University, Doctorate, 1977.

6299. **Thompson, Charles Herbert.** *The History of the National Basketball Tournaments for Black High Schools.* Louisiana State University, Doctorate, 1980.

6300. **Thompson, George Logan, Jr.** *A Survey of County Basketball Tournaments in North Carolina.* University of North Carolina, Master's, 1948.

6301. **Thompson, Robert J.** *The Relationship to Kinesthetic Sense of the Jump Shot in Basketball.* University of Wisconsin–La Crosse, Master's, 1967.

6302. **Thomsen, Theron P.** *An Investigation of the Relative Accuracy of Standardization of Free Throws in Basketball.* University of Iowa, Master's, 1948.

6303. **Thornes, Ann (Brown).** *An Analysis of a Basketball Shooting Test and Its Relation to Other Basketball Skill Tests.* University of Wisconsin, Master's, 1963.

6304. **Thornton, Jack Murray.** *Building and Maintaining Strength and Condition for Basketball Players.* Henderson State Teachers College, Master's, 1964.

6305. **Tibbitts, Huse Norwood.** *The Development and Evaluation of Potential Basketball Ability Variables and Tests.* Springfield College, Master's, 1940.

6306. **Ticcony, George A.** *An Annotated Bibliography of Basketball Literature, 1947–1951.* Springfield College, Master's, 1952.

6307. **Timmermann, J.** *A Study of the Possible Effect of Basketball on the Feet of College Freshman Men.* University of Iowa, Master's, 1939.

6308. **Tippett, Terrell.** *The Choking Phenomenon: The Effect of Stress on Complex Motor Skill Performance of Individuals With Differing Ego-Strengths.* Memphis State University, Master's, 1972.

6309. **Tissaw, Joseph D.** *A Plan for the Purchase and Care of Athletic Equipment for High Schools of Northern Arizona.* Northern Arizona University, Master's, 1957.

6310. **Toien, Per.** *The Effects of Dehydration and/or Fatigue on the Free Throw Shooting Accuracy of Varsity College Basketball Players.* Northeast Missouri State University, Master's, 1982.

6311. **Tomayko, John Robert.** *The Relationship of Psychological Climate to the Performance of Male and Female Intercollegiate Head Basketball Coaches.* University of Pennsylvania, Doctorate, 1982.

6312. **Tomlinson, Stanley Joseph.** *A Comparison of Various Practice Methods Used in Learning to Shoot Free Throws.* Eastern Illinois University, Master's, 1973.

6313. **Toner, Mark Keven.** *The Relationship of Selected Physical Fitness, Skill, and Mood Variables to Success in Female High School Basketball Candidates.* Boston University, Doctorate, 1981.

6314. **Toney, Davis R.** *An Analysis of Selected Factors in the Study of a Freshman Basketball Squad.* Purdue University, Master's, 1961.

6315. **Toohey, Dawn Margaret.** *Basketball: Its Dramatic Ritual, Ceremonies, and Social Function.* Ohio State University, Doctorate, 1975.

6316. **Tooze, Gerald Eldridge.** *A Survey of Current Rating Practices Used by Basketball Officials Associations in Selected Areas of the United States.* San Diego State College, Master's, 1963.

6317. **Torrey, Lynette Imo.** *An Analysis of Selected Factors of Basketball Dribbling Ability in Women.* University of Arizona, Master's, 1973.

6318. **Tracy, S.W.** *A Comparative Analysis of the Individual Fundamental Skills of Basketball.* New York University, Master's, 1940.

6319. **Trefilek, Thomas Joseph.** *Behavioral Analysis Study on Coach Ray Meyer of DePaul University.* George Williams College, Master's, 1980.

6320. **Treglown, Bill M.** *The Relationship of Elbow Extension Strength, Wrist Flexion Strength, and Grip Strength to Basketball Set Shooting Accuracy in Selected Intercollegiate Basketball Participants.* Chico State College, Master's, 1967.

6321. **Treu, Lawrence Leo.** *A Survey to Determine the Duties of a Supervisor of Basketball Officials.* University of Utah, Doctorate, 1974.

6322. **Truesdale, John C.** *Measurement of Athletic Intelligence.* University of Iowa, Master's, 1953.

6323. **Trujstad, Grant M.** *A Comparison of Personalities of Lake Conference Basketball Players for the Year 1970–71.* Bemidji State College, Master's, 1973.

6324. **Trumbo, James K.** *The Personality of Basketball Officials.* West Chester State College, Undergraduate research report, 1980.

6325. **Tubbs, Jeffrey Lynn.** *A Comprehensive Manual of Basketball Statistics.* Middle Tennessee State University, Doctorate, 1982.

6326. **Turnbull, Carol Ann.** *A Coaching Manual for Women's Competitive Basketball.* University of North Carolina, Master's, 1971.

6327. **Turnbull, William Ivan.** *Construction of a Basketball Official's Test Presented by Videotape.* University of North Carolina, Master's, 1974.

6328. **Turner, Edward Thomas.** *The Effects of Viewing College Football, Basketball and Wrestling on the Elicited Aggressive Responses of Male Spectators.* University of Maryland, Doctorate, 1968.

6329. **Turpin, Kathy J.** *The Role of the Family in the Socialization of Female College Basketball Players.* Western Illinois University, Master's, 1981.

6330. **Tylka, Dale.** *The Relationship of Basketball Skill Ability as Compared to Physical Education Grade Point Average and Overall Grade Point Averages of 6th and 7th Grade Boys at Woodside Elementary School.* University of North Dakota, Master's, 1971.

6331. **Uhrlaub, Ernest A.** *A Study of the Amount of Activity of High School Players in the Game of Basketball.* University of Kansas, Master's, 1940.

6332. **Umbles, Lee R., Jr.** *Developing and Utilizing the Ability of the Small Player to Play Consistent Winning Basketball.* George Williams College, Master's, 1972.

6333. **Umfress, Lynda Sue.** *The Reliability and Validity of a Basketball Skills Battery for Secondary Girls.* Eastern Kentucky University, Master's, 1977.

6334. **Ummus, David L.** *An Attempt to Validate a Developed Basketball Skill Test Battery.* University of Wisconsin–La Crosse, Master's, 1967.

6335. **Urlaub, E.A.** *A Study of the Amount of Activity of High School Players in the Game of Basketball.* Kansas University, Master's, 1940.

6336. **Valenti, Joseph.** *A Survey of Completeness and Methods of Recording Data in Basketball Scouting Reports.* Western Illinois University, Master's, 1966.

6337. **Valenti, Paul Bartholomew.** *History of Basketball at Oregon State College From 1928 Through 1949.* Oregon State University, Master's, 1957.

6338. **Valliere, Donald D.** *A Study to Determine the Advantage of the Home Court in Basketball.* University of Kansas, Master's, 1950.

6339. **Vancisin, Joe.** *The Relation of Quickness and Jump Spring to Basketball Success.* University of Minnesota, Master's, 1956.

6340. **Vander Velden, Lee R.** *Relationships Among Member, Team, and Situational Variables and Basketball Team Success: A Social-Psychological Inquiry.* University of Wisconsin, Doctorate, 1972.

6341. **Van Dresser, Doris.** *A Comparison Study of Two Types of Shooting Skills in Girls Basketball: the Underhand Shot and the Chest Shot.* University of Wisconsin–La Crosse, Master's, 1968.

6342. **Van Eman, Lanny E.** *Pressure Basketball and the Speed Game.* Western Kentucky University, Master's, 1979.

6343. **Van Housen, Constance Jayne.** *A Comparative Study of Passing Interaction in Relation to Sociometric Standing and Perceiving Skill Between Male and Female Collegiate Varsity Basketball Players.* East Stroudsburg State College, Master's, 1973.

6344. **Van Kyke, Clyde Stacy.** *Bilateral Transfer of Training in Basketball Dribbling.* University of Maryland, Master's, 1970.

6345. **Van Tassel, Anna M.** *A Written Self-Instructional Program for Learning the Lay-up Shot in Basketball.* Southern Illinois University, Master's, 1969.

6346. **Varichak, Richard Warren.** *An Investigation of the Relationship Between Certain Fundamental Physical Abilities and Ball Handling Skill in Basketball and Volleyball.* University of Texas, Master's, 1960.

6347. **Vennari, Paul J.** *Interscholastic Basketball Officiating.* West Virginia University, Master's, 1954.

6348. **Vennochi, Julius J.** *A Battery of Tests to Compare the Ability in Basketball of Selected Boys in Junior High School and a Boy's Club.* Boston University, Master's, 1956.

6349. **Vergamini, Carl.** *A Study of the Effects of the Twelve-Foot Free-Throw Lane Upon College Basketball.* University of Iowa, Master's, 1958.

6350. **Vinson, Joseph J.** *A Comparison of Accuracy in Sixth and Seventh Grade Girls Using the One Hand Set Shot Versus the Two Hand Set Shot in Basketball.* Montana State University, Master's, 1971.

6351. **Viramontes, James Raymond.** *A Grading System for Varsity Basketball Players.* University of Texas, Master's, 1953.

6352. **Vizard, Thomas Charles.** *The Effects of Increased Emotional Pressure on Foul Shooting Performance in College and High School Basketball Tournaments.* University of Massachusetts, Master's, 1967.

6353. **Voege, Robert A.** *A Comparison of Norms Among Elite Male and Female Basketball Coaches at Division I and Division III Colleges With Regard to the Recruitment of Student-Athletes.* University of Pittsburgh, Doctorate, 1982.

6354. **Vogel, Robert J.** *Development of an Off-Season Weight Training Program for Men's Basketball for Northern State College.* Northeastern State University, Master's, 1986.

6355. **Vorland, Dean H.** *A Comparison of Practice Methods in Free Throw Shooting.* University of North Dakota, Master's, 1972.

6356. **Wachob, R.** *Survey of the Methods and Contents of Basketball Teaching.* New York University, Master's, 1931.

6357. **Wagner, Cloyd George, Jr.** *The Effects of Different Lengths of Practice on the Learning of Certain Basketball Skills Among Junior High School Boys.* Temple University, Master's, 1962.

6358. **Wahlgren, Dennis A.** *A Comparison of Practice Plans and Team Statistics as Factors of Success in NAIA Basketball.* University of Kansas, Master's, 1977.

6359. **Wakefield, Markham Churr.** *A Study of Mortality Among Men Who Have Played in the Indiana High School State Final Basketball Tournaments.* Indiana University, Doctorate, 1944.

6360. **Walbert, Earl F.** *The Effects of Mixed Lateral Dominance on Basketball Foul Shooting.* West Chester State College, Master's, 1970.

6361. **Walker, Penny.** *A Cinematographic Comparison of the Body Mechanics of the Basketball Jump Shot.* University of Toledo, Master's, 1974.

6362. **Walker, Robert J.** *An Investigation of Points Scored, Shooting Accuracy, and Turnovers in Terms of Possession Time for College Basketball Games.* East Tennessee State University, Master's, 1973.

6363. **Walker, Robert Louis.** *An Investigation of the Athletic Training Practice of Selected Varsity Coaches in Utah.* University of Utah, Master's, 1968.

6364. **Walker, Thomas Vaughn.** *Aggression in Sport: A Study of Fouling in University Basketball.* Oregon State University, Doctorate, 1979.

6365. **Wall, Bobby Russell.** *Influence of Women's Intercollegiate Basketball Competition on Anxiety and Aggression.* University of Kentucky, Master's, 1982.

6366. **Wallace, James Franklin.** *The Influence of Relaxation Upon Shooting Percentages in Basketball.* California State University, Long Beach, Master's, 1971.

6367. **Wallace, Kathey.** *The Relationship of Personality and Motivation Factors to Free Throw Performance.* Northeast Missouri State University, Master's, 1981.

6368. **Wallace, Robert, Jr.** *The Three Second Rule in High School Basketball.* Northern Illinois University, Master's, 1961.

6369. **Walley, Colleen Paige.** *A Comparative Study of the Values of Female and Male Intercollegiate Basketball Players at Central Washington State College.* Central Washington State College, Master's, 1976.

6370. **Wallis, John D.** *Comparison of the Effects of Isotonics and Isometric Exercises on the Jump-Reach Ability of Basketball Players.* East Tennessee State University, Master's, 1963.

6371. **Walor, John.** *A Time Study of the Activity During a Basketball Game.* Wichita State University, Master's, 1962.

6372. **Walsh, Herschel.** *An Investigation of the Effects of Practice With a Weighted Basketball on the Development of Selected Basketball Skills.* East Tennessee State University, Master's, 1969.

6373. **Walter, Ronald J.** *A Comparison Between Two Selected Evaluative Techniques for Measuring Basketball Skill.* Western Illinois University, Master's, 1968.

6374. **Walters, Betty L.** *Response Accuracy of Female Collegiate Basketball Players in Complex Situations.* Southern Illinois University, Master's, 1978.

6375. **Waltz, Barbara Ann.** *An Analysis of the Improvement in Cardiovascular Efficiency of Junior High School Girls When Using Different Rules of Basketball.* San Diego State College, Master's, 1971.

6376. **Wampler, M. Keith.** *Developing the Young Basketball Player Through Ball Handling.* Ashland College, Master's, 1981.

6377. **Ward, Leroy O.** *The Effect of Wrestling and Basketball Contests Upon the Emotional State of the Coaches.* University of Maryland, Master's, 1970.

6378. **Wardwell, Nancy Weltheimer.** *Rachel E. Bryant: Contributions to Physical Education and Girls' and Women's Sports.* University of Toledo, Doctorate, 1979.

6379. **Warnock, Ronald H.** *A Comparative Analysis Between Two Methods of Executing a Center Jump in Basketball.* Washington State University, Master's, 1960.

6380. **Warren, Beverly J.** *The Relationship Between Self-Concept and Performance on Tests of Skill in Basketball.* Southern Illinois University, Master's, 1971.

6381. **Washburn, L.P.** *Effect of Basketball on Blood Pressure and Albuminuria.* Springfield College, Master's, 1911.

6382. **Wasser, Richard Joseph.** *The Effect of General Basketball Practice on Free Throw Shooting Ability.* California State University, Los Angeles, Master's, 1970.

6383. **Watkins, Mary Frances.** *Development and Use of Game Statistics for Girls' Basketball at Three Rivers, Texas.* University of Texas, Master's, 1966.

6384. **Waugh, Gerald R.** *The Importance of Free Throwing and Personal Fouls in Winning Basketball Games.* University of Kansas, Master's, 1959.

6385. **Wech, Michael J.** *A Self-Instruction Program for Teaching Rules and Concepts of Basketball to Fourth Grade Students.* State University of New York at Buffalo, Master's, 1966.

6386. **Weick, Lucinda Kathryn.** *Achievement Scales in Basketball for College Women.* University of Nebraska, Master's, 1967.

6387. **Weigel, William F.** *The Production of a Film Strip Dealing With the Basic Pattern of the Five Man Figure Eight Offense Used in Basketball.* Florida State University, Master's, 1952.

6388. **Weiner, Helen Jane.** *A Study to Determine the Effect of the Limited and Continuous Dribble in Girls' Basketball on the Number of Fouls or Passes.* Springfield College, Master's, 1953.

6389. **Weishaupt, Heidi M.** *The Effect of Interscholastic Basketball Competition on the Self-Concept of High School Girls.* University of Northern Colorado, Doctorate, 1977.

6390. **Weiss, Bernard E.** *A Comparative Study of the Contents of Basketball Coaching Books Published 1891-1967.* Ohio State University, Master's, 1968.

6391. **Wendedbow, Stephen.** *The Coefficient of Friction of a Basketball Shoe Upon Various Floor Surfaces.* Western Illinois University, Master's, 1977.

6392. **Wermager, Donald V.** *A Comparison in Two Methods of Aiming Basketball Shooting.* Bemidji State College, Master's, 1972.

6393. **Werner, Robert Charles.** *Major Factors That Have Affected the Game of Basketball Since Its Inception.* Central Washington State College, Master's, 1969.

6394. **West, Thomas Lee.** *State Personality Characteristics of Male Basketball Officials at Different Levels of Competition.* Sam Houston State University, Master's, 1980.

6395. **Weston, Arthur John.** *A Study of the Validity of an Objective Test as a Predictor for Selecting a Basketball Team Compared with Pre- and Post-Season Subjective Judgment of Coaches.* University of the Pacific, Master's, 1969.

6396. **Wheaton, Garrett Eugene.** *A Study of the Reactions of Coaches, Athletes and Spectators to Situations Occurring in Football and Basketball Contests.* University of Kansas, Master's, 1966.

6397. **Whitacre, William K.** *Effect of Mental Practice on the Acquisition of a Certain Motor Skill.* Northeast Missouri State University, Master's, 1964.

6398. **White, James A.** *Visual Aids in the Teaching of Basketball.* University of Arizona, Master's, 1946.

6399. **Whitford, Linda Ann.** *The Effect of Interscholastic Competition on Selected Personality Traits of Female High School Basketball Players.* Slippery Rock State College, Master's, Date unknown.

6400. **Widad, Al-Mufti.** *The Effect of the Use of a Selected Incentive Upon Improving Performance of Shooting Free Throws in Basketball.* Southern Illinois University, Master's, 1972.

6401. **Widdoes, Paul J.** *Effects of Alcohol Upon the Basketball Free Throw for Accuracy.* Wayne State University, Master's, 1976.

6402. **Wiegand, Robert L.** *A Comparison of Acquisition of Basketball Dribbling Skills Among Normal and Socially Maladjusted Boys, Ages 12 and 13, Through Use of the Individually Prescribed Instructional System.* Slippery Rock State College, Master's, 1972.

6403. **Wiegman, Fred B.** *An Investigation of the Existing Methods of Approving High School Basketball Officials in the Various States.* University of Michigan, Master's, 1951.

6404. **Wienbergen, Harry J.** *Basketball: A Study of Performance in Four Fundamentals.* University of Wisconsin, Master's, 1936.

6405. **Wierzal, Dennis.** *Comparison Between Two Approaches of Measuring Basketball Ability.* Purdue University, Master's, 1960.

6406. **Wiesner, Betty Anita.** *A Study of the Effect of Playing Official Boys' Rules Basketball and Modified Girls' Rules Basketball on Selected Women Students.* Springfield College, Master's, 1958.

6407. **Wigle, William P.** *The Professional Preparation of Secondary Coaches in the State of Ohio.* Utah State University, Master's, 1970.

6408. **Wiley, Roland L.** *A Pre-Game Warm-Up Procedure Based on Methods Employed by Outstanding College and High School Basketball Coaches.* University of Iowa, Master's, 1958.

6409. **Wilkins, Max L.** *A Survey and Analysis of High School Basketball Rebounding.* University of Wyoming, Master's, 1955.

6410. **Wilkinson, Earl Keith.** *A Survey of the Methods of Organizing State High School Basketball Tournaments.* Mankato State University, Master's, 1955.

6411. **Wilkinson, William Dale.** *The Effect of Playing Time on Free Throw Shooting Accuracy.* University of Illinois, Master's, 1951.

6412. **Willard, S.** *A Comparison of the Bank and Rim Shots and Various Combinations From Selected Shooting Angles for College Students.* Central Washington State College, Master's, 1972.

6413. **Williams, Anita R.** *The Effect of Biological Rhythms Upon Female High School Basketball Players.* Brigham Young University, Master's, 1980.

6414. **Williams, Brent E.** *Effect of Selected Kinds of Music and Music Intensity on Basketball Shooting.* Utah State University, Master's, 1967.

6415. **Williams, Elvins Thomas.** *A Study of Flexibility in Basketball Players.* University of Oregon, Master's, 1950.

6416. **Williams, Jerry T.** *An Investigation of the Effects of Wrist Weights on Basketball Shooting Accuracy.* East Tennessee State University, Master's, 1971.

6417. **Williams, Liburn Lane.** *A Survey of Procedures in the Organization and Administration of Invitational Basketball Tournaments for High School Boys.* Louisiana State University, Master's, 1947.

6418. **Wilson, Allen S.** *Predicting Team Success from a Basketball Skill Test.* University of Massachusetts, Master's, 1967.

6419. **Wilson, Floyd S.** *A Cinematographical Analysis of the Rebounds of an Official Laceless, a Last-Bilt, and a Rubber Basketball From a Glass, a Wooden, and a Steel Backboard.* Springfield College, Master's, 1949.

6420. **Wilson, Gilbert E.** *A Study of the Factors and Results of Effective Team Rebounding in High School Basketball.* University of Iowa, Master's, 1948.

6421. **Wilson, Shirley Annette.** *A Study to Determine the Grade Placement of Basketball for Girls in Georgia.* Springfield College, Master's, 1966.

6422. **Winsor, Gordon C.** *Selection and Assignment of College Basketball Officials.* University of Iowa, Master's, 1958.

6423. **Wissel, Harold Robert.** *The Effects of Three Physical Conditioning Programs for Junior High School Basketball Players.* Springfield College, Doctorate, 1970.

6424. **Wissen, Theodore Donald.** *The Effect of the Use of the Loop Film on Accuracy in Free Throw Shooting.* Northern Illinois University, Master's, 1966.

6425. **Wold, Allan H.** *The Effect of a Systematic Conditioning Program on Body Density and Anthropometry of Varsity High School Basketball Players.* Mankato State University, Master's, 1969.

6426. **Wolfarth, Robert.** *The Role of the Coach, Athletic Director and Officials in High School Basketball Confrontation, Essex County, New Jersey.* Montclair State College, Master's, 1972.

6427. **Wood, Robin Carlton.** *Organized Instruction in Basketball.* Columbia University, Doctorate, 1955.

6428. **Wooden, John Robert.** *Study of the Effect of the Abolition of the Center Jump on the Height of Outstanding College Basketball Players.* Indiana State Teachers College, Master's, 1947.

6429. **Woollumm, C.J.** *The Relationship of Selected Data to Team Success in the Marshall University Basketball Seasons, 1972–76.* Marshall University, Master's, 1977.

6430. **Woudstra, James D.** *The History of Men's Basketball in the Netherlands.* South Dakota State University, Master's, 1981.

6431. **Wright, Deborah.** *A Guide to Recognizing and Dealing With Stress and Burnout in Coaches for the High School Athletic Director.* Virginia Polytechnic Institute and State University, Master's, 1985.

6432. **Wright, Richard Alan.** *Self-Concept and Interpersonal Perception Change in Basketball Teams.* University of Montana, Master's, 1971.

6433. **Wright, Robert L.** *An Experimental Study of Shot Charts as an Aid in Coaching Basketball in Secondary Schools.* Indiana State Teachers College, Master's, 1937.

6434. **Wright, William Tyson, Jr.** *The Effect of Ability and Gender on the Rating of Team Cohesion Within Successful Intercollegiate Basketball Teams.* Pennsylvania State University, Master's, 1981.

6435. **Wyatt, Thomas.** *Social Distance Between Black and White Athletes Participating in Interscholastic Athletics at Integrated High Schools in Durham and Wake Counties.* North Carolina Central University, Master's, 1970.

6436. **Yerles, Magdaleine.** *Social Status and Group Status in High School Basketball Teams.* University of Illinois, Master's, 1973.

6437. **York, Norman.** *A Comparison of Certain Reaction Times of Basketball Players and Non-Athletes Sixteen to Eighteen Years of Age.* University of Oregon, Master's, 1951.

6438. **Young, G.** *The Construction of a Short Battery of Tests to Measure Playing Ability in Women's Basketball.* University of California, Master's, 1950.

6439. **Young, Judith Corbett.** *The Relationships Among Leader Characteristics of Male and Female Basketball Coaches and Team Performance.* University of Maryland, Doctorate, 1981.

6440. **Young, Stephen B.** *The History of Professional Basketball 1946–1979.* Western Illinois University, Master's, 1981.

6441. **Yow, Sandra Kay.** *A Study of the Reasons for Continuing or Not Continuing Post-High School Participation of All-Conference Women Players.* University of North Carolina, Master's, 1974.

6442. **Yukelson, David Paul.** *Group Cohesion in Sport: a Multidimensional Approach.* North Texas State University, Doctorate, 1982.

6443. **Zappa, Ermine Anthony.** *Guidelines to Aid the Coach in the Selection of Interscholastic Basketball Defenses.* California State University, Los Angeles, Master's, 1962.

6444. **Zarnum, Drake.** *Pre-Season and Season Conditioning Programs and Their Relationship to Injuries in Basketball.* Ithaca College, Master's, 1973.

6445. **Zaugg, Maxwell Kay.** *Superstitious Beliefs of Basketball Players.* University of Montana, Master's, 1980.

6446. **Zentner, Rod W.** *The Soft Touch Basketball Training Glove as a Method to Improve Free Throw Accuracy.* University of Wisconsin–La Crosse, Master's, 1973.

6447. **Ziegler, Randolph.** *A Coach's Guide for Selected High School Varsity Basketball Candidates.* Wayne State University, Master's, 1973.

6448. **Ziemer, Gladys L.** *Estimation of the Energy Cost of the Roving Player Position in Women's Basketball.* University of New Mexico, Master's, 1968.

6449. **Zillmer, William J.** *Cardio-Vascular Tests as Measures of Athletic Conditioning in Basketball.* University of Iowa, Master's, 1937.

6450. **Zimmer, William R.** *Comparisons of Selected Personality Traits Between Intramural Basketball Officials and Athletes.* West Virginia University, Master's, 1976.

6451. **Zimmerman, Glen B.** *A Study of the Variabilities of Certain Physiological Tests as They Relate to the Participants in a Five Day Basketball Tournament.* Utah State University, Master's, 1954.

6452. **Zimmerman, Patricia Ann.** *The Relationship of Kinesthesis to High and Low Levels of Basketball Ability Among College Women.* University of Illinois, Master's, 1961.

Index

The index is categorized by the primary topics indicated in the titles of the reference materials. In numerous instances, a specific reference is listed under two or more headings.

5980, 5987, 6045, 6070, 6109, 6110, 6138, 6172, 6185, 6206, 6228, 6257, 6281, 6342, 6379, 6387

passing game, 192, 850, 1039, 1541, 2465, 2478, 2505, 2591, 2683, 3125, 3193, 3198, 3309, 3311, 3322, 3337, 3351, 3352, 3356, 3392, 3402, 3452, 3513, 3832, 3905, 3947, 4248, 4274, 4434, 4520, 4538, 4592, 4610, 4740, 4752, 4800, 4837

post, 101, 350, 434, 495, 641, 815, 817, 1276, 1420, 1615, 1863, 1864, 2079, 2207, 2258, 2265, 2305, 2317, 2333, 2341, 2421, 2426, 2454, 2464, 2496, 2508, 2556, 2586, 2602, 2621, 2622, 2653, 2671, 2690, 2711, 2759, 2770, 2784, 2821, 2837, 2930, 3000, 3058, 3060, 3062, 3080, 3113, 3231, 3245, 3249, 3255, 3288, 3331, 3380, 3383, 3522, 3635, 3697, 3705, 3714, 3722, 3865, 3924, 3984, 4077, 4088, 4107, 4147, 4166, 4193, 4196, 4202, 4223, 4227, 4229, 4230, 4240, 4243, 4256, 4263, 4266, 4326, 4327, 4361, 4373, 4394, 4396, 4410, 4430, 4449, 4456, 4458, 4462, 4469, 4507, 4626, 4642, 4648, 4658, 4660, 4666, 4667, 4674, 4694, 4820

press, 2266, 2419, 2557, 2558, 2583, 2592, 2628, 2705, 2719, 2750, 2805, 2812, 2838, 2848, 2872, 2876, 2922, 2994, 2998, 3025, 3033, 3035, 3045, 3199, 3215, 3217, 3252, 3269, 3283, 3285, 3300, 3308, 3343, 3390, 3410, 3459, 3464, 3487, 3518, 3520, 3888, 4024, 4046, 4111, 4150, 4173, 4189, 4214, 4217, 4218, 4239, 4247, 4262, 4282, 4293, 4340, 4378, 4391, 4405, 4416, 4421, 4431, 4435, 4452, 4479, 4503, 4508, 4551, 4570, 4602, 4603, 4605, 4632, 4659, 4695, 4716, 4727, 4748, 4775, 4818

pressure, 236, 820, 2775, 2859, 2904, 3216, 3510, 3512

shuffle, 191, 198, 199, 374, 1356, 1412, 2691, 2699, 2787, 2789, 2825, 2854, 2946, 2959, 2968, 2974, 2975, 3076, 3113, 3221, 3232, 3289, 3419, 3892, 4064, 4139, 4152, 4192, 4195, 4209, 4213, 4256, 4336, 4337, 4365, 4543, 4694

zone, 323, 408, 538, 805, 1077, 1123, 1191, 1218, 1373, 1484, 1822, 1969, 2164, 2181, 2182, 2216, 2217, 2287, 2310, 2344, 2359, 2407, 2442, 2458, 2467, 2469, 2473, 2493, 2520, 2530, 2532, 2533, 2597, 2603, 2607, 2614, 2625, 2656, 2666, 2668, 2687, 2688, 2712, 2713, 2736, 2745, 2751, 2758, 2776, 2794, 2800, 2806, 2811, 2817, 2822, 2830, 2846, 2851, 2887, 2890, 2897, 2912, 2918, 2923, 2931, 2974, 2980, 2988, 2999, 3003, 3010, 3019, 3022, 3023, 3034, 3093, 3103, 3122, 3130, 3139, 3147, 3148, 3172, 3203, 3204, 3212, 3219, 3263, 3270, 3273, 3287, 3295, 3297, 3321, 3335, 3358, 3360, 3376, 3382, 3396, 3402, 3415, 3424, 3437, 3438, 3444, 3459, 3460, 3490, 3495, 3501, 3528, 3682, 3731, 3737, 3779, 3811, 3830, 3888, 3945, 3946, 3962, 4011, 4028, 4032, 4041, 4050, 4056, 4065, 4070, 4087, 4091, 4094, 4104, 4108, 4109, 4130, 4163, 4178, 4183, 4200, 4251, 4275, 4281, 4286, 4300, 4307, 4309, 4320, 4331, 4340, 4349, 4351, 4355, 4390, 4396, 4401, 4410, 4430, 4437, 4444, 4445, 4482, 4504, 4513, 4516, 4526, 4533, 4568, 4572, 4579, 4638, 4656, 4675, 4684, 4685, 4689, 4698, 4709, 4715, 4769, 4783, 4806, 4816, 4820, 4836

Offensive theory, 66, 357, 2700

Officials and officiating, 4, 195, 202, 380, 603, 901, 908, 940, 980, 989, 1081, 1270, 1315, 1444, 1478, 1499, 1535, 1681, 1700, 1707, 1724, 1735, 1823, 1842, 1857, 2083, 2099, 2125, 2126, 2502, 2744, 3083, 3098, 3687, 3753, 3760, 3768, 3773, 3796, 3809, 3813, 3821, 3852, 3860, 3878, 3881, 3898, 4129, 4422, 4617, 4947, 4953, 4959, 4989, 5012, 5018, 5032, 5044, 5045, 5049, 5090, 5108, 5115, 5150, 5172, 5210, 5227, 5282, 5305, 5341, 5342, 5351, 5399, 5447, 5526, 5585, 5603, 5616, 5621, 5624, 5625, 5632, 5713, 5783, 5791, 5808, 5815, 5829, 5880, 5895, 5898, 5910, 5919, 5921, 5923, 5926, 5930, 5955, 5998, 6043, 6103, 6108, 6113, 6183, 6190, 6216, 6229, 6266, 6316, 6321, 6324, 6327, 6347, 6394, 6403, 6422, 6450

Ohio State University, 640

Olympics, 139, 230, 506, 507, 508, 559, 611, 1199, 1260, 1332, 1395, 1827, 3626, 3634, 6084

Oregon, University of, 604

Pitino, Rick, 1065, 1115, 4870
Pittsburgh, University of, 992
Politics and basketball, 1333, 1334, 2073
Portland Trailblazers, 153, 275, 287, 522, 840, 885, 1211
Practice organization, 4929, 5330, 5465, 5548, 5639, 5643, 5932, 5939, 5941, 6051, 6078, 6115, 6175, 6189, 6242, 6357
Professional basketball, 57, 68, 201, 279, 311, 313, 314, 342, 349, 381, 485, 552, 588, 595, 596, 597, 598, 605, 606, 612, 614, 617, 618, 667, 680, 709, 715, 716, 717, 718, 726, 743, 783, 793, 800, 962, 963, 967, 972, 990, 991, 1000, 1015, 1016, 1017, 1028, 1043, 1070, 1072, 1122, 1141, 1150, 1170, 1173, 1175, 1176, 1177, 1178, 1179, 1180, 1182, 1216, 1227, 1257, 1258, 1264, 1265, 1266, 1267, 1292, 1298, 1352, 1380, 1381, 1382, 1383, 1384, 1391, 1418, 1422, 1542, 1903, 3222, 5311, 5575, 5637, 5971, 6160, 6278, 6440
Psychological factors and tests, 5086, 5100, 5685, 6237, 6311, 6340
Publications, commercial, 4893, 4894, 4895, 4896, 4897, 4898, 4899, 4900, 4901, 4902, 4903, 4904, 4905, 4906
Purdue University, 921

Q

Quickness, 5013, 5209, 5220, 5283, 5391, 5402, 5480, 5624, 5785, 5879, 5909, 6020, 6339, 6374, 6437. *See also* Conditioning, motor learning

R

Ramsay, Jack, 1092, 1093, 1094, 1281, 3880, 3901, 3930, 3945, 3963, 3991, 4013, 4122, 4177, 4205, 4329, 4755
Reaction time. *See* Conditioning, motor learning
Rebounding, 4946, 5075, 5091, 5096, 5135, 5208, 5270, 5312, 5314, 5380, 5387, 5481, 5495, 5576, 5613, 5697, 5759, 5963, 5995, 6009, 6187, 6212, 6221, 6409, 6420
Recruiting, 1139, 4454, 4455, 4704, 4789, 5030, 5065, 5165, 5316, 5445, 5597, 5607, 5735, 5872, 5933, 6071, 6353
Reed, Willis, 438, 439, 1048, 1107, 1108
Robertson, Oscar (Big "O"), 146, 1132, 1133
Rules, 6, 79, 149, 195, 263, 635, 661, 1078, 1159, 1231, 1244, 1445, 1485, 1487, 1489, 1491, 1492, 1493, 1497, 1498, 1500, 1502, 1524, 1530, 1546, 1576, 1592, 1627, 1644, 1672, 1677, 1699, 1714, 1735, 1767, 1773, 1797, 1801, 1816, 1837, 1839, 1844, 1845, 1849, 1850, 1854, 1864, 1870, 1871, 1914, 1981, 1986, 2014, 2098, 2117, 2146, 2155, 2300, 2319, 2321, 2366, 2369, 2507, 2538, 2633, 3558, 3561, 3569, 3579, 3580, 3588, 3593, 3604, 3605, 3613, 3620, 3631, 3633, 3636, 3637, 3642, 3645, 3652, 3658, 3674, 3685, 3686, 3692, 3713, 3727, 3746, 3762, 3769, 3780, 3783, 3796, 3814, 3815, 3826, 3827, 3853, 3870, 3906, 3929, 3936, 3951, 4276, 5014, 5024, 5037, 5041, 5111, 5119, 5130, 5178, 5231, 5259, 5325, 5347, 5348, 5363, 5659, 5748, 5775, 5810, 5873, 5885, 5933, 5956, 5963, 5983, 6058, 6106, 6225, 6251, 6255, 6349, 6368, 6375, 6406
Rupp, Adolph F., 249, 525, 744, 1160, 1161, 1162, 1163, 1846, 2139, 2173, 2286, 2360, 2639, 3784, 3797, 3848, 3882, 3902, 3964

S

Safety, 5010, 6253
Sampson, Ralph, 750
San Antonio Spurs, 933
San Diego Clippers, 934
San Francisco Warriors, 1002
Scandals, basketball, 642, 788, 960, 1143, 1362, 3822, 6082
Scheduling, 1652
Scholastic achievement, 5265, 5284, 6165, 6209, 6252, 6330

V

Valvano, Jim, 1339
Van Arsdale, Tom and Dick, 1340
Vanderbilt University, 969
Versace, Dick, 1272, 1349, 1350, 3516
Vertical jumping, 4914, 4933, 4934, 4957, 5042, 5069, 5167, 5198, 5226, 5300, 5340,
    5345, 5379, 5381, 5489, 5504, 5529, 5551, 5553, 5557, 5562, 5566, 5660, 5752,
    5840, 5844, 5849, 5950, 6041, 6060, 6080, 6093, 6097, 6105, 6155, 6203, 6215, 6370
Villanova University, 995
Violence and sport, 1243, 5534
Virginia, University of, 309, 751, 1336
Vision, 4970, 5061, 5117, 5241, 5260, 5289, 5309, 5349, 5376, 5436, 5554, 5675,
    5814, 5854, 5879, 6065, 6132, 6232, 6240, 6258
Visual and instructional aids, 1964, 2221, 2339, 2831, 3592, 3598, 3627, 3628,
    3629, 3630, 3650, 3678, 3679, 3680, 3681, 3700, 3701, 3702, 3719, 3735, 3736,
    3904, 3905, 3950, 3952, 3953, 3970, 3971, 3972, 3998, 4000, 4001, 4018, 4019,
    4020, 4038, 4061, 4079, 4080, 4131, 4132, 4133, 4158, 4159, 4241, 4367, 4670,
    4842, 4843, 4844, 4845, 4846, 4847, 4849, 4850, 4851, 4852, 4853, 4854, 4855,
    4856, 4857, 4858, 4859, 4860, 4861, 4862, 4863, 4864, 4865, 4866, 4867, 4868,
    4869, 4870, 4871, 4872, 4873, 4874, 4875, 4876, 4877, 4878, 4879, 4880, 4881,
    4882, 4883, 4884, 4885, 4886, 4887, 4888, 4889, 4890, 4891, 4892, 4966, 4978,
    5022, 5046, 5079, 5090, 5093, 5115, 5133, 5175, 5233, 5235, 5247, 5269, 5334,
    5368, 5411, 5443, 5449, 5521, 5592, 5632, 5776, 5837, 5895, 6016, 6065, 6120,
    6144, 6156, 6197, 6229, 6246, 6270, 6278, 6295, 6327, 6361, 6387, 6398, 6424, 6433
Visualization, 4925, 5078, 5992, 6186
Vitale, Dick, 714, 1353, 3240

W

Walton, Bill, 100, 207, 520, 521, 772, 1134, 1211, 1268
Warming up, 4963, 4964, 5171, 5372, 5523, 5644, 5849, 5882, 6167, 6408
Washington Bullets, 936
Webb, Spud, 1236, 1379
Weight training, 4914, 4933, 4934, 4957, 4999, 5003, 5063, 5143, 5153, 5226, 5254,
    5307, 5340, 5345, 5365, 5476, 5501, 5512, 5529, 5611, 5617, 5660, 5669, 5682,
    5828, 5844, 5866, 5891, 5902, 5925, 6018, 6027, 6053, 6054, 6066, 6093, 6129,
    6155, 6187, 6215, 6222, 6226, 6265, 6354
West, Jerry, 775, 1392, 1393
Wheelchair basketball, 1022, 5219, 5692, 5693, 6195
Wilkens, Lenny, 1405
Women's/girls' basketball, 1, 2, 15, 19, 31, 78, 133, 140, 160, 162, 193, 263, 276,
    359, 426, 436, 457, 458, 631, 641, 672, 704, 746, 877, 887, 891, 896, 899, 902,
    1031, 1053, 1078, 1103, 1164, 1197, 1200, 1231, 1254, 1269, 1283, 1307, 1320,
    1323, 1354, 1438, 1443, 1675, 3532, 3567, 3591, 3605, 3620, 3640, 3652, 3711,
    3741, 4502, 4655, 4708, 4915, 4917, 4930, 4938, 4942, 4945, 4955, 4969, 4978,
    4984, 4994, 4995, 4999, 5005, 5019, 5022, 5025, 5027, 5029, 5046, 5059, 5061,
    5071, 5077, 5080, 5090, 5100, 5102, 5104, 5106, 5109, 5115, 5129, 5137, 5144,
    5148, 5151, 5155, 5163, 5169, 5171, 5181, 5185, 5188, 5190, 5191, 5195, 5201,
    5205, 5207, 5212, 5215, 5232, 5233, 5235, 5238, 5241, 5243, 5258, 5259, 5261,
    5263, 5266, 5281, 5283, 5284, 5298, 5315, 5326, 5332, 5333, 5335, 5338, 5341,
    5349, 5354, 5356, 5357, 5360, 5368, 5371, 5392, 5395, 5401, 5410, 5416, 5420,
    5421, 5427, 5432, 5435, 5441, 5442, 5444, 5452, 5453, 5461, 5462, 5466, 5485,
    5489, 5493, 5496, 5498, 5506, 5508, 5514, 5520, 5535, 5542, 5563, 5564, 5567,
    5568, 5573, 5580, 5585, 5596, 5597, 5599, 5607, 5611, 5612, 5615, 5617, 5626,

5629, 5630, 5632, 5635, 5646, 5650, 5652, 5653, 5656, 5660, 5663, 5664, 5665, 5667, 5674, 5682, 5683, 5685, 5701, 5710, 5719, 5720, 5722, 5723, 5724, 5727, 5732, 5736, 5737, 5743, 5766, 5776, 5786, 5793, 5800, 5802, 5803, 5810, 5823, 5833, 5835, 5840, 5847, 5854, 5863, 5870, 5875, 5880, 5884, 5890, 5892, 5895, 5899, 5903, 5915, 5917, 5918, 5931, 5939, 5944, 5947, 5959, 5962, 5966, 5975, 5976, 5979, 5981, 5983, 5992, 6000, 6007, 6012, 6014, 6017, 6022, 6032, 6035, 6044, 6057, 6058, 6059, 6083, 6086, 6113, 6131, 6145, 6149, 6152, 6153, 6161, 6162, 6164, 6180, 6181, 6182, 6184, 6203, 6211, 6221, 6222, 6227, 6229, 6235, 6248, 6251, 6254, 6259, 6261, 6263, 6283, 6288, 6298, 6313, 6317, 6326, 6329, 6333, 6341, 6343, 6346, 6350, 6353, 6365, 6369, 6374, 6375, 6378, 6383, 6386, 6388, 6389, 6399, 6406, 6413, 6421, 6438, 6439, 6441, 6448, 6452
Wooden, John, 252, 406, 1085, 1190, 1226, 1430, 1431, 1432, 1433, 3866, 3884, 3968, 4474, 4487, 4770, 4771
Wootten, Morgan, 465, 480, 1319, 1435, 1436, 1437, 4561, 4582

Y

Youth basketball, 33, 50, 51, 63, 87, 161, 177, 242, 268, 274, 289, 433, 470, 471, 483, 733, 851, 1018, 1282, 1343, 1371, 1440, 2306, 2318, 4931, 5288, 5322, 5479, 5494, 5539, 5612, 5832, 5848, 5866, 5871, 5902, 5924, 5957, 5969, 5997, 6035, 6098, 6122, 6156, 6177, 6239, 6294, 6330, 6376, 6385, 6402

Z

Zaharias, Babe Didrikson, 1035, 1447

About the Editors

Jerry V. Krause, EdD, has coached at all levels—from elementary school to college. A recognized authority on coaching education and a leader in collegiate basketball circles, he has served on the board of directors of the National Association of Basketball Coaches (NABC) and has chaired the Research Committee of the NABC since 1969. He has also served on the board of trustees of the Naismith Basketball Hall of Fame. Dr. Krause was a member of the NCAA Basketball Rules Committee for 10 years and chaired the committee in 1986-87. Dr. Krause is also a past president of the National Association of Intercollegiate Athletics (NAIA) Basketball Coaches Association.

An accomplished basketball clinician and scholar, Dr. Krause regularly appears at clinics for teaching coaching around the country. He has written four basketball books, including the first edition of this one, and has published many articles on the subject.

Dr. Krause heads the department of physical education at Eastern Washington University and serves as assistant basketball coach at Gonzaga University in Spokane, WA.

Dr. Krause's teams have won over 500 games. In 1981, he served as assistant coach for the Gold Medal West Team in the U.S. Olympic Committee's National Sports Festival III. His international experience includes serving as assistant coach for the U.S. team in the 1977 Pan American Junior Games as well as being head coach of the U.S. team in the 1976 Jones Memorial Cup Competition in Taiwan.

Stephen J. Brennan is a former teacher-coach at the high school and collegiate levels and a long-time NABC member. He holds master's degrees in educational administration and sport psychology. Brennan is the founder and managing partner of Peak Performance Consultants, an Omaha, Nebraska-based company specializing in motivation and education. As such he conducts corporate workshops in motivation, goal setting, and stress management. He has addressed international, national, and regional educational and psychological conferences and is often a featured speaker at Converse and MacGregor coaches' clinics nationwide, addressing the mental aspects of competition and coaching.

Brennan has written numerous basketball articles in professional journals and is the author of *The Mental Edge: Basketball's Peak Performance Workbook*. He developed "The Mental Edge Clinic," a one-day mental training workshop for high school and collegiate student athletes and coaches. He has been employed by professional basketball scouting services and is currently a performance consultant with the Kansas City Royals baseball organization.